# Intervention and State Sovereignty in Central Europe, 1500–1780

# STUDIES IN GERMAN HISTORY

*Series Editors*
Neil Gregor (Southampton)
Bridget Heal (St Andrews)

*Editorial Board*
Simon MacLean (St Andrews)
Frank Rexroth (Göttingen)
Ulinka Rublack (Cambridge)
Joel Harrington (Vanderbilt)
Yair Mintzker (Princeton)
Svenja Goltermann (Zürich)
Maiken Umbach (Nottingham)
Paul Betts (Oxford)

# Intervention and State Sovereignty in Central Europe, 1500–1780

PATRICK MILTON

# OXFORD
UNIVERSITY PRESS

Great Clarendon Street, Oxford, OX2 6DP,
United Kingdom

Oxford University Press is a department of the University of Oxford.
It furthers the University's objective of excellence in research, scholarship,
and education by publishing worldwide. Oxford is a registered trade mark of
Oxford University Press in the UK and in certain other countries

© Patrick Milton 2022

The moral rights of the author have been asserted

First Edition published in 2022

Impression: 1

All rights reserved. No part of this publication may be reproduced, stored in
a retrieval system, or transmitted, in any form or by any means, without the
prior permission in writing of Oxford University Press, or as expressly permitted
by law, by licence or under terms agreed with the appropriate reprographics
rights organization. Enquiries concerning reproduction outside the scope of the
above should be sent to the Rights Department, Oxford University Press, at the
address above

You must not circulate this work in any other form
and you must impose this same condition on any acquirer

Published in the United States of America by Oxford University Press
198 Madison Avenue, New York, NY 10016, United States of America

British Library Cataloguing in Publication Data
Data available

Library of Congress Control Number: 2022940195

ISBN 978–0–19–287118–3

DOI: 10.1093/oso/9780192871183.001.0001

Printed and bound by
CPI Group (UK) Ltd, Croydon, CR0 4YY

Links to third party websites are provided by Oxford in good faith and
for information only. Oxford disclaims any responsibility for the materials
contained in any third party website referenced in this work.

*To my mother, in loving memory of my father.*

# Acknowledgements

I am very grateful to the following persons:

Brendan Simms, Moni and Phili and Marcus, Hamish Scott, Bridget Heal, Ali Ansari, Simon Wadsworth, Hannah Doyle, Stephanie Ireland, Neil Gregor, Christoph Kampmann, Anuschka Tischer, Peter Wilson, Jessica Gienow-Hecht, Daniela Hacke, Alexander Schunka, Len Scales, Gregor Walter-Drop, Tom Peak, Malik Dahlan, Andrew Thompson, Maria-Elisabeth Brunert, Heinz Duchhardt, Sebastian Ballard, Christopher Clark, Max Fenner

and to the following institutions:

the Master and Fellows of Peterhouse, Cambridge; the Centre for Geopolitics, Cambridge; the Deutscher Akademischer Austauschdienst (DAAD); the Leibniz-Institute of European History, Mainz; the German History Society, London; the History Department of the John F. Kennedy Institute of North American Studies, Berlin.

# Contents

*Abbreviations*   xi
*Notes on the Text*   xiii
*Maps*   xiv

Introduction   1

1. Legal Foundations: Imperial Constitutional Law and the Law of Nations and Nature   22

## PART ONE: EUROPEAN INTERVENTIONS IN CENTRAL EUROPE, c.1500–1780

2. Interventions in Central Europe I: c.1500–1618   55
3. Interventions in Central Europe II: 1618–1645   85
4. Guarantees and Interventions: European Powers and the Empire, 1645–1780   127

## PART TWO: INTERVENTION AS JUDICIAL EXECUTION WITHIN THE HOLY ROMAN EMPIRE

5. Interventions in Defence of Mediate Subjects: The Smallest Territories, c.1500–1780   161
6. Intervention in Small Principalities: The Case of Nassau-Siegen, 1699–c.1724   186
7. Intervention in Medium-Sized Principalities: The Case of Mecklenburg-Schwerin, 1713–1730   223

Epilogue   267

*Bibliography*   273
*Index*   295

# Abbreviations

| | |
|---|---|
| Add. MSS. | 'Additional Manuscripts' class series of files at British Library London |
| *AVNAG* | *Annalen des Vereins für Nassauische Alterthumskunde und Geschichtsforschung* |
| *APW* | *Acta Pacis Westphalicae*. Ed., Konrad Repgen (Münster, 1962–present). |
| Ausw.-Bez. | 'Auswärtige Beziehungen' class series of files at LHAS |
| BL | British Library, London |
| Cal. Br. | 'Calenberg Brief' class series of files at NHStAH |
| *CEH* | *Central European History* |
| *EHQ* | *European History Quarterly* |
| *EHR* | *The English Historical Review* |
| *ESR* | *European Studies Review* (now *EHQ*) |
| *EStC* | *Europäische Staats-Cantzley* (Anton Faber, ed.) |
| *GH* | *German History* |
| Hann. | 'Hannover' class series of files at NHStAH |
| HHStA | Österreichisches Staatsarchiv, Abteilung Haus-, Hof- und Staatsarchiv, Vienna |
| *HJ* | *The Historical Journal* |
| *HZ* | *Historische Zeitschrift* |
| IPO | Instrumentum Pacis Osnabrugensis (Treaty of Osnabrück, 1648) |
| IPM | Instrumentum Pacis Monasteriensis (Treaty of Münster, 1648) |
| *IHR* | *The International History Review* |
| *JEMH* | *Journal of Early Modern History* |
| *JHIL* | *Journal of the History of International Law* |
| *JMH* | *Journal of Modern History* |
| *JhVFL* | *Jahrbuch des Historischen Vereins für das Fürstentum Liechtenstein* |
| JRA | Jüngster Reichsabschied, 1654 |
| LANRW | Landesarchiv Nordrhein-Westfalen, Abteilung Rheinland, Standort Düsseldorf |
| LHAS | Landeshauptarchiv, Schwerin |
| MEA | Mainzer Erzkanzlerarchiv class series of files at HHStA |
| *MIöG* | *Mitteilungen des Instituts für österreichische Geschichtsforschung* |
| *MöStA* | *Mitteilungen des österreichischen Staatsarchivs* |
| NA | The National Archives, Kew, London |
| nd | no date |
| NHStAH | Niedersächsisches Landesarchiv—Hauptstaatsarchiv Hannover |
| np | no place |
| *NtS* | *Neues teutsches Staatsrecht* (by Johann Jacob Moser) |
| NW Kreis | 'Niederrheinisch-Westfälisches-Kreisarchiv' class series of files at LANRW |

| | |
|---|---|
| REO | Reichsexekutionsordnung (1555) |
| RHR | Reichshofrat |
| RHRO | Reichshofratsordnung(en) |
| RK | Reichskanzlei (when used in reference to class series of files at HHStA) |
| RKG | Reichskammergericht |
| RKGO | Reichskammergerichtsordnung |
| Rtlr | Reichstaler monetary unit used in Germany |
| SA | 'Staatenabteilungen' class series of files at HHStA |
| *SCJ* | *Sixteenth Century Journal* |
| SK | Staatskanzlei (when used in reference to class series of files at HHStA) |
| *TRHS* | *Transactions of the Royal Historical Society* |
| *ZHF* | *Zeitschrift für Historische Forschung* |

# Notes on the Text

Archival references are provided in the following sequence: document (including, where available, author and addressee, place, and date), archive, class series, file or carton number, folio numbers (where available).

Between the late sixteenth and the beginning of the eighteenth century most of Europe switched from the Julian Calendar ('Old Style') to the Gregorian Calendar ('New Style'), which is ten days ahead until 1700 and eleven days ahead after 1701. Most dates in the text from the late sixteenth century onwards are in 'New Style'. Dates in 'Old Style' have been indicated by 'OS' in the footnotes.

Quotations from original sources in German and French have been translated by the author. Quotations from original sources in English have been left unaltered.

'Imperial' is used to refer to the Holy Roman Emperor (*kaiserlich*), and to the Holy Roman Empire itself including to its central institutions (*Reichs-*). Reflecting contemporary usage, terms such as 'the Palatinate' are used as shorthand instead of the formally correct appellation 'county Palatine of the Rhine'. Names of places and people have been left in their German form unless a commonly used English version exists.

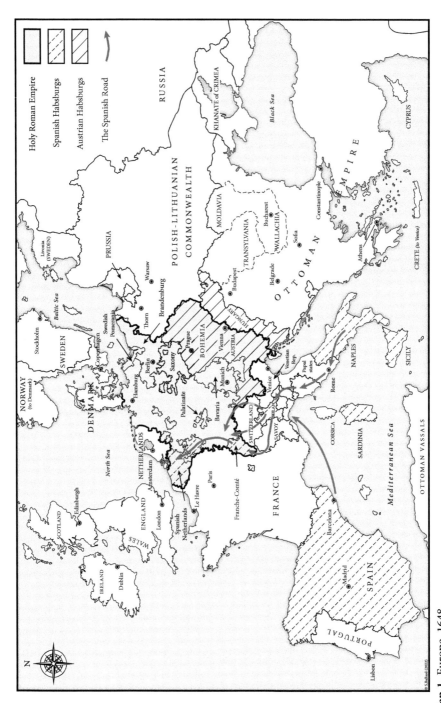

Map 1. Europe, 1648.

Map 2. Central Europe 1648.

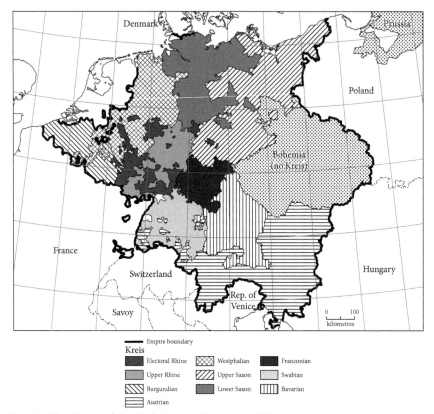

**Map 3.** The Kreise of the Holy Roman Empire, *c.*1700.

# Introduction

In April 1719, the Hanoverian envoy at Vienna, Daniel von Huldenberg, sent a letter to his master George I, British king and elector of Hanover, concerning the negotiations he was conducting with the Emperor's ministers at the Imperial court. A month earlier, Hanoverian forces had intervened in the conflict between the estates and the ruler of Mecklenburg-Schwerin, ensuring the defence of the noble subjects against the ruling duke Carl Leopold. Huldenberg reported with satisfaction on the favourable disposition of the Emperor Charles VI and his ministers, who were reported to be 'eager to relieve the oppressed nobility, to punish the great scandal of the duke's tyranny, and to vindicate the Emperor's authority'. However, while they were glad the intervention had taken place, they thought it necessary to stress that it was not simply a Hanoverian intervention against a distasteful ruler resulting in minor military hostilities, but that it was an execution of a legal verdict of one of the supreme judicial tribunals of the Holy Roman Empire (the Old German Reich). Accordingly, when reporting on the intervention to Vienna, the Hanoverian government should avoid the language and the arguments of *raison de guerre*, because 'what we are dealing with here is not a war, but an execution of Imperial verdicts by the Imperial Kreis (circle/district)'.[1]

While these comments show how leading German statesmen viewed princes accused of tyranny, they also reflect the nature of intervention in the Reich. For while intervention in sovereign, independent states amounted to an act of war (albeit permissible under certain circumstances according to many early modern theories of the law of nations), interventions against territorial princes were largely regulated, and provided for, by German constitutional law of the Empire. The veteran diplomat Huldenberg alludes to a distinction between the two types of intervention in support of subject populations which are the topic of this book: those conducted within the decentralised constitutional structure of the Empire, and those conducted by outside powers into central Europe for the protection of foreign subjects.

---

[1] Huldenberg to George I, Vienna, 12 April 1719, NHStAH, Cal.-Br.24, 4915, i, fols 146r–7r at fol. 147r.

*Intervention and State Sovereignty in Central Europe, 1500–1780*. Patrick Milton, Oxford University Press.
© Patrick Milton 2022. DOI: 10.1093/oso/9780192871183.003.0001

# Topic and Topicality

At first glance it might appear that this topic is a rather modern one. This impression is understandable because the majority of scholarly literature and journalistic work on international intervention treats it as a novel departure in geopolitical practice and international relations, and as a phenomenon without a history.[2] Most works that do consider historical precedents do so cursorily.[3] Historians have only very recently begun to argue that a universalist, normative discourse underpinned a series of 'humanitarian' interventions from the beginning of the nineteenth century. These included the British-led interventions against the international slave trade, a series of interventions by the European great powers for the protection of Christian minorities under Ottoman rule (Greece in 1827–29, Lebanon and Syria in 1860–61, the Balkans in 1876–78), and the US intervention in the Cuban war of independence at the end of century. A leading historian of these events, Fabian Klose, concluded that the nineteenth-century was therefore a genuine 'century of humanitarian intervention'.[4]

However, the fact that interventions for the protection of foreign subjects also occurred frequently throughout the early modern period from the beginning of the sixteenth century, is virtually unrecognised in works on intervention, particularly by political scientists.[5] By focusing on early modern interventions, this book highlights a phenomenon which is much older than often assumed. Naturally these early modern precedents did not have the same normative foundations as the equivalent interventions that occurred from *c*.1800. The term 'humanitarian intervention' itself was a neologism of the nineteenth-century.[6] This book will incidentally show, though, that references to universalist notions of humanity that transcended confession and race were *occasionally* made in the theoretical debate and political rhetoric surrounding these interventions from the sixteenth century onwards, yet this was far from the norm. While they may not adequately be described as humanitarian—what was ostensibly being defended through these interventions were certainly not 'human rights' in the modern sense—they might aptly be termed 'proto-humanitarian' interventions. In the words of Simms and Trim, the early modern period was a time of 'incubation... the modern phenomenon known as "humanitarian intervention" is like a river formed from the combination of several different tributaries:... confessional

---

[2] E.g., Noam Chomsky, 'Humanitarian intervention', *Boston Review* (Dec. 1993–Jan. 1994).
[3] E.g., Anne Orford, *International Authority and the Responsibility to Protect* (Cambridge, 2011).
[4] Fabian Klose, *'In the cause of humanity'. Eine Geschichte der humanitären Intervention im langen 19. Jahrhundert* (Göttingen, 2019), 15.
[5] E.g., Michael Ignatieff, *Empire Lite: Nation-building in Bosnia, Kosovo and Afghanistan* (London, 2003), 57–9.
[6] Fabian Klose, 'The emergence of humanitarian intervention. Three centuries of "enforcing humanity"', in Klose (ed.), *The Emergence of Humanitarian Intervention. Ideas and Practice from the Nineteenth Century to the Present* (Cambridge, 2016), 1–27.

solidarity, opposition to "tyranny", abolitionism that transcended race, and belief in a variety of values, including liberty, civilisation, democracy, and (eventually) human rights'.[7]

Questions surrounding intervention have been especially topical in the last three decades, in the context of both the failure to intervene effectively and possibly prevent genocide in Rwanda and Bosnia in the mid-1990s, and of numerous implemented interventions—the supposed humanitarianism of which varied widely—in Iraq (1991/98), Somalia (1992–93), Kosovo (1999), Sierra Leone (2000), Georgia (2008), Libya (2011), Ukraine (2014/2022), and elsewhere. In response to a prompt during the 1999 speech to the UN General Assembly by the Secretary-General Kofi Annan, in which he famously expressed the dilemma between state sovereignty and non-intervention in other states' domestic affairs on the one hand, and the external defence of human rights through intervention on the other hand, the global community adopted a seemingly novel conception of sovereignty.[8] The final report of the International Commission on Intervention and State Sovereignty (ICISS), convened by Canada, proposed a 'Responsibility to Protect' (R2P) in 2001. According to this concept, states retained sovereignty and the rights to manage their own domestic affairs; however, 'sovereignty implies responsibility, and the primary responsibility for the protection of its people lies with the state itself. Where a population is suffering serious harm, as a result of internal war, insurgency, repression or state failure, and the state in question is unwilling or unable to halt or avert it, the principle of non-intervention yields to the international responsibility to protect.'[9] At the 2005 World Summit, a somewhat watered-down version of this principle was then adopted, according to which possible R2P cases were to be referred to the existing regular channels of the UN Security Council.[10]

While R2P has often been conflated with humanitarian intervention—this was supposed to be a measure of last resort—and this in turn has been associated with a US-led programme of 'liberal interventionism' (especially since the 2003 Iraq invasion), R2P is clearly conceptually linked to intervention.[11] The 2011 intervention in Libya against Muammar Gaddafi was authorised by a UN Security Council resolution which referred to the responsibility to protect.[12] Other uprisings and conflicts sparked by the Arab Spring have continued to keep

---

[7] Brendan Simms and D.J.B. Trim, 'Towards a history of humanitarian intervention', in Simms and Trim (eds), *Humanitarian Intervention: A History* (Cambridge, 2011), 21, 24.

[8] The argument was elaborated in Kofi A. Annan, *'We the Peoples': The Role of the United Nations in the Twenty-first Century. Report of the Secretary-General* (New York, 2000), 48.

[9] International Commission on Intervention and State Sovereignty, *The Responsibility to Protect* (Ottawa, 2001), xi.

[10] Resolution 60/1, 2005 World Summit Outcome, 24 October 2005, UNGA A/RES/60/1, 30.

[11] Thomas Peak, *Westphalia from Below. Humanitarian Intervention and the Myth of 1648* (London, 2021).

[12] Resolution 1970 (2011), 26 Feb. 2011, UNSC S/RES/1970, 2, and Resolution 1973 (2011), 17 Mar. 2011, UNSC S/RES/1973, 3.

interventionism—whether humanitarian or not—on the agenda in the Middle East over the last decade, especially in the context of numerous external powers' military interferences in the civil wars of Syria and Yemen. These interlocking conflicts have led numerous commentators to compare them to the Thirty Years War in early modern Europe, along with its domestic rebellions which escalated into general wars largely through foreign interventions.[13] The parallels, however, in some ways go further than most people recognise.

Commentators have often portrayed R2P as a ground-breaking reinterpretation of the concept of sovereignty.[14] But how new was it really? Scholars have pointed out that sovereignty has long entailed notions of responsibility.[15] This book will argue that a remarkably similar conception of sovereignty and territorial rule already existed in early modern Europe and especially in central Europe. It will attempt to show that the conditionality of sovereignty and territorial rule was in some ways even more pronounced (or, severe) in early modern Europe than in the twenty-first century theory as embodied in the modern concept of R2P. While applied history may well be of value, this book does not aim to draw lessons from historical interventions for the current world.[16] Instead, it is a history of an early modern phenomenon for its own sake.

The period with which this book deals is still often misunderstood. The seventeenth and eighteenth-centuries are traditionally portrayed as falling within the age of absolutism, in which European states and German territories had largely freed themselves of the constraints of higher worldly power, while asserting an unrivalled domestic authority, especially after 1648.[17] While this old view of absolutism has largely been replaced by a more nuanced picture,[18] it is still a widespread belief in the existing historiography that in the period after the Peace of Westphalia (1648) the scope for and occurrence of such interferences in other states' domestic affairs were significantly reduced.[19] This book challenges this prevailing view, which is largely a by-product of the Westphalian sovereignty myth that identifies the treaties of Westphalia as the starting-point of an international system of state sovereignty and non-intervention.

---

[13] E.g., Richard Haass, 'The new Thirty Years War', *Project Syndicate*, 21 July 2014; Patrick Milton, Michael Axworthy, and Brendan Simms, *Towards a Westphalia for the Middle East* (London, 2018).

[14] E.g., Gareth Evans, *The Responsibility to Protect: Ending Mass Atrocity Crimes Once and For All* (Washington, 2008).

[15] Luke Glanville, *Sovereignty and the Responsibility to Protect. A New History* (Chicago, 2014), 31–59.

[16] Margaret MacMillan and Patrick Quinton-Brown, 'The uses of history in international society', *International Affairs* 95/1 (2019), 181–200.

[17] E.g., James Sheehan, *German History 1770–1866* (Oxford, 1994), 16.

[18] E.g., Heinz Duchhardt and Ronald G. Asch (eds), *Der Absolutismus—ein Mythos? Strukturwandel monarchischer Herrschaft in West- und Mitteleuropa (ca. 1550-1700)* (Cologne, 1996).

[19] E.g., Wilfried Hinsch and Dieter Janssen, *Menschenrechte militärisch schützen. Ein Plädoyer für Humanitäre Intervention* (Bonn, 2006), 58, 88; Klaus Malettke, *Hegemonie—multipolares System—Gleichgewicht. Internationale Beziehungen, 1648/1659–1713/1714* (Paderborn, 2012), 50–1.

Looking at the public justifications and private deliberations of decision-makers and commentators surrounding such cases of interventions can reveal the attitudes of contemporaries to notions of good governance and to the treatment of subject populations, and how these could or could not be enforced by outsiders. The hypothesis from which this book proceeds is that the defence of other rulers' subjects formed part of the motivation for interventions, while usually merging with, or serving as a pretext for, geopolitical motives. The empirical focus is on early modern central Europe—primarily the Holy Roman Empire, including chiefly Germany, and at times the Netherlands, Switzerland, and northern (Imperial) Italy,[20] as well as Hungary and Poland. This book also explores the ways in which attitudes towards intervention shifted over the course of the period. By expanding the geographical scope to include some limited supplementary analysis of cases in central Europe outside of Germany, this book will also contribute towards a comparative understanding of the enforcement of norms of governance in early modern international society.

## Research Context and Historiography: The Empire, European International Relations, Intervention, and the Myth of Westphalia

The topic of this book is situated on the intersection of two strands of research: research into the Holy Roman Empire, specifically its political, constitutional, and confessional history; and the history of early modern European international relations and law. As the Peace of Westphalia was both the most important fundamental constitutional law for the Empire during its last 150 years, and an international peace treaty, the impact of its mythologising bridges both strands. This is because different components of the myth have contributed towards a particular—and largely inaccurate—interpretation of interventions both within the Empire, and in broader European international politics and law. Building on the growing body of historiography that questions the 'Westphalian myth', this book is the first detailed investigation of intervention for the protection of other rulers' subjects in early modern central Europe.

According to different versions of the Westphalian sovereignty myth, Westphalia established the principle of sovereignty and non-intervention either among German princes or among European states or both. That myth has long been engrained in the disciplines of political science, particularly International Relations (IR), but also in international law and the history of international law,

---

[20] Imperial Italy (*Reichsitalien*) consisted of northern Italian Imperial fiefs – territories that were under the Emperor's feudal jurisdiction but which were not represented at the Reichstag. These included Milan, Savoy, Genoa, Parma, Mantua, Tuscany, and others.

and to a lesser extent in the discipline of history. The myth has been so powerful that 'Westphalia' has become a well-known metonym for a system of sovereign nation states. The ideas associated with the myth are also a standard trope among journalists[21] and politicians.[22] It has even been identified as the origin of the globalised market economy.[23] The Peace of Westphalia is simultaneously one of the most thoroughly researched, and one of the most misunderstood peace settlements in history—albeit not by the same people. The Westphalian myth consists of several assumptions and notions but these can be grouped into two main interrelated aspects. Firstly, there is the 'internal-constitutional' aspect which posits that the treaties of Westphalia granted the princes, in other words, the territories or Imperial Estates of the Empire, sovereignty.[24] Derived from this is the 'international' aspect of the myth which assumes that the Peace enshrined the principle of state sovereignty and non-intervention in the internal affairs of other states in the broader European arena, and the principle of the legal equality of states.[25] Related to both aspects is the notion that the Peace abolished the hierarchical elements of the European order by negating the secular and spiritual leadership of the Emperor and the Pope, respectively, and instead installing the system of secular international law.[26]

As I will argue, Westphalia had little to do with sovereignty. It neither granted sovereignty to the Imperial princes, nor enshrined such general principles for Europe as a whole. In many ways the individual princes and the Empire as a whole were subject to a greater degree of external supervision and intervention post-Westphalia, than before 1648. Sovereign states existed well before 1648, and interventions in the domestic affairs of other states (and other Imperial Estates) continued well after 1648. Both the Emperor and the Pope had lost their pretensions to universal authority long before 1648. Of course, I am not the first to question the traditional view of Westphalia. Numerous contributions by historians,[27] IR scholars,[28] and international law scholars[29] have convincingly refuted the myth, including several pieces which explicitly provide correctives to

---

[21] E.g., 'Die Geschichte der Deutschen', *Stern Extra* 3 (2010), 81–2.

[22] E.g., May 2017 speech by the German foreign minister Sigmar Gabriel (https://www.auswaertiges-amt.de/de/newsroom/170522-bm-friedensverantwortung-religionen/290118).

[23] Susan Strange, 'The Westfailure system', *Review of International Studies* 25 (1999), 345–54.

[24] E.g., Michael Hughes, *Law and Politics in Eighteenth-Century Germany. The Imperial Aulic Council in the Reign of Charles VI* (Woodbridge, 1988), 16–17.

[25] E.g., Daniel Philpott, *Revolutions in Sovereignty. How Ideas Shaped Modern International Relations* (Princeton, 2001), 85.

[26] Robert Gilpin, *War and Change in World Politics* (Cambridge, 1981), 29f.

[27] Peter H. Wilson, *The Holy Roman Empire. A Thousand Years of Europe's History* (London, 2016), 127–9, 174–5.

[28] Andreas Osiander, 'Sovereignty, international relations, and the Westphalian myth', *IO* 55 (2001): 251–87.

[29] Stephane Beaulac, 'The Westphalian legal orthodoxy – myth or reality?', *JHIL* 2 (2000): 148–77.

the misperceptions.[30] But such corrections have only partially dented the potency of the Westphalian myth. In its international aspect, the myth forms the core of a model of the so-called 'Westphalian System', particularly in anglophone political science and IR.[31] The Peace was indeed ground-breaking in terms of its bridging of international law with the domestic constitutional law of the Empire, but its immediate effects on international law have been widely misconstrued. The notion that 1648 marks a watershed moment in international law, by enshrining state sovereignty and non-intervention is also widespread in legal history and the international law literature.[32] It has even recently been suggested that the mythical notion of the Westphalian System is so central to IR that it forms part of its foundational myth and that revising it would entail a reinvention of the discipline itself.[33]

The standard view of the Peace of Westphalia as a watershed in international politics is related to the way in which the history of European international relations has been written. Along with the misperception that Westphalia was an epochal caesura which secularised politics and enshrined the principle of a balance of power, the period between the Reformation and 1648 has traditionally been portrayed as the age of confessional conflict.[34] The later seventeenth and eighteenth centuries by contrast have been regarded as an age in which religion ceased to be an important factor in international relations. Instead, international politics in this period was the story of the interactions and relations between formally equal sovereign state units represented by their rulers and diplomats, according to principles of raison d'état and the balance of power, largely devoid of confessional and other ideological factors, much like a set of billiard balls.[35] The classic school of diplomatic history often implicitly shared such assumptions, with its almost exclusive focus on wars, diplomatic negotiations and the conclusion of treaties between princes and other rulers, along with their ministers and diplomats.

---

[30] Derek Croxton, 'The Peace of Westphalia of 1648 and the origins of sovereignty', *IHR* 21 (1999): 569–91.
[31] E.g., Anthony McGraw, 'Globalization and global politics', in J. Baylis et al. (eds), *The Globalization of World Politics* (Oxford, 2011), 23. It has also been repeated by French and German political scientists: Arnaud Blin, *1648, La Paix de Westphalie, ou la naissance de l'Europe politique moderne* (Brussels, 2006); Herfried Münkler, *Der Dreissigjährige Krieg. Europäische Katastrophe, deutsches Trauma, 1618–1648* (Berlin, 2017), 22–31, 36–9, 817–43.
[32] E.g., O. Kimminich, *Deutsche Verfassungsgeschichte* (Baden-Baden, 1987), 215–28.
[33] Benjamin de Carvalho and Jörg Kustermans, 'The modern Westphalian peace impasse in International Relations and what to do about it', in Dorothée Goetze and Lena Oetzel (eds), *Warum Friedenschliessen so schwer ist. Frühneuzeitliche Friedensfindung am Beispiel des Westfälischen Friedenskongresses* (Münster, 2019), 93–106.
[34] E.g., Luise Schorn-Schütte, *Konfessionskriege und europäische Expansion. Europa 1500–1648* (Munich, 2010).
[35] E.g., Evan Luard, *The Balance of Power: The System of International Relations, 1648–1815* (Basingstoke, 1992).

Diplomatic history with a focus on geopolitics and the shifting balance of power has and continues to produce valuable research.[36] But there has been an increasing shift towards seeking to explain the history of international relations by reference to the influence of a number of structural factors such as communication channels, political culture and norms, language, personal networks, and religion.[37] This 'new diplomatic history' has eschewed the analysis of international relations solely on the basis of high politics and grand strategy. Some historians have focussed on the social networks of diplomats as an important element in an 'actor-centric' view of international relations.[38] Others have emphasised the cultural and normative elements of a 'society of princes'.[39] The recognition that non-sovereign, sub-state actors, such as Imperial Estates, possessed agency in international relations, has led to analysis of 'asymmetrical political relationships'. Protection (in Latin, *protectio*), as an early modern concept denoted a variety of different practices involving the defence or sponsorship of weaker by stronger actors, and the rights that accrued to the protector as a result of his relationship with the 'protectee'.[40] *Protectio* often had similar inter-personal qualities to the contemporaneous practice of patronage, a reflection of the foundation of early modern statehood and 'foreign', or external, policy resting to a large degree on a complex and overlapping set of personal relationships.[41]

According to the traditional picture of post-Westphalian international relations, especially as portrayed by scholars of political science and international law, interventions for the protection of other rulers' subjects have hardly any precedent in period before the twentieth century, as mentioned above.[42] Historians, too, have only recently ventured into a rigorous historical understanding of the phenomenon. Mar Swatek-Evenstein has produced a synthesis of interventions since the 1820s.[43] Davide Rodogno, Alexis Heraclides, and Ada Dialla—and with a clear present-day political agenda, Gary Bass—have published monographs of the history of post-1815 interventions by Christian European powers in the Ottoman Empire, while Fabian Klose has written an impressive history of humanitarian intervention across the globe during the nineteenth-century.[44] Prior to that he

---

[36] E.g., Brendan Simms, *Three Victories and a Defeat. The Rise and Fall of the First British Empire, 1714–1783* (London, 2007).
[37] E.g., Charlotte Backerra, *Wien und London, 1727–1735. Internationale Beziehungen im frühen 18. Jahrhundert* (Göttingen, 2018).
[38] Hillard von Thiessen et al. (eds), *Akteure der Außenbeziehungen* (Cologne, 2010).
[39] Lucien Bély, *La Société des Princes XVI^e–XVIII^e-siècle* (Paris, 1999).
[40] Tilman Haug et al. (eds), *Protegierte und Protektoren. Asymmetrische Beziehungen zwischen Partnerschaft und Dominanz* (Cologne, 2016).
[41] Hillard von Thiessen et al. (eds), *Nähe in der Ferne. Personale Verflechtung in den Außenbeziehungen der Frühen Neuzeit* (Berlin, 2005).
[42] E.g., Thomas G. Weiss, *Humanitarian Intervention* (Cambridge, MA, 2007).
[43] Mar Swatek-Evenstein, *A History of Humanitarian Intervention* (Cambridge, 2020).
[44] D. Rodogno, *Against Massacre: Humanitarian Interventions in the Ottoman Empire, 1815–1914* (Princeton, 2012); G.J. Bass, *Freedom's Battle: The Origins of Humanitarian Intervention* (New York, 2008); Klose, *'In the cause of humanity'*.

edited a collection of essays on the same topic. While noting the existence of early modern precedents (and sometimes dismissing their conceptual relevance), these books do not include detailed empirical analysis of the sixteenth, seventeenth, and eighteenth centuries.[45]

Several historians of early modern Europe have encouragingly carried out first steps towards an historicised empirical understanding of the history of the state practice of intervention in early modern Europe. Brendan Simms and David Trim published a collection of essays in 2011 which was the very first step towards the long history of intervention that included cases from early modern Europe.[46] According to Trim, early modern statesmen contemplated and implemented interventions only in reaction to 'extreme atrocities...massacres, or egregious abuse by a prince'.[47] While this book argues that such abuses were certainly considered valid pretexts and or reasons for interventions, they were also discussed and carried out in response to 'lesser' infractions, including the violation of legal procedures and rights, such as rights of worship and property rights, and unconstitutional practice, which did not necessarily involve killings. Andrew Thompson has highlighted the involvement of Britain in the Holy Roman Empire, including Britain's role as a protector of German Protestants.[48] Renate Wieland has examined the policies of the elector-King of Brandenburg-Prussia towards Protestants in the Reich in similar terms.[49] Anuschka Tischer has investigated how rulers justified and legitimated their interferences in other states' domestic affairs, while also arguing that there was an absence of clear divisions between the internal and external spheres of early modern states.[50] Gabriele Haug-Moritz and Fabrice Micaleff have written about the interventions by Queen Elizabeth I's England and other states in the sixteenth-century French Wars of Religion.[51] Christoph Kampmann headed a project which sought to undertake a 'diachronic' investigation of the history of intervention evolving into the modern

---

[45] Klose (ed.), *Emergence*.
[46] Brendan Simms and D.J.B. Trim (eds), *Humanitarian Intervention: A History* (Cambridge, 2011).
[47] David J.B. Trim, '"If a prince use tyrannie towards his people": interventions on behalf of foreign populations in early modern Europe', in Simms and Trim (eds), *Humanitarian Intervention*, 29–66 at 29, 41.
[48] Andrew C. Thompson, 'The Protestant interest and the history of humanitarian intervention, c.1685–c.1765', in Simms and Trim (eds), *Humanitarian Intervention*, 67–88.
[49] Renate Wieland, *Protestantischer König im Heiligen Reich. Brandenburg-preußische Reichs- und Konfessionspolitik im frühen 18. Jahrhundert* (Berlin, 2020).
[50] Anuschka Tischer, 'Grenzen der Souveränität: Beispiele zur Begründung gewaltsamer Einmischung in "innere Angelegenheiten" in der Frühen Neuzeit', *Historisches Jahrbuch*, 131 (2011), 41–64.
[51] Gabriele Haug-Moritz, 'Schutz fremder Glaubensverwandter? Die Intervention des elisabethanischen England in den ersten französischen Religionskrieg (1562/1563)', in Haug et al. (eds), *Protegierte und Protektoren*, 165–86; Fabrice Micaleff, 'Strategie der Schwäche. Die provenzalischen Katholiken und ihre auswärtigen Protektoren in der Zeit der katholischen Liga (1589–1596)', in ibid., 187–200.

phenomenon of humanitarian intervention.[52] In this context he interestingly reinterpreted the Glorious Revolution of 1688 as an example of a proto-humanitarian intervention which was justified by the need to uphold English Liberties.[53] On the basis of this example, he has also argued that there was a 'responsibility to protect' in early modern Europe, even after Westphalia.[54] Scholars of the history of political thought and international law have recently pointed out that military interventions for the protection of foreign subjects were in fact debated and theorised by early modern political philosophers and thinkers, in terms which were sometimes similar to current discourses.[55] The above-mentioned articles and chapters are valuable contributions but none of these deal specifically with central Europe, and furthermore there is no detailed monograph on the history of early modern intervention (in central Europe or beyond).

The Holy Roman Empire has undergone a dramatic reassessment among historians. The older negative assessment of the Reich among Prussian-influenced German historians from the nineteenth century shifted from the 1960s onwards.[56] The idealisation of the Reich which peaked around 25 years ago has since been tempered by more balanced assessments[57] and studies of oppressive aspects of early modern German history.[58] The foremost anglophone historians of the Reich, Peter Wilson and Joachim Whaley, have demonstrated its continued dynamism, capacity for inner reform and external defence, and have elucidated the complex system of governance in the Empire.[59] Christopher Close has recently investigated the politics of alliance in the Empire, arguing that leagues among Estates drove state formation and were at the heart of a system of shared sovereignty. Rather than conflict or rivalry between the Emperor and the Imperial Estates, there was 'an ongoing debate about how [the] regions could best support the centre and vice versa. Corporate alliances formed one of the chief nexus points around which this

---

[52] Christoph Kampmann, 'Vom Schutz fremder Untertanen zur Humanitären Intervention. Einleitende Bemerkungen zur diachronen Analyse einer aktuellen Problematik', *Historisches Jahrbuch* 131 (2011), 3–10.

[53] Christoph Kampmann, 'Das "Westfälische System", die Glorreiche Revolution und die Interventionsproblematik', in *Historisches Jahrbuch* 131 (2011), 65–92.

[54] Christoph Kampmann, 'Kein Schutz fremder Untertanennach 1648? Zur Akzeptanz einer responsibility to protect in der Frühen Neuzeit', in Haug, et al. (eds), *Protegierte und Protektoren*, 201–16.

[55] E.g., S. Recchia and J. Welsh (eds), *Just and Unjust Military Interventions: European Thinkers from Vittoria to Mill* (Cambridge, 2013); Wilhelm G. Grewe, *The Epochs of International Law* (Berlin and New York, 2000), 487–96; Simon Chesterman, *Just War or Just Peace? Humanitarian Intervention and International Law* (Oxford, 2001), 8–21.

[56] For a historiographical overview, see Tim Blanning, 'The Holy Roman Empire of the German Nation past and present', *Historical Research*, 85 (2012), 57–70.

[57] Barbara Stollberg-Rilinger, *The Emperor's Old Clothes: Constitutional History and the Symbolic Language of the Holy Roman Empire* (New York, 2015).

[58] Research has shown that household slavery of trafficked foreigners (usually Africans from overseas colonies) existed in the Empire, was on occasion explicitly affirmed by the courts: Rebekkavon Mallinckrodt et al. (eds), *Beyond Exceptionalism—Traces of Slavery and the Slave Trade in Early Modern Germany, 1650–1850* (Berlin/Boston, 2021).

[59] Wilson, *Empire*; Joachim Whaley, *Germany and the Holy Roman Empire* (2 vols. Oxford, 2012).

debate revolved.'[60] This approach is innovative and illuminates the dispersed nature of sovereignty in the Empire. However, it underestimated the role and importance of the Imperial judiciary and its capacity for interventions into the regions, even though this phenomenon would strengthen Close's argument, because judicial executions were not simply unilateral intrusions by the centre into the regions, but resulted from a calibrated interplay between the Emperor/ supreme courts and the Imperial Estates organised through the *Kreise*. The highest courts of the Imperial judiciary usually acted as the vehicle through which the Empire intervened in the internal affairs of the territories and mediated in conflicts between them, and upholding basic rights of subjects.[61] A considerable amount of research has been conducted on legal conflicts between princes and their subjects carried out at the supreme courts.[62] The present work contributes to our understanding of the Empire's judicial system by assessing the normative basis of its principles of the dispensation of justice with regard to the protection of persecuted subjects. That only a small proportion of the many relevant cases can be examined here in meaningful detail, with many more surveyed cursorily, goes without saying.

In the context of the positive reappraisal of the Reich, historians have often noted the capacity of the Empire's central institutions to intervene in the territorial affairs of the princes and other Imperial Estates for the benefit of the subject populations.[63] The supreme judicial tribunals provided a measure of legal security and access to judicial recourse for the various corporate groups of mediate (and immediate) subjects of the Empire, including territorial estates, citizens of Imperial cities, women, confessional groupings including Jews, while also generally defending the Imperial constitutional order predicated on peaceful interterritorial relations.[64] Peter Wilson noted that 'judicial intervention stabilized the Empire, both curbing violence and perpetuating gross inequality'.[65] Michael Geyer recently made some interesting remarks on both Westphalia and the kind of interventions within the Empire ordered by its supreme courts which this book investigates in detail. He argues that 'these incidents fit the concept of "humanitarian intervention" very well ... However, the salient point of these interventions

---

[60] Christopher W. Close, *State Formation and Shared Sovereignty. The Holy Roman Empire and the Dutch Republic, 1488–1696* (Cambridge, 2021), 8.

[61] Siegrid Westphal, *Kaiserliche Rechtsprechung und herrschaftliche Stabilisierung. Reichsgerichtsbarkeit in den thüringischen Territorialstaaten 1648–1806* (Cologne, 2002).

[62] E.g., Rita Sailer, *Untertanenprozesse vor dem Reichskammergericht. Rechtsschutz gegen die Obrigkeit in der zweiten Hälfte des 18. Jahrhunderts* (Cologne, 1999).

[63] Werner Trossbach, 'Power and good governance: the removal of ruling princes in the Holy Roman Empire, 1680–1794', in J.P. Coy et al. (eds), *The Holy Roman Empire, Reconsidered* (New York, 2010), 191–209.

[64] E.g., Whaley, *Germany*, i, 11; ii, 125, 140, 147–8, 248; Gabriele Haug-Moritz, *Württembergischer Ständekonflikt und deutscher Dualismus. Ein Beitrag zur Geschichte des Reichverbands in der Mitte des 18. Jahrhunderts* (Stuttgart, 1992).

[65] Wilson, *Empire*, 636.

is that they occurred in a system of courts...and thus settled conflicts short of military intervention'.[66] However, as this book demonstrates, executions of judicial decisions in the Empire were occasionally implemented militarily. The chapters that follow provide a deeper analysis than has been provided before, of how interventions against perceived tyrannical rule were assessed by contemporaries. This enables a better understanding of the normative underpinning of the system of rule in the Empire and beyond.

## Method and Interpretative Framework

This study derives some insights from IR theories and political science in general. In the last decade, IR scholars have attempted to reach a 'historicised' understanding of the phenomenon of intervention.[67] One IR scholar has claimed that intervention cannot really be viewed as a distinct category of state practice in the early modern period.[68] To an extent this makes sense, when one considers that supporting other rulers' oppressed and rebelling subjects almost inevitably occurred among rival states, especially when these were at war or on the brink of war. However, the argument is ultimately unconvincing because there was certainly a debate among early modern statesmen, commentators, and jurists about the justness and legality of such interventions—even when they occurred between polities that were on different levels of the hierarchy of rank among the early modern community of princes and states—and interferences in other states' internal affairs were indeed conceptualised by contemporaries as 'interventions'.

Realist and neorealist theories of IR, under the influence of classical expositions of the reason of state, view states as being motivated solely by power-accretion and survival, and thus would argue that interventions are aimed at furthering power-political and security interests only.[69] The premise of this study, however, is that realist theories underestimate the extent to which rules and norms shape states' perception of their self-interest. Separating power and security factors from other—primarily socio-cultural factors—often fails to represent states' beliefs about their interests. Notions of security and strategy can fuse with more ideological impulses. Therefore, power-political and strategic factors should not be considered in a vacuum, in isolation from cultural, societal, and ideological influences. Often a genuine concern for subjects' rights was inseparable from a

[66] Michael Geyer, 'Humanitarianism and human rights: a troubled rapport', in Klose (ed.), *Emergence*, 31–55, at 41–2.
[67] E.g., John MacMillan, 'Intervention and the ordering of the modern world', *RIS* 39 (2013), 1039–56.
[68] Edward Keene, 'International hierarchy and the origins of the modern practice of intervention', ibid., 1077–90.
[69] J. Moses, 'Sovereignty as irresponsibility? A realist critique of the responsibility to protect', ibid., 113–35.

power-political appraisal of interests. Legitimations provided by the interveners (often propagandistically) and the reactions and perceptions of contemporaries to political events such as interventions, and discourses surrounding them, largely reflect the normative content of a political culture.

This book proceeds from the hypothesis that a range of norms relating to good governance, the adherence to law, and the measured treatment of subjects, constituted a set of shared assumptions and implicit rules. These ran parallel to the primary emphasis on strategic and power considerations associated with realist assumptions, and which exerted a systemic influence in international politics.[70] Lasting political rule was only viable if it was based on prevailing normative belief. Political and social norms were closely intertwined and usually defined in broadly religious terms in early modern Europe.[71]

Combining case studies from two considerably different contextual backgrounds—'international' interventions and Imperial interventions within the Empire—requires explanation. After all, the Imperial interventions by the Emperor against the Imperial Estates (i.e. the territorial princes) can be viewed as internal policing exercises which were conceptualised as the Emperor carrying out his judicial and protective duty towards his own mediate subjects by enforcing Imperial law. Interventions against independent, sovereign rulers often in the context of large-scale wars, on the other hand, were for the defence of truly 'foreign' subjects. Arguably, the essence of intervention is the external violation of state sovereignty for the protection of foreign subjects, whereby the target government's title to rule the subjects being aided is not denied in principle.

Nevertheless, incorporating the broader European state system into the analysis has much to commend it. Despite the diverging legal contexts (Imperial constitutional law on the one hand, and the Law of Nations on the other), in both cases the attendant debates and deliberations concerned the protection of subjects under another ruler, be it a sovereign or a (princely) Imperial Estate. And while an intervention in an Imperial Estate by the Emperor as overlord can hardly be viewed as a 'foreign' intervention, according to legal regulations such interventions were subcontracted to neighbouring Imperial Estates, whose intervention against fellow-princes could and was seen as 'foreign' interference.[72] On the other hand, when dealing with early modern Europe, it is misleading to see a binary dichotomy between 'foreign' and 'domestic', especially in central Europe, with its multiple, overlapping jurisdictions, shared intersecting sovereignty, and mediated

---

[70] See also M. Schulz, *Normen und Praxis. Das Europäische Konzert der Großmächte als Sicherheitsrat 1815–1860* (Munich, 2009), 4–20.
[71] Hillard von Thiessen, *Das Zeitalter der Ambiguität. Vom Umgang mit Werten und Normen in der Frühen Neuzeit* (Cologne, 2021), 163–77.
[72] See also Fabian Frommelt, 'Vom kaiserlichen Kommissar zum Hohen Repräsentanten— Zwangsadministrationen im historischen Vergleich', in Frommelt (ed.), *Zwangsadministrationen. Legitimierte Fremdverwaltung im historischen Vergleich*(Berlin, 2014), 9–43, at 13.

14  INTERVENTION AND STATE SOVEREIGNTY

subjecthoods.⁷³ Furthermore, the German Imperial Estates were not comparable to estates within other polities, due to their dual capacity as both subjects of the Emperor, and subjects, or entities, under international law, possessing legally-enshrined foreign-political and military capacities. As such they were restricted by certain duties towards the Empire, the Emperor, and their own subjects, but were nevertheless capable of conducting their own diplomatic relations and concluding alliances with outside powers, maintaining armies, and waging war. In any case, military force was mooted and employed in both sorts of intervention.

Similar questions arising during these crises within the Reichand beyond are addressed: could a 'responsibility' to protect the subjects of other rulers be justified? If so, did this only apply to the Emperor and princes among themselves within the Empire, or was it a broader responsibility among European rulers? To what extent were princes and governments expected to adhere to any common codes of conduct and how far could one intervene to enforce compliance with such norms? Who was permitted to intervene against whom? What was the role of strategic security considerations in the motivation for intervention and how did these interact with other factors, such as upholding legal rights and treaty terms? Was the defence of legal rights and stipulations through intervention an end in itself or a means to an end? Can any 'universalist' sentiment be detected in such undertakings? Was the defence of weaker, lower-ranking princes by higher ranking, stronger ones conceptualised in a similar fashion as the protection of other rulers' subject populations? Was intervention a form of 'state-building' and did it often lead to foreign rule and imposed external administrations?

## At the Heart of Europe: The Holy Roman Empire and Interstate Relations

This book is mainly concerned with events and debates that occurred in the Holy Roman Empire. It is therefore useful to briefly explain this entity and how it interacted with its neighbours as well as European states further afield. Despite an unresolved historiographical debate about whether or not the Empire was a state, and if so, what kind of state, most historians now agree on the basics.⁷⁴ It was, in the words of Peter Wilson, 'a mixed monarchy where the Emperor shared power to differing degrees with a complex hierarchy of Imperial Estates'.⁷⁵ Authority was collectively arranged at three complementary levels.⁷⁶ 1. The complex hierarchy of

---

⁷³ Kenneth Pennington, *The Prince and the Law, 1200–1600* (Berkeley, 1993), 284.
⁷⁴ Brief overviews: Barbara Stollberg-Rilinger, *The Holy Roman Empire. A Short History* (Princeton, 2018); Joachim Whaley, *The Holy Roman Empire. A Very Short Introduction* (Oxford, 2018).
⁷⁵ Wilson, *Empire*, 116, 171.
⁷⁶ This section uses some material written by the author in Patrick Milton, Michael Axworthy, and Brendan Simms, *Towards a Westphalia for the Middle East* (London, 2018).

around 250 Imperial Estates (princely territories and Imperial cities represented at the Reichstag) at the lower level; 2. The ten regional districts (*Kreise*—'circles') encompassing several neighbouring Imperial Estates at the intermediary level; and 3. the handful of central Imperial institutions—the Imperial Diet or Reichstag (assembly representing Imperial Estates), the supreme courts (Imperial judicial tribunals—the 'Imperial Aulic Council' or Reichshofrat, and the 'Imperial Cameral Court' or Reichskammergericht) and the office of the Emperor—at the higher level. The Empire can be conceived as a hierarchical multi-level system of governance, 'a sophisticated form of early modern consociationalism'.[77] At least among the aristocratic political and social elites of the Empire, there was a strong sense of belonging and of nationhood which developed over the course of a millennium, and in which the recognition of the Emperor's overlordship was virtually unchallenged for most of the Empire's long history. The Emperors' overlordship existed in three capacities: as the head of a *political* hierarchy of Estates, as the *judicial* apex of a legal system,[78] and as the *feudal* overlord over all fief-holders.[79]

The Emperor was not, as is well known, an absolute ruler over a centralised monarchy. According to the protean body of treaties, laws, and customary practice collectively constituting the Imperial constitution, the numerous constituent territories of the Empire—the Imperial Estates—possessed considerable prerogatives associated with statehood. These included the ability to conduct individual foreign policies (including the right to wage war, conclude peace and alliances, dispatch embassies), and the right to rule over their subject populations. During the early modern period, almost all Emperors were provided by the German branch of the Habsburg dynasty centred in Austria. The elective nature of the monarchy was confirmed and enshrined in the Golden Bull of 1356, which specified that the Emperor was elected by seven of the highest-ranking Imperial Estates, the prince-electors, described by one historian as the 'pillars of the Empire', who collectively possessed an elevated corporate dignity that was considerably higher than ordinary princes.[80] These princes were the archbishops of Mainz, Trier, and Cologne, the king of Bohemia, the count-Palatine of the Rhine, the duke of Saxony, and the margrave of Brandenburg. The dukes of Bavaria and of Braunschweig-Lüneburg were added in the seventeenth century. The Imperial Estates were the 'immediate' subjects of the Emperor (their subjecthood to the Emperor was not mediated through any intervening lord), while the population groups within the Imperial Estates were subjects both of their territorial prince or

---

[77] Brendan Simms, '"A false principle in the Law of Nations": Burke, State Sovereignty, [German] Liberty, and Intervention in the Age of Westphalia', in Brendan Simms and D.J.B. Trim (eds), *Humanitarian Intervention: A History* (Cambridge, 2011), 89–110, at 92.

[78] Dietmar Willoweit, 'Das Reich als Rechtssystem', in Schilling et al. (eds), *Altes Reich und Neue Staaten 1495 bis 1806*, 81–91.

[79] Barbara Stollberg-Rilinger, 'Das Reich als Lehnssystem', in ibid., 55–67.

[80] Axel Gotthard, *Säulen des Reiches. Die Kurfürsten im frühneuzeitlichen Reichsverband* (Husum, 1999).

Imperial city council, but also the 'mediate' subjects of the Emperor. These groups of subjects within the territories were often arranged into corporate entities known as territorial estates (*Landstände*) which in Germany usually consisted of nobles, clerics, and towns.

The Empire was not run through centralised bureaucracies as modern states are. Rule was largely negotiated and carried out through personal bonds of loyalty and patronage. Corporate bodies of subjects, such as territorial estates, had considerable rights and privileges within most territories, based on positive treaty laws and long-standing customary practice. They usually had the right to approve taxation collected by the ruling prince. If their rights were consistently disregarded, any subject or groups of subjects had the right to sue their ruler at the supreme judicial tribunals, at the level which was higher than their prince in the Imperial hierarchy. If the ruler in question continued to rule 'tyrannically', and to ignore verdicts from the supreme courts, the Emperor could mandate an armed intervention against the offending prince for the protection of his subjects, and such mandates could be executed, provided this was politically feasible. Such interventions form a large part of this study. Imperial and territorial law incidentally also provided for analogous interventions by ruling princes within their own territories, whereby territorial courts in the name of the prince could intervene against noble landowners who were mistreating their peasants.[81] In addition to 'regular' Imperial interventions, there existed 'irregular' interventions which were not carried out under Imperial authority, but in which princes or corporate groups of princes asserted the right to intervene themselves, chiefly on the basis of the mutual guarantee clauses of Westphalia. If the former are conceived as 'vertical interventions' carried out by the Emperor against lower levels of the Imperial hierarchy, then the latter could aptly be described as 'horizontal interventions' as they were carried out against fellow princes, and therefore equals (more or less), in the Imperial hierarchy. These terms are used in a constitutional-juridical sense; naturally an unauthorised Prussian intervention was quite different in power-political terms than collective measures by local Kreis authorities, for example.

Just as the Imperial system of limited, rights-based rule was supposed to inhibit arbitrariness on the part of the princes against their subjects, so it prevented arbitrary rule by the Emperor over his immediate subjects, the princes. These also had considerable rights and privileges based in treaty and customary law, the famous 'German Liberties' (*deutsche Freiheit*), which primarily related to their right to share in the governance and management of the Empire. Rights were generally not universal and individual, as they are conceptualised today, but rather corporate—in other words attached to specific groups with a recognised status.[82] Indeed, one of the chief functions of the Empire was the mutual protection of

---

[81] Whaley, *Germany*, ii, 254.   [82] Wilson, *Empire*, 265.

these corporate rights. Thus, the Empire was a highly decentralised system, based on checks and balances, and structurally less capable of aggressive external power-projection and expansion than more centralised states. Instead, it was an association of heterogeneous corporate parts geared towards mutual defence.[83] At the end of the fifteenth-century the political elites of the Empire completed a reform process which restructured it as a defensive order of peace and legality. In 1495 a public peace ('Eternal Territorial Peace') was declared in which the use of force was made illegal (punishable by a 'ban'—the secular equivalent to the excommunication of Canon law) within the Empire, unless mandated by the newly established Imperial judiciary. All members of the Empire were placed under the protective umbrella of this public peace.

In sum, the Empire was a system based on tradition and legality, and this system depended for its smooth functioning on a high degree of cooperation, consensus, and the willingness to compromise on the part of its constituent political parts. It was precisely this willingness to compromise, cooperate, and seek consensus that broke down in the decades leading up to and during the Thirty Years War (1618–1648), which was in part an Imperial civil war in which neighbouring states intervened.[84] It was arguably the single most important event in our period. This war, and the peace settlement which ended it, cast a long shadow over the remainder of the early modern period. They also highlight the close interlinkages between Imperial politics and European international relations.

European statesmen, rulers, and diplomats were conscious of their shared Christian heritage—a continuation of the notion of a *respublica Christiana* from the Middle Ages—and considered themselves mutually bound as a community by shared rules of the 'law of nations' (*ius inter gentes*, or *ius gentium*).[85] Despite this sense of community bounded by the law of nations, war and conflict were endemic in early modern international relations—historians refer to the 'bellicosity' of the age.[86] It might therefore be surprising that there was an almost universally accepted norm of the high value of peace and the belief that it should be the basic condition among Christian powers.[87] Yet the 'sub-'norm of readiness to make peace was often in conflict with other norms of princely conduct which risked causing war, such as promoting the glory and honour of the dynasty and rulers' personal reputations, and defending one's subjects (and, more controversially, other rulers' subjects). Early modern European rulers justified their wars

---

[83] Helmut Neuhaus, '"Defension" – Das frühneuzeitliche Heilige Römische Reich als Verteidigungsgemeinschaft', in Stephan Wendehorst et al. (eds), *Lesebuch Altes Reich* (Munich, 2006), 119–26.
[84] Christoph Kampmann, *Europa und das Reich im Dreißigjährigen Krieg* (Stuttgart, 2013), 17.
[85] Anuschka Tischer, *Offizielle Kriegsbegründungen in der Frühen Neuzeit. Herrscherkommunikation in Europa zwischen Souveränität und korporativem Selbstverständnis* (Münster, 2012), 58–78.
[86] Johannes Burkhardt, 'Die Friedlosigkeit der Frühen Neuzeit. Grundlageniner Theorie der Bellizität Europas', *ZHF* 24 (1997), 509–74.
[87] Irene Dingel et al. (eds), *Handbook of Peace in Early Modern Europe* (Berlin/Boston, 2020).

against each other on a variety of grounds, which often overlapped. These could include self-defence against threats or aggression, defending dynastic succession rights, responding to insults against honour and reputation, upholding the law of nations, punishment for injuries committed, and defending one's own subjects.[88] The protection of *other* rulers' subjects and of legal-constitutional rights in another state was also used to legitimate wars of intervention, to an extent that has previously been underappreciated. Theoretically, the Pope possessed the function of an 'arbiter' between warring Christian princes, although the practical limitations in the papal ability to perform this role were considerable, even before the Protestant Reformation in the sixteenth century. Despite the Emperor being the highest-ranking secular prince in Christendom, public debates in post-Reformation Europe largely rejected his suitability as such an arbiter, and instead focussed on the potential for the kings of France or England to assume that mantle, while also recognising that the role of arbiter could disguise hegemonic ambitions.[89]

During much of the sixteenth and seventeenth-centuries, the geopolitics of the interstate system were structured predominantly around the rivalry between France and the Habsburgs. While this rivalry persisted almost as a constant until the mid-eighteenth century, the international system was generally highly volatile on account of its growing pluralisation and alliance fluidity.[90] While this is true for most of the period, there were shifts in the nature of conflict. Most of the wars of the eighteenth century were 'symmetrical conflicts', in other words, classic state-on-state wars or 'cabinet wars'. Many of the most prominent wars during the sixteenth and first half of the seventeenth century, however, have been interpreted by historians as 'state-building wars', and as asymmetrical conflicts.[91] Such conflicts stemmed from an attempt by individual component entities of larger conglomerates of states which shared the same monarch in personal union, to break away and assert their independence from these 'composite monarchies', which dominated Europe.[92] Although the international system was not widely conceptualised as an integrated whole until the eighteenth century, European statesmen and diplomats were already aware of the interconnected nature of the various regional balances, or sub-systems, as seen for example in the practice of 'leapfrog diplomacy' whereby one power would entice a distant state to put pressure on a

---

[88] Tischer, *Kriegsbegründungen*, 132–209.

[89] See Christoph Kampmann, *Arbiter und Friedensstiftung. Die Auseinandersetzung um den politischen Schiedsrichter im Europa der Frühen Neuzeit* (Paderborn, 2001).

[90] Heinz Schilling, *Konfessionalisierung und Staatsinteressen. Internationale Beziehungen 1559–1660* (Paderborn, 2007), 385–92.

[91] Johannes Burkhardt, 'Wars of State or Wars of State-Formation?', in Olaf Asbach et al. (eds), *War, State and International Law in Seventeenth-Century Europe* (Farnham, 2009), 17–34.

[92] John H. Elliott, 'A Europe of composite monarchies', *P&P* 137 (1992), 48–71; Dorothée Goetze and Michael Rohrschneider, 'Imperien und "composite states" in der Frühen Neuzeit', *Europäische Geschichte Online (EGO)*, Feb. 2022.

more proximate rival from the rear, to improve its own geopolitical position in its own region of interest.[93]

The Holy Roman Empire was central to the European international system. Despite its legal-constitutional order of peaceful inter-territorial relations, the Reich was far from untouched by the predatory international environment; in fact, German and European politics were highly intertwined.[94] Located at the geopolitical heart of Europe, Germany was where the interests of all the major European powers, including France, Spain, the Netherlands, Denmark, Sweden, and even England intersected.[95] This was not just a question of geography. As a decentralised polity with a multitude of power centres, the Empire was incapable of harnessing its vast resources behind a unified programme of power-projection and expansion. Preventing the decentralised Empire from falling under the domination of a rival power within or outside Germany was a vital security interest for European powers, and one that many states were willing to go to war for, as they did during the Thirty Years War. The central position and manpower resources of the Empire were such that it could not be ignored by outside (especially neighbouring) powers. Its constitutional structure gave its numerous neighbours manifold opportunities to establish links and networks of patronage, sponsorship and protection with local princes or groups of princes, all of which increased the propensity of outside powers to intervene in the Empire, and for members of the Empire to appeal for external intervention during conflicts originating within the Empire. This, along with the princes' own jealous guarding of their liberties and privileges, helped to ensure the continuation of the Empire's decentralised constitutional set-up. The web of European-Imperial interconnections was strengthened by the numerous dynastic links between German and European princely and royal families, such as the personal unions that existed at various times between Saxony—Poland, Brandenburg—Prussia, Hanover—Britain, and Hessen-Kassel—Sweden. Almost all European international problems therefore also had a German dimension.[96]

Rival powers intervened in each other's domestic affairs throughout the early modern period, with *part* of the aim almost always being to gain geopolitical advantage. French armies and diplomacy supported rebellions against Spanish rule—Spain being under Habsburg rule from 1516 until 1700—at various times in the Netherlands, Catalonia, Naples, and Portugal, and supported states that were hostile to Spain in Italy (primarily Venice). France also had a long tradition of setting up patronage networks and relationships of protection of clients within the Empire that were directed against the Habsburg Emperor. Spain in turn also

---

[93] Brendan Simms, 'Europe's shifting balance of power', in Hamish Scott (ed.), *The Oxford Handbook of Early Modern European History, 1350–1750* (Oxford, 2015), ii, 638–62, at 649–50.
[94] Johannes Arndt, 'Deutsche Territorien im europäischen Mächtesystem', in Heinz Schilling et al. (eds), *Heiliges Römisches Reich Deutscher Nation 962 bis 1806* (Dresden, 2006), 135–43.
[95] Simms, *Europe*, 7–42. [96] Ibid., chs 1–2.

intervened in France's domestic affairs, for example by aiding enemies of the crown and co-religionists during the sixteenth-century French Wars of Religion. In 1617, the two branches of the Habsburgs signed a treaty which facilitated the rapid Spanish intervention in support of the Austrian Habsburg Emperor soon after the outbreak of the Thirty Years War. Spain's support of its Austrian cousins was largely aimed at securing the 'Spanish road' military corridor supplying their theatre of war in the Low Countries, but the family and religious ties were also still significant. In the Netherlands, the Spanish were fighting a rebellion by the largely Protestant northern provinces from 1568, a conflict in which outside powers, such as England under Elizabeth I, also intervened.

Broadly speaking European statesmen and diplomats considered the Habsburgs (especially its Spanish branch) to be the biggest threat to the balance of power until the mid-seventeenth century, and France for the century or so thereafter. During the later seventeenth and first half of the eighteenth centuries, an alignment of England/Britain, the Emperor, and the Dutch directed against France was viewed by contemporaries as more or less constant. From the mid-eighteenth century the number of great powers in the international system had increased to form a 'pentarchy' of Britain, France, Austria, Prussia, and Russia, which replaced the old Franco-Habsburg dualism as the main structuring principle in European geopolitics. In this later period the implacable inner-German enmity between Austria and Brandenburg-Prussia became an important feature of Imperial and international politics, and in general the centre of gravity in terms of the dynamism of European politics had shifted to the east. The German great powers and especially Russia overshadowed the western powers of Britain, France, and Spain from the mid-eighteenth-century.[97]

## Sources and Outline

The main sources that underpin this study include diplomatic correspondence (reports and instructions), the litigation records, official state papers, memoranda, and the private papers of statesmen, rulers, diplomats, and politicians of the European states and German territories involved in the relevant cases of intervention. Similar material from other states which were not directly involved in the crises, but whose statesmen nevertheless commented and discussed the (potential) interventions are also relevant to discern normative evaluations, perceptions, and assessments. Along with the works of contemporary theorists of German public (Imperial constitutional) law and the Law of Nations and Nature, the chief publications of the public sphere (pamphlets, journals, newspapers)

---

[97] Expertly analysed in H.M. Scott, *The Emergence of the Eastern Powers, 1756–1775* (Cambridge, 2001).

which deal with and debate the relevant cases of intervention also form useful original source material.

The remainder of this book is structured as follows. The opening chapter will address the parameter conditions and legal foundations of intervention in early modern central Europe, including Imperial constitutional law, and the theories of writers of the Law of Nations and Nature which discuss the legitimacy—or lack thereof—of interventions in other European states. The main empirical material then begins with Part One which analyses the 'international' interventions of European powers into central Europe before, during, and after the Thirty Years War. In Part Two, the analysis then 'zooms' into central Europe by addressing the Imperial interventions that were carried out as judicial executions within the Empire. Cases of interventions in very small territories such as Hohenems-Vaduz (modern Liechtenstein) in 1679–86 will be investigated. But the main empirical focus will be on interventions in a small and in a medium-sized territory, with Nassau-Siegen (1705–22) and Mecklenburg-Schwerin (1714–30) selected as detailed case studies.

# 1
# Legal Foundations
## Imperial Constitutional Law and the Law of Nations and Nature

Various constitutional arrangements formed the legal foundations for interventions, as did the writings of theorists. Fundamental laws and treaties possessing constitutional status, customary law, and the office of the Emperor formed the basis of the Imperial courts' jurisdiction in the territories. They also stipulated the mechanisms through which interventions could take place, usually in the form of executions of judicial decisions. They also laid down many of the corporate and individual rights which could be protected by intervention.

### The Reichsabschiede of Worms (1495) and Augsburg (1555)

The laws passed at the Reichstag of Worms in 1495 as the culmination of the Imperial reform movement had the effect of establishing a public peace for the Empire and an order of legal security, whereby disputes would be settled judicially at the newly established Imperial judiciary, rather than through violent self-help measures.[1] They set up the Empire as an order of public peace until its dissolution.[2] The Imperial Cameral Court (Reichskammergericht) was founded as a supreme judicial tribunal and highest court of appeal, capable of invalidating territorial litigation.[3] The 'Eternal Territorial Peace' outlawed the use of violence and banned the right of the Imperial Estates to conduct violent feuds. Instead of conducting violent self-help, legal complaints would be lodged at the Reichskammergericht. Anyone contravening this established public peace was to be declared 'banned', whereby he would forfeit all rights, possessions, and territories.[4] The effect of these measures was summed up by the jurist Karl-Friedrich Häberlin: 'In bygone ages,

---

[1] Matthias Schnettger, *Kaiser und Reich. Eine Verfassungsgeschichte (1500–1806)* (Stuttgart, 2020), 44–54.

[2] Siegrid Westphal, 'The Holy Roman Empire of the German nation as an order of public peace', *GH* 36 (2018), 401–14.

[3] Karl Zeumer (ed.), *Quellensammlung zur Geschichte der Deutschen Reichsverfassung* (Tübingen, 1913), 228–35.

[4] Ibid., 226.

the law of the fist prevailed. Disputes which are now settled by the pen at court, were then decided by the sword on the field of battle.'[5]

The Eternal Peace could be cited to justify interventions against rulers who used excessive force against their subjects. It therefore came to encompass general calm and peace within territories because the intervening Imperial authorities understood unrest within a territory could easily spread disturbances beyond its frontiers.[6] Conversely, victims of intervention would seek to support their own position by claiming the interveners had themselves committed a breach of the peace.[7]

This next big reform package passed at the 1555 Augsburg Reichstag included the ordinances of the Imperial Cameral Court (*Reichskammergerichtsordnung*)[8] and the 'Imperial Ordinance of Execution' (*Reichsexekutionsordnung*),[9] two important pieces of legislation affecting the regulation of regular Imperially-sanctioned interventions. They stipulated what kinds of appeals could be received at the high courts and specified how their decisions were to be executed. They enshrined the right of subjects to appeal against their rulers to a higher court, thereby extending legal security to mediate subjects. A major impetus behind this had been the Peasants' Revolt of 1525.[10] After massacring the rebellious subjects, the princely elites formalised the criminalisation of subjects' armed rebellions in legal codes such as the *Constitutio Criminalis Carolina* of 1532.[11] But they undertook innovative steps towards granting subjects the right of legal resistance through litigation: the right to sue their territorial princes or seignorial lords at higher courts. The Reichstag of 1526 ruled that appeals, including by subjects, against the territorial judiciaries could be heard by the Imperial judiciary and the procedural elements were regulated at the 1555 *Reichskammergerichtsordnung*.[12]

Historians have rated this 'juridification' of social conflict as a significant success story for the rule of law, and it was arguably a safety valve against violent protest.[13] This provision resulted in a profusion of subjects' appeals against their princes at the highest courts over the next two-and-a-half centuries. A quarter of cases before the Reichshofrat over the course of its existence were lodged by

---

[5] Karl-Friedrich Häberlin, *Handbuch des deutschen Staatsrechtes* (Berlin, 1797), iii, 399.
[6] E.g. RHR-report, 3 Nov. 1722: HHStA, RHR, Vota 34.
[7] E.g. RHR-report, 14 Feb. 1728: HHStA, RHR, Vota 36.
[8] Adolf Laufs (ed.), *Die Reichskammergerichtsordnung von 1555* (Cologne, 1976).
[9] Hanns Hubert Hofmann (ed.), *Quellen zum Verfassungsorganismus des Heiligen Römischen Reiches Deutscher Nation* (Darmstadt, 1976), 105–23.
[10] Peter Blickle, *The Revolution of 1525*, transl. Thomas A. Brady, Jr (Baltimore, 1981).
[11] Peter Blickle, 'The criminalization of peasant resistance in the Holy Roman Empire', *JMH* 58 (1986), 88–97.
[12] Wilson, *Empire*, 632; Winfried Schulze, *Bäuerlicher Widerstand und feudale Herrschaft in der frühen Neuzeit* (Stuttgart, 1980), 76; Laufs (ed.), *Reichskammergerichtsordnung*, 167–8 (part 2, art. 1, §1), 203–4 (part 2, art. XXVI, §2).
[13] Winfried Schulze, *Einführung in die Neuere Geschichte* (Stuttgart, 1987), 61.

ordinary inhabitants.[14] However, an ordinance of 1613 stipulated that the accused prince would have to be given the chance to present his case before mandates were issued against him. There remained a fundamental presumption of the prince's innocence and good governance.[15] The twin features of the criminalisation of violent (or other non-legal) resistance on the one hand, and the possibility of subjects' resistance through litigation remained a key element of the Empire's politico-legal culture until its end. A prince facing violent rebellions could hope for the Empire's support in suppressing his rebellious subjects. Conversely, a prince who mistreated his subjects, denied them their legal rights, or sought to undercut their legal appeals could face an Imperial intervention against his regime in support of his subjects.

The Imperial Kreise—associations of neighbouring territories in charge of organising common defence—were charged with the execution, militarily if necessary, of Reichskammergericht-verdicts in 1522, and in the 1555 *Reichsexekutionsordnung*.[16] There was a long-standing dispute between the Emperor and the princes, the princely conception of judicial executions being that the heads of the Kreis had to be appointed to intervening execution-commissions according to the *Reichsexekutionsordnung*, whereas the Reichshofrat and the Emperor maintained that the latter had the freedom to appoint whichever prince he wanted on the basis of his supreme judicial office.[17]

The reforms passed at the 1555 Reichstag are usually remembered for the Augsburg Religious Peace. After a series of relatively limited wars in the 1540s and 1550s the ruling princes and the Emperor's court came to the recognition that the religious schism could not be solved theologically or militarily. In 1552/1555, they therefore moved towards accepting and legally regulating confessional co-existence by shelving intractable questions of theological truth. This embodied, for the first time, a recognition of the importance of creating a legal-political framework to manage religious co-existence.[18] The protection of the Public Peace was extended to Lutheran rulers, but not to Reformed-Calvinists and other religious groups. The secular princes were granted the right to choose between the Catholic and the Lutheran faith, the so-called Right of Reformation (*ius reformandi*). Subjects could be forced to convert to the religion which their prince had chosen.[19] Subjects who did not wish to follow the confession of their prince were granted to the right to emigrate to a territory which shared their faith—the first basic individual right granted to the vast majority of German subjects.[20] Partially designed to undercut the tendency of princes to intervene on their own

---

[14] Wilson, *Empire*, 287.     [15] Schulze, *Widerstand*, 78.
[16] Zeumer, *Quellensammlung*, 268–71; Hofmann (ed.), *Quellen*, 111.
[17] E.g.: RHR-report, 7 Sep. 1718: HHStA, RHR, Den.-Rec. 699(14).
[18] Luise Schorn-Schütte, *Die Reformation* (Munich, 2011), 88–90.
[19] See *NtS* 15, 646; Zeumer, *Quellensammlung*, 284–9.
[20] Axel Gotthard, *Der Augsburger Religionsfrieden* (Münster, 2004).

authority 'horizontally' on behalf of co-religionist subjects of other princes of a different confession, the Religious Peace sought to consign confessional affairs to an inviolable domestic sphere.[21] In this vein, the treaty text stated: 'No Estate [territory] should protect and shield another Estate or its subjects against their government in any way'.[22] The 1555 reforms therefore tried to undercut horizontal intervention while simultaneously strengthening the mechanisms of regular 'vertical' Imperial intervention.

## The Reichshofrat Ordinances

In addition to the Reichskammergericht, the Reichshofrat served as an alternative supreme court, one of 'the two tribunals at which Imperial Estates can be sued'.[23] The Reichshofrat was founded by Maximilian I in 1497 as a second supreme court beholden entirely to the Emperor and revived by Ferdinand I in 1559.[24] The Reichshofrat was less closely bound to an order of proceedings than the Reichskammergericht, and enjoyed greater freedom of action to seek a mediated settlement of disputes between conflicting parties. This, along with its close ties to the Emperor, who staffed and paid its members, from whom it derived its authority, and who was its official head, gave the Reichshofrat a greater political and diplomatic role than the Reichskammergericht.[25] Various ordinances of the Reichshofrat contained numerous stipulations relevant to the legal basis of Imperial interventions. Dispensation of justice was to be aimed at upholding the rights and privileges of all members of the Reich, including subjects, territorial estates, Imperial Estates, and the Emperor himself.[26] The ordinances of 1637 and 1654 explicitly provided for the appeal of subjects—regardless of social standing or religion—against their rulers.[27] Not only could subjects appeal against the territorial authorities' judicial rulings, but also against governmental and administrative measures.[28] Reaching definitive verdicts was not the primary aim of the Reichshofrat. Instead, it was to seek to mediate an amicable settlement between the conflicting parties in the first instance.[29] A confessional representation of both Protestants and Catholics was reaffirmed in the ordinance of 1654: six of the eighteen Reichshofrat-members were to be Protestants.[30]

---

[21] Joachim Whaley, 'Religiöse Toleranz als allgemeines Menschenrecht in der Frühen Neuzeit?', in Georg Schmidt et al. (eds), *Kollektive Freiheitsvorstellungen im frühneuzeitlichen Europa (1400–1850)*, (Frankfurt, 2006), 403–5.
[22] Zeumer (ed.), *Quellensammlung*, 287.
[23] Häberlin, *Handbuch des deutschen Staatsrechtes*, iii, 398.
[24] Eva Ortlieb, 'Die Entstehung des Reichshofrats in der Regierungszeit der Kaiser Karl V. und Ferdinand I.', *Frühneuzeit-Info* 17 (2006), 11–26.
[25] Sellert, *Prozessgrundsätze*, 175–7; Sellert (ed.), *Ordnungen*, ii, 49.
[26] RHRO 1637, §2: Hofmann (ed.), *Quellen*, 167.   [27] Sellert (ed.), *Ordnungen*, ii, 39ff.
[28] RHRO 1654: Sellert (ed.), *Ordnungen*, ii, 107.
[29] RHRO 1637, §5: Hofmann (ed.), *Quellen*, 167.   [30] Sellert (ed.), *Ordnungen*, ii, 56.

The ordinances also provided for the Reichshofrat's dispatch of commissions. Commonly, princes of the Kreis in which the disputed case occurred were instructed by the Reichshofrat to form a commission and act under the authority of the Emperor, on behalf of the Kreis. Their tasks could include mediating between conflicting parties, implementing protective measures over persecuted parties, executing Reichshofrat-verdicts or decisions, executing treaty stipulations, administering a territory, or simply investigating and gathering further evidence. Such commissions are important for the topic under investigation, because they were often the vehicle through which potentially military Imperial interventions in the affairs of the territories occurred. The ordinances of the Reichshofrat proclaimed 'the advancement of justice and the rescuing of the persecuted' as one of the purposes of its commissions.[31]

## The Treaties of Westphalia (1648) and the Latest Imperial Recess (1654)

The Peace of Westphalia which ended the Thirty Years War in 1648 consisted of the Treaty of Münster (*Instrumentum Pacis Monasteriensis*—IPM) between France and the Emperor together with the Empire (i.e. the Imperial Estates), and the Treaty of Osnabrück (*Instrumentum Pacis Osnabrugensis*—IPO) between Sweden and the Emperor together with the Empire. The Peace consisted of three main elements: a reformed Imperial constitution; related to this, a revamped religious settlement for the Empire; and an international peace treaty. It was therefore both a document of international and constitutional law.

Although the 'Westphalian myth' of princely sovereignty has largely been debunked, it is often not recognised that the Peace in many ways *increased* the scope for external interference in the affairs of the territorial states and the Reich as a whole. Its mutual guarantee clauses and its confessional arrangements provided greater opportunities for legally-backed intervention than before.[32] The official recognition and toleration of the three major confessional groups, the freezing of confessional conditions within each territory according to a 'normative year', and the guarantee clauses formed the legal basis of the Protestant princes' claimed right of intervention on behalf of co-religionists under Catholic rule—which could be described as 'horizontal intervention'. Nevertheless, it also helped the proponents of princely liberties argue for freedom from interferences in internal territorial affairs.

---

[31] RHRO 1654, art. 2 §6: Sellert (ed.), *Ordnungen*, ii, 117.
[32] Although see Brendan Simms, 'A false principle in the Law of Nations', at 92, where Westphalia is described as 'a charter for intervention'.

LEGAL FOUNDATIONS 27

The chief provisions which were often cited by proponents of princely prerogatives and opponents of interventions in the territories were those which affirmed princely rights: the free exercise of *ius territoriale* (territorial 'rights' i.e. rule), the right to participate and be consulted in decisions relating to all important Reich affairs, the *ius foederum*, and the confirmation of the terms of the Augsburg Religious Peace of 1555.[33] Yet, as Burkhardt has demonstrated, 'territorial Right' cannot be and was not interpreted as signifying sovereignty.[34] The reaffirmed right of the princes to conclude alliances among themselves and with external powers was one of the main provisions contributing to the sovereignty myth.[35] However, the *ius foederum* was subject to an important caveat: 'provided nevertheless, that these Alliances be neither against the Emperor, nor the Empire, nor the Publick Peace, nor against this Transaction especially'.[36]

A further provision which was often cited in support of the princely conception of far-reaching princely authority over territorial subjects, and hence an opposition to interferences in the internal affairs of the territories, was the confirmation of the Right of Reformation for the princes.[37] Despite this confirmation, serious limitations to the territorial rulers' authority over their subjects in confessional matters were also introduced in 1648, which were regularly cited by those intervening on behalf of persecuted co-religionists in other territories. The subjects' right of emigrating (*ius emigrandi*) was reaffirmed,[38] while the introduction of the normative year (*Normaljahr*) constituted a more far-reaching curtailment of princely authority over subjects. As a religious compromise settlement, confessional possessions, the right of worship and the official confessional status of each territory were fixed to the state it had been in, on 1 January 1624.[39] A graded form of toleration was applied to all adherents of the recognised confessions, based on the situation that had existed in the normative year. Although the princely Right of Reformation was reaffirmed for secular princes, this now largely became a private matter for the prince in question and it was thereby effectively negated.[40] The confessional rights of subjects would therefore no longer be affected by a princely conversion. Additionally, no subject in the Empire could be prevented from converting to Catholicism, Lutheranism, or Calvinism. No adherent of the three confessions could be discriminated against based on religion.[41]

In general, Westphalia laid the foundation for an improved 'juridification' of sectarian conflict, especially because Calvinism was finally recognised. At the level

---

[33] Clive Parry (ed.), *CTS* i, 241.
[34] Johannes Burkhardt, 'Der Westfälische Friede und die Legende von der landesherrlichen Souveränität', in Jörg Engelbrecht et al. (eds), *Landes- und Reichsgeschichte*(Bielefeld, 2004), 199–220, at 213–15.
[35] E.g. Albrecht Randelzhofer, *Völkerrechtliche Aspekte des Heiligen Römischen Reiches nach 1648* (Berlin, 1967), 162.
[36] Parry (ed.), *Consolidated Treaty Series*, vol. 1, 241.   [37] Hofmann (ed.), *Quellen*, 173.
[38] IPO art. V, § 30: Hofmann (ed.), *Quellen*, 181.   [39] *CTS* 1, 215.
[40] Ibid., 222.   [41] IPO, Art. 5, § 41: ibid., 231.

of the Empire, the principle of full equality (parity) between Catholicism and Protestantism was enshrined. One of the Protestants' chief grievances about being outvoted by the Catholic majority was addressed. Protestant representation was stipulated for both supreme judicial tribunals.[42] This strengthened the Empire's regular channels of intervention because henceforth the dispensation of justice at the courts, and supervision by the Diet, was viewed as more legitimate by Protestants.

The guarantee clauses (IPO XVII §4–5/IPM §115–116) bridged international and Imperial-constitutional law. These clauses formed the most important foundation of interventions by the external guarantors and the claimed right of intervention by the Protestant princes. They stated that each contracting party (France, Sweden, the Emperor, the Imperial Estates) was obliged as a guarantor to uphold each and every aspect of the peace settlement, even those that did not directly affect them.[43] That this granted France and Sweden the right to intervene to uphold all rights and terms of Westphalia after the prescribed steps was generally accepted.[44] The question of whether these clauses gave the Imperial Estates the right to enforce the stipulations of the treaties militarily through a 'horizontal intervention' was far more controversial.

The Latest Imperial Recess of 1654 was the set of laws passed by the last intermittent Reichstag before it became permanent at Regensburg from 1663. Westphalia was confirmed, but the system of executing high court verdicts was amended.[45] The requirement of placing the executee under the ban was dropped given the difficulty in securing its implementation.[46] The executee would be placed under the ban if he resisted the execution by force.[47] This provision was sometimes considered a legal justification for removing princes from power who had resisted Imperial executions using force.[48]

## The Capitulations of Election (1519–1792)

The capitulations of election (*Wahlkapitulationen*) were contracts between the electors and the Emperor-designate, the conclusion of which constituted a precondition for the election of an Emperor by the electors from 1519.[49] They tended to reflect a desire to limit the capacity of the Emperor and of the Imperial courts to intervene in the territories. Leopold I's capitulation sought to limit the extent to

---

[42] IPO, Art. 5, § 54–5: Müller (ed.), *Instrumentum Pacis Westphalicae*, 130.
[43] IPO, Art 17, §4–7 = IPM, §114–17 (Parry: IPM §122–4): CTS 1, 354.
[44] Johann Jacob Moser, *Von der Garantie des Westphaelischen Fridens* (np, 1767), 39.
[45] JRA §193: Adolf Laufs (ed.), *Der jüngste Reichsabschied von 1654* (Bern, 1975), 94.
[46] JRA §15: Hofmann (ed.), *Quellen*, 200.   [47] Ibid., 212.
[48] E.g. RHR-report, 3 Nov. 1722: HHStA, RHR, Vota 34.
[49] Gerd Kleinheyer, *Die kaiserlichen Wahlkapitulationen* (Karlsruhe, 1968), 123.

which the Reichshofrat could initiate proceedings against princes based on complaints by their subjects, although the subsequent trend was the opposite. The ban was seen as particularly inimical to princely authority as it provided for the deposition of princes, and could be declared by the Emperor and the Reichshofrat after consulting the electors.[50] Despite being a legal instrument, it had always been more of a political tool.[51] Numerous high-profile depositions of banned princes contributed to a princely reaction in Charles VI's capitulation (1711), according to which the banning of ruling princes was henceforth bound to the consent of the Reichstag.[52] This effectively ended the institution. The 'suspension' from power of the duke of Mecklenburg in 1728 contributed to a further tightening of the mechanisms of deposition in 1742 when Charles VII had to promise 'to preserve the free seat and vote of all Estates of the Empire at the Reichstag... they shall not be deposed from their territorial government, be it provisionally, or in contumacy, or in any other way'.[53] Conversely, article 15 of Charles VI's *Wahlkapitulation* was sometimes cited[54] by proponents of Imperial protective intervention: 'The... Emperor shall maintain the mediate subjects of the Empire and the territorial subjects of the Estates under his Imperial protection'.[55]

## Customary Law and the Office of the Emperor

In the context of regular Imperial interventions, references to customary law and practice were often used to legitimise the *desired outcome* of an intervention.[56] This was usually the return to the *status quo ante* within targeted territories. The office of the Emperor, on the other hand, legitimised *the act of intervening*. Customary practice enjoyed constitutional validity. Its importance reflected Germany's conservative political culture and an aversion towards the unprecedented.[57] The leading eighteenth-century public law jurist Johann Jacob Moser explained that German princes' authority was never absolute. It was subject to a two-way limitation: by Imperial fundamental laws and by their territory's customary practices.[58]

The office of the Emperor was a crucial legitimating factor for Imperial interventions. Even in cases of considered or requested interventions which

---

[50] Matthias Weber, 'Zur Bedeutung der Reichsacht in der Frühen Neuzeit', *ZHF* Beiheft-19 (1997), 55–90.
[51] Dorothee Mußgnug, *Acht und Bann im 15. Und 16. Jahrhundert* (Berlin, 2016).
[52] *Europäische Fama* 324 (1729), 1026ff.
[53] Quoted in Zeumer (ed.), *Quellensammlung*, 408–12.
[54] RHR-report, 22 Oct. 1720: HHStA, RHR, Vota 34.
[55] Zeumer (ed.), *Quellensammlung*, 419.
[56] See also Eva Ortlieb, *Im Auftrag des Kaisers. Die kaiserlichen Kommissionen des Reichshofrats und die Regelung von Konflikten im Alten Reich (1637–1657)* (Cologne, 2001), 34–41.
[57] Roeck, *Reichsherkommen*, parts 2–3. [58] Moser, *NtS* 14, 9.

were not to be carried out or authorised by the Emperor, but by the princes or external European powers, the authority of the Emperor was rarely explicitly denied. Such interventions were portrayed by their advocates as restitutive measures, which normally should have been carried out under the Emperor's authority, but were carried out by others in his place, as the Emperor was either unable or unwilling to do so.[59] The Emperor's legal mandate to intervene in the territories derived from his authority over the Imperial Estates, which existed in three capacities. Firstly, as head (*Oberhaupt*) of the Imperial hierarchy; secondly, as the highest judge of the Empire possessing the supreme judicial office, with the dispensation of justice carried out in his name; finally, as feudal overlord of the Empire, whereby the Imperial Estates' territories theoretically reverted to the Emperor's possession after the extinction of a ruling dynasty, and fiefs had to be invested to each new ruler. Fiefs could also technically be withdrawn if an Imperial Estate rebelled against its feudal overlord.[60] In practice little distinction was made between these three capacities and they were routinely referred to in conjunction with one another.[61]

An important concept which underpinned Imperial interventions and derived from the Emperor's high office was the idea that as the highest judge he represented the source of all justice in the Reich and that, as the head of the Empire, it was his 'paternal' responsibility to protect the weak and the persecuted and to maintain all his subjects' rights, both mediate and immediate. Thus, he was regularly referred to as 'the highest protector',[62] whose general tasks in the Empire included 'the protection of the princely houses of the Empire and their subjects, and the re-establishment and consolidation of... territorial constitutions, and of complete calm'.[63] He was widely expected to 'protect... against violence and injustice, by virtue of Imperial high judicial decrees'.[64] These duties derived from 'high judicial duty and paternal care over the Empire'.[65] On receipt of complaints of persecution and violence at the hands of territorial rulers, the Reichshofrat would routinely remind the Emperor that his 'supreme judicial office... requires the mediate Imperial subjects and the territorial subjects of the Estates... to be kept under the Emperor's protection'.[66] The Emperor himself was keen to present his role in the Reich as its 'highest lord-protector'.[67]

---

[59] E.g. *Corpus Evangelicorum*-resolution, 16 Nov. 1720: *EStC*37 (1721), 626–8.
[60] See Moser, *NtS*14, 261.   [61] Westphal, *Kaiserliche Rechtsprechung*, 89.
[62] RHR-report, 9 Sep. 1708: HHStA, RHR, Den.-Rec. 694(4).
[63] RHR-resolution, 17 Jan. 1729: HHStA, RHR, Prot.-xviii,71, fol. 26.
[64] Emperor Charles VI to duke of Mecklenburg-Schwerin, Vienna, 26 July 1715: HHStA, RK, Kl.-Reichsstände 347, fols 136–40.
[65] RHR-resolution, 17 Jan. 1729: HHStA, RHR, Prot. xviii, 71, fol. 27.
[66] RHR-report, 22 Oct. 1720: HHStA, RHR, Vota 34.
[67] Emperor Charles VI to Cardinal von Sachsen-Zeitz, Vienna, 10 June 1717: HHStA, RK, PK-Weisungen 5a, fol. 259.

The Emperor's protective function also derived from his role as the '*Supremus Executor Pacis*', the highest authority responsible for the execution and implementation of Westphalian terms and rights.[68] The Reichshofrat argued that as 'overlord'[69] of the Reich, territorial subjects' duty of obedience towards the Emperor took precedence over their duty of obedience towards their territorial rulers, thereby further legitimising territorial interventions.[70] Even territorial rulers accused of insubordination by ignoring the Emperor's mandates, would without fail assert their loyalty and obedience to the head of the Empire.[71] According to Moser, as the head of the Empire, the Emperor was authorised to order interventions even before the supreme courts had reached decisions or verdicts.[72] He was even argued—controversially—to be permitted to depose a prince in consultation with the Reichstag, 'if the territorial ruler...neglects his duties to such an extent, that one must fear the ruin of his house or of his territory'.[73]

## Types and Mechanisms of Intervention in the Empire and their Intellectual Foundations

The body of law outlined above was not merely used as a rhetorical justification for largely political acts. It directly determined the mechanisms of intervention in a political culture which was geared towards the maintenance of the rule of law. There were two broad types of intervention in the Empire: 'regular' intervention under the Emperor's authority, and 'irregular' intervention which was not carried out under his command. The office of the Emperor as the highest judge and head of the Imperial hierarchy formed the basis of regular interventions carried out in his name and under his authority. In combination with an overlap between three different areas of Imperial law, it determined how the 'regular' channel of Imperial interventions could take place: firstly, the jurisdiction of the supreme judicial tribunals in inter- and intra-territorial disputes; secondly, the system of executing the decisions of the Imperial judicial tribunals through the participation of the Kreise and commission; and finally, the basic individual and corporate rights of German subjects. The so-called *privilegia de non appellando* were concessions that more powerful princes sought to limit the capacity of territorial subjects to appeal to the Imperial courts. However, the *privilegia* could not provide the princes with a complete exemption from the jurisdiction of the Imperial courts, even when a *privilegia illimitata* had been granted. No type of *privilegium* could prevent

---

[68] Quoted in RHR-report, 5 Nov. 1726: HHStA, Staatenabteilung, Nationalia-Palatina 34.
[69] Moser, *TRSL*, 19. [70] RHR-statement, 14 May 1723: HHStA, RHR, Den.-Rec. 699(7).
[71] E.g. Duke of Mecklenburg-Schwerin to Charles VI, Rostock, 5 Feb. 1718: *EStC32* (1719), 144–50.
[72] Moser, *NtS* 14, 263–4. [73] Ibid., 264.

subjects from appealing against their rulers in cases of a denial (or delay) of justice (*denegate justitia*).[74]

On receipt of an accusation against territorial rulers the supreme courts could then appoint princes to form an Imperial commission to investigate the complaints and, if necessary, to execute judicial decisions. The task of intervening was therefore delegated by the Reichshofrat in the name of the Emperor to the Imperial Estates acting on behalf of their Kreis. Approval by the Reichstag was not required for such executions. Most Imperial interventions required an appellant to have addressed complaints to the courts—the role of the Emperor therefore being largely reactive.[75] However, in cases of patent and 'notorious' violations, the Emperor and the Reichshofrat could directly mandate an execution-commission, through a so-called *Mandatum sine-clausula*, a fast-track protective measure in cases in which the illegality was plain, without preceding litigation at the judicial tribunals. This was an important instrument for armed interventions because they could be issued on the basis of the 'common good', whereby the courts had much interpretative leeway.[76]

The basic individual rights of subjects which could be protected by these mechanisms were summed up by Moser:[77] freedom of conscience for all Catholics, Lutherans, and Reformed post-1648, the freedom to emigrate (except in areas where serfdom was customary), the freedom to enter an external power's military service as long as it was not at war with the Reich, the right to appeal against one's territorial ruler's judicial verdicts, and to sue a ruling prince. Finally, all subjects were deemed to be 'free people...both with regard to their persons and their property'.[78] These individual rights which largely derived from Imperial law overlapped with different sets of corporate and customary rights at the territorial level.

Analogous interventions could also occur within the territorial level by princes against landlords mistreating peasants. The Emperor was at the apex of a hierarchical set of reciprocal inter-personal and inter-corporate relationships based on a social contract of protection in return for obedience and counsel. These reciprocal duties existed along the Imperial hierarchy: between Emperor and Imperial Estates, between Imperial Estates (usually ruling princes) and territorial estates (usually noble landlords), between seignorial landlords and tenant peasants. In general, lordship in each of these relationships entailed a responsibility to protect

---

[74] Ulrich Eisenhardt, *Die kaiserlichen Privilegia de non Appellando* (Cologne, 1980), 25–7.
[75] Sellert, *Prozessgrundsätze*, 195–203.
[76] Manfred Uhlhorn, *Der Mandatsprozess sine-clausula des Reichshofrats* (Cologne, 1990).
[77] Moser, *TRSL*, 937–9.
[78] Moser, *TRSL*, 939. Recent research has shown, however, that some foreign slaves were kept in the Empire and that this was explicitly affirmed by the courts at least once in the late eighteenth-century: Rebekka von Mallinckrodt, 'Slavery and the Law in Eighteenth-Century Germany', in von Mallinckrodt et al. (eds), *Beyond Exceptionalism—Traces of Slavery and the Slave Trade in Early Modern Germany, 1650–1850* (Berlin/Boston, 2021), 137–62.

those subject to the lord in question, upon which the subjects' provision of counsel and obedience depended.[79]

This principle of monarchical rule legitimised by the provision of protection existed throughout Christendom.[80] As early as 1275, the authors of the *Schwabenspiegel* legal code wrote 'we shall serve the lord so that he shall shield us, and if he shields us not, then by right we are not obliged to serve him'.[81] Influential fifteenth- and early sixteenth-century Italian humanist writers shared a belief that the exercise of power had to be justified and legitimised through the consent and trust of the ruled.[82] There was a general belief in Germany, France, and England, that rulers who carried out violence against those that they should naturally love—primarily their subjects and children—were acting illegitimately and therefore guilty of tyranny, or *rex crudelis*. Violence by rulers against others guilty of *rex crudelis* was considered legitimate.[83] This duty to protect found expression in numerous territorial treaties or contracts between the prince and his subjects, such as one from Nassau-Siegen in 1596 in which the prince promised to 'protect and shield the subjects from unjust violence'.[84] The reciprocal duties between rulers and ruled was also expressed in the numerous written appeals that early modern subjects routinely addressed to their princes.[85]

The failure to provide protection or, worse, the victimisation of one's own subjects could lead to interventions against lords, including the deprivation of fiefs, by the higher level across the feudal hierarchy. Research has shown that central European peasants were not merely passive, oppressed subjects, but could often take the initiative legally and politically by lodging appeals against their landlords and/or rulers. The multitude of intersecting rivalries and conflicts along different levels of the Reich hierarchy (subjects—territorial estates—Imperial Estates—Emperor) and rivalries between princes, confessional groupings, other corporate entities, and foreign European powers, meant that parties to conflict always had plenty of opportunities to appeal for support outside of the immediate context of the dispute. Thus, in the Empire conflicts between two parties would inevitably draw in additional parties at different levels of the Imperial hierarchy

---

[79] Christoph Kampmann, *Reichsrebellion und kaiserliche Acht. Politische Strafjustiz im Dreissigjährigen Krieg und das Verfahren gegen Wallenstein 1634* (Münster, 1993), 226.

[80] Rainer Babel, *Garde et Protection. Der Königsschutz in der französischen Außenpolitik vom 15. bis zum 17. Jahrhundert* (Ostfildern, 2014), 30-3.

[81] F.L.A. Lassberg (ed.), *Der Schwabenspiegel* (Tübingen, 1840), 133.

[82] Joseph Canning, *Conciliarism, Humanism and Law. Justifications of Authority and Power, c.1400-c.1520* (Cambridge, 2021), 92-143, 179-82.

[83] Jean-Marie Moeglin, '"Rex crudelis". Über die Natur und die Formen der Gewalt der Könige vom 11. zum 14. Jahrhundert', in Martin Kintzinger et al. (eds), *Gewalt und Widerstand in der politischen Kultur des späten Mittelalters* (Ostfildern, 2015), 19-51, at 21.

[84] Werner Conze, 'Sicherheit, Schutz', in Brunner et al. (eds), *Geschichtliche Grundbegriffe* (Stuttgart, 1984), v, 839.

[85] Cecilia Nubola et al. (eds), *Bittschriften und Gravamina Politik, Verwaltung und Justiz in Europa (14.-18. Jahrhundert)* (Berlin, 2005).

(and beyond). The manifold opportunities of appeal and external protection and intervention engendered a sense of consciousness of subjects' legal rights, which in turn strengthened their resolve to mount legal resistance through litigation at the supreme tribunals and appeals for external protection.[86]

Regular Imperial interventions can be broadly grouped into three types. Firstly, there were interventions for the protection of territorial subjects against the actions of their territorial ruler (Chapters 5–7). Secondly, there were interventions for the protection of Imperial Estates against victimisation by other, more powerful Imperial Estates.[87] The relevant mandate in such cases often took the form of a *Conservatorium*, or *Protectorium*, which was an order to protect a specific person, subjects or territorial estates, or one or more princes or other Imperial Estates.[88] Thirdly, some interventions were aimed at improving territorial governance by rectifying bad governance through the imposition of an Imperial administration in cases of governments' chronic, insurmountable debt or princes' insanity (Chapter 5). The 'irregular interventions' which were not carried out under the Emperor's authority, but instead under that of the princes themselves or by external European powers into the Empire (Chapters 2–4), also drew heavily on laws and constitutional arrangements when they were being justified.[89] This was more so in the former than the latter case because interventions of the former type occurred largely within the Empire, whereas in the latter case the Law of Nations was an additional area of interveners' repertoire of argumentation.

## Legal Theorists on Interventions within the Empire

The rest of this chapter will address the writings of theorists regarding intervention. A related topic that theorists addressed is the relative balance between subjects' rights and rulers' prerogatives, and the nature of sovereignty. The assessment of the Peace of Westphalia by early modern writers is important in this context because of Westphalia's central role in defining subjects' and princes' rights within the Empire, and in legally empowering outside powers to intervene into the Empire. Theorists of numerous legal traditions dealt with these topics. These included writers of the public law of the Empire,[90] and of the 'law of nations and nature' (the predecessor of international law). Theorists of the law of nations

---

[86] Peter Blickle, *Landschaften im Alten Reich* (Munich, 1973).
[87] For this, see Patrick Milton, 'Imperial law versus geopolitical interest: the Reichshofrat and the protection of smaller states in the Holy Roman Empire under Charles VI (1711–40)', *I* 130 (2015), 831–64.
[88] Moser, *NtS* 14, 265.
[89] For horizontal interventions by princes against their peers, see Patrick Milton, 'The early eighteenth-century German confessional crisis: the juridification of religious conflict in the re-confessionalised politics of the Holy Roman Empire', *CEH* 49 (2016), 39–68.
[90] See Michael Stolleis, *Geschichte des öffentlichen Rechts in Deutschland* (Munich, 1988), i.

were less concerned with the minutiae of the Imperial constitution, and more with the general principles governing interstate relations.[91] While the authors of theoretical texts were generally not cited in official declarations of war and official justifications for interventions—mainly because such theorists did not create binding law with their texts—there is some evidence that their writings influenced princes who carried out interventions.[92]

In general, public law writers favoured the rights of subjects' corporate bodies within territories along with the Emperor's right and responsibility to intervene on their behalf, whereas natural law writers emphasised the prerogatives of territorial princes, with the concomitant illegitimacy of Imperial intervention in their domestic territorial affairs. This disagreement expressed itself in diverging interpretations of the Peace of Westphalia and its specific role in the mutual protection of individual and corporate rights. According to many writers of natural law, Westphalia chiefly enshrined the corporate rights of the Imperial Estates, whereas public law writers generally emphasised the importance of upholding the corporate rights of mediate subjects. They therefore placed greater emphasis on Westphalia's role in safeguarding and regulating the broader Imperial structure and its provisions for intervention against princely absolutism in defence of mediate subjects. By contrast, natural law theories were routinely used as an ideological tool by early modern rulers in the pursuit of princely absolutism.[93]

Some theorists of natural law were more in favour of territorial estates' rights, such as Johann-Salomon Brunnquell, who insisted that princes must adhere to compacts concluded with subjects. Many German natural law writers such as Nikolaus-Hieronymus Gundling, and Christian Wolff ostensibly supported near-absolutist territorial rule despite this being very much the exception in the Empire, and despite being critical of the theories of Hobbes. They also rejected the notion of the divine right of territorial princes, but they construed the mere obedience of subjects as their consent to an implicit contract of rule. However, they argued that princely powers were not without bounds, as they were always subject to *limites naturales* (limits set by natural law), to *limites practitiis* (practical limitations), and to the fundamental Imperial constitutional laws. The natural law that imposed restrictions on princely freedom of action primarily related to the necessity of pursuing the 'common good' (*salus publica*), but according to these theories, its pursuit usually entailed an expansion of princely governmental authority vis-à-vis subjects and territorial estates, and it was up to the prince to define the

---

[91] Knud Haakonssen, 'Early-modern natural law', in George Duke et al. (eds), *Cambridge Companion to Natural Law Jurisprudence* (Cambridge, 2017).
[92] Tischer, *Kriegsbegründungen*, 75–6; Ragnhild Hatton, *George I. Elector and King* (London, 1978), 224.
[93] Notker Hammerstein, 'Christian Thomasius', in *Politische Theorien des 17. und 18. Jahrhunderts*, ed. Bernd Heidenreich et al. (Darmstadt, 2011), 123–4.

common good.[94] Other theorists of both natural and public law, especially those of the tradition of 'universal public law' (*ius publicum universal*) such as Justus Henning Böhmer, went further and ascribed to the prince the power to determine which fundamental territorial laws were compatible with the common good.[95] The existing literature underappreciates that discourses grounded in natural law were cited not only by territorial princes intent upon state-building and extending their authority over their subjects, but also by the Imperial authorities (chiefly the Reichshofrat) when intervening against ruling princes for the protection of the traditional customary rights of their territorial estates and other subjects. In suspending the duke of Mecklenburg-Schwerin from power, for example, the Reichshofrat argued that the duke's disregarding of the obligations detailed in treaties concluded by his predecessors with their subjects was contrary to natural law.[96]

Public law jurists were largely critical of drive towards absolutism by some princes, especially those ruling larger, militarised territories, and lamented the disunity that this brought to the Empire. They instead emphasised the rights and privileges of corporate entities and subjects within territories and the role of the Emperor as a protector of this plethora of rights, if need be through intervention. Personal circumstances sometimes played a role. Johann Jacob Moser had been a legal counsellor in the employment of the territorial estates of Württemberg, who were conducting a bitter, decades-long conflict with their duke, and in this context Moser was arrested and imprisoned by ducal authorities for five years without trial.[97] This personal experience of princely arbitrariness undoubtedly affected Moser's stance on Imperial interventionism. He agreed that in principle, subjects were obliged to obey their princes, but 'one must not take subjecthood and slavery or blind subservience for one and the same thing; instead subjecthood must be understood in such a manner as is appropriate to the original German liberty'.[98]

This reference to German Liberty is instructive. Traditionally historians have equated the concept of German Liberties, or *Deutsche Freiheit*, with an assertion of princely liberties and freedom from Imperial interference, which is how it was mainly understood in the eighteenth-century. Leonard Krieger argued that this contributed to German authoritarianism, as liberty became synonymous with the authority of the (territorial) state.[99] Michael Hughes defined it as 'the princes' winning of internal sovereignty within their states'.[100] However, as Georg Schmidt

---

[94] See Diethelm Klippel, 'Staat und Souveränität', in *Geschichtliche Grundbegriffe* (Stuttgart, 1990), vi, 112–14.
[95] E.g. Justus Böhmer, *Introductio in ius publicum universale* (Magdeburg, 1710).
[96] RHR-report, 3 Nov. 1722: HHStA, RHR, Vota 34.
[97] Mack Walker, *Johann Jacob Moser and the Holy Roman Empire* (Chapel Hill, 1981).
[98] Moser, *TRSL*, 1149.
[99] Leonard Krieger, *The German Idea of Freedom* (Chicago, 1957), 5–7.
[100] Michael Hughes, 'The Imperial Aulic Council as Guardian of the Rights of Mediate Estates', in Rudolf Vierhaus (ed.), *Herrschaftsverträge, Wahlkapitulationen, Fundamentalgesetze* (Göttingen, 1977), 192–204, at 195.

has demonstrated, the concept applied equally to German subjects, mainly on the basis of individual property rights, and later also confessional rights, from the time of its inception in the fifteenth-century.[101] Some early modern public law writers stressed that the concept reflected a German tradition of rights being respected across the Imperial hierarchy, including those of the territorial estates and other subjects. The polymath Hermann Conring, for example, stressed the historical legitimacy of the territorial estates' rights as an essential component of German politico-legal culture.[102] This tradition was often used in nationalist discourse to contrast German freedoms with the tyrannies of Turkey and France.[103] According to Moser, 'the Germans were free people, from the top right down to the peasant, and were governed as such, in contrast to the Russians and Turks'.[104] He noted 'when a German ruler ruins his own territory or lands, the Emperor and the Reich are authorised to put a check on him, and to render him incapable of carrying out sinister designs to the detriment of Reich'.[105] Similarly, the public law theorist G.D. Strube argued 'that it is forbidden to annul the treaties made with [the subjects], and to harass the subjects with unusual taxes under the pretext of an unprovable territorial necessity'.[106]

The jurist Johann Jacob Schmauss argued that subjects' labour and taxes were supplied in a contractual expectation of good and just governance and that the Empire was the guarantor of the princes' good treatment of their subjects.[107] While the basic assumption of *Landeshoheit* was that the territorial rulers were permitted 'to command ... everything in their territory and lands', this authority was always subject to restrictions. Such prerogatives could only be exercised by the princes 'in so far as their hands are not tied by Imperial laws, the customary law of the Empire, the treaties with their territorial estates and subjects, ... traditional freedoms and customs'.[108] Thus, in addition to being subject to the authority of Emperor and Empire, the princes' duties and restrictions curtailing their authority with regard to their own subjects were also clearly articulated by contemporary legal experts.[109] Such notions were central to the justifications of Imperial interventions, as expressed by Moser: 'If an Imperial Estate ... oppresses its territorial estates and subjects in violation of the freedoms they possess, the Emperor has the right and responsibility to provide them with protection against this.'[110] The public law jurist Christian Jacob von Zwierlein stressed that must have recourse

---

[101] Georg Schmidt, 'Die "deutsche Freiheit" und der Westfälische Friede', in Ronald G. Asch et al. (eds), *Frieden und Krieg in der Frühen Neuzeit* (Munich, 2001), 323–47.

[102] Hermann Conring, *Exercitatio de Germanici Imperii civibus* (Helmstedt, 1641), sec. 33.

[103] Martin Wrede, *Das Reich und seine Feinde. Politische Feindbilder in der reichspatriotischen Publizistik* (Mainz, 2004), 538–9.

[104] Moser, *TRSL*, 347.   [105] Ibid., 285.   [106] G.D. Strube quoted in Moser, *TRSL*, 318.

[107] J. Heldmann (ed.), *J. J. Schmaussens academische Reden über das teutsche Staatsrecht* (Lemgo, 1766), 660f.

[108] Both quotations Moser, *NtS* 14, 9.   [109] Moser, *NtS* 15, 61.   [110] Moser, *TRSL*, 285.

to judicial appeal, otherwise 'most of our Imperial Estates will become despots, and the subjects will become akin to slaves, while the little bit of German Freedom that remains will be lost entirely'.[111]

The natural law theorist and political philosopher Samuel Pufendorf discussed the Imperial judiciary in his work *Monzambano*. While he approved of its ideals and its ability to intervene in local conflicts, he argued in 1667 that its functioning was woefully deficient:

> There [is] scarce any Trace of Justice... left in the Empire... if [litigating parties] commence a Suit in the [Reichskammergericht], it is an Age before they can hope to see an end of it. In [the Reichshofrat] it is feared that there is too much opportunity for Partiality and Bribery.[112]

Many of the interventions against ruling German princes accused of tyranny, bad governance, and ruinous expenditures resulted in their depositions from power, even after the successive restrictions imposed by the Emperors' capitulations of election. Yet Pufendorf—representing a mainstream view on this topic—argued that depositions of Imperial princes were unconstitutional:

> Much less is it in the Power of the Emperor alone to take away or deprive any Prince of his Dignity, or expel any of the States out of his Dominions, though they are guilty of a great Crime against the Empire, but even in the most notorious case he must obtain the Consent of the Electors, before he can interdict the meanest of the offender.[113]

There was a discussion among German public law jurists and other writers about the extent to which the mutual guarantee of the Peace of Westphalia permitted irregular 'horizontal interventions' by princes on their own authority within the Empire. At the beginning of the eighteenth century, the umbrella organisation of Protestant princes represented at the Reichstag, the *Corpus Evangelicorum*, developed a constitutional vision which asserted that, as a contracting party of the treaties of Westphalia, they were entitled on the basis of the guarantee to execute the treaty terms by force if necessary, if Westphalian terms were violated and if the Emperor refused to immediately dispatch execution-commissions. They were therefore asserting a right to intervene in the domestic territorial affairs of Catholic princes for the protection of the latter's Protestant subjects. The principle of non-interference in domestic affairs was argued to be dangerous:

---

[111] Christian Zwierlein, *Vermischte Briefe und Abhandlungen* (Berlin, 1767), 105–13.
[112] Samuel Pufendorf, *The Present State of Germany*, ed. Michael Seidler (Indianapolis, 2007), 206.
[113] Ibid., 120.

Territorial rulers refusing to accept that other fellow Estates of the Reich protect foreign inhabitants and subjects was one of the greatest causes which led to the wretched Thirty Years' War. It is precisely this wound which has been healed by the Peace of Westphalia.[114]

The Protestant understanding, therefore, was that stability could not be achieved by an absence of external intervention. Westphalia was, according to this view, a corrective measure because it opened domestic affairs up to mutual and reciprocal scrutiny of religious rights. Thus, at the end of 1719 during a confessional crisis in the Empire, the *Corpus* issued—without reference to the Emperor's authority—the duke of Württemberg with a *Protectorium* over the city of Speyer, which was complaining of violations of its rights by the prince-bishop of Speyer.[115] The *Corpus* received ample intellectual support in its interpretation from several of their co-religionists in the field of public law and natural law, such as Moser[116] and Nicolaus Hieronymus Gundling,[117] while the Emperor and the Catholics rejected this expanded scope of intervention.

In general, theorists from the late seventeenth-century onwards were influenced by the intellectual trends and rights-based discourse of the Enlightenment, which itself built on earlier natural law traditions.[118] Johann Leonard Hausschild wrote in 1738 that all subjects and serfs possessed 'rights of humankind' which should be guaranteed and must not be violated.[119] However, although many Protestant writers generally applauded Westphalia for, among other things, its provision (as they saw it) of an expanded right of horizontal intervention, which could benefit Protestant communities, as outlined above, some of the same writers also considered the confessional terms of Westphalia to be inadequate and anachronistic as judged by the later standards of Enlightenment toleration. Writers such as Gundling,[120] and Renatus Karl von Senkenberg disapproved of Westphalia's rigid freezing of confessional conditions and the ability of princes to expel subjects whose religion had not been practised in the relevant territory in 1624, and the continued ban on 'sects' and religions other than Catholicism, Lutheranism, and Calvinism.[121]

One early modern European and German tradition of writing provided an idealised picture of princely and civic duties for instructional purposes in the form

---

[114] *Corpus* to principal-commissioner, 14 Apr. 1720, in *EStC*, vol. 36 (1721), 610–16624ff.
[115] *Corpus* Conclusum, 22 Dec. 1719: Schauroth (ed.), *Vollständige Sammlung*, vol. 3 (1752), 673.
[116] Moser, *NtS* 7: 202–3, 426–7.
[117] Nicolaus Hieronymus Gundling, *Ausführlicher Discours über das Natur- und Völcker-Recht*, 332.
[118] Vincenzo Ferrone, *The Enlightenment and the Rights of Man* (Liverpool, 2019); Dan Edelstein, *On the Spirit of Rights* (Chicago, 2019).
[119] Schulze, *Widerstand*, 140.
[120] Gérard Laudin, 'Le Gründlicher Discours über den Westfälischen Frieden de Nicolaus Hieronymus Gundling', in Jean-Paul Cahn et al. (eds), *De la guerre juste à la paix juste* (Villeneuve, 2008), 136–7. I thank Prof. Anuschka Tischer for this reference.
[121] Renatus Karl von Senkenberg, *Darstellung des... Westfälischen Friedens, nach der Ordnung der Artikel* (Frankfurt, 1804), 146.

of manuals for rulers (*Fürstenspiegel/speculum principium*, 'mirror of princes') and the ruled (*Untertanenspiegel*, 'mirror of subjects'). According to many German writers, a severe failure to conform to these would warrant an extra-territorial enforcement by the Empire. While the latter prescribed subjects' obedience and instructed them to limit complaints to legal channels, the former expounded the responsibility of territorial princes to rule in a measured and restrained manner while respecting the territorial and Imperial constitutions.[122] Such manuals on princely virtues shared a theme of an aversion towards 'tyranny' and a princely responsibility to protect one's subjects. Subjects were entrusted to princes by God and ensuring the well-being of these subjects therefore legitimised their rule. One such manual from 1622 stated that a prince must consider 'how he can protect his subjects from external violence and his territory from wantonness'.[123] Johann Schramm's *Politica Historica* (1606) argued that princes who sought to excessively burden their subjects and keep them in poverty were 'afflicted by tyranny and avarice'. Veit Ludwig von Seckendorff argued in 1685 that rulers who disregarded the 'welfare of the people' were guilty of tyrannical rule.[124] Johann Joachim Becher also tended towards stressing princes' responsibilities towards subjects in his *Politischer Discurs*. He complained that in practice, many subjects are being treated as 'serfs and slaves'; yet despite claiming that many princes were tyrants, he denied subjects a right of resistance, as did most early modern theorists.[125] The Jurist Anton Wilhelm Ertel was unusual in arguing that subjects possessed a right of active, non-judicial resistance, 'when no regular legal remedy remains', in other words, when they were suffering under tyrannical rule.[126]

A similar discourse against tyrannical rule was often expressed by writers from other traditions too. Samuel Gottlieb Treuer published a treatise in 1719 at the time of the Imperial intervention in Mecklenburg-Schwerin. He argued that respecting subjects' rights was essential for domestic peace within territories and that all subjects should enjoy natural rights which went beyond positivist codified law. Based on empirical historical enquiry, he submitted that absolute government usually resulted in tyranny and that this could justly be curtailed through external intervention.[127] Similarly, and in the context of the same case, the historian Hans Heinrich Klüver wrote in 1740 that 'an Imperial Estate cannot arbitrarily alter its territorial governmental constitution and disregard the rights of its estates. Consequently, His Imperial Majesty has sufficient authorisation and power to

---

[122] Bernd Kremer, *Der Westfälische Friede in der Deutung der Aufklärung* (Tübingen, 1989), 73–6.
[123] Georg Löhneiss, *Aulico-politica oder Hof-, Staats- und Regierkunst* ([1622–24] Frankfurt, 1679), 93.
[124] Veit Ludwig Seckendorff, *Christen-Stat* (Leipzig, 1685), 264.
[125] Quotations in Peter Blickle, 'Untertanen in der Frühneuzeit', *Vierteljahrsschrift für Sozial- und Wirtschaftsgeschichte*, 70/4 (1983), 504.
[126] Schulze, *Widerstand*, 253–6.
[127] Robert von Friedeburg, 'Natural jurisprudence, argument from history and constitutional struggle in the early enlightenment: the case of Gottlieb Samuel Treuer's polemic against absolutism in 1719', in T.J. Hochstrasser et al. (eds), *Early Modern Natural Law Theories* (Dordrecht, 2003), 141–64.

restore the form of government of a territorial prince's lands to a footing that is in accordance with the Imperial and territorial constitutions, and to protect the mediate subjects in their rights.'[128]

This eighteenth-century discourse against arbitrary and tyrannical rule had a long lineage. In the 1570s the jurist Andreas Gail wrote a legal treatise which discussed 'how the tyranny of rulers against their subjects may be impeded and eliminated' by the Imperial supreme courts. In this influential text, Gail posited a clear responsibility of princes to protect subjects' rights, and failing this, a responsibility of the Empire to intervene against abuses of power. He argued that a prince who 'acted against his subjects with excessive fury and torments them beyond measure', and who imposes taxes far beyond customary levels 'without the consent and will of the subjects', was guilty of 'wantonness and tyranny'. Subjects owed their princes obedience, but a prince also owed his subjects 'loyalty' and was responsible for their 'protection and the maintenance of their rights'. If a prince failed in this responsibility to protect his subjects' rights, 'the subjects may certainly appeal for and requisition help and protection from a higher authority'. The Imperial judiciary may determine 'that a prince may be deprived of his jurisdiction and rule on account of great and dreadful encumbrances and tyranny... also that a prince's fief may be withdrawn and he may be deposed because of the abuse of his jurisdiction or power'. However, he also stressed that the Reichskammergericht should ensure that subjects are not incited to rebel against their princes and that mandates should not be issued to princes rashly.[129]

Similar arguments relating to the combination of subjects' own lack of a right of resistance in the face of tyranny with a duty of a higher authority to intervene against this were made by Johannes Althusius in the early seventeenth century. But his theory of intervention was far more expansive than that of most other theorists because of his broad conception of who was encompassed as possible interveners: the electors could intervene against the Emperor and even territorial estates could resist princes within the territories.[130]

## Theorists of the Law of Nations and Nature on International Interventions on Behalf of Foreign Subjects

Many of the period's most prominent theorists of the Law of Nations and Nature considered the question of whether or not intervention for the protection of a tyrannical ruler's subjects was legitimate, in addition to discussing its occurrences

---

[128] Hans Klüver, *Beschreibung des Herzogthums Mecklenburg* (Hamburg, 1737–1740), vol. 5, iii–iv.
[129] Andreas Gail, *Deß kaiserlichen Kammergerichts sonderliche Gerichtsbreuche und Rechtsregeln* (Hamburg, 1601 [1578]), extract printed in Schulze, *Widerstand*, 200–3.
[130] Johannes Althusius, *Politica Methodice* (Herborn, 1614).

as a political phenomenon without assessing its permissibility per se. This is unsurprising given that such interventions (or interventions justified as such) have occurred throughout modern history. The Europe in which sixteenth-century theorists were writing was undergoing and had undergone far-reaching changes. The notion of a single Christian political and cultural-religious entity (*Christianitas*) with the Emperor and Pope at its secular and spiritual apex was making way for a more pluralistic international order.[131] Nevertheless, the recognition among Europe's Christian political actors of being part of a shared community of cultural values and norms persisted throughout the early modern period.[132] The emergence of dynastic and (proto-)nation states from the fourteenth-century initiated a development which was largely completed by the sixteenth-century (before Westphalia!), namely the relocation of external sovereignty to a number of kingdoms and other polities. Similarly, the Reformation broke the spiritual unity of western Christendom, adding further fractures which compounded the political pluralisation of the continent. In light of this relocation of sovereignty to the national level (a process to which some theorists such as Jean Bodin and Renaissance humanists had themselves contributed), what did law of nations thinkers write about intervention in the internal affairs of other states?

At the beginning of the sixteenth century, Niccolò Machiavelli's writings noted the widespread existence of interventions in the domestic affairs of other 'republics', without coming to an explicit verdict about whether they were legitimate. He was more concerned with expounding the necessary steps for state survival and for the pursuit of rulers' self-interest; preventing hostile interventions by outside powers formed an important part of each state's interests because such interventions were inimical to true freedom and self-governance. To forestall such interventions, Machiavelli argued, outside powers needed to be deprived of a pretext to intervene, and this could be aided by reducing the risk of subjects' rebellions and complaints, which might be used as an excuse by outside powers to intervene. He therefore advised princes and republican governments to ensure the existence of the rule of law and legal appeals possibilities in their polities, in order to remove the grounds for foreign intervention against them. 'Whenever one finds outside forces called in by a party of men residing in a city, it may be taken for granted that this is due to a defect in its constitution, in that it comprises no institution which provides an outlet for the malignant humours to which men are prone, without their taking unconstitutional action.'[133]

Most other theorists paid more attention to the question of what kind of military force was legitimate, including interventions. Many Law of Nations

---

[131] Heinz Duchhardt, *Balance of Power und Pentarchie. Internationale Beziehungen 1700–1785* (Paderborn, 1997), 73.
[132] Tischer, *Kriegsbegründungen*, 219–22.
[133] Niccolò Machiavelli, *The Discourses* ([1517] London, 1970), 228–9 (I.7.2–3, 7).

writers of this period considered intervention in the context of the 'just war' doctrine (*bellum iustum*); the conditions that needed to be in place for military action to be considered just. Just war was influentially defined by the thirteenth-century scholastic thinker St Thomas Aquinas as a publicly declared war, conducted as a last resort under princely authority, arising from a just or material cause, and carried out with a good intention, namely to establish a just peace.[134] Whether interventions for the protection of foreign subjects constituted a just cause for war was discussed by some writers. Some, such as the early sixteenth-century humanist Erasmus of Rotterdam, considered almost any application of military violence unjust and espoused an irenic world view, on the basis that any use of force would have unpredictable consequences.[135] Most theorists, however, argued that war could be just if it was aimed at the promotion of the common good and caused by the desire to punish injuries inflicted or by exercising the rights of self-defence. In this context early modern thinkers debated whether punishing other rulers' tyranny towards their own subjects constituted a good intention and just cause. Similarly, whether the right to self-defence extended to the defence of others was an important question in discussions about the legitimacy or justness of military interventions for the protection of foreign subjects.[136]

The debate around the European conquest and colonisation of the New World was relevant to thinking on interventions for the protection of foreign subjects.[137] Francisco de Vitoria, the founder of the Spanish late scholastic tradition argued that the basic principle in international law was non-intervention except when 'sins against nature' were committed within other kingdoms and empires.[138] In such cases outside powers were entitled to intervene, based on, *inter alia*, Proverbs 24:11 ('Deliver them that are drawn unto death, and forbear not to free those that are being dragged to destruction'), Leviticus 19:18, Romans 13:8, and God's command to be concerned about neighbours and to love them as one loves oneself. Because the Indigenous Americans were neighbours, he argued that 'anyone, especially princes, may defend them from tyranny and oppression' which he argued were being perpetrated in Indigenous empires in the Americas[139] Avenging offences against the law of nature was less important to Vitoria than the defence and protection of subjects in danger. According to Vitoria, Indigenous rulers' jurisdiction rights over their subjects was subordinated

---

[134] St Thomas Aquinas, *Summa Theologiae* (Cambridge, 2006), vol. 35, 81–2.
[135] Jan Sperna-Weiland et al. (eds), *Erasmus von Rotterdam* (Hamburg, 1988).
[136] J.T. Johnson, 'The idea of defense in historical and contemporary thinking about just war', *Journal of Religious Ethics* 36 (2008), 543–56.
[137] Mariano Delgado, 'Die Kontroverse über die Humanitäre Intervention bei der spanischen Expansion im 16. Jahrhundert', *Historisches Jahrbuch* 131 (2011), 93–118.
[138] For the following: G.P. van Nifterik, 'Religious and humanitarian intervention in sixteenth- and early seventeenth-century legal thought', in Randall Lesaffer et al. (eds), *Sovereignty and the Law of Nations 16th–18th centuries*, in *Iuris Scripta Historica* 20 (2006), 35–60, at 39–43.
[139] Quoted in William Bain, 'Vitoria: the laws of war, saving the innocent, and the image of God', in Welsh, *Military intervention*, 71.

to other (Christian) rulers' right to intervene for the protection of innocents, because for a just cause to exist, the motivation had to be to stop the inhumane treatment of humans. This was based not only on religion, but also on 'friendship and bond of humankind'.[140]

Writing under the impression of the chaos of the French Wars of Religion, Jean Bodin sought to buttress the authority of the prince as sovereign, while stressing that sovereigns remained bound to divine and natural law.[141] His *Six books of a Commonweale* (1576) was seminal in strengthening the theoretical foundation of an idealised 'internal' sovereignty as concentrated in the person of the monarch.[142] As part of Bodin's aim of strengthening the legitimate monarch's domestic control and authority over all subjects, he emphasised the absence of a right of resistance by subjects, even against the most evil and tyrannical of sovereigns. However, *other* Christian sovereigns were entitled to intervene for the protection of foreign subjects suffering under the tyranny of a prince, by acting defensively on their behalf. By doing so, the intervening sovereign prince was exercising one of his rights of sovereignty (freedom of action in foreign policy and acting defensively on behalf of others) and moreover engaging in a laudable undertaking by protecting persecuted innocents.[143]

Bodin characterised such external protection as 'a holie anchor for people uniustly tyranized'. Given his approval of interventions for the protection of foreign subjects, Bodin felt obliged to stress that 'I do not meane that it shall be lawfull for forraine princes to thrust their neighbours subiects into rebellion, under coulor of protection or amitie'. But he also argued that if 'a wise prince... finds that the outrageous proceeding of a Tyrant against his subjects be irreconcilable, then ought he to take upon him the protection of the afflicted with a generous resolution'[144] Bodin also discussed the more specific treaties of protection that could be signed between weaker and stronger entities (both states and sub-state actors such as territorial estates or towns). For it to be true *protection*, Bodin stressed that the protector would need to act selflessly, and treaty terms would need to ensure that the protectee does fall under the protector's rule.[145]

Intervention against tyrannical rule was discussed extensively in sixteenth-century treatises, most prominently in those of the 'monarchomach' tradition which tried to justify Protestant resistance against the Catholic monarchy in France during the wars of religion and against Spanish rule in the Netherlands.[146]

---

[140] Francisco de Vitoria, *Political Writings*, ed. Anthony Pagden et al. (Cambridge, 1991), 233, 286–8.
[141] Sophie Nicholls, *Political Thought in the French Wars of Religion* (Cambridge, 2021), 171–84.
[142] Grewe, *Epochs*, 177–80.
[143] Nifterik, 'Intervention', 46–8; Tuck in Recchia and Welsh, *Intervention*, 105.
[144] Jean Bodin, *The Six Bookes of a Commonweale* ([1576] London, 1606), 632.
[145] Bodin, *Six Bookes* (Paris, 1986), book 1, 151–2, book 5, 167–8, 172–3.
[146] See Robert Kingdon, 'Calvinism and resistance theory, 1550–1580', in J.H. Burns et al. (eds), *Cambridge History of Political Thought* (Cambridge, 1991), 193–218.

One of the most famous was the pseudonymously published *Vindiciae contra Tyrannos* (Basel, 1579), which devoted the last of its four chapters to the question of 'whether neighbouring princes may by right, or ought, to render assistance to subjects of other princes who are being persecuted on account of pure religion, or oppressed by manifest tyranny'.[147] The first three chapters attempted to justify internal resistance by subjects of the true (i.e. Protestant) religion against oppression by their tyrannical government (which was assumed to be Catholic), while the final chapter turned towards international relations by arguing in favour of intervention for the protection of tyrannised subjects of other princes. In advocating a right of resistance by subjects against their own rulers, the argument was unusual among theoretical works. It was not a purely theoretical work, though, because it was probably aimed at encouraging Protestant states' interventions in the French Wars of Religion and in the Dutch Revolt.[148]

The author's argument in favour of intervention is based on two arguments. Firstly, he argues that the (Protestant) Church constitutes a single corporate body that transcends borders, and that each constituent part is therefore entitled and obliged to provide assistance and protection to other parts of the body, regardless of state boundaries.[149] Secondly, the author then goes beyond narrow Protestant solidarity by arguing that Christian princes have a right and an duty to defend innocents suffering under tyranny: 'a prince who idly observes the wicked acts of a tyrant and the slaughter of innocents, which he can prevent ... is more guilty than the tyrant'.[150]

The author addresses the opposing argument, namely that rulers should not interfere in other states' domestic affairs by quoting the Roman playwright Terence: 'I am a man, I think that nothing human is alien to me.' The author makes clear that princes should not use protective intervention as a spurious pretext for self-aggrandisement, which is how he viewed the French intervention by Henry II against Charles V in 1552. He nevertheless advises rulers, when appropriate, to

> confine a tyrant within his borders, and extend a helping hand to stricken people... In this way you should show that you are entirely concerned for human society, not your own welfare... If a prince practise tyranny against a people, a neighbouring prince should be no less zealous in rendering assistance to it, than he would be to the prince if the people engaged in sedition.[151]

The author of the *Vindiciae* therefore exceeded earlier writers' espousal of intervention by fashioning it as not only a right but also a duty of Christian princes,

---

[147] For the following: Nifterik, 'Intervention', 43–6; David J.B. Trim, '"If a prince use tyrannie towards his people"', in Simms et al. (eds), *Humanitarian Intervention*, 29–66, at 32–6.
[148] George Garnett, 'Introduction', in *Vindiciae, contra tyranos* (Cambridge, 1994), liii.
[149] *Vindiciae*, 175.   [150] Ibid., 180–3.   [151] Ibid., 183–4.

and by adopting a highly prescriptive tone: 'Contemporary princes ought to follow these examples in repressing tyranny...justice binds us to check tyrants...and charity to succour and lend a helping hand to the oppressed'.[152]

One of the most important theorists of the law of nations prior to Grotius was the Italian humanist Alberico Gentili, who was a convert to Protestantism and had fled Spanish Habsburg rule in his native Italy to take up a professorship of law in Oxford. He devoted a considerable part of his seminal work *De iure belli libri tres* (1588) to the topic under consideration. In some ways his arguments on intervention were similar to those of the Protestant author of the *Vindiciae*: both were in favour of intervention for the protection of other rulers' subjects, specifically in support of the rebellions against Spanish Habsburg rule, on the basis that the failure to protect others when it entails no risk to oneself is morally objectionable.[153] Unlike the arguments put forward in the *Vindiciae* however, Gentili, similar to Bodin before him, denied subjects a right of resistance against their ruler, while sovereigns were entitled to act defensively on the behalf of foreign subjects. The basic underlying principle was that 'kingdoms were made not for kings, but kings for their kingdoms', and that all kingdoms or polities were bound together in a universal community of humanity, governed by natural law.[154] This derived from the 'natural fellowship of [the] human race'.[155]

Gentili argued that when disputes arose between private subjects within a polity, or between subjects and their rulers, there were existing mechanisms of litigation or adjudication within that state which could settle the matter. But if subjects had organised themselves to an extent to which they could carry out a general armed rebellion against their ruler, then 'they are public characters and on an equality with the sovereign, just as one sovereign is said to be on an equality with another'. Gentili viewed such a dispute as having left the internal sphere; instead, it was played out at an anarchical level whereby there were no higher adjudicating authorities. Under such circumstances, other sovereign rulers could step in to support either the ruler or his subjects. The subjects could be defended against their ruler if he had committed a 'violation of the common law of mankind', just as one should 'defend sons against fathers who are unjust'.[156] Gentili therefore stressed that '[i]t is not lawful...to do to subjects whatever one wishes' because all men, even sovereigns, were subject to natural law.[157] Because subjects possessed no right of resistance, he argued that 'aid may be given to the subjects of another even when they are unjust, but only with the purpose of saving them from immoderate cruelty and unmerciful punishment; for it is the part of humanity to do good even to those who have sinned'.[158]

---

[152] Ibid., 185.  [153] Nifterik, 'Intervention', 50.
[154] Alberico Gentili, *De Iure Belli Libri Tres* (Oxford, 1933), 76.  [155] Ibid., 74.
[156] Ibid., 75.  [157] Ibid., 78.  [158] Ibid., 76.

Gentili also discussed the geopolitical realities of intervention. He came to the recognition that interventions usually only took place when they reinforced a strategic self-interest on the part of the intervener. In the recent case of the English intervention in support of the Dutch anti-Spanish revolt (1585), Gentili argued that apart from the question of its justness, there was a consideration of self-interest on the part of the English which made the intervention compelling. Given the 'many bonds of kinship between the English and the Belgians' and the physical proximity of the Netherlands, it was in England's interest to ensure that this neighbouring country did not fall 'from its former state of liberty [to become] grievously oppressed with garrisons and ruled by the mere nod of a sovereign. Now this condition their neighbours are not able to endure. And no one else ought to be prevented from fostering liberty... from good neighbours come good things, from bad ones, evil'.[159] This points to the strategic importance attached by England to the Low Countries. Preventing the erasure of traditional Dutch Protestant liberties and the Netherlands' complete subjugation under Habsburg control would further the geopolitical aims of halting the advance of Philip II's looming universal empire: 'the great hero [Earl of] Leicester wisely realised that the defence of the Belgians was most expedient and necessary for his own country... for fear that if that bulwark of Europe... should be broken down by the Spaniards, nothing would be left as a bar against their violence'.[160]

Hugo Grotius, a Dutch Protestant, was arguably the most influential theorist of the early modern law of nations. He also discussed intervention and devoted a section of his seminal *De jure belli ac pacis libri tres* (1625) to the question 'Whether we have a just cause for war with another prince, to relieve his subjects from their oppression under him'. Repeating earlier arguments by Gentili and by Bodin, he argued that subjects had no right of resistance against tyrannical rulers, and he similarly argued that other Christian sovereign princes could act defensively on their behalf: 'though it were granted that Subjects ought not... to take up Arms against their Prince... we should not yet be able to conclude from thence, that others might not do it for them'.[161] In comparison with previous theorists, though, Grotius places greater emphasis on the punitive nature of the resulting interventions, punishment being inflicted for serious violations of the law of nature: 'Kings... have a Right to exact Punishments, not only for Injuries committed against themselves, or their Subjects, but likewise, for those which do not peculiarly concern them, but which are, in any Persons whatsoever, grievous Violations of the Law of Nature or Nations'. And as was the case with previous thinkers on the subjects, he stressed that such interventions should not be used as a cover for self-aggrandisement: '... not with an ambitious Design of gaining them

---

[159] Ibid., 77.   [160] Ibid., 78.
[161] Grotius, *The Rights of War and Peace* ([1625] Indianapolis, 2005), 1161–2.

[the target countries] for himself, but for the Sake of vindicating the Cause of the Oppressed'.[162]

The theorists considered so far had a rather favourable attitude towards intervention. However, not all sixteenth- and seventeenth-century political thinkers agreed. The late scholastic Jesuit writer of the Salamanca School, Francisco Suárez, was generally opposed to intervention in the internal affairs of states. In the early seventeenth century, he wrote that 'the assertion that sovereign kings have the power of avenging injuries done in any part of the world, is entirely false, and throws into confusion all the orderly distinctions of jurisdiction'.[163] An exception to this rule, according to Suárez, could be made if subjects possessed a legally-secured right of resistance according to the constitutional arrangements of the state in question. In such cases, and if the subjects were already actively revolting, and consented to and requested intervention, other sovereign princes could support them, if there were ties of 'friendship' or alliance between them.[164] The late sixteenth-century writer Balthazar Ayala intended to delegitimise the Dutch rebellion and the interventions in support of the rebels. He therefore argued that neither subjects possessed a right of resistance, nor did other rulers have a right to support them against their lawful superiors. Instead, the Papacy was the only authority permitted to intervene against Christian rulers in their domestic affairs, for example by deposing a prince and relieving his subjects of their oath of loyalty to him.[165]

The theoretical positions in the law of nations on intervention considered so far were written before the Peace of Westphalia. After the supposed watershed of 1648, theorists' writings on intervention does ostensibly seem to have shifted. Writing in the 1650s, Thomas Hobbes argued that such interventions for the protection of another prince's subjects were impermissible.[166] According to Samuel Pufendorf's theory from 1672, the right to intervene existed, but was more restricted than in the theories of his predecessors Bodin, Gentili, and Grotius. It could take place only if specifically requested by the oppressed subjects. In answer to the question 'whether it be lawful to take arms in defence of the subjects of a foreign commonwealth, against the invasions and oppressions of their sovereign', he wrote 'that we cannot lawfully undertake to defend the subjects of a foreign commonwealth, in any other case, than we they themselves may lawfully take arms to repress the insupportable tyranny and cruelties of their own

---

[162] Ibid., 1021. See also R.J. Vincent, 'Grotius, Human Rights and Intervention', in Hedley Bull et al. (eds), *Hugo Grotius and International Relations* (Oxford, 1992), 241–56.
[163] Quoted in Pärtel Piirimäe, 'Just war in theory and practice: the legitimation of Swedish intervention in the Thirty Years War', *HJ* 45 (2002), 499–523, at 515.
[164] J. Soder, *Francisco Suárez und das Völkerrecht* (Frankfurt, 1973).
[165] Balthasar de Ayala, *De Jure et Officiis bellicis et disciplina militari* (Washington, 1912), sec. 1.2.11.
[166] See Jonathan Havercroft, 'Was Westphalia 'all that'? Hobbes, Bellarmine, and the norm of non-intervention', *Global Constitutionalism* 1 (2012), 120–40.

governors'. According to Pufendorf, rulers had a responsibility to protect, but only toward their own subjects, not foreign ones.[167]

In the mid-eighteenth century, Christian Wolff's theory was similarly disinclined towards intervention: 'to interfere in the government of another...is opposed to the natural liberty of nations'.[168] However, Wolff's theory hypothetically permitted collective intervention if it was carried out by a so-called *civitas maxima*. He conceived of this fictitious body as a commonwealth encompassing a series of smaller associations and political units. On contractarian grounds, collective intervention by this overarching body could be legitimate, since the member states were joined to this larger unit and committed themselves to its laws.[169] It is possible that Wolff was influenced by the Holy Roman Empire in devising this theory, as internal interventions within the Empire were legally possible. Another mid eighteenth-century German theorist of the law of nations, Johann Gottlieb Heineccius, also argued against any kind of intervention in the internal affairs of sovereign princes, on the basis that 'sovereignty is sacred and... Sovereigns are sacred'.[170]

Emer de Vattel was the most influential theorist of the law of nations in the eighteenth century and his normative ideas on the international order—expressed primarily in his *Droit des Gens* of 1758—were seminal in shaping the standard view of modern international relations and legal order. Vattel's conception of intervention was even more restrictive than that of his contemporary Wolff. According to his theory, the international system should consist of legally equal and politically independent sovereign states, which adhere to the attendant rule of non-intervention in each other's domestic affairs.[171] Intervention was allowed only under extraordinary conditions, such as to aid tyrannised subjects who appeal for help and who are actually already in a state of revolt, or in the context of a civil war when the state has collapsed into warring factions, in which case the factions have in effect become distinct polities and it is therefore not truly an intervention within a state.[172] For such theorists, therefore, cases of intervention for the protection of foreign subjects was conceptualised less as intervention, and more as an internationalised escalation of a civil war.

These exceptions on the part of Vattel and Wolff notwithstanding, the fact that theories of natural law and the law of nations appear to become increasingly

---

[167] Pufendorf, *The Law of Nature and Nations* (London, 1729), 843–4.
[168] Quoted in Jennifer Pitts, 'Intervention and sovereign equality: legacies of Vattel', in Recchia, *Military Intervention*, 143.
[169] Ibid., 142, 144–5.
[170] Johann Gottlieb Heineccius, *A Methodical System of Universal Law, or: the Laws of Nature and Nations* ([1741] Indianapolis, 2008), 442.
[171] Simone Zurbuchen, 'Vattel's "Law of Nations" and the principle of non-intervention', *Grotiania* 31 (2010), 69–84.
[172] Richard Tuck, *The Rights of War and Peace. Political Thought and the International Order from Grotius to Kant* (Oxford, 2001), 193–4.

anti-interventionist after 1648 seems to lend credence to a key aspect of the 'Westphalian system'. However, these theories were an ideal-type normative narrative, rather than an accurate depiction of post-Westphalian state practice. Nor did they accurately reflect the positive European law of nations, at least with regard to the possibility of French and Swedish intervention in the Empire. Pitts has therefore astutely remarked that the 'Westphalian' model of equal, independent sovereign states should more accurately be termed a 'Vatellian' model.[173]

## Conclusion

Early modern jurists of various traditions discussed the legality and justness of interventions against princes and kings for the protection of their subjects and came to different conclusions. Proponents of the right of intervention emphasised the inherent liberties and rights of subjects and the foreign political freedoms of princes to act defensively on behalf of foreign subjects. This was based on a responsibility to protect not only one's own subjects but also others, especially when bound by common religion or by alliance or 'friendship'. Opponents of intervention emphasised princes' prerogatives (in the case of Imperial Estates) and sovereignty (in the case of kings and republics) which made interference from outside impermissible.

When writing about interventions within, or into, the Empire, there was a much stronger argumentative reliance upon positive (codified) constitutional and treaty law because there was an extraordinarily extensive body of laws and treaties which could be used to legitimise intervention, in many cases as judicial execution. Discussions about interventions by one state in another state other than the Empire, by contrast, invoked abstract principles supposedly inherent in the law of nature and nations, although there was some overlap.

Most theorists of the law of nations and nature—both Catholic and Protestant—allowed for interventions for the protection of other rulers' subjects to a greater or lesser degree, albeit as an exception rather than as the norm in interstate relations. Most early modern theorists argued strongly in favour of a high degree of princely sovereignty and prerogatives, but this did not preclude the right to intervene for the protection of other princes' subjects. Indeed, an emphasis on sovereignty, the absence of a right of resistance by subjects, and intervention for the latter's protection reinforced each other.[174]

The conclusion of the Peace of Westphalia in 1648 was in some regards a watershed, although not for the reasons commonly asserted in the 'Westphalian myth'. It legally codified the possibility of intervention into the Empire by France

---

[173] Pitts, 'Intervention and sovereign equality: legacies of Vattel', 134–5.
[174] Kampmann, 'Glorreiche Revolution und die Interventionsproblematik', 69 n. 11.

and Sweden and thereby conceptually bridged the gap that existed between Imperial intervention within the Empire and 'international' intervention. Contrary to the claims of the Westphalian myth, the Peace increased the legal scope of external involvement in the Empire and its individual territories, by providing for (and in the case of internal Imperial interventions, strengthening) a juridification of intervention.

When comparing the writing by public law scholars with authors from the natural law tradition, some differences emerge in their attitude towards intervention. Most natural law writers argued that interventions for the protection of foreign subjects were permissible in the law of nature and nations. While stressing the legality of judicial interventions in the Empire, many public law scholars who focussed more on positive treaty law, such as Moser, denied a right of international intervention for the defence of foreign subjects. They argued that such interventions were possible only if explicitly provided for in positive treaty law, as opposed to being permissible in the underlying normative framework of natural law, and it was precisely the guarantee of Westphalia which provided the only permissible form of foreign intervention. The next part of the book turns to the history of interventions in European state practice both before and after that important peace settlement.

PART ONE
# EUROPEAN INTERVENTIONS IN CENTRAL EUROPE, c.1500–1780

# 2
# Interventions in Central Europe I: c.1500–1618

It is hardly surprising that the theorists we encountered in the last chapter discussed intervention so extensively, considering the geopolitical context in which they were writing. Interventions in the domestic affairs of other rulers, often justified by the need to protect the target ruler's subjects, were common in early modern state-practice. A conceptual risk of considering such policies as interventions in the 'domestic' affairs of other states is that, in early modern Europe, the boundaries between polities' internal and external spheres were slightly blurred. Instead of conceiving of a sharp division between 'internal/domestic' and 'external/foreign', it would be less anachronistic to recognise the existence of a princely community of shared norms and values grounded in Christianity and the Law of Nations.[1] Nonetheless, it is mainly the justificatory arguments of the interveners that give rise to this impression; statements from the princes and authorities targeted by intervention had a pronounced sense of a norm of non-intervention in disputes between a ruler and his subjects.

Yet the distinction between internal and external was indeed less pronounced than in the modern age. 'Sub-state' entities such as territorial estates and other corporate bodies often carried out activities that would today be considered 'international' such as dispatching and receiving diplomatic representation and maintaining armed forces.[2] Territorial estates often also performed governmental functions within their broader polities and ruled over landed peasant and serf populations, who would on occasion mount rebellions against their noble lords. Some possessed the right of armed resistance against the monarch.[3] From this perspective, an intervention in support of territorial estates' armed rebellions against their prince could conceivably be construed as a regular form of support by an allied power, rather than the saving of passive subjects.[4] This impression is

---

[1] Tischer, *Kriegsbegründungen*, 219–22.
[2] Thus: Anuschka Tischer, 'Grenzen der Souveränität: Beispiele zur Begründung gewaltsamer Einmischung in "innere Angelegenheiten" in der Frühen Neuzeit', *Historisches Jahrbuch* 131 (2011), 41–64.
[3] Robert von Friedeburg, 'Widerstandsrecht im Europa der Frühen Neuzeit', in von Friedeburg (ed.), *Widerstandsrecht in der Frühen Neuzeit* (Berlin, 2001), 11–60.
[4] Barbara Stollberg-Rilinger, *Vormünder des Volkes? Konzepte landständischer Repräsentation in der Spätphase des Alten Reiches* (Berlin, 1999), 77–81.

in part created by the ways in which some intervening powers and the subjects they were assisting sought to justify such cases of intervention. It is certainly not how the target ruler viewed them; instead, he regarded them as illegitimate, plain *interventions* in conflicts between himself and his own subjects. In order to delegitimise the English intervention in the French wars of religion for example, the French ambassador to London declared in 1562:

> It is very apparent that if neighbouring kings support the complaints of rebels, they will open the door to their great prejudice and certain ruin, and to numerous seditions and divisions within their own countries and kingdoms, which would be something greatly damaging to the common good, security and profit of all those who God has elevated to the status and grandeur of kings and princes.[5]

One of the reasons why interventions were so commonplace is that they were often a structural feature of the escalation of conflicts within polities. Dissent would lead to rebellion and this to civil war, which then very frequently became internationalised through intervention and the external provision of protection to factions in order to weaken rival governments. Princes and governments rarely ignored conflict within neighbouring polities, as it usually affected their interests. Many of the crises addressed below were connected by a chain of interventions. Thus, military interventions were rarely stabilising or de-escalating, nor did they often go according to plan or reduce violence (apart from most Imperial judicial interventions in the smaller territories). To the contrary, a common feature of the external provision of military protection or support for one group of subjects was the imperilment of another. Even in peacetime, to gain the edge over geopolitical rivals, a common foreign policy strategy of rulers was to attempt to prop up the rights and powers of territorial estates and religious minorities within rival states, while simultaneously reducing estates' and religious minorities' influence within one's own polity. The seventeenth-century English Whig MP Richard Hampden, for example, argued that it was necessary to undercut English Catholics' ability to 'make application to foreign princes, and solicit their aid', while in the same breath imploring his king 'to be the head and protector of all Protestants, as well abroad as at home'.[6] Many of the 'international' interventions for the protection of oppressed subjects were directed against the Habsburgs and were justified in part as resistance against the threat of a Universal Monarchy. For most of our period this threat was associated with the house of Habsburg, which, according to the

---

[5] Paul de Foix's declaration, Hampton Court, 19 Oct. 1562, in David Potter (ed.), *The Letters of Paul de Foix, French Ambassador at the Court of Elizabeth I, 1562-1566* (Cambridge, 2019), 117-24.

[6] 'Commons Address in Answer to the King's Speech', 30 Dec. 1680, William Cobbett (ed.), *Parliamentary History of England* (London, 1806-20), 32, col. 1256.

Dutch rebel-leader William of Orange, was 'the greatest & the mightiest of all Christendome'.[7]

Numerous other interventions for the protection of foreign subjects outside of the geographical scope of this book occurred or were mooted during the sixteenth century. Revolts by Balkan Christians in areas such as Albania and the Peloponnese either were triggered, or existing rebellions were supported, by Venetian interventions.[8] In the 1530s the Emperor encouraged the Christian Maronites of Mount Lebanon to start a rebellion against the Ottomans. He promised a Spanish naval assault, however, the intervention failed to materialise during the ensuing revolt.[9] Numerous neighbouring powers, most importantly England, Spain, Savoy, the Dutch rebels, and several German princes, intervened in France during the wars of religion of the 1560s–90s. After intervening in Scotland in support of an armed revolt by Protestant Scottish 'Lords of the Congregation' against the Queen Regent of Scotland from the House of Guise in 1560, Queen Elizabeth I again targeted the power of the ardently Catholic, Spanish-backed Guise faction of France when she mounted a somewhat feeble intervention in support of the French Protestants in 1562/63. In justifying her intervention 'against the violence and tyranny of the House of Guise...to relieve the poor churches of the iniquities and cruel oppressions', Elizabeth stressed she was launching a 'defence for the protection of her crown and of her closest neighbours against a true tyranny'.[10] Because the Guise faction had usurped power from the young king, Elizabeth, as a neighbouring Christian sovereign, was sending forces to France to act as a surrogate on his behalf in order 'to defend and guard the subjects of [the French king] against tyranny, massacre, & ruin'.[11] Although the justification tended to conceal her ambitions for returning Calais to English rule, this general line of argument reflected the idea that sovereigns and princes lived in community of shared Christian values, and that they could intervene in order to secure peace and calm in Christendom, or to proffer protection of each other's subjects, when the latter's own prince was incapable or unwilling to do so.[12] Persecuted Catholics throughout Protestant Europe viewed Spain as their natural protector until the mid-seventeenth century, a role which Philip II in particular was ready to accept and act upon, for example in Ireland and France.[13] In what follows, the most prominent cases of interventions in central Europe up until the Thirty Years War will be surveyed.

---

[7] *Apologie of Prince William of Orange* (1581), 55.
[8] Noel Malcolm, *Agents of Empire. Knights, Corsairs, Jesuits and Spies in the Sixteenth-Century Mediterranean* (London, 2015), 123–50.
[9] Sam Kennerly, *Rome and the Maronites in the Renaissance and Reformation* (London, 2022), 86–93.
[10] *Protestation faite et pvbliee de par la Roine d'Angleterre...* (1562), 3–4.   [11] Ibid., 9.
[12] Haug-Moritz, 'Schutz fremder Glaubensverwandter', 183; Tischer, *Kriegsbegründungen, passim*.
[13] José Javier Ruiz Ibáñez, 'Les acteurs de l'hégémonie hispanique, du monde à la péninsule Ibérique', *Annales* 69/4 (2014), 927–54.

## The European State System at the Beginning of the Early Modern Period

One of the main changes that occurred between the mid-fifteenth and the mid-seventeenth centuries is that the European system became more integrated. Largely distinct regional sub-sets, or sub-balances, gradually came to merge, and governments increasingly started to consider European geopolitics in the round, taking into account not only relations with neighbours, but the sum of diplomatic, political, and economic linkages across the entire European system, and beyond. In the fifteenth and sixteenth centuries, the various regional sub-theatres of Europe had not yet integrated fully into a single overarching system; events in the north and east of Europe for example occurred largely in isolation from developments in western or southern Europe. The process of diplomatic integration was not yet fully complete by the beginning of the eighteenth century. This is one of the reasons why interventions were usually carried out by neighbouring polities within the context of relations within a specific sub-theatre.

Many of the interventions ostensibly for the protection of other rulers' subjects occurred as attempts to redress (subjectively perceived) imbalances in the equilibrium of power, especially between the Habsburgs and France. They were aided by the dense networks of contacts between governments and their rivals' subjects in west-central Europe. Franco-Habsburg rivalry was the main structuring element of European geopolitics until the mid-eighteenth-century. The Habsburgs dynasty's acquisition of the Imperial throne in the mid-fifteenth century and its rapid accretion of territories around the turn of the sixteenth century was a cause for alarm in France. It set the scene for its rivalry with the French Valois and later Bourbon dynasty, fought out mainly in the contested zones of influence in Italy, the Low Countries, and Germany, along with attendant interventions and counter-interventions. The Habsburgs secured the rich Burgundian Netherlands by the 1490s; Spain plus Sardinia, Naples, and Sicily fell to King Charles in 1516, who became Holy Roman Emperor Charles V in 1519, and under whose Spanish kingship vast new lands in the Americas were conquered. Additionally, the Jagiellonian inheritance of Bohemia, Silesia, and parts of Hungary and Croatia came under Habsburg rule in 1526, while Milan was secured in 1535/59. France perceived the rise of the Habsburgs to be a major geopolitical threat owing to a sense of being encircled: Spain-proper was located to its south across the Pyrenees, the Spanish Netherlands were along France's northern border, while its eastern borders were in the vicinity of Spanish possessions in Italy and the Franche-Comté. Nor were French fears allayed by the propagandistic ideology of 'universal monarchy' proclaimed at the court of Charles V under his chancellor Mercurino Gattinara.[14]

---

[14] Franz Bosbach, *Monarchia universalis. Ein politischer leitbegriff der Frühen Neuzeit* (Göttingen, 1988); Geoffrey Parker, *Emperor. A New Life of Charles V* (New Haven, 2019).

## Interventions in the Age of Charles V and Francis I

Simultaneous challenges on multiple fronts to this perceived threat of Habsburg 'universal monarchy' interacted geopolitically. The Turkish onslaught against the Habsburgs resulted in an unprecedented French alliance with the Ottomans in 1536, for example.[15] Numerous strategically-driven interventions, ostensibly for the protection of the opposing side's subjects, were part and parcel of these geopolitical confrontations. Thus, Emperor Charles V supported a rebellion by the duke of Bourbon in France in the 1520s.[16] Interventions in the other direction, by France (and other powers) into the Empire were more frequent, due in large part to the highly decentralised structure of that polity, along with the plentiful opportunities of tapping into opposition to the Emperor. This ever-present potential channel for intervention and faction-sponsoring within the Empire was enhanced by the Reformation. France thus supported rebellions by various Protestant princes against the Emperor despite persecuting French Protestants.

In general, the Protestant Reformation increased an interventionist impulse in European inter-state relations by creating a sense of a shared spiritual, and 'corporate', belonging and a community of fate among rulers and foreign subjects. Princes would therefore often take the side of persecuted subjects of other princes if those subjects were co-religionists, thereby enhancing the proclivity of princes to intervene on behalf of co-religionist subjects of other rulers.[17] A member of the Catholic Guise party in the French Wars of Religion declared in 1565: 'These days a Catholic prince must befriend all Catholics in all countries, just as a heretical prince must befriend all heretics, be they his own subjects, or the subjects of others.'[18] Of course this was hyperbole which did not always apply, although shared confession could certainly create a sense of commonality between rulers and others' subjects. This trend was especially pronounced in the Empire because the religious schism enhanced and overlaid its polycentric and decentralised constitutional power structure.

The fact that the new faith attracted many important princes, but not a majority, within the Empire, greatly increased the potential scope and occurrence of intervention and external protection of immediate and mediate subjects, both within the Empire (Imperial princes supporting the subjects of other princes), and from without. This was because the incomplete spread of the Reformation created a whole new set of potential conflicts—between princes and subjects of opposing

---

[15] De Lamar Jensen, 'The Ottoman Turks in sixteenth-century French diplomacy', *SCJ* 16 (1985), 451–70.
[16] Kohler, *Expansion und Hegemonie*, 354–5.
[17] David Trim, 'Intervention in European history, c.1520–1850', in Stefano Recchia and Jennifer Welsh (eds), *Just and Unjust Military Interventions. European Thinkers from Vittoria to Mill* (Cambridge, 2013) 21–47, at 27.
[18] Quoted in Schilling, *Konfessionalisierung*, 396.

confessions, between princes of opposing confessions among themselves, between the Catholic Emperor and the Protestant Imperial Estates, and between the Emperor and his Protestant subjects in the Habsburg hereditary lands—on top of a multitude of pre-existing and overlapping conflict constellations. France and other powers could therefore use the new confessional antagonism as an additional lever for interference, external protection, and intervention, or threaten to do so.

The Knights' Revolt of 1522–23 and the Peasants' Rebellion of 1524–26 were expressions of social and political grievances combined with religious impulses engendered by the early Reformation.[19] In both cases, links with outside powers were causing the princes (the main target of the revolts) and the Emperor concern, as they raised the spectre of foreign intervention in support of the rebellions. This was less serious in the case of the Knights' Revolt, for although its leader Franz von Sickingen held occasional negotiations with King Francis I of France, he remained essentially loyal towards the Habsburgs.[20] During the Peasants' Rebellion, the risk of towns and communities in southwest Germany 'turning Swiss', seemed to be exacerbated by an intervention from Zurich in support of nearby rebels.[21] French involvement also came at an inopportune time when the Emperor was busy fighting France in Italy. The rebel duke Ulrich of Württemberg—who had been banned and deposed by the Emperor but was allied with France—intervened in the rebellion in the hope of regaining his territory. He was supported by France and by Swiss mercenaries. The indirect Franco-Swiss intervention had to be called off after the severe French defeat at the Battle of Pavia in Italy (1525).[22] Over the next century-or-so France and other powers would continue to intervene in conflicts within the Empire resulting from the consequences of the Reformation, both to gain a strategic advantage, and to stave off perceived geopolitical threats, and in some cases this meshed with an ideological desire to aid co-religionists.

The princes were able to see off the challenges posed by the peasants and the knights in the 1520s. Some more powerful princes used the opportunity of the rebellion to expand their control at the expense of weaker neighbouring rulers, under the guise of 'protecting' the latter.[23] In order to reduce the likelihood of future revolts, the soundly defeated peasants (along with all other subjects) were granted rights of appeal against their rulers, thus enhancing their legal security. However, the princes' victory also ensured their leadership of the Reformation,[24] a development which made external support and intervention more likely, because

---

[19] Christian Peters, 'Das Widerstandsrecht als Problem reformatorischer Theologie', in Friedeburg, *Widerstandsrecht*, 113–40.
[20] Whaley, *Germany*, i, 216.
[21] Thomas Brady, *Turning Swiss: Cities and Empire 1450–1550* (Cambridge, 1985).
[22] Whaley, *Germany*, i, 224–5.
[23] Thomas Sea, 'Predatory protectors? Conflict and cooperation in the suppression of the German Peasants' Revolt of 1525', *SCJ* 39 (2008), 89–111.
[24] Wilson, *Empire*, 738.

foreign states generally sought alliances with German princes rather than groups of mediate subjects. The Protestant princes of the Schmalkaldic League,[25] managed to achieve an alliance with Denmark in 1538 and also entered into talks with England, but these links could not prevent the League's eventual suppression by Emperor Charles V.[26] He was generally more interested in the Mediterranean, but in central Europe he sought to pursue the twin goals, firstly of altering the constitutional balance in the Empire towards a more monarchical and centralised one, which also entailed the extirpation of the Protestant heresy, and secondly, of shutting out France.[27]

The two goals were intertwined because France was continually intervening on behalf of anti-Habsburg rebellions in the Empire and supporting opponents of Imperial authority. French kings clearly distinguished between the Emperor and the Empire and presented themselves as the protectors of the latter—as represented collectively by the Imperial Estates—against the former.[28] In May 1532, the king of France concluded the first of many treaties of protection with Bavaria at Scheyern Abbey. The Lutheran elector of Saxony and landgrave of Hessen were also contracting parties. Ten years later, France and Denmark intervened on behalf of the rebellious Duke William of Kleve-Mark who had contested the Habsburg claim to the inheritance of Guelders. In the resulting announcement of war against Charles V in 1542, the French king explicitly excluded 'the subjects of the Holy Empire' from his declaration of war, in recognition that these constituted a potential reservoir of support against their Emperor.[29] The military subjugation of the duke of Kleve-Mark in 1543 was a step towards the Emperor's goal of a more monarchical and uniformly Catholic Empire. Duke William was forced to renounce his alliance with France.[30] Emperor Charles V tried to deflect French intervention into the Empire, but at the same time conceded that the Empire was more decentralised and estates-based than other polities, and therefore—paradoxically—more prone to external intervention. Thus, in 1535 he instructed his statesmen in Germany to refute the accusations of Habsburg tyranny made by Francis I by allowing for a right of resistance by the Imperial Estates 'against him who ... for his tyrannical ambition and monarchical affection' was suppressing their rights, while of course stressing that he represented no such danger himself.[31]

---

[25] Gabriele Haug-Moritz, 'Widerstand and "Gegenwehr". Die schmalkaldische Konzeption der "Gegenwehr" und der "gegenwehrliche Krieg" des Jahres 1542', in Friedeburg (ed.), *Widerstandsrecht*, 141–62.

[26] Rory McEntegart, *Henry VIII, the League of Schmalkalden and the English Reformation* (Woodbridge, 2002), 26–130.

[27] Aurelio Espinosa, 'The grand strategy of Charles V. Castile, war, and dynastic priority in the Mediterranean', *JEMH* 9 (2005), 239–83.

[28] Babel, *Garde*, 261–314.   [29] Quoted in Tischer, *Kriegsbegründungen*, 49 n. 7.

[30] Babel, *Garde*, 207–22.   [31] Quoted in Tischer, 'Grenzen der Souveränität', 56.

Having successfully concluded the war with France at Crépy in 1544, the bulk of Charles V's forces were freed for an assault against the Schmalkaldic League, whose leaders were accusing Charles V of 'governmental tyranny and unjust violence'.[32] After defeating the Saxon-led Protestants in 1547, the Emperor rewarded Duke Moritz of the Albertine branch of the Saxon Wettin dynasty, who had supported him, by transferring to Moritz the electoral dignity and lands of the defeated Ernestine branch of John Frederick, who had led the Schmalkaldic League. Such unilateral rearrangements of the Imperial constitution alarmed many of the princes concerned for their rights, the German Liberties, and contributed to the next princes' rebellion in 1552. Princely concerns were further raised when the Emperor attempted to enforce more monarchical constitutional arrangements, while imposing Catholicism with the so-called Interim in 1547–48.[33] He had overreached at the latest with his attempt to secure an alternating emperorship between Vienna and Madrid. The anti-Habsburg propagandistic image of the *leyenda negra* ('black legend') and its slogan *spanische Servitut* ('Spanish servitude') drew on this princely aversion to many of Charles V policies.[34]

## King Henry II of France's Intervention in the Empire, 1552

Several princes (Brandenburg, Mecklenburg, Prussia) that had formed a Protestant defensive alliance in 1550 mounted a renewed rebellion, the so-called Princes' Revolt, in 1552. The Emperor's erstwhile ally, the newly elevated Elector Moritz of Saxony, defected and decided to lead the rebellion, while also seeking French intervention. Despite being a brutal persecutor of his own Protestant subjects, the new French king Henry II (r. 1547–1559) was receptive to the German princes' overtures, having just instigated a rebellion against Habsburg rule in Siena.[35] A treaty was signed at Chambord in January 1552.[36] In return for a military intervention against the Emperor and large subsidies, the rebel princes promised to assist France 'in regaining his deprived hereditary possessions' lost to the Habsburgs, and to grant the king of France, as 'Imperial vicar', control over the Imperial towns of Metz, Verdun, and Toul despite having no constitutional

---

[32] Quoted in Tischer, *Offizielle Kriegsbegründungen*, 117 n. 41.
[33] Georg Schmidt, ' "Teutsche Libertät" oder "Hispanische Servitut": Deutungsstrategien im Kampf um den evangelischen Glauben und die Reichsverfassung, 1546–1552', in Luise Schorn-Schütte (ed.), *Das Interim 1548/50* (Gütersloh, 2005), 166–91.
[34] Peter Schmidt, *Spanische Universalmonarchie oder 'teutsche Libertet'. Das spanische Imperium in der Propaganda des Dreißigjährigen Krieges* (Stuttgart, 2001).
[35] Kohler, *Expansion und Hegemonie*, 380.
[36] For the following: August Druffel (ed.), *Briefe und Aktenzur Geschichte des sechzehnten Jahrhunderts*, iii: 1546–1552, 340–8.

authority to make such cessions.[37] These terms were significant because the possession of the towns could serve as a territorial bridgehead for intervention into the Empire, while the promised permanent position of Imperial vicar could undergird such intervention legally, thus raising the prospect of perpetual French involvement in the Empire. Moreover, the German princes promised to vote for King Henry's candidate in an Imperial election, or indeed for the French king himself if he decided to stand for election.[38]

The treaty not only set out in detail the planned French military contribution, it also tried to justify the intervention by adopting legitimation strategies that would be repeated in subsequent centuries. Nonetheless, the degree of hostility expressed here by Imperial Estates against their Emperor was certainly unusual. The accusation of Spanish-style tyranny towards both princely subjects and common inhabitants is levelled against the Emperor. The alleged tyranny consisted of his wish to suppress the Protestant religion, along with long-standing rights and liberties:

> The...actual hostile measures, with which our opponents...limit, and in the end even destroy our religion, is manifest. His Imp.-Majesty has implemented measures aimed at depriving not only the princes and electors of the Empire, but also the cities and...common subjects of our highly-beloved fatherland of the German nation, of their old liberties and freedom, with the goal of placing us under such a beastly, unbearable and eternal subjugation, as exists in Spain.

The signatories also argued that the Emperor's imprisonment of the landgrave of Hesse was a violation not only of Imperial law and Imperial Estates' rights, but also 'of justice and the law of nations'. In ceding Imperial territories to the French king and speaking on behalf of the interests of the Empire as a whole, the princes claimed to be the true representatives of the 'fatherland of the German nation', a position which the Emperor himself had forfeited on account of his alleged tyranny. According to the signatories, this is what permitted and obliged them to seek the 'protection' of the king of France, 'whose forefathers have always done a lot of good for the German nation'. The planned intervention was therefore designed to 'rescue and vindicate the old liberties and freedom of our beloved fatherland'. The prospect of entering into a formal asymmetrical treaty of 'eternal protection' with the French king was also envisaged, and indeed this agreement can be seen as a high point of France's policy of *protectio* towards the Imperial Estates.[39]

---

[37] For the consequences for these areas: Christine Petry, *'Faire des sujets du roi'. Rechtspolitik in Metz, Toul und Verdun unter französischer Herrschaft (1552–1648)* (Munich, 2006).
[38] Babel, *Garde*, 222–42, esp. 231.
[39] Anuschka Tischer, 'Protektion' (2014), in *Enzyklopädie der Neuzeit Online* (Stuttgart/Weimar, 2009), 471–4.

Henry II released a declaration addressed to the Imperial Estates to present the rationale for his intervention. He explained that because of the close ties and neighbourhood of the German and French nations, disturbances and oppressions within the Empire necessarily affected the well-being and security of France. Moreover, the Empire was characterised as the 'outer works' (*Vorburg*) of European security and therefore any European sovereign ought to intervene if German Liberties were being undermined:

> our ancestors have always lived in highest friendship with the estates of the Holy Empire... which has contributed to our benefit and to the security of the French crown. Then we easily understood that such transformations from freedom to a perpetual servitude could not occur without a... demise of the whole German nation of the Holy Empire. In the meantime, we know full well that the German nation is a firm bulwark, whose unsubverted maintenance [is in the interest] not only of the French crown, but also of the whole of Christendom.[40]

Although the French military intervention failed to achieve an early victory (largely because of the failure to bring about a simultaneous Ottoman attack), the rebel princes were able to sufficiently beleaguer the Emperor's forces as to cause his flight from his court at Innsbruck and to eventually force him to come to terms with the Protestant princes at the Peace of Passau (1552).[41] The hypocrisy and geopolitical contingency of French 'protection' of Protestants and intervention on their behalf, is revealed not only by the simultaneous persecution of French Protestants, but also by king Francis I's promise to help Charles V extirpate German Protestantism in the secret annex of Meudon, attached to the Franco-Habsburg peace of Crépy in 1544, seven years before Henry II's protection treaty with the Protestants.[42]

## Interventions in the Dutch Revolt 1568–c.1600

The Dutch Revolt and its foreign interventions occurred in territories which were still part of the Empire, constituting its Burgundian Kreis, although in practice the Netherlands was already somewhat removed from Imperial affairs by the sixteenth century. Apart from its location in the Empire's northwest, the Dutch revolt also posed a threat to the stability of central European and Imperial politics through the dynastic links of the main conflicting parties. The leader of the Dutch

---

[40] Printed in Wolfgang Lautemann et al. (eds), *Geschichte in Quellen* (Munich, 1996), iii, 199–203.
[41] Parker, *Charles V*, 433–9; James D. Tracy, *Emperor Charles V, Impresario of War. Campaign Strategy, International Finance, and Domestic Politics* (Cambridge, 2002), 230–40.
[42] Alfred Kohler (ed.), *Quellenzur Geschichte Karls V.* (Darmstadt, 1990), no. 84, 315.

rebels, William of Orange, was an Imperial prince of the house of Nassau-Orange. He possessed a dense network of familial links among numerous ruling Imperial counts, some of whom intervened in support of the rebels alongside their relative in 1568. William was also allied to more substantial princes such as John Casimir of the Palatinate, who launched an English-funded military intervention against Spanish forces in the Brabant in 1572.[43]

King Philip II of the Spanish Habsburgs was of course closely dynastically linked to the German Habsburgs whose head was the Emperor. The king of Spain was keenly interested in events and developments within the Empire: not only were his Dutch provinces fiefs of the Empire, as mentioned, but they were also adjacent to the territories of numerous fully-fledged Imperial Estates. Furthermore, the fact that Germany was a site of geopolitical between the French and Habsburgs heightened Philip II's awareness of the importance of the Empire. While France sough to break free from its perceived Habsburg encirclement by supporting anti-Habsburg Calvinist Imperial Estates such as the Elector-Palatine, the Spanish conversely needed allies in the vicinity, not least to secure the Spanish Road (which passed through the Empire) and a steady supply of German mercenaries, and to maintain an advantageous position from which to prosecute the war against the Dutch rebels. For these reasons, Philip II maintained a well-functioning clientele network of protégés and allies among Imperial princes who ruled lands near the Netherlands and along the Spanish Road, and councillors at the Imperial and the various German princely courts.[44]

The Emperor's position in this conflict was precarious because on the one hand he was the feudal overlord of lands in which a rebellion and war were occurring, yet he was also part of the wider Habsburg dynasty, whose Spanish branch was being targeted by rebellion. A reflection of his dual position as Imperial overlord and Habsburg ruler is that he was called upon to intervene on both sides. His Spanish cousins repeatedly requested Emperor Maximilian II's support based on Habsburg dynastic solidarity, while the Elector-Palatine organised a collective appeal to the Emperor by the Rhineland electors in 1568, calling upon him to exercise his traditional function of a protector of territorial estates by defending the traditional rights of the Burgundian/Dutch estates. In the end, the Emperor supported neither side, opting to offer mediation instead. The Empire itself also remained neutral, with the Reichstag turning down requests for assistance by both the rebels and the duke of Alva in 1570.[45]

---

[43] J. Raitt, 'The Elector John Casimir, Queen Elizabeth, and the Protestant League', in D. Visser (ed.), *Controversy and Conciliation. The Reformation and the Palatinate, 1559–1583* (Alison Park, 1986), 117–45.
[44] Friedrich Edelmayer, *Söldner und Pensionäre. Das Netzwerk Philipps II. im Heiligen Römischen Reich* (Munich, 2002).
[45] Johannes Arndt, *Das Heilige Römische Reich und die Niederlande 1566 bis 1648. Politisch-konfessionelle Verflechtung und Publizistik im Achtzigjährigen Krieg* (Cologne/Weimar/Vienna, 1998), 46–66.

The Dutch crisis was one of the consequence of the division of the Habsburg dynasty at the end of Emperor Charles V's reign, and the subsequent attempts of his son Philip II, the head of the Spanish Habsburg branch, to centralise his new 'composite monarchy'. The rebellion which broke out in 1566 was essentially the result of a crisis of estrangement between the Dutch noble estates and burghers on the one side, and the new Spanish regime of Philip II, who, along with his newly introduced governors and military commanders, were perceived as foreign, whereas his father, Emperor Charles V, a native Dutch-born prince of Burgundy had not. The introduction of new Spanish garrisons, the scheme to introduce numerous new bishoprics, the persecution of Protestants by an Inquisition, were all resented by the various social groups of the Seventeen Provinces. Rather than pursuing a unified programme of national resistance aiming at independence, Parker and others have shown that the pursued goals were more particularist and aimed at the restoration of an eclectic multitude of local privileges and rights, which were of a corporate rather than national nature. Instead of a single revolt movement spanning eighty years (as might be implied by the term 'Eighty Years War'), there were a series of different rebellions which only gradually coalesced.

From its beginning, the Dutch Revolt had significant European geopolitical implications and became internationalised early on, through a series of interventions, but also numerous inter-personal contacts and networks fostered by exiles. Along with the protagonists' above-mentioned dynastic connections, and a potent ideological component and personal network of the 'Calvinist international' decisively supporting the Dutch rebels, the Revolt's wider geopolitical implications derived from its occurrence at a time of Spanish near-hegemony in Europe and in the overseas. Yet it also became clear that the Revolt was becoming insurmountable for Spain, as it was drawing increasingly large Spanish forces at a time when Philip II was actively engaged in multiple other theatres of conflict, such as his interventions in the French Wars of Religion, an overstretching of resources which contributed to the financial crisis and Spanish state bankruptcy of 1596. This, along with the logistical difficulty of supplying his troops in the Netherlands along the Spanish Road made the whole Spanish engagement in the Low Countries appear as a viable site for geopolitical rivals to challenge Spain. A relatively low-cost way of doing so was by intervening in support of the anti-Spanish Dutch rebels. This was particularly feasible—and at times indeed imperative—for new enemies such as England and traditional rivals such as France (albeit constrained by its Wars of Religion), because the Netherlands were in the immediate vicinity of their heartlands and were therefore a vital region in terms of their geopolitical interests, whereas it was located more at the periphery of the newly truncated Spanish Habsburg monarchy.[46]

---

[46] Geoffrey Parker, *The Army of Flanders and the Spanish Road, 1567–1659* (Cambridge, 1972), 80–105.

Given that the events in the Netherlands were closely embedded into the broader geopolitical context, it is unsurprising that the conflict would become internationalised almost from the start. The above-mentioned relatives of William of Orange from the Wetterau association of Imperial counts along with other Protestant Imperial Estates in the Rhineland, such as Count Johann of Nassau-Dillenburg and the duke of Zweibrücken, intervened in support of the rebels from 1568 when William took refuge in Nassau. Philip II on occasion used international intervention as a tool to strengthen the Spanish Road. Thus in 1571, he incited a rebellion against the ruling counts of Finale as a pretext to intervene in the resulting conflict between ruler and subjects for the latter's protection, by occupying the County and its neighbouring territories with troops from Milan.[47] The Dutch rebels in turn benefitted from intervention by both the French (until French civil war escalated in 1572) and the Huguenot opposition, the latter to assist their co-religionists, and both in order to weaken France's traditional Habsburg rival.[48] The internationalised context also meant that the main actors frequently addressed the wider European public, while simultaneously justifying their actions to domestic audiences. Following the appointment of William of Orange as Stadholder in 1572, the provinces issued a proclamation 'that we should forsake the king and seek foreign assistance'.[49]

Five years later, the Stadholder published his *Apology*, a tract justifying Dutch resistance. He recalled 'how haughtily, insolently and with what contempt for our whole nation' the Spanish governed the Netherlands. Their actions were said to reveal 'the secret purpose of Spain, to wit, to destroy and enslave us...trampling underfoot so haughtily our liberties and ancient freedoms'.[50] The 'true barbarism' of Spanish rule, their attempts 'to establish the cruel Spanish Inquisition' in the Netherlands, and the execution of 'the leading citizens of Brussels', were all argued to provide Orange and the States of Holland and Zealand 'just causes...to resort to arms'.[51]

The following year, the States-General of the United Provinces published a declaration, aimed at a wider European audience, the Act of Abjuration, in which they announced and justified their deposition of the king of Spain, using arguments reminiscent of some of the Monarchomach resistance literature. A revival of interest in the writings of Tacitus, whose portrayal of the Batavian revolt against the Roman Empire lent itself to obvious contemporary parallels, and whose writings were popularised by the well-known Brabantine philosopher Justus Lipsius, is likely to have influenced the authors.[52] Without citing authorities,

---

[47] Whaley, *Germany*, i, 374.   [48] Schilling, *Konfessionalisierung und Staatsinteressen*, 438.
[49] Parker, *Revolt*, 146.
[50] Alistair Duke, 'William of Orange's apology (1580)', *Dutch Crossing* 22 (1998), no. 1, 3–96, at 56.
[51] Ibid., 58–9.
[52] Simon Schama, *The Embarrassment of Riches – an Interpretation of Dutch Culture in the Golden Age* (New York, 1987), 75.

they argued that according to natural law, princes' right to rule and sovereignty were conditional upon them fulfilling their responsibility to protect their subjects, and that if the prince failed to fulfil this duty, he could be replaced by his subjects. To do so they would thereby seek external protection, which was moreover argued to permissible under the law of nations.

> ...a prince is constituted by God to be ruler of a people, to defend them from oppression and violence...and whereas God did not create the people slaves to their prince...but rather the prince for the sake of the subjects...to govern them according to equity...And when he does not behave thus, but, on the contrary oppresses them...then he is no longer a prince, but a tyrant...[W]hen this is done...they may not only disallow his authority, but legally proceed to the choice of another prince for their defence.[53]

They pointed out that the Dutch provinces had 'always been governed according to their antient privileges...for most of the provinces receive their prince upon certain conditions, which he swears to maintain; which if the prince violates, he is no longer sovereign'. Philipp II's rule was managed by advisors who 'conceived a secret hatred to this land and to its liberty' and sought to 'make himself absolute...to reduce this country to slavery'. This was done 'under the mask of religion', while in fact the motive was not religious, but 'to annul all the privileges of this countrey, [to] govern it tirannically as in the Indies'.[54] The declaration went to lengths to describe the 'inhumane crueltys' of the Spanish forces, who 'massacred the inhabitants in a most barbarous manner'. It stressed that before considering the deposition of the king and the seeking of external protection, 'we used all possible means...to be reconciled to our king...like good subjects'.[55] With this being to no avail, the estates declared the king of Spain deposed. A corollary of the subjects' resistance was their seeking of foreign protection by requesting external intervention. Thus, at the same time as declaring the king deposed, the estates announced that they would 'seek some other powerful and more gracious prince to take us under his protection'.[56]

For this purpose, the estates looked primarily to Spain's traditional rival France, and later to England. The States-General did not initially seek to achieve sovereignty over the Netherlands themselves. Instead, they wanted to transfer sovereign authority from the king of Spain to another prince. Francis, duke of Anjou, the brother and heir of King Henry III of France, appeared a suitable candidate. He had negotiated an end to the fifth French war of religion in 1576 which had introduced confessional co-habitation arrangements in France, measures which

---

[53] *Declaration of the States-General*, in Walter Scott (ed.), *Somers' Tracts* (London, 1809), i, 323–29, at 323.
[54] Ibid., 324–5.   [55] Ibid., 326–7.   [56] Ibid., 327.

many in the Netherlands hoped to see established there too. In 1578, Anjou was proclaimed by the States-General as 'Defender of the Liberties of the Low Countries', who in turn pledged to intervene against Spanish forces in the Netherlands with 12,000 troops. The French intervention of the duke of Anjou was a failure. He could not secure the allegiance of all the Provinces. Seeking to assert his authority, French forces began to attack Ostend, Dunkirk, and Antwerp, where the resulting 'French fury' of January 1583 was so violent that Anjou became irreparably discredited in the eyes of most Netherlanders, and had to withdraw permanently in June 1583.[57] The intervening would-be protector had instead attacked those he had promised to assist.

The English intervention in the Netherlands was more substantial. Before her main intervention in 1585, Queen Elizabeth had provided some support from the early 1570s onwards. She supplied several hundred men in 1572 and allowed her ports to be used as bases by Dutch naval forces. In response to the recognition of the duke of Anjou as the Defender of the Liberties of the Low Countries, she paid the elector-Palatine to send 12,000 mercenaries in support of the Dutch rebels in 1578 as mentioned above. In the same year she paid the rebels one million Florins.[58] This was an example of a geopolitical 'protection competition', which in this case was driven by the Queen's fear of allowing the southern Netherlands to be taken over by her French rival. Indeed, from the English perspective, an extension of French control into the Low Countries was just as dangerous as a strong Spanish military domination of those provinces. The Earl of Sussex, one of the Queen's courtiers, warned in 1578 that 'the case will be hard with the Queen and with England if ever the French possess or the Spaniards tyrannise the Low Countries'.[59]

In 1576 two rebel provinces, Holland and Zealand, had offered Elizabeth sovereignty. Although she declined the offer, she accepted their embassies formally and conceded that 'being so hardly treated as they have been...there is appearance of reason in their defending themselves and seeking aid other ways'. Elizabeth's sentiments matched those of the English public. Pamphlets published during the Dutch Revolt portrayed the Spanish Habsburg regime in the Netherlands under the absolutist, 'Turk-like' Philip II as an unconstitutional military tyranny. Many authors argued, in political rather than confessional terms, that it was necessary to intervene against the Habsburgs in the Netherlands, lest 'the great Spanish Leviathan' were to extend its absolutist domination to 'all Christendom together', thus establishing a 'universal monarchy'.[60] In the mid-1570s, Elizabeth's principle secretary Walsingham drafted a

---

[57] Parker, *Revolt*, 176, 191–7, 205–6; Schilling, *Konfessionalisierung*, 442.
[58] Parker, *Revolt*, 191–2.
[59] The Earl of Sussex to Walsingham, Bury, 6 Aug. 1578, *Calendar of State Papers Foreign, Elizabeth*, 13 (1578–79), 120–1.
[60] Quoted in Hugh Dunthorne, *Britain and the Dutch Revolt 1560–1700* (Cambridge, 2013), 33–4.

statement indicating that she would protect the provinces if Philip II refused to accept that 'sooche placards, inquisytyons... [which] tende to the molesting of them for the professyon of the rrelygyon... in the countreys of hol. And zelande shall be... abolyshed'.[61]

The English court's views on potential intervention were thus informed by a combination of a confessional solidarity and a perceived geopolitical threat. These two elements were in fact almost inseparable. Instead of full independence, or an extension of English rule to the Netherlands, Elizabeth I hoped for the 'Burgundian solution'; a return of the Netherlands to their previous state of self-rule replete with traditional local corporate rights, which although under Spanish sovereignty, would nevertheless be a limited, or conditional, sovereignty without the presence of Spanish troops or the centralising ambitions of foreign (i.e. Spanish) governors. The retention of Calvinist rights of worship and the cessation of tyrannical rule were an integral part of this reversion to the kind of Netherlandish autonomy that had existed under Charles V. This solution would ensure that the Low Countries—described by Elizabeth's interventionist advisor William Cecil as 'the very counter-scarp of England', because it was vital to English shipping and trade, and adjacent to the seat of English government—would remain in friendly hands.[62] Failure to ensure this would risk the Netherlands being turned into the centre of Spain's Catholic-absolutist military power, or of being added to the French monarchy, thus giving France complete control of the opposite coastline along the English Channel.[63]

At the time of the offer of sovereignty in 1576 Elizabeth had opted to mediate and intercede rather than intervene militarily on the rebels' behalf. Her calculus changed in 1584–85. The assassination of William of Orange in 1584 plunged the Provinces further into constitutional disarray, which the Spanish were keen to exploit. Impressive Spanish advances, including the capture of Bruges and Ghent and the besieging of Antwerp, caused alarm in London.[64] It was compounded by the uncovering of a Spanish plot to assassinate the Queen. Without William of Orange, the rebels were deprived of the only leader capable of rallying a united Dutch front against the Spanish. At the same time, the death of the childless French king's heir, the duke of Anjou, left the Protestant Henry (IV) of Navarre as heir presumptive of France. This led to renewed upsurge of anti-royalist opposition by the Catholic League and the Guises who placed themselves under Spanish protection at the treaty of Joinville on 31 December 1584.[65] The prospect of

---

[61] Quotations in Simon Adams, 'Elizabeth I and the sovereignty of the Netherlands 1576–1585', *TRHS* 14 (2001), 309–19 at 315–16.
[62] Quoted in Simms, *Britain's Europe*, 30.
[63] R.B. Wernham, 'English policy and the revolt of the Netherlands', in J.S. Bromley et al. (eds), *Britain and the Netherlands* (The Hague, 1960).
[64] Parker, *Revolt*, 207–16.
[65] Printed in Frances Davenport (ed.), *European Treaties Bearing on the History of the United States and its Dependencies to 1648* (Clark, 2004), 225–8.

French assistance for the Dutch rebels thereby vanished at a time when the Spanish forces in the Netherlands seemed on the brink of final victory. If the Catholic side, now under Spanish protection, emerged victorious in France, that kingdom would effectively become a Spanish client and Philip II would dangerously extend his power from Iberia across France and the Netherlands and into Italy and Germany where his Habsburg cousins were in control.[66] This prospect of a Catholic-absolutist Habsburg universal monarchy was so intolerable to England, that the Queen was compelled to act.[67] Yet she remained fundamentally hesitant about aiding rebels against their sovereign, which might account for the limited nature of the military intervention.[68]

In October 1584, a decision was taken in London to send forced to the Netherlands, but at this time the Estates-General were still hoping for French protection and had offered King Henry III sovereignty. After the French king declined, the English ministry informed the States-General in March 1585 that Elizabeth I 'is fullie resolved to take the protection of them'. The States-General then formally requested England's intervention and offered Elizabeth sovereignty over the Netherlands on 12 May 1585. The Queen declined the offer of sovereignty, being opposed in principle to territorial expansion, and instead opted for a vaguely-defined position of a 'protector' of the Netherlands.[69] Following negotiations Elizabeth I and the States-General signed the Treaty of Nonsuch in August 1585.[70] The Queen agreed to intervene in support of the United Provinces with 4,000 soldiers and 500 cavalry. In addition, she pledged to pay an annual subsidy of 600,000 florins to the States-General, and to appoint a lieutenant-general for the Netherlands, who would also perform civil functions. In return, the Dutch were to hand over Flushing, Rammekens, and Brill as 'cautionary towns' (sureties) until English expenses had been repaid. In September 1585, 4,100 English troops led by the earl of Leicester arrived at Flushing (too late to prevent the fall of Antwerp to the Spanish on 17 August), a force which increased to 8,000 men by December.[71]

In October 1585 the Queen published a tract, the *Declaration of the Causes Mooving the Queene of England to give aide to the Defence of the People afflicted and oppressed in the Lowe Countries*,[72] in which the intervention was legitimised. The *Declaration* posited three main interconnected justifications: firstly, the longstanding close diplomatic, commercial, and cultural ties between England and the Netherlands; secondly, the consequent obligation of the English to protect the Netherlanders in their violated traditional rights and liberties and defend them

---

[66] For Spain's rationale: Parker, *Grand Strategy of Philipp II*, 147–203.
[67] Thus: Wernham, 'Elizabethan war aims', 344–5.
[68] Charles Wilson, *Queen Elizabeth I and the Revolt of the Netherlands* (Basingstoke, 1970).
[69] Adams, 'Elizabeth I and the sovereignty of the Netherlands', 317–318, quotation on p. 318.
[70] *A General Collection of Treatys, Manifesto's . . . and other Publick Papers 1495–1712* (London, 1732), 83–8.
[71] Parker *Revolt*, 217–18.   [72] Printed in *Somers' Tracts*, i, 410–19.

from Spanish tyranny; and thirdly, a right to intervene against Spain to forestall a geopolitical danger, as a form of self-defence against anti-English plots and aggression.

The *Declaration* began by establishing a right of resistance among subjects under certain circumstance and a concomitant right of intervention on the part of other princes. It noted that in principle, 'kings and soveraignes, are... not bounde to yield account... to any others but to God their only soveraigne lorde'. However, if 'just and reasonable groundes' existed, then certain neighbouring powers were authorised and indeed obligated to intervene for the protection of other sovereigns' subjects if these, like the Dutch, were 'lamentablie afflicted, and in present danger to be brought into a perpetuall servitude'.[73] In general, if a prince allowed 'tyranny' to reign in his dominions, whereby violences were committed against the subjects and they were deprived of their traditional 'liberties', then

> in such cases of general injustice, and upon such violent breaking of their privileges, they are free from their former homages, and at libertie... to seek the protection of some other forreyne lord, or rather to yield themselves to the soveraigntie of some mightie prince...[74]

What made the Queen of England particularly interested in the condition of the Netherlands was 'the natural situation of those Lowe Countries and our realme of Englande, one directly opposite to the other', and the existence of 'mutuall bondes'. The links and reciprocal duties between the two countries were such that they 'resembled... man and wife'.[75] These interconnections meant that both nations were bound up in a community of fate and owed each other protection should the need arise. Shared religion, by contrast, was hardly mentioned. Providing her Dutch neighbours with such protection became a necessity since the introduction of a novel, tyrannical, and illegitimate Spanish regime by Philip II, who 'appoynt[ed] Spaniards, forreiners... men more exercised in warres then in peaceable government... to be chiefest governours of [the] Low Countries, contrary to the ancient lawes and customes thereof'. Under Spanish rule, the conventional governance of the Netherlands was argued to have been completely overturned and corrupted. The Spanish governors 'being exalted to absolute government... have violently broken the ancient laws and liberties of all the [Dutch provinces], and in a tyrannous sort have banished, killed... many of the most ancient and principall persons of the naturall nobilitie that were most worthie of government'. In addition to murdering the traditional local elites, the Spanish were accused of having killed 'a great part of the natural people'. Although the 'cruell persecutions' of the Spanish were carried out under 'pretence... [of the] maintenance of the Romish religion', the fact that Catholics such as the counts of

[73] Ibid., 410–11.   [74] Ibid., 413.   [75] Ibid., 413.

Hoorn and Egmont were also executed was argued to demonstrate that religion was merely a fig leaf to mask the true Spanish objective in the Netherlands, namely 'to bring these whole countries in servitude to Spayne'.[76] The *Declaration* noted that other neighbours, such as France, had also promised to 'ayde the oppressed people of the lowe countries against the Spaniards', and recalled that this was thwarted by the Spanish-backed House of Guise. In any case, England was argued to be a more suitable protector, because the Dutch were 'more straightly knitt in aunsient friendship to this realme then to any other countrie'. The declaration stressed that military intervention was a measure of last resort, decided upon only after the Spanish ignored the Queen's warnings.

Having addressed the more ideological arguments of the need to defend corporate rights and a limited, estates-based form of government in a neighbouring country, the next part of the justification turned to more geopolitical arguments which made the intervention compelling. These related to the Queen's right to intervene as a form of self-defence (which was more closely aligned to ideas of the just war doctrine), and as a way of preventing a grave strategic threat to her kingdom. The *Declaration* listed a number of Spanish-supported or instigated invasion plots, including a Spanish-Papal intervention in Ireland, and conspiracies against her person.[77] The tract then went on to connect the violent oppression of the Netherlanders with a strategic threat to England: if the king of Spain's

> chieftaines in his low countries increased their cruelties towards his owne afflicted people...[and] if the nation of Spayne shoulde make a conquest of those countries...wee...manifestly see in what danger our selfe, our countries, and people, might shortly bee, if in convenient time wee did not speedily otherwise regard to prevent or stay the same.[78]

This combined and interconnected threat of an accretion of large Spanish forces in the Low Countries—which itself entailed the illegal suppression of the traditional liberties and privileges of the Netherlanders—and the Spanish plots to 'procure sundry invasions of our realme, by their forces out of Spayne and the Lowe Countries' necessitated swift measures of pre-emptive defence. It required the Queen

> more carefully to look to the safety of our selfe and our people: and finding our own dangers indeed very great and imminent, we have been the more urgently provoked to attempt and accelerate some good remedy...to withstand and prevent this present common danger to our realme and themselves [the Dutch], evidently seene...by planting the Spanish nation and men of warre, enemies to our countries, there so nere unto us.[79]

---

[76] Ibid., 412.   [77] Ibid., 414–15.   [78] Ibid., 414.   [79] Ibid., 416.

The *Declaration* stressed that although the Queen had taken over some cautionary towns for safekeeping, she had no intention of holding on to them permanently, nor did she intend 'to make any particular profit hereof to our selfe or to our people'. She also emphasised that the Netherlanders themselves had frequently requested her intervention by making 'continuall lamentable requests... for our succours'. Recalling her intervention in Scotland in the 1560s, Elizabeth I concluded that she was now carrying out a similar protective intervention in her eastern neighbour. If she failed to procure such urgent protection for the Dutch, they would have 'no hope of relief of these their miseries, but rather an increase thereto, by daily conquests of their townes and slaughter of their people'.[80]

The English military intervention in the Netherlands in the autumn of 1585 had important short-term and longer-term implications for the subsequent development of the Dutch Revolt and European history. It marked the beginning of the undeclared Anglo-Spanish war of 1585–1604. It encouraged the Dutch to continue resisting Spain at a critical moment when many were in favour of seeking terms with the duke of Parma, and thereby arguably saved the rebellion. In 1586 the States-General fielded a larger army than they had for many years. Because it amounted to a declaration of war against Spain, the English intervention persuaded Philip II to strike at England directly with the Spanish Armada of 1588. Apart from damaging Philip's prestige and finances, the failure of the Armada also marked a turning point in the Dutch Revolt. It contributed to the survival of the United Provinces and Spain's eventual recognition of the Netherlands as an independent state in 1609/48. From the Dutch perspective, the intervention was therefore a success, furnishing vital assistance at a crucial moment. In the statement issued by the States-General in February 1586 conferring the office of governor-general of the Netherlands on the commander of the English forces, the earl of Leicester, the Queen was thanked for her decision 'to support and defend us... to settle things on their ancient foundation, that we may be better able to defend ourselves against the violence and tyranny' of Spanish rule.[81]

Elizabeth I was disgruntled with Leicester for having accepted (or instigated) this position, because it implied that she was claiming sovereignty over the Netherlands. This points to a clash in objectives between the Dutch rebels and their English protector. As mentioned above, Elizabeth I did not seek to facilitate the Netherlands' independence with her intervention, nor did she wish to annex the provinces, which is why she turned down the offer of full sovereignty over the Netherlands in 1585. Instead, she wished to see the provinces restored to their traditional political and religious liberties but under continued Spanish sovereignty, which the Dutch were of course unable to accept after 1581 when they deposed Philip II. In December 1587, Elizabeth reiterated to her negotiators in

---

[80] Ibid., 417.   [81] Proclamation (6 Feb. 1586), *Somers' Tracts*, i, 420–1.

the Netherlands that 'our purpose, and...all...our actions...have concurred herewith, [is] the relief of the people of those Low Countries, who were of long time sought by foreign forces to be extirped and conquered'. In particular, she wished 'to establish the Low Countries in peace and lawful government by natural born subjects as in former times, without oppression by Spaniards...that all the provinces be restored to their ancient liberty and privileges wherein they lived before the persecutions and oppressions begun by the Duke of Alva'.[82]

This divergence in aims increasingly caused a breakdown of trust between the English and the Dutch rebels, especially as Elizabeth was pressurising the States-General to join her in the negotiations with the Spanish to force them to come to terms with Philip II, which they did not desire. Relations were also strained by English commanders' abandonment of several key forts to the Spanish in 1587 and by Elizabeth's recalling of her troops in the Netherlands to defend England against the Armada.[83] With English commitment to their cause lagging, the Dutch launched a diplomatic drive in Germany aiming at securing the protective intervention of Protestant princes. Dutch envoys argued that all Protestants across western and central Europe, and beyond, were tied up in a shared community of fate and that by intervening on behalf of the Dutch, Protestant princes would in fact be promoting their own interests.[84] While England's intervention in the Netherlands was by no means a failure—it saved the Dutch from complete subjugation to Spain and helped the Netherlands retain their corporate rights and liberties—it did contribute to a development which ultimately resulted in Dutch independence, contrary to English plans, and to a greater vulnerability to France further down the line.

## Tensions, Crises, and Interventionist Trends in the Empire c.1570–1615

With the end of the French Wars of Religion in 1598, the survival of the new Dutch republic, the conclusion of an Anglo-Spanish peace in 1604 (in which England promised to stop intervening in the Netherlands), and the conclusion of a twelve-year truce between the Spanish and the Dutch in 1609,[85] the focus of European interventionism shifted back to the German heartlands of the Empire. As we have seen, the Empire, with its decentralised power structure and confusing array of corporate rights and liberties had long been the site (or target) of outside

---

[82] Elizabeth I to commissioners, December 1587, *Calendar of State Papers Foreign: Elizabeth*, 21/3 (London, 1929), 474–5.
[83] Parker, *Revolt*, 220–1.
[84] Uwe Sibeth, 'Gesandter einer aufständischen Macht. Die ersten Jahre der Mission von Pieter Cornelisz. Brederode im Reich (1602–1609)', *ZHF* 30 (2003), 19–52.
[85] See Randall Lesaffer (ed.), *The Twelve Years Truce (1609)* (Leiden, 2014).

intervention by more unitary neighbouring state actors, a trend that was exacerbated by the Reformation and the conflicts it produced in the first half of the sixteenth century. Yet a period of calm and cross-confessional cooperation in the Empire after the abdication of Charles V largely removed the German parts of the Empire from 'international' interventionist activity (i.e. discounting the judicial interventions within the Empire), especially from the mid-1550s until the 1580s. During this period the civil wars in France and in the Spanish Habsburg monarchy temporarily redirected interventionist activity towards western Europe and the westernmost (Burgundian-Dutch) parts of the Empire as we have seen. At the turn of the century, however, the focus of intervention returned to Germany with a vengeance, starting with some small-scale interventions in disputes from the late-sixteenth-century, continuing with a more serious succession dispute over Jülich-Kleve-Berg in 1609–10/1614, and then erupting with a cascading set of interventions in the great Imperial civil war from 1618. This shift in interventionist focus was not just related to an upsurge in confessional tensions—whether these made a war in 1618 inevitable is doubtful[86]—but more importantly, to the shift of perceived hegemonic menace emanating from the German Habsburgs during the Thirty Years War.

In the 1580s, Justus Lipsius wrote 'Do you behold the large country of Germany? There were lately in her great sparks of civil dissension, which do begin to burn again, and unless I am deceived will grow to a more consuming flame.'[87] In hindsight, this prediction seems apposite. The Thirty Years War and the interventions which sustained it, although not inevitable, were made more likely by a preceding gradual breakdown in confessional relations and by political-institutional deadlock, especially from the 1580s. Before examining the interventions of 1618–48—arguably the 'crescendo' of early modern European interventionism—we shall survey the preceding increase in tensions within the Empire, tensions which produced several crises and small interventions.[88]

The Augsburg settlement was a good working solution, which brought peace for many decades. From the mid-1550s until the late 1570s the Imperial institutions—predicated on consensus, compromise, and cooperation—functioned smoothly, reflecting the Imperial constitution's consolidation.[89] But the 1555 settlement was nevertheless structurally deficient and left several issued unresolved and subject to nagging disputes, the result of irreconcilable interpretations by the Catholics on the one hand, who viewed the Peace as a provisional expedient, and the Protestants on

---

[86] E.g., Axel Gotthard, 'Die Ursachen des DreißigjährigenKrieges', in Robert Rebitsch (ed.), *1618: Der Beginn des Dreißigjährigen Krieges* (Cologne, 2017), 47–76.

[87] Justus Lipsius, *On Constancy – De Constantia* (Exeter, 2006), 128.

[88] An overview of this period: Joachim Whaley, 'Imperial politics, 1555–1618', in Olaf Asbach et al. (eds), *The Ashgate Research Companion to the Thirty Years War* (New York, 2014), 13–24.

[89] Thus, Maximilian Lanzinner, *Friedenssicherung und politische Einheit des Reiches unter Kaiser Maximilian II* (Göttingen, 1993).

the other hand, who considered it a fundamental legal basis of co-existence.[90] These diverging interpretations increasingly caused tension during the reign of the withdrawn and mentally unstable Emperor Rudolf II (1576–1612) who was unwilling and/or unable to act as a mediator between the two confessional parties.[91]

The first deficiency was that the Augsburg peace only granted Lutheran rulers protection under the Territorial Peace, the other major branch of Protestantism, Calvinism, and other sects remained banned and were officially heresies. Secondly, the princes only granted each other toleration between themselves, not among subjects within their territories. The Right of Reformation meant that subjects could be forced to convert to the religion which their prince had chosen (either Catholicism or Lutheranism). This was a form of religious compulsion later encapsulated in the phrase *cuius regio eius religio* ('the religion of the prince is the religion of the territory'). Thirdly, even from a state-centric perspective, it was increasingly unsatisfactory for Protestant Imperial Estates, because the Right of Reformation of ecclesiastical rulers was contested. According to the Catholic interpretation, ecclesiastical territories were excluded from the Right of Reformation and their Catholic status was thereby fixed. The Imperial cities' Right of Reformation was similarly contested by the Catholics. Ferdinand had issued an informal declaration in 1555 (*Declaratio Ferdinandea*), which stipulated that Protestant noble subjects living in ecclesiastical territories could remain Lutheran. This exemption (*Freistellung*) of certain subjects from the restrictions of the Religious Peace was controversial, with the more radical Protestant interpretations positing—in an argument that presaged Enlightenment thinking—that it could imply a right of all subjects of all Imperial Estates to possess freedom of worship.[92] From this position it was not a big step to argue that the rights of these subjects could be protected by external intervention. From the later sixteenth century many Catholic rulers questioned the validity of the *Declaratio Ferdinandea*, while Protestant rulers believed that by interceding on those nobles' behalf, they were simply enforcing a binding pledge.

The fourth deficiency of the Religious Peace was that the Ecclesiastical Reservation helped ensure an inbuilt Catholic majority in the Reichstag and the Kreis diets. The increasing willingness of the Catholic Imperial Estates to resort to majority voting, thereby marginalising Protestants and overruling their concerns, led to a fundamental paralysis of the Imperial constitution and its institutions.[93] The smooth functioning of the system depended upon negotiated consensus,

---

[90] Matthias Pohlig, 'The Peace of 1555 – A failed settlement?', in Asbach, *Ashgate Research Companion*, 193–204.
[91] R.J.W. Evans, *Rudolf II and His World, 1576–1612* (Oxford, 1973).
[92] Nikolaus Paulus, 'Religionsfreiheit und Augsburger Religionsfriede', in Heinrich Lutz (ed.), *Zur Geschichte der Toleranz und Religionsfreiheit* (Darmstadt, 1977), 17–41.
[93] Winfried Schulze, 'Majority decision in the Imperial Diets of the sixteenth and seventeenth centuries', *JMH* 58 (1986), 46–63.

cooperation, and compromise, which could not be achieved by an absolute reliance upon majorities.[94] The Catholic domination of the legislature at the Reichstag and the general atmosphere of sectarian tension had a knock-on effect on the functioning of the Imperial judiciary. The Reichskammergericht gradually became deadlocked in religious cases, particularly from 1600,[95] although it had functioned well in confessional cases during the 1550s–1580s.[96] The Emperor's Reichshofrat was increasingly used as a more swift alternative but the Protestants considered it biased,[97] and were reluctant to recognise the legitimacy of judicial interventions in confessional cases, most notoriously, its rulings in the cases of Aachen in 1593/98 and Donauwörth in 1607.[98] This growing paralysis of the Imperial judiciary increased the willingness of activist princes to threaten or carry out irregular 'horizontal' interventions on their own authority.

Another destabilising development was the rise of Calvinism from the 1560s, which disrupted the existing balance and contributed to a culture of disruptive confessional interventionism.[99] The new recruits of the banned faith included a handful of leading princes such as the electors of the Palatine and of Brandenburg, and the landgrave of Hessen-Kassel. This caused a serious intra-Protestant fissure, as the new recruits usually converted from Lutheranism. Lutheran Imperial Estates of the later sixteenth century were informally led by the moderate elector Augustus of Saxony (r. 1553–86).[100] They were more status-quo and compromise oriented, displayed greater loyalty to the Emperor, and were more willing to cooperate with the Catholics in Imperial politics than their Calvinist counterparts, because the Lutheran position had large been secured at Augsburg in 1555. The Calvinists, on the other hand, became more radical, and were determined to confessionalise disputes and thereby paralyse the system, precisely because the existing system did not accept their faith and put them in a legally precarious position. This heightened the willingness of Calvinist princes such as the elector-Palatine Frederick V to disrupt through threatened or implemented irregular interventions in support of their co-religionists. In the resulting climate of confessional polarisation, conflicts which were not originally (or not mainly) sectarian

---

[94] Peter H. Wilson, *Europe's Tragedy. A History of the Thirty Years War* (London, 2009), 43–6, 197–238; Christoph Kampmann, *Europa und das Reich im Dreißigjährigen Krieg* (Stuttgart, 2013), 20–2.

[95] Martin Heckel, *Deutschland im konfessionellen Zeitalter* (Göttingen, 2001), 84–5.

[96] Bernhard Ruthmann, *Die Religionsprozesse am Reichskammergericht (1555–1648)* (Cologne, 1996).

[97] Stefan Ehrenpreis, 'Die Tätigkeit des Reichshofrats um 1600 in der protestantischen Kritik', in Wolfgang Sellert (ed.), *Reichshofrat und Reichskammergericht: ein Konkurrenzverhältnis* (Cologne, 1999), 27–46.

[98] Stefan Ehrenpreis, *Kaiserliche Gerichtsbarkeit und Konfessions konflikt. Der Reichshofratunter Rudolf II. 1576–1612* (Göttingen, 2006), 187–96.

[99] Heinz Schilling (ed.), *Die reformierte Konfessionalisierung in Deutschland. Das Problem der 'Zweiten Reformation'* (Gütersloh, 1986).

[100] Jens Bruning, 'August (1553–1586)', in Frank-Lothar Kroll (ed.), *Die Herrscher Sachsens 1089–1918* (Munich, 2007), 110–25.

in nature could easily become confessionalised, and risked drawing in the intervention of co-religionist princes and European powers who were not originally affected.[101]

This is what occurred during several crises from the 1580s. These included conflicts over electoral-Cologne and the cities of Emden and Aachen in the 1580s, the bishopric of Strassburg in the 1590s, and the city of Donauwörth and the duchy of Jülich-Kleve-Berg in the 1600s–10s. In some of these cases, especially those in proximity to the Spanish Road and those in the north-west of Germany, local controversies became enmeshed with and even subsumed by the broader great power struggles of the Spanish–Dutch war, while others were of more narrow German-Imperial import. In the former case, many of the conflict and intervention constellations presaged the subsequent alignments of the Thirty Years War whereby the Spanish and German Habsburgs together with the Catholic Imperial Estates faced off the mainly Calvinist Protestant princes together with France and the Dutch.

The interventions in Cologne[102] and Strassburg[103] were carried out for strategic and religious-constitutional reasons in conflicts between rival claimants to the government of these prince-bishoprics, arising from irreconcilable interpretations of the 1555 Religious Peace. The pretext (and motivation) of the interventions in these cases was to defend a particular constitutional interpretation. The disputes in the cities of Emden and Aachen were similarly strategically salient and also related to conflicting interpretations of the Religious Peace (in the case of Aachen), but manifested in part as a conflict between rulers and subjects, and could therefore fall into the category of interventions or intercessions for the protection of subjects.

In the mid-late sixteenth century, there was a generalised fear that the civil wars in France and in the Spanish Habsburg territories would spread further and further into the Empire.[104] Yet the structural propensity of members of the Empire to seek external support and intervention, exacerbated by increasingly debilitating confessional tensions, caused collective attempts to seal off Germany from the French wars and the Dutch Revolt to stall. Thus, a conference of the five western Imperial Kreise at Koblenz in 1599 failed to agree upon a statement protesting Spanish military incursions into the Lower-Rhenish-Westphalian Kreis, because the Catholic princes were wary of seeming to want to shut out

---

[101] Elisabeth Müller-Luckner et al. (eds), *Konfessionsfundamentalismus in Europa um 1600* (Munich, 2007).
[102] Friedrich Beiderbeck, *Zwischen Religionskrieg, Reichskrise und europäischem Hegemoniekampf. Heinrich IV. von Frankreich und die protestantischen Reichsstände* (Berlin, 2005), 62–73; Whaley, *Germany*, i, 401–3; Wilson, *Tragedy*, 207–10.
[103] Beiderbeck, *Religionskrieg*, 215–67; Wilson, *Tragedy*, 210–11; Whaley, *Germany*, i, 411–13.
[104] Jonas van Tol, *Germany and the French Wars of Religion, 1560–1572* (Leiden, 2018); Whaley, *Germany*, i, 406–7.

Spanish intervention for their protection against perceived Calvinist conspiracies.[105] Local disputes that occurred deep in the interior of the Empire, such as Donauwörth, were less prone to attract intervention by foreign powers than those that occurred at the periphery, closer to France and the Spanish Netherlands, and were instead more likely to draw in interventions by the Empire's judiciary and by neighbouring princes. Yet the way in which the Imperial intervention in Donauwörth was badly mishandled made it explosive and further escalated confessional polarisation in the Empire. It contributed to an accelerated disenchantment with the perceived viability of regular mechanisms of conflict-regulation via the Imperial judiciary and Imperial institutions in general. This in turn contributed to a greater desire among the more confessionally radical princes such as Christian of Anhalt to erect confessional alliances, seek foreign support, and intervene on behalf of co-religionist subjects.[106]

Donauwörth had become predominantly Protestant by the beginning of the seventeenth century and Protestants controlled the city council. There remained a small but vocal Catholic minority, but their citizenship rights were increasingly denied by the council despite the city being officially biconfessional according to the Augsburg settlement. Encouraged by the radical prince-bishop Heinrich Knöringen of nearby Augsburg, the abbot and monks of the Catholic Benedictine monastery of the Holy Cross reintroduced the St Mark's Day procession and together with local Catholics, conducted the procession in a provocative, demonstrable manner, in defiance of a city council ruling. This led the city's Protestant leadership to ban the procession in 1605, and it was accused of allowing a Protestant mob to violently disperse the monks' procession the following year, despite the Catholics' procession rights having been confirmed in a preliminary ruling by the Reichshofrat. As a result, the Emperor placed the city council under the ban and commissioned the duke of Bavaria to execute the verdict in 1607 and to thereby protect the rights of the Catholic minority.[107]

This caused consternation among Protestants Empire-wide, because they viewed the Reichshofrat's dispensation of justice in confessional matters as biased. The Reichshofrat's interventions in Aachen and in the small Swabian Imperial city of Weil der Stadt,[108] which were seemingly designed to shield the minority Catholic city councils against the majority Protestant population acquiring a stake in the civic government, had already alienated the Protestants. They therefore viewed the Reichshofrat as the wrong instance of appeal in this case. Secondly, they deemed imposition of the ban—the most severe judicial penalty designed for

---

[105] Heinz Duchhardt, *Der Weg in die Katastrophe des Dreißigjährigen Krieges. Die Krisendekade 1608–1618* (Munich/Berlin, 2017), 120.
[106] Volker Press, 'Fürst Christian I. von Anhalt-Bernburg, Haupt der evangelischen Bewegungspartei vor dem Dreissigjährigen Krieg', in Konrad Ackermann et al. (eds), *Staat und Verwaltung in Bayern* (Munich, 2003), 193–216.
[107] Ban proclamation printed in Wilson (ed.), *Sourcebook*, 10–11.
[108] For the RHR's treatment of this case, see: Ehrenpreis, *Kaiserliche Gerichtsbarkeit*, 214–36.

notorious rebellion—as excessive. Thirdly, instead of appointing the convening prince of the Kreis in which the case was located—in Swabia this was the Lutheran the duke of Württemberg—as stipulated by the *Reichsexekutionsordnung*, the Emperor had appointed the unofficial head of the radical Catholic party, Duke Maximilian of Bavaria to carry out the intervention instead. In the eyes of the Protestants, Rudolf II had exposed himself as confessionally biased and willing to abuse his high judicial office to curry political favour with Bavaria, whose support he wanted during his conflict with his Austrian relatives during the Habsburg Brothers' Quarrel.

What caused real Protestant outrage, however, was that the Emperor seemed to acquiesce in the duke of Bavaria not only militarily occupying the city, but also annexing it to his own duchy and forcibly re-Catholicising it—flagrant violations of Imperial law giving an impression of 'might is right'.[109] The Protestant princes and Imperial cities of the south-west of the Reich held several crisis meetings in response, at which military counter-intervention for the protection of the majority Protestant citizens of Donauwörth and its liberation from illegal Bavarian rule was considered. In the end they could not yet bring themselves to take matters into their own hands and opted to appeal.[110] The crisis contributed to the paralysis of the Imperial institutions and overlapped with the crisis of Austrian Habsburg leadership, and the consequent inability of the Emperor to perform his traditional role as a neutral judicial overlord, arbiter and protector. As a result, opportunities were now given to radical sectarian alliances, the Protestant Union (1608) and the Catholic League (1609), to poise themselves seemingly in readiness for irregular horizontal intervention for the protection of co-religionists in other territories, while also spreading their networks beyond the Reich.[111]

The crisis over Jülich-Kleve-Berg, which coincided with the beginnings of the Union and the League, was a dynastic succession crisis, but it acquired such an explosive potential because of its international geopolitical and confessional dimensions.[112] In combining a confusing array of different conflict and interest constellations, the crisis may be seen as a microcosm of politics and conflict in the Empire, not least because compromise and cooperation prevailed after limited fighting and intervention, preventing the episode from escalating into a general war. The crisis, which erupted in two fits in 1609–10 and 1614, featured a dynastic succession dispute between rival claimants (Wolfgang Wilhelm of Pfalz-Neuburg

---

[109] Dieter Albrecht, *Maximilian I. von Bayern 1573–1651* (Munich, 1998), 397–403.
[110] C. Scott Dixon, 'Urban order and religious coexistence in the German imperial city: Augsburg and Donauwörth, 1548–1608', *CEH* 40 (2007), 1–33 (p. 23 for mooted Protestant counter-intervention).
[111] Treaty documents in Wilson (ed.), *Sourcebook*, 12–20. See Wilson, *Europe's Tragedy*, passim; Albrecht Ernst et al. (eds), *Union und Liga 1608/09. Konfessionelle Bündnisse im Reich* (Stuttgart, 2010); Simon Adams, 'The Union, the League and the Politics of Europe', in Geoffrey Parker (ed.), *The Thirty Years' War* (New York, 1987), 25–38.
[112] Manfred Groten et al. (eds), *Der Jülich-Klevische Erbstreit 1609* (Düsseldorf, 2011).

and elector Johann Sigismund of Brandenburg), underlining the crucial importance of dynastic inheritance rights in early modern geopolitics, but also a conflict over the balance of prerogatives between Imperial Estates and the Emperor, especially after the latter tried to impose his authority by sequestrating the contested territory and having it administered by an Imperial commissioner. Additionally, there were tensions within the territory between the largely Protestant territorial estates on the one hand, and princely authority on the other, while the Catholic privy-councillors at Düsseldorf had long been under the influence of the Catholic party in the Reich and Spain.[113]

Thus, these 'base-conflicts' were overlain, to varying degrees, by a confessionalised antagonism, especially during the second run of the crisis. And all these sets of conflict risked sucking in—more or less willingly—the intervention of outside powers, particularly Spain, the Dutch republic and France. Even more so that the afore-mentioned, initially intra-German conflicts in Cologne, Strassburg, and Aachen, the location of Jülich-Kleve was of great strategic importance to the Habsburg-Dutch rivalry and the Franco-Spanish rivalry, which had been revitalised after Henry IV's consolidation of power. This geopolitical salience gave the crisis an even greater potential to become 'Europeanised' than the previous German conflicts along the Rhine.[114]

The contested territorial complex of Jülich-Kleve-Berg protruded into Dutch territory at the end of the Spanish Road, and the Rhine flowed between Jülich and Berg, while these two duchies also enveloped the important electorate of Cologne. It was of great economic and commercial importance and its large population was confessionally mixed. When Duke Johann Wilhelm died in March 1609, there was anxiety among the privy councillors and the Catholic party in the Reich that this important collection of territories would come under Protestant rule because the two most credible contenders were both Lutheran. As the Habsburgs also had a vague claim, many Catholics hoped that the territories would be sequestered by the Emperor before he, as feudal overlord, decided whom to enfeoff. The two Lutheran contenders pre-empted any such take-over by the Emperor, or indeed by the regency that was set up under the duke's (Catholic) widow and the privy councillors, when they occupied the territories and established joint rule as the 'possessing princes', in cooperation with the territorial estates in June 1609. They declared that they would refuse to accept the jurisdiction of the Reichshofrat or the Emperor in this case (it occurred not long after the Donauwörth outrage) and would only submit to a collective decision by a panel of neutral Imperial Estates. In response, Emperor Rudolf II declared their arrangement to be invalid,

---

[113] For the internal dynamics: Rolf-Achim Mostert, 'Der jülich-klevische Regiments- und Erbfolgestreit—ein Vorspielzum Dreißigjärigen Krieg?', in Stefan Ehrenpreis (ed.), *Der Dreißigjährige Krieg im Herzogtum Berg und in seinen Nachbarregionen* (Neustadt, 2002), 26–64.

[114] Alison Anderson, *On the Verge of War. International Relations and the Jülich-Kleve Succession Crises (1609–1614)* (Boston, 1999), 74–95.

sequestrated the fiefs, and appointed his cousin archduke Leopold as Imperial commissioner to take over the administration of the territories. Leopold occupied the fortress of Jülich and his forces engaged in some skirmishes with those of the 'possessing princes'. At this stage, the succession dispute had assumed the character of a feudal conflict between the Emperor as overlord and two of his immediate subjects who were contesting his right to dispense fiefs and were thereby positioning themselves as champions of princely liberties. Each side sought to establish a power-base within the territories by allying with the lower-level protagonists of the conflict within the contested lands: the Imperial commissioner with the representatives of the princely government in Düsseldorf (the privy councillors and the duke's widow) who wished to see the continuation of Catholic rule, and the Lutheran possessing princes with the largely Protestant territorial estates.[115]

However, external assistance was surprisingly hard to come by, a fact which paints a different picture than that of irreversible confessional polarisation and internationalisation inevitably leading to war. Some historians portray the Jülich–Kleve conflict as fitting nearly into this pattern, for example as a mere prelude to, or even first salvo of the Thirty Years War.[116] Although external forces did intervene and there was some limited fighting, what is more striking about the crises is the absence of full-blown escalation. The newly formed Catholic League turned down the support requested by the Imperial commissioner archduke Leopold, despite a Catholic would-be administrator being besieged and denied rule over territories mandated to him under Imperial authority by two Protestant princes acting on their own authority. Duke Maximilian of Bavaria refused to put the topic on the agenda of the League because he had no interest in facilitating Habsburg rule over this crucial territorial complex in the northwest of Germany.[117] In general, most princes in the Empire hoped for a peaceful settlement and impressed upon the Emperor the importance of mediating a solution under a more moderate commissioner. But Rudolf II's mishandling of yet another crisis and his loss of authority in the Empire in general, contributed to the Europeanisation of the conflict and to Imperial politics in general.[118]

Yet, when it did occur, the foreign powers' intervention was limited. There were loud calls for intervention among Puritan war-mongers at Westminster and among the Dutch Orangist war party that was dissatisfied with the truce, but

---

[115] These internal dynamics within the territories are covered by Rolf-Achim Mostert, 'Der jülich-klevische Regiments- und Erbfolgestreit—ein Vorspielzum Dreißigjärigen Krieg?', in Stefan Ehrenpreis (ed.), *Der Dreißigjährige Krieg im Herzogtum Berg und in seinen Nachbarregionen* (Neustadt an der Aisch, 2002), 26–64.
[116] E.g., Heinz Ollmann-Kösling, *Der Erbfolgestreit um Jülich-Kleve: Ein Vorspiel zum Dreissigjährigen Krieg* (Regensburg, 1996).
[117] Alison, *Verge of War*, 211ff; Wilson, *Tragedy*, 238.   [118] Duchhardt, *Krisendekade*, 133.

these hawkish voices were not in control of foreign policy.[119] Both the Dutch and the Spanish were reluctant to intervene aggressively because they did not wish to risk endangering their recently concluded twelve-year-truce of 1609.[120] Their cautiousness allowed France to take the lead until the death of Henry IV.[121] The reluctance of the European powers to risk war permitted an intra-German preliminary settlement of the dispute.[122] During a second, more confessionalised flare-up of the dispute in 1614, foreign powers were again drawn in, and again they opted to cease intervening before the situation escalated into a general war.[123]

---

[119] Magnus Rüde, *England und Kurpfalz im werdenden Mächteeuropa (1608–1632)* (Stuttgart, 2007), 185.
[120] For Dutch and Spanish cautiousness: Helmut Gabel, 'Sicherheit und Konfession. Aspekte niederländischer Politik gegenüber Jülich-Berg vor und während des Dreißigjährigen Krieges', in Ehrenpreis (ed.), *Berg*, 132–79.
[121] Henry IV's intervention: Volker Press, *Kriege und Krisen. Deutsche Geschichte 1600–1715* (Munich, 1991), 174–84; J. Michael Hayden, 'Continuity in the France of Henry IV and Louis XIII: French foreign policy, 1598–1615', *JMH* 45 (1973), 1–23.
[122] Ollman-Kösling, *Erbfolgestreit*, 90; Wilson, *Tragedy*, 235.   [123] Anderson, *Verge*, 163–93.

# 3
# Interventions in Central Europe II: 1618–1645

### The Thirty Years War

One reason why Emperor Rudolf II did not deal with the Jülich-Kleve crisis effectively is because it occurred during a period of infighting within the German branch of the Habsburg dynasty, and internal unrest within the Austrian hereditary lands. This internal unrest culminated in the rebellion of the Protestant Bohemian territorial estates against the Habsburgs which marked the beginning of the great war that some commentators in the Reich had come to expect since around the turn of the century. The sense of anxious anticipation is reflected in a letter sent in 1615 by Landgrave Moritz of Hessen to the French king Louis XIII: 'I fear greatly that the states of the Empire, which are in such a state of quarrel among themselves, will spark a disastrous fire, that will not only engulf themselves but also all those countries which are in any way connected with Germany.'[1] This prediction was grim but prescient. Yet despite a multitude of crises in the decade prior to 1618, the years between the Spanish-Dutch truce and the Bohemian rebellion were an unusually peaceful period of European history.[2]

The outbreak of the rebellion in Prague, its escalation into an Imperial civil war fought over the Empire's constitution, and its subsequent 'internationalisation' into a general European war, was a result of three overlapping problem areas: 1. The crisis of the Austrian Habsburg dynasty; 2. The crisis of the Imperial constitution, in particular as it pertained to its confessionalised law and the balance of prerogatives between Emperor and princes; and 3. The manifold connections between European powers and the members of the decentralised and polycentric Empire. What linked these different problem areas in practice and what caused the conflict to escalate from one level to the next, in the sequence above, were interventions. The Thirty Years War was therefore at its core a series of successive interventions, usually justified and/or motivated by a desire to defend the rights of the target ruler's subjects (both immediate and mediate). The Bohemian rebellion could not have morphed into a European general war had

---

[1] Quoted in Duchhardt, *Krisendekade*, 10.
[2] Lucien Bély, *Les relations internationals en Europe. XVIIe-XVIIIe siècles* (Paris, 1992), 3–57.

it not been for the numerous Imperial-European interconnections.[3] The war certainly overlapped with the ongoing great-power rivalries when it became internationalised, but it was not simply one stage or iteration of a long-term Franco-Habsburg contest that lasted from 1477 to 1756 as some historians have argued.[4] Others downplay the importance of foreign intervention.[5] More persuasive interpretations portray the war as a distinct conflict over Imperial (i.e. constitutional) issues, which then became increasingly internationalised when it merged with great power rivalries in the Empire's vicinity, while never losing its Imperial-German focus.[6] This chapter will focus on the crucial moments of intervention, including the Palatine intervention in Bohemia (1619); the counter-interventions in support of the Emperor (1619); the Danish (1625), Swedish (1630), Transylvanian (1619 and 1644), and French (1635) interventions in support of the anti-Habsburg rebels.

## Rebellion and Intervention in Bohemia and Germany 1618–1623

During the succession dispute in the German Habsburg branch, the so-called Brothers' Quarrel of 1606–12, between the Emperor Rudolf II and his rivals Matthias and Ferdinand, both sides felt compelled to make considerable concessions of religious and political rights to the Protestant territorial estates of their territories in return for money and support.[7] The most consequential concession granted to the estates was Rudolf's 'Letter of Majesty', which the Protestant territorial estates of Bohemia and Silesia extorted from the Emperor in 1609 during a military emergency. The Letter placed them in a very influential, autonomous position and granted all subjects of Bohemia religious freedom. After the successful power-grab by archduke Matthias, soon followed by his election as Emperor in 1612, the dynasty began to scale back the concessions granted to the territorial estates earlier, and to crack down on Protestantism, by denying Protestants access to public office and banning Protestant worship in towns on church land. By this stage about three-quarters of the inhabitants of the Habsburg hereditary lands had become Protestant.[8]

---

[3] Anuschka Tischer, 'Dynamik durch Gewalt? Der Dreißigjährige Krieg und die Wandlungsprozesse der Frühen Neuzeit', in Tischer et al. (eds), *Dynamic durch Gewalt? Der Dreißigjährige Krieg als Faktor der Wandlungsprozesse des 17. Jahrhunderts* (Münster, 2018), 13–39, at 38.

[4] Nicola M. Sutherland, 'The origins of the Thirty Years War and the structure of European politics', *EHR* 107 (1992), 587–625.

[5] Georg Schmidt, *Die Reiter der Apokalypse. Geschichte des Dreißigjährigen Krieges* (Munich, 2018).

[6] Peter H. Wilson, 'The causes of the Thirty Years War 1618–48', *EHR* 123 (2008), 554–86; Christoph Kampmann, *Europa und das Reich im Dreißigjährigen Krieg* (Stuttgart, 2013).

[7] Václav Bůžek et al. (eds), *Ein Bruderzwist im Hause Habsburg* (Budwar, 2010).

[8] Geoff Mortimer, *The Origins of the Thirty Years War and the Revolt in Bohemia, 1618* (New York, 2015); Wilson, *Tragedy*, 106–16, 269–71; Whaley, *Germany*, i, 428–37.

It would be erroneous to characterise the rebellion of the Habsburg territorial estates as a solely religious revolt, although religion was certainly a factor. It was primarily an assertion of traditional liberties, corporate privileges and autonomy.[9] Confession was blended into this motivation because the asserted constitutional and political corporate rights included confessional elements, such as the freedom to worship and erect churches. The Bohemian and Austrian territorial estates were moreover representative of a vast central and eastern European zone of territorial entities—stretching from the Empire (including the Netherlands and Imperial Italy) to Poland and Hungary—which was characterised by noble estates' extensive claims of autonomy, liberty, and participation in governance, claims which often clashed with the centralising ambitions of the zone's ruling princes. The estates in this zone often claimed to be the true 'representatives' of their countries, and varyingly claimed to possess the right not only to approve princely taxation and to be consulted in all important matters of government, but also to elect the monarch, and to mount armed resistance against any ruler seeking to undermine their traditional privileges and liberties.[10]

Seeking external protection through intervention and links with other territorial estates were by-products of their political vision. The Bohemian territorial estates possessed links with Protestant Imperial Estates such as the neighbouring Palatinate, which contributed to their elevated self-perception and to their professed inspiration by 'German freedom'.[11] There had been an alliance between the Calvinist estates of Transylvania and the Protestant nobility of Poland, while Bohemian estates made efforts in the 1610s to set up an international estates-confederation with those of Hungary aimed at mutual defence of their rights.[12] Although these efforts failed, they succeeded in securing the participation of the Silesian, Moravian, and Lusatian estates in the *Confoederatio Bohemica* in July 1619, during the rebellion.[13]

Tensions between the Bohemian estates and the Habsburgs increased after Emperor Matthias moved the Imperial court from Prague back to Vienna in 1612 and his stadholders in Prague continued the centralising, anti-Protestant policies. Relations further deteriorated after Emperor Matthias got archduke Ferdinand of Inner Austria appointed as king of Bohemia in 1617. Ferdinand

---

[9] Klaus Gerteis (ed.), *Monarchie oder Ständestaat. Der böhmische Aufstand von 1618* (Trier, 1983).
[10] Arno Strohmeyer, *Konfessionskonflikt und Herrschaftsordnung. Widerstandsrecht bei den österreichischen Ständen (1550-1650)* (Mainz, 2006), 62-198; Barbara Stollberg-Rilinger, *Vormünder des Volkes? Konzepte landständischer Repräsentation in der Spätphase des Alten Reiches* (Berlin, 1999), 92-111.
[11] Whaley, *Germany*, i, 453.
[12] Duchhardt, *Krisendekade*, 56, 150; Joachim Bahlcke, 'Calvinism and estate liberation in Bohemia and Hungary (1570-1620)', in Karin Maag (ed.), *The Reformation in Eastern and Central Europe* (Aldershot, 1997), 72-91.
[13] Winfried Becker, 'Ständestaat und Konfessionsbildung am Beispiel der böhmischen Konföderationsakte von 1619', in Dieter Albrecht et al. (eds), *Politik und Konfession* (Berlin, 1983), 77-99. Document printed in Wilson, *Sourcebook*, 41-6.

had already made a name for himself with aggressive counter-Reformation drives in Styria which were now extended to Bohemia. The rebellion which began on 23 May 1618 was carried out by a minority radical wing of the Bohemian nobles, led by count Heinrich Matthias von Thurn.[14] On 25 May 1618, the estates published a justification for their act of rebellion, the so-called *Apologia*, which attempted to legitimise their actions as a just form of defence against the illegal and unjust actions of the king's maverick ministers and advisers and the Jesuits, which was therefore not an act of rebellion at all:

> Inhabitants of the kingdom have faced...many kinds of terrible hardships in both political and ecclesiastical affairs... [Habsburg councillors] evilly plagued the subjects in diverse ways on account of religion, had them banished under the pretence of secular malfeasances...and used unheard-of atrocities to force people to convert to the Catholic religion against their will and against the clear language of the Letter of Majesty.[15]

Armed hostilities between the Habsburg and rebel Bohemian forces began in June 1618. By the end of August 1619, the estates had declared King Ferdinand as deposed and had formed the *Confederatio Bohemica* union of the rebellious estates under Habsburg rule. The treaty text designated Bohemia as an elective monarchy, prohibited the election of a new king while the incumbent was still alive, and asserted the estates' right of armed resistance against a king who violated their rights.[16] This was diametrically opposed to the Habsburgs' conception of the Bohemian monarchy which they considered to be hereditary in their house. In the context of this escalated rebellion, the Bohemian rebels tried to attract external support.

There was a flurry of interventions in the Habsburg lands in 1618–1619. Both sides were militarily weak and needed to call on outside assistance. Several powers intervened because their rivals seemed preoccupied by internal troubles making intervention appear low-risk.[17] By accepting the Bohemian crown offered to him following the royal election, elector-Palatine Frederick V in effect intervened in support of the rebels against their king in late 1619 to be elected king himself. Something similar occurred with Prince Bethlen Gábor of Transylvania (r.1613–29) in respect to Habsburg Hungary. In 1616 he had already carried out a small intervention in defence of the rights of Protestants in the Habsburg hereditary lands. Three years later, in alliance with the rebelling Bohemians, Austrians, and Hungarians, he launched daring and brutal invasions of Hungary

---

[14] Hans Sturmberger, *Aufstand in Böhmen. Der Beginn des Dreißigjährigen Krieges* (Munich, 1959).
[15] Quoted in Tryntje Helfferich (ed.), *The Thirty Years War. A Documentary History* (Indianapolis, 2009), 21–9.
[16] Wilson, *Sourcebook*, 41–6.    [17] Thus: Wilson, *Tragedy*, 269.

and Austria, including ineffective sieges of Vienna, and had himself elected (counter-)king of Hungary in 1620 by anti-Habsburg rebel Hungarians.[18] In 1618, Duke Charles Emanuel of Savoy—a bitter rival of the Spanish Habsburgs in northern Italy—financed an expedition of anti-Habsburg mercenary forces in Bohemia led by count Ernst von Mansfeld, to deal a blow against the Habsburgs and to improve his chances of being elected king of Bohemia himself.[19] The Habsburgs meanwhile received support from Bavaria, Saxony, Spain, and the Papacy in 1619.

The elector-Palatine's intervention in the Bohemian rebellion, in the form of his acceptance of the crown offered to him by the rebel estates in September 1619, was a momentous decision. It amounted to a declaration of war against the Habsburgs, whose most aggressive and anti-Protestant archduke, the deposed king of Bohemia, was elected Emperor almost simultaneously as Ferdinand II; a dangerous constellation. It spread the war to south and west Germany and turned a local rebellion in the Habsburg lands into a civil war of the Empire. It had catastrophic consequences for the intervener, who lost his lands, titles, and dignities. Frederick V's decision to intervene was informed by politico-dynastic ambitions and religious and providential considerations. It was also influenced by his overconfidence in the Palatinate's German and international Protestant networks of support.[20]

The dynastic rewards of becoming king of Bohemia were enticing. The large kingdom bordered his territory of Upper Palatinate. Ruling both the Palatinate and the Bohemian kingdom in personal union would give Frederick a very sizeable chunk of lands stretching from the Moselle and Rhine rivers in the West to the borders of Hungary and Poland in the East. Such an accretion of lands would certainly give him the edge over his rival Catholic Wittelsbach cousins of Bavaria who coveted the Palatine Wittelsbachs' electoral dignity. Furthermore, apart from the obvious rank elevation, possession of the Bohemian crown would create the constitutional anomaly of uniting two Imperial electoral votes in Frederick V's person and giving the Protestants a majority in the electoral college, thus raising the possibility that he might become Emperor himself.[21] His ambitions for the Imperial crown (either for himself or for his successor) were later seemingly

---

[18] Andrea Schmidt-Rösler, 'Princeps Transilvaniae – Rex Hungariae? Gabriel Bethlens Außenpolitik zwischen Krieg und Frieden', in Heinz Duchhardt et al. (eds), *Kalkül—Transfer—Symbol. Europäische Friedensverträge der Vormoderne* (Mainz, 2006), sec. 80-98, http://www.ieg-mainz.de/vieg-online-beihefte/01-2006.html.

[19] Ruth Kleinman, 'Charles-Emmanuel I of Savoy and the Bohemian election of 1619', *European Studies Review* 5 (1975), 3-29, at 10.

[20] Brennan Pursell, 'The Palatinate and its networks in the Empire and in Europe', in Olaf Asbach and Peter Schröder (eds), *The Ashgate Research Companion to the Thirty Years War* (New York, 2014), 25-37.

[21] Heinz Duchhardt, *Protestantisches Kaisertum und Altes Reich. Die Diskussion über die Konfession des Kaisers in Politik, Publizistik und Staatsrecht* (Wiesbaden, 1977), 131-47.

confirmed when he named his son after the only Emperor of the Palatine dynasty, Ruprecht.[22]

Frederick's wife, Princess Elizabeth of England, gave him misguided assurances that her father King James I would intervene in support of the Palatinate, possibly to defend Frederick's planned acquisition of Bohemia, and at the least to defend his hereditary electorate, which probably contribute to his decision-making. His uncle, the new Stadholder of the United Provinces, Prince Maurice of Orange, encouraged him to accept the crown and promised financial and military assistance. Probably also important in Frederick's decision, was his providential belief that God had selected him to do His work on earth, in this case to rescue the oppressed Bohemian Protestants from Habsburg persecution. Such millenarian fantasies allowed him to turn a blind eye to the significant risks involved, and to ignore the more prudent voices at his court in Heidelberg and among Protestant Union members. These cautioned that accepting the crown amounted to intervening in a rebellion against his Imperial-feudal overlord on the side of the rebels and therefore risked exposing the elector to the Imperial ban and the loss of his territories. Nonetheless, Frederick V wrote to the Bohemian rebels before definitively accepting: 'we must notice...the special providence and predestination of God'. Without awaiting confirmation of an English commitment to support the undertaking, and egged on by Christian of Anhalt—who had been pressing the Union members for intervention since the beginning of troubles in Bohemia—Frederick accepted the offer definitively at the end of September 1619, writing to the Bohemians that he was driven 'to follow the will of the Almighty'.[23]

Frederick V's public justification of the intervention, issued in November 1619, omitted mention of his own dynastic and geopolitical ambitions and toned down the millenarian-providential reasoning.[24] Instead it emphasised that the intervention was just and legitimate, carried out to rescue the Bohemians from oppression, and deriving from a right of resistance of the estates and a right of intervention by neighbouring princes, arguments which were seemingly deemed to be more acceptable to the princely public. The 'un-Christian, heinous persecution of the poor subjects, with the threat of great hardship, insult and danger to life and limb' was portrayed in disturbing detail: 'robbery, murder, arson, and ruination of the territory, and the spilling of much innocent Christian blood, hacking of suckling babies and the like inhuman, barbarous excesses, maliciousness and atrocities' were argued to have been carried out by the regents of Bohemia and the Jesuits. In addition to general violence, they were accused of carrying out an illegal counter-Reformation programme in violation of the Letter of Majesty, even though

---

[22] Wilson, *Tragedy*, 284–5.
[23] Quoted in Brennan Pursell, *The Winter King. Frederick V of the Palatinate and the Coming of the Thirty Years War* (London, 2016), 76–80.
[24] Printed in Wilson, *Sourcebook*, 47–52.

'people's consciences cannot be commanded'.[25] The Bohemian estates' acts of resistance against such governmental crimes, which 'they were entitled to make under divine and natural law' were therefore argued to be justified; moreover, they aimed 'to stabilise and promote defence', and 'had many well-founded, legitimate and sufficient reasons to change their government', as permitted by the constitution and traditions of Bohemia.

In accepting the crown, Frederick stressed that 'we do not seek unjustly to dispossess or deprive any other person... and so never sought elevation'. Instead, his intervention was aimed at furnishing the protection of lives, consciences, and rights that the Bohemian subjects so desperately needed: 'to legitimise those who desire their liberty, privileges, the Letter of Majesty, the free exercise of the Evangelical religion... to protect and preserve them against unjust violence... to rescue and emancipate [Bohemia] from further suffering and eventual ruin'. The means by which he acquired the crown were by a constitutionally correct election: 'thus the affair is in itself legal, Christian and worthy'.[26] Frederick V claimed that he also decided to intervene because he considered it a 'divine vocation' and because by providing the requested protection, he was acting 'in God's name, for the advancement of His holy honour'.[27] He summarised that 'for the consolation and protection of those that are so greatly distressed, for the maintenance of the common liberty and welfare... and especially their ardent desire for our intervention, we finally approved the unanimous election they offered us'.[28] In addition to referring to a norm of the duty of protective intervention, he also argued that his intervention and rule over Bohemia would further the strategic defence interests of the Empire, because previously, so he argued, the large taxes that had been raised in the country had not been spent where they were needed, namely on border defences against the Turks. Frederick also argued that his acquisition of Bohemia tied it more effectively into the Empire and its mutual defence mechanisms: 'were the worthy kingdom of Bohemia... a bulwark against foreign nations, not immediately assisted in some way, it might well have fallen into other foreign hands, and into such a state that it would have become detached from the Holy Empire'.[29]

Emperor Ferdinand II published an edict in January 1620 in which he annulled the Bohemian royal election of Frederick V. The broader aims of this publication were to publicly respond to the rebels and the elector-Palatine by delegitimising both the Bohemian rebellion and the Palatine intervention.[30] The actions of the Bohemian estates were unsurprisingly portrayed as an illegal act of rebellion, rather than justified resistance.[31] He argued that their actions were in fact 'arbitrary acts... against their duly determined authority', in short, 'a public and

---

[25] Ibid., 47–8.  [26] Ibid., 49–50.  [27] Ibid., 50–1.  [28] Ibid., 51.
[29] Ibid., 48, 50–1.  [30] Printed in ibid., 39–46.  [31] Strohmeyer, *Widerstandsrecht*, 449.

hostile defiance and rebellion'.[32] A few radical members of the estates had 'clothed their odious rebellion under the mantle of religion', but then proceeded 'also to repress both Protestant and Catholic members of the estates who remained loyal', and to illegally establish 'an entirely new constitution'. Ferdinand parried Frederick's geopolitical point about securing Bohemia for the Empire with a counter-argument: in enabling the intervention of an Ottoman vassal, the Bohemians and Palatines were accused of having treasonously 'abetted Prince Bethlen Gábor of Transylvania, who was under the protection of our archenemy [the Ottomans]... thereby placing into extreme danger this bulwark of the Empire'.[33]

The edict adopted classic anti-interventionist arguments by criticising Frederick V's acceptance of the Bohemian crown as illegal interference, which set a dangerous precedent. The wider objective of this line of argument was to persuade the Protestant princes not to support Palatine actions. The Empire possessed a functioning system of the rule of law with judicially regulated interventions mandated by the Imperial courts. If princes such as the elector-Palatine took the law into their own hands by carrying out irregular horizontal interventions, the entire order of peaceful co-existence regulated by the Public Peace risked unravelling:

> For another [prince] to assume our hereditary kingdom, to take our subjects up into a new oath of fealty, to violate all laws and regulations of the Empire, and especially to go against the greatly affirmed Public Peace, creates a completely invidious and highly prejudicial example for all potentates and regents.[34]

Furthermore, the Palatine intervention risked encouraging further insurrections against legitimate rulers, which was not in the collective interests of princes: 'all potentates, princes, and authorities... are also endangered by such an invidious example, since the same treason by subjects could occur against them as well'.[35]

In October 1619, Frederick and his forces arrived in Prague and he was crowned the following month. At this stage the rebels were making headway against the Habsburgs. The rebels were certainly emboldened and possibly further radicalised by the Palatine intervention.[36] It also raised the prospects of further international interventions in support of their rebellion, considering Frederick's dynastic links with England, the Netherlands, and Sweden. Such hopes were to be largely disappointed, however. Sweden and Denmark were still fully concentrating on the Baltic. The Protestant Union similarly declined to support the Bohemian

---

[32] Helfferich (ed.), *Documentary History*, 40.  [33] Ibid., 41, 43–4.
[34] Ibid., 43–4; Tischer, *Kriegsbegründungen*, 63.  [35] Helfferich (ed.), *Documentary History*, 45.
[36] Joachim Bahlcke, 'Konfessionalisierung der Außenpolitik? Die Rolle der Konfession in den Außenbeziehungen der böhmischen Stände', in Friedrich Beiderbeck et al. (eds), *Dimensionen der europäischen Außenpolitik zur Zeit der Wende vom 16. zum 17. Jahrhundert* (Berlin, 2003), 265–83.

rebels and the Palatinate, even though it was led by Frederick V.[37] While it did raise an army 'to protect liberty and law...to maintain our religion like true patriots', it refused to deploy it in the Habsburg hereditary lands, and instead intended to restrict its use to defensive purposes, although it never fought the Catholic League.[38]

Hoped-for intervention by the Dutch only occurred in a limited manner. Dutch intervention on behalf of the rebels and the subsequent Spanish counter-invention in support of the Emperor were related to the expected expiry of the Spanish-Dutch truce in 1621: the Dutch wished to thereby keep the Habsburgs distracted by prolonging the war in Bohemia, while the Spanish hoped for a quick end to that war so that their Austrian cousins might assist them in their own war against the Dutch.[39] The Spanish envoy to Austria had warned in 1618 that it would become exceedingly difficult to retain Spanish possessions in Flanders and Italy if anti-Habsburg rebels emerged victorious in Bohemia and the Empire.[40] In the summer of 1619, a Dutch agent wrote to an envoy of the Protestant Union: 'the Bohemian war will decide the fates of all of us, but especially yours, since you are the neighbours of the Czechs. For the present we shall seek out all ways of bringing you help'.[41] The belligerent new Dutch Stadholder Maurice of Orange had urged his nephew Frederick to accept the Bohemian crown and even promised support. But in the end the Dutch supplied only 5000 men for action in Bohemia in 1620, and provided far less money than pledged.[42]

James I's failure to intervene robustly on behalf of his Bohemian co-religionists and his son-in-law, their new rebel king, caused the greatest disappointment at Prague and Heidelberg. He was more interested in becoming arbiter of Europe by mediating between the conflicting parties on the continent. His immediate objective was the 'Spanish match'—to find a Catholic, preferably a Spanish, bride for his son—a goal which would be hampered by an anti-Habsburg intervention.[43] Yet the king found himself under intense pressure from the interventionist war lobby of Puritans at Westminster and a lively public sphere, especially as the

---

[37] Gregor Horstkemper, 'Die Protestantische Union und der Ausbruch des Dreißigjährigen Krieges', in Winfried Schulze (ed.), *Friedliche Intentionen—kriegerische Effekte: war der Ausbruch des Dreissigjährigen Krieges unvermeidlich?* (St. Katharinen, 2002), 21–51.
[38] Quoted in Geoffrey Parker, *Global Crisis. War, Climate Change and Catastrophe in the Seventeenth Century* (New Haven, 2013), 213.
[39] Josef V. Polišenský, *Tragic Triangle: the Netherlands, Spain and Bohemia 1617–1621* (Prague, 1991).
[40] Peter Brightwell, 'Spain and Bohemia: the decision to intervene, 1619', *European Studies Review* 12 (1982), 117–41; Eberhard Straub, *Pax et Imperium. Spaniens Kampf um seine Friedensordnung in Europa zwischen 1617 und 1635* (Paderborn, 1980), 116–17, 131–63. Ulrich Nagel, *Zwischen Dynastie und Staatsräson. Die habsburgischen Botschafter in Wien und Madrid am Beginn des Dreißigjährigen Krieges* (Göttingen, 2018), 342–79.
[41] Quoted in Wilson, *Sourcebook*, 52.
[42] Jonathan Israel, *The Dutch Republic. Its Rise, Greatness, and Fall 1477–1806* (Oxford, 1998), 645–74.
[43] Rüde, *England und Kurpfalz*, 165–77.

Palatine-Bohemian military position became increasingly dire.[44] Many English and Scots viewed the defence of foreign Protestants as their new shared monarch's duty.[45] During debates in the Commons in June 1620, Sir Edward Cecil argued in favour of intervention. He noted 'we are not insensible of the sufferance of those of our religion, nor of the wrong done to the count Palatine', and urged that MPs take

> into their most serious consideration the present estate of the king's children abroad, and the general afflicted estate of the true professors of the same Christian religion, professed by the Church of England, in foreign parts; and, being touched with a true sense and fellow-feeling of their distresses, as members of the same body.[46]

Sir James Perrott argued more forcefully against 'the slackness shewn in... the Affair of the Palatinate' and connected the security of Protestant subjects abroad with the position of Protestantism in England. He implored his colleagues to issue a declaration concerning 'the danger of religion in general, and of the Palatinate in particular', which asserted that 'if religion and right may not be restored by peaceable means... we would be ready to adventure the lives and estates of all that belong unto us'. Measures ought to be undertaken and funds approved, which 'enable his maj. To relieve the distressed, to rescue religion, to recover the Palatinate, with the patrimony of his daughter's children'.[47] Despite pleas from his daughter, and exhortations from the Dutch, all King James could bring himself to provide his son-in-law was a volunteer force of under 8,000 troops to defend his ancestral Lower (Rhenish) Palatinate.[48] In any case, geographical and strategic factors made effective Stuart military intervention in central Europe almost impossible.[49] The English and French non-intervention at this crucial moment—which was even mocked in some German Catholic pamphlets[50]—arguably prevented the complete collapse of the German Habsburgs, who were in a highly perilous position in 1619/20.[51]

---

[44] Dunthorne, *Britain and the Dutch Revolt*, 49.
[45] Jason White, *Militant Protestantism and British Identity, 1603–1642* (London, 2012).
[46] William Cobbett, *Parliamentary History of England* (London, 1806–20), 19, col. 1294.
[47] Ibid., cols 1292–3.
[48] Elmar Weiss, *Die Unterstützung Friedrichs V. von der Pfalz durch Jakob I. und Karl I. im Dreißigjährigen Krieg (1618–1632)* (Stuttgart, 1966), 17–54.
[49] Thus: Peter H. Wilson, 'The Stuarts, the Palatinate, and the Thirty Years' War', in Valentina Caldari and Sara J. Wolfson (eds), *Stuart Marriage Diplomacy. Dynastic Politics in their European Context, 1604–1630* (Woodbridge, 2018), 141–56.
[50] Esther-Beate Körber, 'Deutschsprachige Flugschriften des Dreißigjährigen Krieg 1618 bis 1629', *Jahrbuch für Kommunikationsgeschichte*, 3 (2001), 1–47, at 10–11.
[51] Thus: Axel Gotthardt, 'Wende des böhmisch-pfälzischen Krieges. Wie Frankreich und England 1620 die Großmachtposition Habsburgs retteten', in Sven Externbrink et al. (eds), *Formen internationaler Beziehungen in der Frühen Neuzeit* (Berlin, 2001), 396–417. Although the importance

What certainly saved the Emperor, however, was his successful rallying of support from Spain, Bavaria,[52] Saxony,[53] and the Bavarian-led Catholic League along with the Papacy. The series of pro-Imperial interventions, designed to forestall Habsburg collapse in central Europe and to counter the Palatinate and Transylvania, allowed the Emperor to suppress the rebellion in the Habsburg lands and defeat the rebel princes in the Empire in 1620–22. This, together with resumption of the Spanish-Dutch war in 1621, and the fact that Spain occupied the Lower Palatinate,[54] while the Dutch continued to call for interventions in support of Habsburg enemies,[55] internationalised the conflict which was fast becoming a generalised war. Now a fugitive, Frederick V refused to accept terms of surrender to give up his claims, which kept the *Causa Palatina* alive.

## Intervention in the Valtelline Uprising, 1620–1623

Spain's presence along the Rhine in turn was considered a threat by France which had hitherto hardly become involved in the war. However, the French had already become concerned about another Spanish initiative to bolster the Spanish Road in the north Italian/Swiss Alpine region. An intervention from Spanish Milan, ostensibly for the protection of persecuted and rebelling Catholic subjects under Calvinist rule, but primarily aimed at securing Alpine passes on the route towards the Low Countries, took place in 1620 in the Swiss-affiliated Valtelline territory of the Grey Leagues (*Graubünden*) confederacy.[56] The Grey Leagues was a free state which was a close ally or 'associate' (*Zugewandter Ort*) of the Swiss Confederation—itself a collection of semi-sovereign states at this time. Spain was very interested in this territory because it contained the valley passes that could be used as an alternative route for the Spanish Road towards Austrian Habsburg-ruled territory in the Breisgau and Alsace, thus avoiding the Franche-Comté, which was dangerously close to France.[57]

---

of English involvement in the war has perhaps been underestimated: Adam Marks, 'Stuart Politics, English Military Networks and Alliances with Denmark and the Palatinate', in Caldari and Wolfson (eds), *Stuart Marriage Diplomacy*, 173–86.

[52] Andreas Edel, 'Auf dem Weg in den Krieg. Zur Vorgeschichte der Intervention Herzog Maximilians I. von Bayern in Österreich und Böhmen 1620', *Zeitschrift für bayerische Landesgeschichte*, 65 (2002), 157–251.

[53] Frank Müller, *Kursachsen und der böhmische Aufstand, 1618–1622* (Münster, 1997), 148–224, 333–49.

[54] Anna Egler, *Die Spanier in der linksrheinischen Pfalz, 1620-1632. Invasion, Verwaltung, Rekatholisierung* (Mainz, 1971), 70–6.

[55] E.g.: Dutch appeal presented to James I of England, 15 February 1621, in Wilson, *Sourcebook*, 77–80.

[56] See Andreas Wendland, *Die Nutzen der Pässe und die Gefährdung der Seelen. Spanien, Mailand und der Kampf ums Veltlin 1620–1641* (Zürich, 1995), 101–37.

[57] See the map in Wilson, *Europe's Tragedy*, 158.

Oppressive tax regimes combined with religious persecution of the majority Catholic, Italian-speaking population of the Valtelline by the German-speaking Calvinist ruling council of the Three Leagues, led the Catholic subjects to plan a revolt in coordination with the Spanish governor of the neighbouring duchy of Milan. Following the outbreak of the revolt in 1620, the Catholic rebels received support from a Habsburg double-intervention of Spanish troops from the south and Austrian-led forces from the east, leading the Grey Leagues to surrender and forcing them to cede lands to Austrian Tyrol in January 1623, while the Spanish held the valley passes.[58]

The French threatened war and achieved a compromise agreement whereby Spanish forces would vacate the valley passes and be replaced with Papal troops. The historiography is largely in agreement that Spain's 1620 intervention, ostensibly to protect the persecuted Valtelline Catholics, was geopolitically motivated and aimed at gaining strategic control over potential routes to the Netherlands, where their planned resumption of war was imminent, and to Austria and Bohemia where they intended to support their dynastic allies. The narrative of confessional solidarity and the protection of brutalised subjects served as 'padding and as a fig leaf to cover political calculations'.[59]

## Danish Intervention in the Empire, 1625–1629

By 1623, the Emperor's enemies in the Habsburg lands and the Empire were defeated, but this was a 'borrowed' victory, because he had relied heavily on support by Spain and more importantly, Bavaria, who would need to be paid back with constitutional favours and lands taken from the defeated enemies.[60] Following a fast-tracked judicial procedure at the Reichshofrat, the elector-Palatine was declared to be under the Imperial ban, and was to be dispossessed, with the usual litigation procedures deemed superfluous on account of the 'notoriety' of his rebellion against the Emperor. This cleared the way for the transfer of his electoral dignity and his Upper Palatinate territory to the duke of Bavaria in 1623 without the consent of the other electors.[61] The Emperor and his allies were careful to present their military campaigns as legal executions of judicial commissions. Yet despite Vienna's best efforts at cosmetically grafting a veneer of legality onto the suppression of the rebellions—and the punishment of

---

[58] See Randolph C. Head, *Early Modern Democracy in the Grisons. Social Order and Political Language in a Swiss Mountain Canton, 1470–1620* (Cambridge, 1995), 191–8.

[59] Quotation: Duchhardt, *Kriesendekade*, 172.

[60] Thus: Kampmann, *Europa*, 47–9; Thomas Brockmann, *Dynastie, Kaiseramt und Konfession. Politik und Ordnungsvorstellungen Ferdinands II. im Dreißigjährigen Krieg* (Paderborn, 2011), 206.

[61] Deed of enfeoffment of 25 February 1623, in Wilson, *Sourcebook*, 91–2. See also Brockmann, *Ferdinand II*, 206–25. For the elector of Saxony's misgivings, see his letter to archbishop-elector of Mainz, 23 February 1623, in Helfferich (ed.), *Documentary History*, 63–6.

the rebels by dispossessing them—it was precisely the unilateral and perceived overweening way in which constitutional shifts were implemented, that created the core of new grievances in the Empire which helped the exiled rebels to rally opposition forces and ultimately resulted in more anti-Imperial interventions from outside powers.[62]

Denmark was the first foreign power to launch a large-scale intervention against the Emperor. Concerns about the overall constitutional balance in the Empire was one reason behind King Christian IV's decision to intervene in 1625. He moreover had a direct stake in the position of princely rights and the Protestant religion in Germany, and in the security and status quo of Lower Saxony, because he was an Imperial Estate and a Lower-Saxon Kreis-estate in his own right, as duke of Holstein. There were other considerations as well. Christian IV had established himself as the dominant power in northern Germany. His German chancellery in Holstein had worked hard to integrate him into the politics and patronage networks of the Lower-Saxon Kreis. He had managed to secure control of an impressive portfolio of secularised Catholic bishoprics in the Kreis (Schwerin, Bremen, Verden, Halberstadt), which were used to provide for his many sons born after his heir.[63]

The great victories of the Emperor and the Catholic League in the Bohemian and Palatine campaigns caused the almost uniformly Lutheran princes of the Lower-Saxon Kreis to fear not only for their princely liberties, but also for the future security of the Protestant-ruled north German bishoprics and of Protestantism itself. Most of the conversions to Protestantism in these bishoprics had occurred after 1552 and were therefore illegal according to the strictly Catholic reading of Augsburg. In light of the bitter disputes over the Ecclesiastical Reservation since the 1580s, the fear that the Emperor might use his newly-won military ascendancy to impose the Catholic interpretation of Augsburg and expel Protestant administrators from the Lower-Saxon bishoprics seemed realistic.[64] Some Kreis-Estates had been opposed to the king of Denmark's growing influence, but the fears arising from the Imperial-Catholic victories created a sense of cohesion around the Kreis' strongest power, which facilitated Christian's appointment as Kreis-director in 1625. Christian IV himself stood to incur heavy losses, both to his sons' positions in the bishoprics and to his political and economic dominance over Lower Saxony, if the feared expansion of Imperial and League forces into the Kreis occurred. As Lockhart has argued, the king's intervention was

---

[62] Nicolette Mout, 'Der Winterkönig im Exil. Friedrich V. von der Pfalz und die Niederländischen Generalstaaten 1621–1632', *ZHF* 15 (1988), 169–94.
[63] Paul Douglas Lockhart, *Denmark in the Thirty Years' War, 1618–1648. King Chrisitan IV and the Decline of the Oldenburg State* (Selinsgrove, 1996), 95–105.
[64] Kampmann, *Europa*, 51.

therefore a 'conservative' undertaking, designed to defend his existing position in north Germany.[65]

Before risking the intervention, Christian would need to be assured of a favourable international context; specifically, backing by England, France, and the Dutch. What made international safeguards even more pressing was the fact that the Danish state would not technically join the undertaking. Christian IV would have to intervene as duke of Holstein because Denmark's Council of the Realm, controlled by the powerful Danish aristocracy which was more worried about Denmark's traditional Swedish rival, refused to sign off on the intervention. This gave the Danish intervention a different character than the Swedish one which occurred five years later. The former could be presented as Imperial policy by an Imperial Estate and as defensive measures by the Kreis, whereas the latter was a more archetypal 'foreign' great power intervention.[66]

But in practice, the Danish undertaking would very much be an intervention by a dominant regional power and therefore the geopolitical conditions in northern and western Europe would be more important in determining Christian's course of action than any constitutional entitlement to intervene. In 1624, both English and French policy became markedly more anti-Habsburg. Under the new cardinal-premier Richelieu, France became increasingly willing to both confront the Habsburgs and to strengthen links with Protestant anti-Habsburg powers. Worried about Spanish occupation forces in the Lower-Palatinate and about Spain's successes in the Netherlands and the Valtelline, France decided to try to break the Habsburg ring that it perceived to be tightening around it. Richelieu intervened indirectly in the Empire by funding the rebel army under Erich von Mansfeld, while an army was sent into northern Italy to challenge the Spanish hold on the Valtelline valley through which Spanish supplies were passing.[67] English policy too underwent a sharp anti-Habsburg turn. After abandoning the Spanish match project at the end of 1623, James I started drastically increasing subsidy payments to Mansfeld's army and demanding a restitution of his son-in-law Frederick V. At the end of 1624, France instigated a joint note to be sent to King Christian IV indicating that France, England, and the Netherlands would support a Danish intervention in the Empire financially, and perhaps also with a diversionary attack from the West. More important in Christian's assessment of the viability of an intervention was the achievement of an accommodation with his rival Sweden, about whom he was most concerned.[68]

---

[65] Paul Douglas Lockhart, 'Denmark and the Empire. A reassessment of Danish foreign policy under King Christian IV', *Scandinavian Studies* 64 (1992), 390–416, at 401–7.
[66] Thus: Schilling, *Konfessionalisierung*, 335.
[67] Sven Externbrink, *Le Coeur du monde. Frankreich und die norditalienischen Staaten im Zeitalter Richelieus 1624–1635* (Münster, 1999), 59–68.
[68] Lockhart, *Denmark*, 106–30.

After initial military setbacks Christian IV was emboldened to continue fighting once England, France, and the Dutch republic signed the treaty of the Hague in November 1625 in which they announced greater financial support for Danish operations in Germany. The signatories intended 'to intervene at the right time to prevent the all too violent and unbearable progress of these bad intentions [the threat to the Imperial constitution] and oppressions, to restore and conserve [German] freedom, the...constitutions of the Empire against the foreseeable ruin'.[69]

Christian IV offered his own justification for intervening, invoking mainly Imperial law but also divine and natural law, in a letter sent to various Catholic electors in February 1626.[70] In it he attempted to appeal to cross-confessional norms related to the protection of German liberties and the constitution, and portrayed his intervention as being aimed 'solely towards the defence of the Kreis'.[71] As Kreis-director, the king felt obliged to respond to 'the princes...of this Kreis [who] sought some help and rescue'.[72] To do so more effectively, he took up the offer of 'assistance that had long been offered to us by our relatives and neighbouring potentates and sovereigns...who are extremely interested in the conservation of the traditional constitution of the Roman Empire' and signed the treaty of the Hague with them, 'which was established for the maintenance of the German Liberties'.[73] The additional intervention of these European powers underlined 'the extent to which it concerns all of Christendom that the standing of the Holy Roman Empire...be restored to its former state'. By implication, interventions for the protection of the Imperial constitution were legitimate and just. He denied that the undertaking was designed to 'oppress you or the adherents of your religion'. Instead, Christian IV intervened:

> to save this Kreis, which...had been attacked contrary to the Imperial constitution and the [Emperor's] sworn capitulations, and to save German Liberty which is everywhere suffering...so that...liberty and the Religious and Secular Peace [of 1555] might not be lost, but conserved through those means allowed by God and nature.[74]

Although the Danish intervention was less welcome among many of the north German Protestant princes (rightly fearing that it could provoke the deposition of Protestant bishopric-administrators) than among Christian' co-signatories of the Hague alliance, the latter's substantive help failed to materialise. France was forced to deal with another Huguenot rebellion in 1625–28.[75] The Dutch lost Breda to the

---

[69] Treaty of the Hague, 29 November 1625, in Wilson, *Sourcebook*, 92–4, quoted at 92.
[70] Printed in Helfferich, *Documentary history*, 78–82.   [71] Ibid., 78–9.
[72] Ibid., 79.   [73] Ibid., 78, 81.   [74] Ibid., 81.
[75] David Parrott, *Richelieu's Army. War, Government and Society in France, 1624–1642* (Cambridge, 2001), 84–91.

Spanish in June 1625 and had to focus on fighting the Habsburgs in their own country, while the death of James I in March 1625 prevented English assistance. Count Tilly's League forces and Albrecht von Wallenstein's new Imperial army scored major victories against the Danes, driving them completely out of Germany and even invading the Danish heartland of Jutland in 1627. By 1629 Denmark had accepted defeat despite French exhortations to continue fighting and promised not to intervene again, in return for relatively generous terms at the Peace of Lübeck in May 1629.[76] The Emperor was at the height of his power, which now extended across Germany including into the far north.

Judged by the aims of Christian IV, the intervention was a disaster. It resulted in the opposite of what the king intended. Instead of securing his sons' hold on the north German prince-bishoprics, they were forced to relinquish them at the peace of Lübeck. Instead of maintaining Danish political ascendancy over the Lower-Saxon Kreis, it was now replaced by that of the Emperor who became the dominant power in this region. Important Danish client princes, such as the dukes of Mecklenburg, were deposed by the Emperor for allying with Christian IV, and the Imperial general Wallenstein was installed as duke in their place.[77] This was indicative of a sharp shift in the constitutional balance away from the princes and towards the Emperor. Instead of furthering Christian's general aim of defending princely liberties, his failed intervention had therefore accelerated a trend that many perceived as growing Imperial absolutism. Christian IV's other general aim of defending the constitutional position of Protestantism in the Empire also utterly failed, because the Emperor's new position of military-political power emboldened him to impose a strictly Catholic interpretation of the Augsburg religious peace with the Edict of Restitution in March 1629. In the longer term it caused a decline in the geopolitical standing of Denmark relative to Sweden and a decline in absolute terms. The failed intervention set the scene for Sweden's subsequent, ultimately successful, intervention thus allowing it to overtake its Danish rival and replace a Catholic-Imperial ascendancy in north Germany with a Swedish one.

This Restitution Edict, with which the Emperor overreached himself in the hubris of victory, ordered the restitution of all Catholic church territories and properties that had been secularised since 1552. Reformed-Calvinists remained excluded from the Religious Peace.[78] The measure is often portrayed as driven by religious bigotry and as the result of an extreme Catholic position. However, research has shown that it was not the policy that the more anti-Protestant group of advisors in Vienna had wished, and it certainly was not aimed at

---

[76] Lockhart, *Denmark*, 204. The treaty printed in Wilson, *Sourcebook*, 97–9.
[77] Kampmann, *Reichsrebellion*, 90–8; Brockmann, *Ferdinand II*, 293–302.
[78] Marc R. Forster, 'The Edict of Restitution (1629) and the failure of Catholic Restoration', in Asbach, *Ashgate Research Companion*, 205–16. The edict printed in Wilson, *Sourcebook*, 114–17.

extirpating Protestantism.[79] Nevertheless it was a major blow to the Protestants' position in the Empire—many secularisations had taken place since 1552—and it was also unpopular among some Catholic princes. This was because, like the transfer of the Palatine electoral dignity and territory, it was carried out unilaterally and by Imperial decree without the consultation or consent of the princes. Most princes viewed this as a worrying sign that the Emperor was taking advantage of his unprecedented power and military ascendancy to disregard *deutsche Freiheit*. The Edict, and the deposition of the dukes of Mecklenburg before it, alienated those important Protestant princes that had hitherto remained loyal to the Emperor, especially the electors of Saxony and Brandenburg. Even the Catholic League was suspicious of Wallenstein and his alarming accretion of power.[80] The reaction at the electors' diet at Regensburg in 1630 was indicative of the mood in the Empire: they forced the Emperor to dismiss Wallenstein and refused to have his son elected as successor.[81]

The basic problem of the paradox of Imperial strength facing the Emperor at the end of the 1620s was the same as it had been at the beginning of the decade. Despite appearing powerful, the Emperor's lack of sufficient strength to deal with his enemies alone compelled him to instead rely on military contractors such as Wallenstein who had to be rewarded and paid off, just like his princely allies in 1623.[82] He was therefore forced to redistribute lands to his supporters in a way that was seen as a threat to the existing constitutional order, creating new grievances. Thus, pursuing the only means of achieving victory that were available to the Emperor caused renewed rounds of anti-Imperial interventions by foreign powers who saw their security interests being served by restoring the constitutional balance and protecting the rights of the rebels and exiles.[83]

## Swedish Intervention in the Empire from 1630

The second major international intervention against the Emperor was carried out by the Swedish king Gustavus Adolphus (r.1611-1632) to defend Sweden's interests and security around the Baltic. France supported the intervention indirectly. Its leadership believed that this would improve its position in the expected showdown with the Spanish Habsburgs. Over the course of 1629 the two main obstacles in the way of Swedish intervention—the continued intervention of

---

[79] Brockmann, *Ferdinand II*, 359–80.
[80] Michael Kaiser, *Politik und Kriegführung. Maximilian von Bayern, Tilly und die Katholische Liga im Dreißigjährigen Krieg* (Münster, 1999), 268–74.
[81] Brockmann, *Ferdinand II*, 390–405, 427–36; Kaiser, *Maximilian*, 279–302.
[82] For private military enterprise during the war, see David Parrott, *The Business of War. Military Enterprise and Military Revolution in Early Modern Europe* (Cambridge, 2012), 101–35.
[83] See also Wilson, 'Causes of the Thirty Years War', 584.

Sweden's rival Denmark and Sweden's ongoing war against Poland—were removed at the Peace of Lübeck in July and the French-mediated truce of Altmark in September, respectively. France's increasingly supportive stance towards Swedish intervention was also an important facilitator.[84]

The propagandistic justification and legitimation did not differ very much from the motivations for interventions as expressed by the Swedish leadership privately, although certain points were omitted publicly. The Swedes tweaked their public legitimations slightly depending on which audience was being addressed. Their most important justification, the *Manifesto* of July 1630, was probably written with just war theories in mind. It referred to the law of nations and nature. There is evidence that Gustavus Adolphus read the works of Hugo Grotius, and therefore must have been aware of his ideas about the permissibility of intervention for the protection of other rulers' subjects.[85] While it is true that it is not completely certain what King Gustavus Adolphus' immediate objectives were, as he did not present demands to the Emperor initially, historians have researched the aims and drivers of the intervention on the basis of the internal discussions between the king and his advisors.[86] Unsurprisingly, Sweden's aims and motives evolved over the course of their 18-year intervention in the Empire.[87] Two related aims which became crucial as the war went on, but were also present from the beginning to a lesser extent,[88] were those of territorial and financial satisfaction: 'compensation' for Sweden's efforts to restore German liberties and to pay off its army. Naturally, these received no mention in the public justification, which flatly claimed that the king had intervened 'not to extend his limits, and enlarge his bounds, but to deliver his relations and friends from oppression'.[89]

The most important reason for the intervention, and the biggest theme in the public justification, was security—primarily Sweden's but also the security of the region and even of Europe as a whole. The protection of German Liberties, of the confessional rights and constitutional liberties of the Emperor's subjects, and of the traditional constitutional balance within the Empire were considered by Sweden as a corollary of Swedish and European security. While the presence of Imperial armies along the Baltic were a direct military threat to Sweden, the perceived emergence of a more centralised military monarchy in the Empire

---

[84] Kampmann, *Europa*, 71–3.

[85] Pärtel Piirimäe, 'Just war in theory and practice: the legitimation of Swedish intervention in the Thirty Years War', *HJ* 45 (2002), 499–523.

[86] For analyses of Sweden's motivations: Erik Ringmar, *Identity, Interest and Action. A Cultural Explanation of Sweden's Intervention in the Thirty Years War* (Cambridge, 1996); Michael Roberts, *Gustavus Adolphus* (London, 1992), 59–72; Sigmund Goetze, *Die Politik des schwedischen Reichskanzlers Axel Oxenstierna gegenüber Kaiser und Reich* (Kiel, 1971), 58–90; Wilson, *Tragedy*, 461–4.

[87] For later Swedish war aims: Sven Lundkvist, 'Die schwedischen Kriegs- und Friedensziele, 1632–1648', in Konrad Repgen (ed.), *Krieg und Politik, 1618–1648* (Munich, 1988), 219–40.

[88] Debates printed in Wilson, *Sourcebook*, 130–1.

[89] Swedish Manifesto, in Wilson, *Sourcebook*, 122–30, at 122.

was deemed to also pose a more general risk to Swedish security and to the European balance. The Swedish king considered these developments to be part of a broader pan-European Catholic Papal-Habsburg plot to erect a despotic hegemony. In April 1628, he wrote to his chancellor:

> All wars which are being fought in Europe are interwoven with each other and form a unity. That can be seen by the actions of the Papacy in Germany, by the Spanish help that was given to La Rochelle... and by... the court of the Emperor, where there is said to be a firm determination to occupy the northern countries and to thereby advance the aspired-to tyranny over people and souls.[90]

The steady northward advance of Imperial and Catholic League troops worried the Swedes and once they reached the Baltic coast and conquered most of Danish mainland in 1627, alarm bells were ringing in Stockholm. The king addressed the estates in November 1627: 'As one wave follows another, so the popish league comes closer and closer to us. They have violently subjugated a great part of Denmark, whence we must apprehend that they may press on into our borders, if they be not powerfully resisted in good time.'[91] He was therefore arguing that a defensive pre-emptive strike was needed, not only against the Emperor's military threat to Sweden but also against the danger that his growing power posed to German Freedoms. In January 1628, the king addressed the Diet, arguing that 'the Emperor and the papist Liga have conquered or oppressed princes and towns one after another', and that to pre-empt Sweden similarly falling victim to Imperial armies, as Denmark had, 'it is both right and good to carry the war and its burdens to the country of the Emperor and the papists'.[92] In 1628 Sweden first became directly involved in the conflict by providing some limited assistance to the Pomeranian town of Stralsund which effectively resisted Wallenstein's siege and officially requested Swedish protection.[93]

The deposition of the dukes of Mecklenburg and the enfeoffment of the Imperial general Wallenstein with that duchy which was located just across the Baltic sea from Sweden, and his appointment as 'admiral of the oceanic and Baltic seas' portended the Emperor's intention to maintain direct military and naval power in the Baltic, where a Spanish-financed naval programme was initiated at the port of Wismar.[94] The Swedes viewed this as a threat to their ambitions to dominate that sea.[95] It also exemplified the seeming decline of German princely liberties. Gustavus Adolphus believed he needed to secure the German Baltic coastline to maintain Sweden's security against potential future Imperial incursions.[96]

---

[90] Quoted in Kampmann, *Europa*, 199 n. 20.
[91] Quoted in Roberts, *Gustavus Adolphus*, 59–60.   [92] Quoted in Piirimäe, 'Just war', 512.
[93] Wilson, *Tragedy*, 423–4.   [94] Ibid., 426–8.   [95] Kampmann, *Europa*, 11–15.
[96] Roberts, *Gustavus Adolphus*, 60–9; Wilson, *Tragedy*, 462.

During private discussions with the state-council in May 1630, the king reiterated that 'our basic war aim is security... if our security is to be assured it must be under our own control and not in the discretion of the enemy'. Later that month, the king wrote to his chancellor Axel Oxenstierna that security was 'the most important point of all', and that Sweden must ensure that the Emperor's armies are 'entirely withdrawn from the Saxon Kreise, and everything (especially the coastlands) restored to a secure and peaceable condition'.[97] After landing with 13,600 troops in Pomerania, Gustavus Adolphus again wrote to the chancellor, mentioning that the intervention had been imperative 'for the security of the fatherland from the designs of our enemies'. Failing to intervene 'would cause us, instead of security, greater danger and a great loss of reputation; and finally, would give our enemies the opportunity—once they have subjugated all of Germany... to attempt to do the same to us'.[98] Oxenstierna expressed the same sentiment, claiming that 'if the Emperor had once got hold of Stralsund, the whole coast would have fallen to him, and here in Sweden we should never have enjoyed a moment's security'.[99]

Similar arguments were made in the public justification. The king's famous *Manifesto*, written under his supervision by his councillor Johan Adler Salvius was quickly translated and published in numerous languages.[100] Throughout the text, the king of Sweden is credited with pursuing the norm of seeking peace, while the Imperials are accused of 'hating the common peace'. In general, the king did not intend 'to meddle in another's affairs', yet the relentless drive of the Imperial-Catholic armies towards northern Germany made an intervention unavoidable.[101] Austria's unprovoked aggression against the Saxon Kreis-estates was related.[102] Further points made to strengthen this portrayal of the intervention as defensive included the Emperor's armed assistance to Sweden's Polish enemy in 1627, and the Emperor's alleged obstruction of a Polish-Swedish peace.[103] This, along with other acts 'contrary to the law of nations', and the refusal to admit Swedish diplomats to the Lübeck peace conference, led the Swedes to conclude: 'are not we instructed by the law of nature to repel force by force?'[104] Also in line with the just war theory was the *Manifesto*'s claim that the king had decided upon armed intervention only as a measure of last resort, on the basis of 'the right of self-defence'.[105]

---

[97] Quoted in Wilson, *Sourcebook*, 130-1.
[98] Gustavus Adolphus to Axel Oxenstierna, Ribnitz, 8 October 1630, Helfferich (ed.), *Documentary History*, 103-7, at 103-4.
[99] Quoted in Ringmar, *Sweden's intervention*, 112.
[100] Heinz Schilling, 'Das schwedische Kriegsmanifest vom Juli 1630 und die Frage nach dem Charakter des Dreißigjährigen Krieges', in Rüdiger Hohls et al. (eds), *Europa und die Europäer. Quellen und Essays zur modernen europäischen Geschichte* (Stuttgart, 2005), 370-7.
[101] Quoted in Helfferich (ed.), *Documentary History*, 100-1.
[102] Swedish Manifesto, Wilson, *Sourcebook*, 122-30, at 124.   [103] Ibid., 123.
[104] Ibid., 129.   [105] Helfferich, *Documentary History*, 102.

The argument that Swedish security depended on German princely liberties and a constitutional balance between the Emperor and the Imperial Estates was made in both the public justifications and in the private deliberations, although it was less pronounced in the former. Protestant rights as a component of German Liberties also received less emphasis in the public legitimation, to avoid alienating the French, upon whose financial support the intervention would depend.[106] The *Manifesto* claimed that the king 'has only taken up arms for the public good, for his own safety, and the preservation of his friends [the Imperial Estates and other subjects] whom he desires to put in the same state and liberty which they were before this war and by the same means to secure...his own kingdom of Sweden'.[107] In other words, Swedish security depended on that of the region, the 'common security',[108] which was threatened by the Habsburgs.

The Habsburgs posed a threat not only to the Empire's constitutional balance but to Europe's balance as a whole: 'the Spaniards and the House of Austria have been always intent upon a Universal Monarchy'. Gustavus Adolphus' intervention, then, served to stem the threatened subjugation of Germany and by implication avert a Habsburg universal monarchy. In the 1640s chancellor Oxenstierna recalled that one of the goals of the intervention had been 'to restore German liberty...and in this manner to conserve the equilibrium in all of Europe',[109] while an official Swedish pronouncement declared that the interests of both Denmark and Sweden depended on 'Germany's wellbeing and freedom'.[110] This link between Swedish security, the European balance and German Liberties is stressed to an even greater degree in the confidential correspondence, with an added emphasis on Protestantism as one aspect of German Freedom. In 1630, the king wrote that

> Austria fully intends to overthrow all of Germany and bring it to another state. And then...the Evangelical Religion will be uprooted...what a danger this is for us...We cannot enter into any reconciliation with our enemies unless a new religious peace can be reached and confirmed for all of Germany, and our neighbours and friends are returned to their previous state and condition, *so that we, through their safety, may be secure and safe in our fatherland.*[111]

Similarly, in a letter to the elector of Saxony in August 1630, the king asserted that 'Our purpose is...the safeguarding of our kingdom, and the re-establishment of

---

[106] Goetze, *Politik*, 64.   [107] Wilson, *Sourcebook*, 130.
[108] Helfferich, *Documentary History*, 102.
[109] Quoted in Derek Croxton, 'The Peace of Westphalia of 1648 and the origins of sovereignty,' *IHR* 21 (1999), 569–91, at 590.
[110] Tischer, *Kriegsbegründungen*, 144 fn. 46.
[111] Gustavus Adolphus to Axel Oxenstierna, Ribnitz, 8 October 1630: Helfferich, *Documentary History*, 103–7, at 104 (emphasis added).

the oppressed liberty of Germany'.[112] The emphasis on Protestantism in the private correspondence does not, however, imply that the intervention was conceived as a religious war by the Swedish leadership. Instead, the protection of Protestant rights formed one aspect of a catalogue of legal-political rights which needed to be protected against encroachments by Imperial tyranny. In 1637 chancellor Oxenstierna explained that Gustavus Adolphus had intervened to ensure 'that the kingdom of Sweden and our co-religionists may remain in security and be in their possessions preserved, both ecclesiastical and political. It is therefore in this case not so much a matter of religion, but rather of public condition, wherein also religion is comprehended'.[113]

This desire to protect the Emperor's (immediate) subjects was also underlined in the public reasoning, but here the reasoning that this provision of protection mainly served Swedish security aims, was downplayed. Instead, the intervention was portrayed as motivated by an altruistic desire to protect the Imperial Estates and towns of north Germany (who happened to be Protestant) from renegades such as Wallenstein and from tyranny and oppression, because the Emperor was failing in his responsibility of protection. The *Manifesto* argues that this duty to protect subjects is passed on to neighbouring princes if the ruling prince fails in his responsibility, an argumentation that is reminiscent of the theories of Bodin, Gentili, and Grotius. The king of Sweden was thus argued to have intervened

> to preserve his friends...before they were entirely reduced...by the tyranny of ambitious...counsellors and generals of the [Habsburgs];...which is truly an effect of the charity and *protection which a prudent and generous prince naturally owes to his own subjects and to his nearest neighbours*, who are ready to fall under the oppression of their enemies.[114]

The *Manifesto* pointed out that the king's intervention was made more compelling 'by the bonds of proximity, common religion, liberty and commerce',[115] and the fact that his intervention had been requested. The king of Sweden only intervened in defence of the town of Stralsund in 1628, after the townspeople realised 'they could not be delivered by the decrees of the Emperor, and perceiving that the duke of Pomerania, their prince, was not able to assist them'.[116] These were points which hardly appeared as motives in the

---

[112] Quoted in Piirimäe, 'Just war', 520. See also documents printed in Gustav Droysen (ed.), *Schriftstücke von Gustav Adolf zumeist an evangelische Fürsten Deutschlands* (Stockholm, 1877).

[113] Quoted in Michael Roberts, *Gustavus Adolphus. A History of Sweden 1611–1632* (London, 1953–58) ii, 419.

[114] Peter H. Wilson (ed.), *The Thirty Years War. A Sourcebook* (Basingstoke, 2010), 122 (emphasis added).

[115] Helfferich, *Documentary History*, 102.    [116] Wilson, *Sourcebook*, 124–5.

confidential correspondence, except as reasons that needed to be presented in the propaganda. Indeed the council of state concluded that without such an invitation, the intervention could hardly be justified, which explains the urgent instructions that were sent to Swedish envoys across northern Germany to procure such invitations from towns and princes.[117] When the king invaded Pomerania in July 1630, having 'come to the assistance of the oppressed, who had so urgently requested help',[118] it was in fact only the town of Stralsund—which was not an Imperial Estate but a Pomeranian territorial town—that had requested Swedish intervention, contrary to the 'several princes and states of the Empire' which the *Manifesto* claims invited him.[119]

Indeed, the reaction in the Empire to the Swedish intervention, even among Protestant princes, was far from enthusiastic. The electors assembled in Regensburg in 1630 rejected the Swedish reasoning for intervention and argued that by supporting the rebels, Sweden was in fact prolonging the war, instead of pursuing peace. The intervention was therefore criticised as 'an unjustified and hostile attack' against the Empire. Appealing to the rival norm of non-interference in other states' domestic affairs, the electors argued that the king of Sweden 'should interfere in the affairs of the Empire...just as little as he would like to see the other foreign princes constraining his regalities and commanding what he should do or forbear from doing'.[120] Astutely recognising that the 'foreign potentates will also interfere in the affair [the crisis in the Empire] and bring misery, ruin and destruction to each Estate regardless of religion', the Protestant electors of Saxony and Brandenburg attempted to set up a group of neutral princes at the Convention of Leipzig in March 1631. This sought to avoid both Imperial and Swedish military domination and instead buttress the Imperial laws which 'do not oppress German Freedom'.[121]

Most of the Protestant princes whose territories were approached or billeted by Swedish armies faced a bleak choice: ally with Sweden or face a violent, exploitative occupation.[122] Hardly any princes joined the Swedes voluntarily; rebel princes who had anyway lost most of their lands to the Emperor, such as the landgrave of Hessen-Kassel and the exiled elector-Palatine were exceptions. Yet gradually most major Protestant princes were bullied into allying with Sweden. Its military campaign was astonishingly successful, to the point of even worrying the French. Richelieu later recalled the rationale for the 1630 intervention in a letter to King Louis XIII: 'the King of Sweden embarked on his enterprise to prevent the oppression of the princes of the Empire in Germany'.[123] To support the intervention, France signed a subsidy treaty with Sweden at

---

[117] Thus: Piirimäe, 'Just war', 516.
[118] Helfferich, *Documentary History*, 102.
[119] Roberts, *Gustavus Adolphus* ii, 432.
[120] Quoted in Piirimäe, 'Just war', 507, 518.
[121] Quoted in Wilson, *Sourcebook*, 119.
[122] Wilson, *Tragedy*, 465–7.
[123] Quoted in Wilson, *Sourcebook*, 214.

Bärwalde in 1631.[124] In return for French money, the Swedes promised they would respect the exercise of the Catholic religion in areas they conquered and refrain from attacking Bavaria and members of the Catholic League. Sweden largely ignored this last commitment; within less than two years, Gustavus Adolphus had conquered most of Germany as far south as Bavaria.[125] The big Swedish victory at Breitenfeld in 1631 persuaded many princes that Sweden was a viable ally, and the massacre in the Protestant town of Magdeburg by Tilly's army in the same year also drove many Protestant princes including Saxony into the arms of the Swedes. Although Gustavus Adolphus was killed at the battle of Lützen in 1632, this did not cause the Swedish position in Germany to collapse completely. However, by 1634, the Emperor, with support from Bavaria and Spain, had recovered and achieved a major victory at Nördlingen against the Swedes and their Protestant German allies.

Before Sweden's intervention in mid-1630, the war had effectively come to a halt after the Emperor's victory in 1629. Gustavus Adolphus' French-sponsored intervention reignited it and prolonged the war for another 18 years. Was the intervention successful? It led to the death of the king of Sweden himself and bled Sweden dry, but by 1648 it had certainly fulfilled the Swedish goals of shutting the Habsburgs out of the Baltic, maintaining and strengthening a Swedish *Dominum Maris Baltici*, and upholding princely German Liberties, while also achieving a more secure footing for Protestantism in the Imperial constitution. Other aims which became more important over the course of the intervention—territorial compensation in north Germany and financial satisfaction for the Swedish army—were also largely achieved at the congress of Westphalia. Sweden furthermore eclipsed its Baltic rival Denmark and secured the rank of a European great power thanks to its campaigns in the war and its subsequent guarantee of the Peace of Westphalia. Yet the price for improved geopolitical security and constitutional adjustments was almost two more decades of abject destruction, mass death, hunger and disease throughout central Europe, not least in the Baltic German lands whose welfare the Swedes claimed to care about. This is not to say that central Europe would have stayed at peace had the Swedish intervention not occurred—the Franco-Spanish conflict would likely have erupted sooner or later and it is quite possible that it would have spread to the Empire again. Nonetheless from the perspective of most central Europeans—propagandistic Protestant panegyrics lauding Gustavus Adolphus as a Protestant saviour notwithstanding[126]—the Swedish intervention was a catastrophic event.

---

[124] Printed in ibid., 140–2. [125] Kaiser, *Maximilian*, 462–510.
[126] See Diethelm Böttcher, 'Propaganda und öffentliche Meinung im protestantischen Deutschland, 1628–1636', in Hans-Ulrich Rudolf (ed.), *Der Dreißigjährige Krieg* (Darmstadt, 1977), 325–67.

## French Intervention in the Empire during the Thirty Years War (and Continued Swedish Intervention)

In 1635 France shifted from a policy of what one historian has termed 'concealed war' to that of open war against Spain.[127] As a corollary of this, it also intervened in the conflict in the Empire to a greater extent, where the Spanish were active anyway and where Franco-Spanish interests clashed. King Louis XIII and his chief-minister Richelieu were careful to present their war as directed only against the Spanish Habsburgs, not the German branch.[128] Yet this amounted to an intervention in the Empire, because it was triggered and justified by events in Germany, and because the first line of attack was in alliance with the Dutch towards the Spanish Netherlands in the Burgundian Kreis, and in alliance with Savoy, Mantua, and Parma against Spanish Milan in Imperial Italy. Both rhetorically and operationally, France directed its main efforts against the Spanish rather than the German Habsburgs, and the Imperial army concentrated mainly on Sweden after the campaign of 1636.[129]

Richelieu essentially pursued a revisionist grand strategy in European geopolitics.[130] In the 1630s Spain was still viewed as the leading European power. Richelieu wished to see France replace it by elevating its king to the status of 'the greatest monarch of the world and the most esteemed prince'.[131] This would ensure he could become 'arbiter of Christendom'—mediating and arbitrating in conflicts between and within other states to thereby maintain French security and ascendancy.[132] He believed that this would necessitate war against Spain sooner or later, and the key to French success would lie in anti-Habsburg alliances. Firstly, avoiding a situation whereby France would have to face Spain alone; and secondly, intervening in support of anti-Habsburg princes and subjects, were the guiding principles of Richelieu's foreign policy and underpinned France's indirect and direct interventions during the war. Yet beyond these hegemonic goals, Richelieu believed that a post-war order of peace, presided over by France, could ultimately be maintained and secured with a system of collective security based on two 'leagues' for Germany and Italy, the two cockpits of Europe. This would entail

---

[127] Hermann Weber, 'Vom verdeckten zum offenen Krieg. Richelieus Kriegsgründe und Kriegsziele 1634/1635', in Repgen (ed.), *Krieg und Politik*, 203–17.

[128] Anja-Victorine Hartmann, *Von Regensburg nach Hamburg. Die diplomatischen Beziehungen zwischen dem französischen König und dem Kaiser 1630–1641* (Münster, 1998), 206–12, 249–62.

[129] Lothar Höbelt, *Von Nördlingen bis Jankau. Kaiserliche Strategie und Kriegführung 1634–1645* (Vienna, 2016).

[130] Klaus Malettke, *Richelieu. Ein Leben im Dienste des Königs und Frankreichs* (Paderborn, 2018).

[131] 'Avis donné au Roy après la prise de la Rochelle', 13 Jan. 1629, printed in Pierre Grillon (ed.), *Les Papiers de Richelieu. Section politique intérieure. Correspondance et papiers d'état IV (1629)* (Paris, 1980), 24–47.

[132] Kampmann, *Arbiter*, 140–83.

mutual and reciprocal guarantees and control mechanisms, and therefore a voluntary limitation on foreign political freedom and sovereignty.[133]

In Richelieu's mind, supplanting the Habsburgs as leading power did not entail large-scale French territorial expansion towards any imagined 'natural frontiers'.[134] Instead, France should confront the continued basic geopolitical threat of Habsburg encirclement by maintaining alliances with anti-Habsburg Protestant powers such as the Dutch republic and Sweden, and by pursuing a policy of protection. Especially in Germany and Italy, the political autonomy, rights, and liberties of the Imperial Estates and the smaller princes should be protected against Habsburg tyranny and guaranteed by the king of France to forestall the emergence of a more centralised, absolutist Habsburg regime there, which would ultimately threaten French security and survival. Defending the liberties and rights of Habsburg feudal subjects therefore advanced a French geopolitical and security self-interest. To be able to better prop up the rights of the smaller princes and the decentralised Imperial constitution, France needed to gain access to a number of strategic 'portals' which could serve as entry points for self-interested, yet protective, interventions into the Reich (including Imperial Italy). In addition to serving as bridgeheads for intervention, these could also serve to cut the Spanish Road. In 1629, Richelieu advised:

> we need to always be mindful of arresting the progress of Spain. Instead of that nation's goal of increasing its domination and extending its boundaries, France must only think of fortifying itself, erecting and opening gateways into its neighbouring states, and being able to protect them from the oppressions of Spain....[135]

This policy direction was backed up by numerous propagandistic pamphlets in the public sphere which lauded the French king's protection policies, such as one from 1625, which stated that it was 'the courage of our excellent monarch which disposes him to great things and supports his glorious design of protecting the afflicted...'.[136] Another pamphlet from 1629 argued that French protection of Imperial Estates was a useful counter against Habsburg tyranny in the Empire, which corresponded to a long-standing French foreign policy tradition towards Germany from the time of Francis I: 'it has always been the glory and grandeur of the French crown that instead of conquering neighbouring lands, she has considered it glorious to avenge injustice and violence that has been inflicted upon her

---

[133] See Fritz Dickmann, 'Rechtsgedanke und Machtpolitik bei Richelieu', in Dickmann, *Friedensrecht und Friedenssicherung* (Göttingen, 1971), 36–78.
[134] Refuting the older interpretation of natural frontiers: Hermann Weber, 'Richelieu et le Rhin', *Revue Historique* 239 (1968), 265–80.
[135] Grillon (ed.), 'Avis donné au Roy', 24–47, at 25–7.
[136] Quoted in Kampmann, *Arbiter*, 151 n. 115.

friends...and to maintain trust and friendship not only among countrymen but also among foreign peoples and kings'.[137] A pamphlet from 1631 stressed that as arbiter of Christendom, the French king advanced the common good across Europe by ensuring 'the reign of justice and the sincere protection of the oppressed'.[138]

Richelieu pursued a dual strategy of weakening the Habsburgs, which was focussed on central Europe where he most feared the consequences of their domination: protection treaties with Imperial Estates and proxy-wars against the Habsburgs. For much of the 1620s, Louis XIII had to focus on internal consolidation, but protection arrangements were already in place in the Alsace, while French support of Denmark's intervention was an example of the anti-Habsburg proxy-war strategy.[139] At the end of the 1620s, Richelieu sent an army to northern Italy to directly challenge both the Spanish and the German Habsburgs for control of Mantua—one of his projected portals—during a succession crisis.[140] The two strategies sometimes clashed. Having supported and funded Sweden's intervention, Richelieu watched with concern how Gustavus Adolphus conquered most of Germany in 1630–32. Richelieu certainly wanted to see Habsburg power reduced in the Empire through the Swedish proxy war but did not wish to enable its complete replacement with Protestant Swedish military hegemony. Moreover, the Catholic Imperial Estates, who had most to fear from the Swedish advance and who were in theory the ideal candidates for French protection arrangements, themselves appealed to Louis XIII for protection against France's own Swedish proxy in December 1631.

With this dilemma, France's indirect intervention seemed to have backfired.[141] To accept the Catholic electors' request for protection would certainly empower Louis XIII in relation to the Emperor but would also necessitate a direct intervention in the Empire to defend his protectees from either the Habsburgs or Sweden. To decline the request would entail a loss of reputation and appear as a resignation of the king's purported role as the protector of German Liberties.[142] Richelieu and Louis XIII decided that a direct intervention was premature and opted instead for a limited set of protection treaties and arrangements with several Estates who occupied key strategic points which they wanted to secure. Thus, in the face of Swedish threat, the duke of Lorraine reluctantly signed a treaty of protection with France in January 1632.[143] In April 1632, France was able to

---

[137] Ibid., 168 n. 196.     [138] Ibid., 153 n. 125.
[139] Roland Mousnier, 'Les crises intérieures françaises de 1610 à 1659 et leur influence sur la politique extérieure française, surtout de 1618 à 1648', in Repgen (ed.), Krieg und Politik, 169–83.
[140] David Parrott, 'The Mantuan succession, 1627–1631: a sovereignty dispute in early modern Europe', EHR 112 (1997), 20–65.
[141] Malettke, Richelieu, 602–76.     [142] Kampmann, Europa, 81–4.
[143] Rainer Babel, Zwischen Habsburg und Bourbon. Außenpolitik und europäische Stellung Herzog Karls IV. von Lothringen (1624–1634) (Sigmaringen, 1989), 141–5.

extract the archbishop-elector of Trier, Philipp Christoph von Sötern,[144] from the pro-Habsburg camp. According to the treaty, France pledged protection, and in return the French were allowed to garrison several key fortresses along the Rhine; Richelieu's strategic portals for further potential intervention.[145]

Developments in the West of the Empire in 1633 and 1634 heightened the risk of the outbreak of a full Franco-Spanish war in the form of a French intervention in the Empire.[146] French 'protection' of the duchy of Lorraine morphed into military conquest and occupation in 1633. The scene was set for a confrontation along the Rhine, especially as France's incursions into Trier and de facto annexation of the Alsace under the guise of protection arrangements with the Estates there, directly threatened the Spanish Road.[147] More ominously, these French bridgeheads were piercing into the Empire and into traditional Habsburg spheres of influence at a time when an army accompanying the new Spanish governor of the Southern Netherlands, the Cardinal-Infante Ferdinand, was moving along the Spanish Road towards Brussels. Both France and Spain were afraid of isolation in the expected war and both sought security through new alliances or strengthened existing ones.[148] Thus, the Austrians and the Spanish signed a new treaty in 1634,[149] while the French signed treaties with the Dutchin 1634 and 1635.[150]

France became alarmed when Spanish-Imperial forces dealt a devastating blow to the Swedes by crushing them at Nördlingen in September 1634.[151] The weakening of Sweden and the greatly increased risk of the total collapse of its position in Germany enhanced its willingness and that of its German collaborators and allies to enter into protection and alliance relationships with France, thereby improving France's preconditions for a direct intervention.[152] More fundamentally, French intervention in the Empire now became more crucial because Richelieu could not stand by while the strengthened Habsburgs completely defeated the Dutch and the Swedes in the Empire—to do so would mean resigning to Richelieu's nightmare scenario of having to face Spain without allies. The Spanish arrest of Louis XIII's protectee the elector of Trier on 26 March 1635 then triggered the intervention, while the subsequent internal peace settlement at Prague between the Emperor and Saxony, and numerous other princes, ensured a

---

[144] Karl Knipschaar, *Kurfürst Philipp Christoph von Trier und seine Beziehungen zu Frankreich* (Marburg, 1895).

[145] Hermann Weber, *Frankreich, Kurtrier, der Rhein und das Reich 1623-1635* (Bonn, 1969), 127–42, 173–96.

[146] Malettke, *Richelieu*, 715–69.

[147] Wolfgang Stein, *Protection Royale. Eine Untersuchung zu den Protektionsverhältnissen im Elsaß zur Zeit Richelieus* (1622–1643) (Münster, 1978), 101–33, 235–353.

[148] Robert A. Stradling, 'Olivares and the origins of the Franco-Spanish war', *EHR* 101 (1986), 68–94.

[149] Hildegard Ernst, *Madrid und Wien 1632–1637. Politik und Finanzen in den Beziehungen zwischen Philipp IV. und Ferdinand II* (Münster, 1991), 79–107.

[150] Wilson, *Tragedy*, 554–7. [151] Malettke, *Richelieu*, 769–818.

[152] Thus: Kampmann, *Europa*, 103.

continuation of Franco-Swedish intervention in the Empire. This was because they believed the Prague peace cemented the constitutional imbalance and centralising tendencies which threatened Franco-Swedish security interests. Because these interests overlapped with the Estates' liberties, the 'foreign crowns' were able to portray their continued intervention as a provision of protection for German Freedom.

A letter written by Richelieu to the king shortly after the Swedish defeat at Nördlingen conveys his sense of inevitability of a conflict with Spain, and the close connection he believed existed between the position of the Protestant German princes and French security:

> It is certain that if the [Protestant] party [in the Empire] is entirely ruined, the brunt of the power of the House of Austria will fall on France. The worst thing that France can do is to conduct herself in such a manner that she would remain alone to bear the brunt of the Emperor and Spain, which will be inevitable if she does not gather up the remainder of this great party that has been subsisting for a while in Germany. Hence there seems to be no doubt that it is necessary to help this party.[153]

The French justified their intervention with several official declarations, whose slightly different emphases reflected the audience that was primarily being addressed (domestic and foreign). As was the case with the Swedish legitimation, the reasoning in the official public French declarations did not deviate much from the sentiments expressed in the private correspondence. The public reasoning was deliberately framed according to prevailing precepts of Thomist Just War theory.[154] As self-defence was undoubtedly a just cause, the French presented their war as an act of pre-emptive defence against imminent Spanish attack. The refusal of the Spanish to release the elector of Trier constituted the casus belli to trigger the pre-emptive war of self-defence. Louis XIII was argued to be duty-bound to act in defence of the elector to fulfil his pledge of protection. The French protection of the elector of Trier was itself justified because the Emperor, as the elector's overlord, was failing in his own responsibility to protect this prince, a duty which the French King then performed instead. The French king was compelled to declare war as a measure of last resort because the Cardinal-Infante 'has refused to restore the Archbishop of Trier...to liberty, who had been placed under the King's protection in the impossibility of the Emperor or any other prince to bestow their protection onto him, and as he holds a sovereign prince prisoner

---

[153] Richelieu to Louis XIII, n.d., printed in Helfferich, *Documentary History*, 151–2.
[154] Randall Lesaffer, 'Defensive warfare, prevention and hegemony. The justifications for the Franco-Spanish War of 1635', *JHIL* 8 (2006), 91–123, 141–79.

who was not at war with him, against the dignity of the Empire and against the Law of Nations'.[155]

Spain's actions against the elector of Trier constituted 'an offence against the interests of all princes of Christendom'.[156] This was a reference to the last component of a Just War: in addition to being publicly declared under princely authority as a last resort and arising from a just cause, the war needed to have a just goal benefitting the common good. The goal was to prevent the emergence of Universal Monarchy and specifically the subjugation of the Empire under an absolutist, centralised, and tyrannical Habsburg monarchy, which would be deleterious for the 'public liberty', in other words, the freedoms and liberties of all European princes and estates.[157] The statement argued that 'with their weapons and practices and intrigues, the Spanish... undermine and overturn all foundations of public freedom, by openly pursuing their highest goal, namely to subject the Empire in the form of an eternal [i.e. hereditary] monarchy under the House of Habsburg'. Spain had done this by exerting control over their Austrian cousins, instigating the Emperor's suppression of Protestants to create disturbances which then gave the Spanish the opportunity to illegally occupy the Lower Palatinate. By undercutting a threat to the overall liberties of Europe, the French therefore presented their own defensive security aims as beneficial to the common good as well. The attack on the Southern Netherlands specifically was potentially harder to justify as defensive, because the terms of the offensive alliance with the Dutch, including its partition plans, were known and it might therefore be viewed as a premeditated assault. It was therefore justified as an intervention for the protection of rebelling subjects against their tyrannical rulers. Because the rebellion of the South Netherlanders against the Spanish was not underway at the time of the attack, it was presented as an intervention in the long-standing Dutch revolt that had begun in the 1560s.[158] In general though, French policy towards the Habsburg—so the declaration claimed—had hitherto desisted from intervening in support of 'those who out of justified fears took up arms against the Emperor for defence of their freedom', even though this would often have been in France's interests.[159]

In their counter-statements, the Spanish meanwhile accused the French themselves of causing 'great harm to the *respublica christiana*', in other words, the common good, by repeatedly intervening in support of illegal rebellions against rightful rulers, both in the Netherlands and in Germany, thereby disrupting the public peace. They also contested the legitimacy of the French protection over Imperial Estates, such as the elector of Trier. By arresting the elector, the Spanish

---

[155] Quoted in ibid., 92.   [156] Ibid.
[157] German translation: *Königl: Majestät in Franckreich/wegen publication deß Kriegs wider den König in Hispanien gethane Schrifftliche Erklärung* (1635), http://www.vd17.de/digitalisierung/masterplan.
[158] See Lesaffer, 'Defensive Warfare', 166–7.   [159] *Königl: Majestät... Erklärung.*

claimed (inaccurately) that they were acting as Imperial auxiliaries under the authority of the Emperor as the elector's overlord. As lord of the Netherlands and duke of Luxemburg, the king of Spain was not only a member of the Empire but also a more legitimate protector of the electorate of Trier as a fellow-Estate. Contrary to the French, who presented the elector as a 'sovereign prince' with a clear right to conclude foreign alliances, the Spanish stressed his feudal and judicial subjecthood to the authority of the Emperor as an Imperial Estate. France's purported protection of the elector was therefore argued to be an illegal intervention in the affairs of the Empire and a usurpation of Imperial authority.[160]

Numerous government-affiliated publicists, writers, and independent commentators published commentary supporting the rationale of the French intervention. Some authors directly addressed and refuted one of the main points made by critics of the intervention—that it constituted unwarranted foreign interference in the Empire's domestic affairs. One pamphlet from 1638 argued that France's protection of the Imperial Estates (who constituted the true representatives of the Empire) and other subjects in the Empire against Spanish and Austrian Habsburg tyranny did not amount to 'interfering in a foreign dominion and depriving the rightful ruler of that which is his'. Instead, it arose from a duty of humanity and served the necessary function of allowing the Empire to achieve self-actualisation through the upholding of German Freedom:

> It is in accordance with all just peoples, and required by the bond of human society in general, that a potentate helps the oppressed. The kings of France... for the last 100 years have on different occasions assisted the German estates against Spanish violence. Thus, King Henry the Second concluded a union in Ao. 1552 with the Protestant princes in Germany and maintained the other estates in their rights and status.[161]

In subsequent years, so the pamphlet continued, the Habsburgs took advantage of favourable circumstances and victories to 'suppress the innocent inside and outside of Germany... Small wonder then, that the king of France brings himself to moderate excessive power.'[162] Many commentators in Germany supported the French argument that it was intervening to defend liberties. The well-known writer Johann Michael Moscherosch, for example, argued it was acceptable for Germans to serve in the armies of the foreign crowns because they intended to

---

[160] German translation: *Declaration, Das ist: Außführliche Darthuung: Darinnen Deß hochlöblichen Ertz-Hauses Oesterreich/gefaster Waffen Billigkeit...* (1635), http://www.vd17.de/digitalisierung/masterplan (reference: VD17 14:005353A).
[161] *Klagrede Uber den zwischen dem Römischen Keyser Ferdinand II. und Churfürsten Johan Georgen zu Sachsen... auffgerichten Vertrag* (1638), http://www.vd17.de/digitalisierung/masterplan reference: 12:191011G.
[162] Ibid., 82.

protect German Freedom.[163] Despite strict censorship, numerous French publications critical of the intervention also appeared, especially from mid-1636 when a combined Spanish-Austrian counter-attack from the Southern Netherlands could only be stopped 150 km from Paris. Critical pamphlets argued that the intervention was reckless because its outcome was unpredictable, and that it was also unjust because France's proxy-war from 1630 had effectively restarted a highly destructive war which was causing unimaginable suffering: 'one can justifiably claim that all ills which have befallen Germany or the Netherlands have come from the side of France'.[164]

\*

While full-scale war was breaking out between France and Spain in the west of the Empire and in Imperial Italy, peace was being made internally between the Emperor and the Imperial Estates that had been fighting him. The unsatisfactory nature—from the perspective of the foreign crowns—of this internal settlement of the Imperial civil war ensured that Sweden and France would continue their intervention by tapping into persisting grievances among the Imperial Estates, most importantly the amnesty question. After the battle of Nördlingen, the Emperor was in position of strength again, but this time he had learned the lessons from his previous mistakes in 1623 and 1628/29, and aimed at reaching a compromise accommodation with the Imperial Estates, without imposing diktats or unilaterally redistributing territory. Most Imperial Estates joined into the resulting Peace of Prague of May 1635, further isolating Sweden.[165] In addition to considerable concessions to the Protestants,[166] the Peace extended an amnesty to many princes, but excluded several other important Imperial Estates (Palatinate, Württemberg, Saxe-Weimar, Baden-Durlach, Hessen-Kassel, Hohenlohe). The Bohemian and Austrian rebels from 1618 were similarly excluded. The Calvinists were still not recognised. The customary right of princes to conclude alliances with each other was abrogated. The princes' armies (such as those of Saxony and Bavaria) became subsumed into a single Imperial army. The orientation of the Prague peace was thus clearly towards a more centralised Imperial monarchy, and most princes' patriotic desire for peace after almost twenty years of war outweighed their constitutional qualms about an erosion of German Liberties.[167]

---

[163] Georg Schmidt, *Der Dreissigjährige Krieg* (Munich, 2010), 62.
[164] Quoted in Kampmann, *Arbiter*, 171–2.
[165] Martin Espenhorst, 'The Peace of Prague – a failed settlement?', in Asbach, *Research Companion*, 285–96.
[166] Ralf-Peter Fuchs, *Ein Medium zum Frieden. Die Normaljahrsregel und die Beendigung des Dreißigjährigen Krieges* (Munich, 2010), 127–49.
[167] Adam Wandruszka, *Reichspatriotismus und Reichspolitik zur Zeit des Prager Friedens von 1635* (Graz, 1955).

Sweden and France, however, were not going to be as acquiescent.[168] Although the peace established several important solutions to the Imperial constitutional crisis that were then optimised at the Peace of Westphalia, the failure to include the crowns in the negotiations and settlement, despite the conflict already been irreversibly 'Europeanised', arguably doomed it to failure.[169] Apart from the fact that they had been excluded from the peace talks, the crowns could not accept the Prague settlement because, in Sweden's case, there was no provision for its territorial satisfaction, nor for the financial compensation of its army, upon which it was existentially dependent, or for adequate Protestant rights.[170] For both Sweden and France, the persisting exclusion of many princes from the amnesty and the centralising, monarchical trend which this reflected, constituted an unacceptable security threat as it portended a stronger, more unified Habsburg-dominated Empire capable of power-accretion and projection.[171] Sweden and France therefore continued their intervention. From a presentational point of view, it was convenient that many of the Franco-Swedish security goals coincided with the Imperial Estates' cherished German Liberties. Their continued and escalated intervention could therefore reasonably accurately be portrayed as carried out for the protection of the Imperial Estates' rights. Richelieu, along with many other French statesmen and leaders, had long recognised the opportunity inherent in 'the fear felt by all the electors, both Catholic and Protestant, that they would be deprived of their estates... [which] made them secretly seek your [King Louis XIII] support'.[172]

The elector of Saxony recognised this danger when he asked the Emperor to redress the amnesty issue. Throughout most of the war Saxony had been a loyal ally of the Emperor and was also opposed, in principle, to the notion of foreign interventions supposedly for the protection of Protestantism in the Reich. He believed the continuation of such interventions needed to be staved off by adequately addressing the amnesty question. It was this issue, so he wrote to Ferdinand II in March 1635, which provided 'the pretexts by which the foreign troops justify their persistent residence and evil start in the Empire,... for many of the estates in Germany that are allied with the crown of Sweden are excluded from the amnesty'.[173] The Saxon elector interceded with the Emperor not only on behalf of excluded princes, but also on behalf of the Emperor's territorial subjects, such as the Protestant inhabitants of Silesia. He argued that by restituting their property and rights one could deprive the crowns of some of the grievances which sustained

---

[168] Wilson, *Tragedy*, 565–73. [169] Kampmann, *Europa*, 116–21.
[170] Meeting report, Council of the Realm, September–October 1635, in Wilson, *Sourcebook*, 209–11.
[171] Christoph Kampmann, 'Peace impossible? The Holy Roman Empire and the European state system in the seventeenth-century', in Olaf Asbach et al. (eds), *War, State and International Law in Seventeenth-Century Europe* (Farnham, 2009), 197–210.
[172] Quoted in Wilson, *Sourcebook*, 214.
[173] Johann Georg, elector of Saxony, to Emperor Ferdinand II, Hall, 15 March 1636, printed in Helfferich (ed.), *Documentary History*, 176–79, at 177.

their destructive interventions: 'you would thereby deflect the objections of the foreigners and give all the world to know that Your Imperial Majesty... does not allow an innocent and loyal subject to be driven out'.[174] The elector stressed that ultimately the amnesty would need to be extended to all princes to end the Swedish intervention: 'the crown of Sweden would not, out of honour and conscience, abandon them [the excluded Estates] before they gained a reliable certainty, nor would it retreat from the Empire before their inclusion in the amnesty'.[175]

Records of government discussions in Stockholm confirm the elector of Saxony's assessment.[176] The regency determined the conditions under which their intervention could end, demonstrating not only the inseparable connection in Swedish statesmen's minds between German Liberties and Swedish security, but also a real concern for the fate of Protestant subjects' confessional rights in Germany. It was decided that

> We ought to pitch the terms...concerning restitution of the oppressed Protestant electors, princes and estates as high as is practicable; for it is our Christian duty to take up their cause...The safety of this country depends upon the liberties of the estates in Germany not being transformed into a servitude, under the absolute domination of the House of Austria, and especially keeping that House away from the Baltic; it is a question of honour [which] gives us the goodwill and affection of all our neighbours and many estates and soldiers in the Holy Roman Empire.[177]

While the Swedes were concerned about the extent of German Liberties, and the extension of the amnesty, this came second to their desire for German land and money. The regency decided that peace terms should be accepted if a satisfactory 'indemnity and contentment of the soldiery' were offered, even without an amnesty provided for the Estates. In that case 'we should leave it to the Estates themselves to deal with. Thereafter we should give them all possible assistance, not with the sword...but by intercession and other amicable means, and without prejudice to our own attempts to find an acceptable means of withdrawing from the war'.[178]

\*

It has recently been questioned whether the traditional picture of a straightforward Franco-Swedish victory is accurate.[179] The eventual peace settlement was

---

[174] Ibid., 179.    [175] Ibid., 177.
[176] See Jenny Öhman, *Der Kampf um den Frieden: Schweden und der Kaiser im Dreissigjährigen Krieg* (Vienna, 2005), 88–90.
[177] Swedish regency resolution, 1 August 1636, in Wilson, *Sourcebook*, 211–13, at 211–12.
[178] Ibid., 212.
[179] E.g.: Robert Rebitsch, Jenny Öhmann, and Jan Kilian, *1648: Kriegführung und Friedensverhandlungen: Prag und das Ende des Dreißigjährigen Krieges* (Innsbruck, 2018).

a compromise in which the Emperor retained key advantages, such as the settlement imposed in the hereditary lands against the defeated Bohemian and Austrian rebels.[180] Ultimately, however, the French intervention was a success: it ensured that the Emperor remained distracted in Germany and unable to provide substantial help to France's main enemy Spain. The Emperor's isolation forced him to grant concessions which meant that intervention in central Europe had largely paid off: it would no longer be possible to transform the Empire into a more centralised Imperial monarchy capable of external power projection and aggression, as the Emperor at times appeared poised to do in the 1620s. By acquiring Alsace, the French succeeded in blocking the Spanish Road. The foreign crowns' security interests were also safeguarded by their acquisition of territorial bridgeheads in Germany, by the separation of the German from the Spanish Habsburgs, and by the defence of German princely and Protestant liberties, and thereby also the decentralised constitutional structure of the Empire. This all would prevent the emergence of a strong monarchy which would upset the balance of power and threaten French and Swedish security. Crucially, as guarantors, France and Sweden secured the right to police and if need be intervene, to uphold the whole settlement in all its constituent elements: the decentralised constitution, the defence of their territorial acquisitions, and the enforcement of the separation of the two Habsburg lines.

## The Intervention by Prince György I Rákóczi of Transylvania in Hungary, 1644

Apart from the big Swedish victories of the 1640s, the Transylvanian re-entry into the war against the German Habsburgs as a Swedish ally in 1644 contributed to the extreme pressure that was exerted on the Emperor, compelling him to make substantive concessions at the Westphalian peace congress. The Transylvanian attack on Habsburg Hungary was the last 'international' intervention in central Europe before the conclusion of peace.[181] Rákóczi's published justification of his intervention was remarkable for several reasons.[182] It was directly addressed to the Emperor's Hungarian subjects as an appeal for their support against the Habsburgs. As 'lord of a part of the Kingdome of Hungarie' and as a Magyar, Rákóczi presented himself to his addressees as part of their 'nation' and as a liberator from Habsburg tyranny. The guiding theme throughout the text was the

---

[180] Franz Brendle, 'Der Westfälische Frieden als Kompromiss. Intentionen, Grundsätze und Inhalte der Friedensverträge', in Claus-Peter Hartmann et al. (eds), *Der Dreißigjährige Krieg. Facetten einer folgenreichen Epoche* (Regensburg, 2009), 173–83.
[181] Wilson, *Tragedy*, 696–8.
[182] *Declaration of George Racokzkie* (1644), in Helfferich, *Documentary History*, 228–32. See also Tischer, *Kriegsbegründungen*, 184–5.

inherent value of freedom—political and spiritual—which Rákóczi claimed to be defending against the Emperor's oppression. The freedom which Rákóczi referred to had a more personal quality than was common in the seventeenth century, when it was normally portrayed as something ascribed to corporate bodies as inherent rights, rather than to individuals. His intervention was also argued to be designed to protect the freedom of all religions. This was probably related to his background as a Calvinist ruler of a multi-confessional principality which was a feudal vassal of the Muslim Ottomans.[183]

Rákóczi's declaration set out to establish the motif of the universal human value and norm of personal freedom: 'How precious, and of what high esteem be with every one the liberty of the soule and body.' This liberty was being asserted through freedom struggles across Europe, including in Germany, Portugal, Naples, and Catalonia. These were all directed against the Habsburg oppressors and designed to restore their 'former condition of liberty'.[184] Rákóczi viewed the supposed oppressions in Hungary as part of this general phenomenon of Habsburg tyranny across Europe. The Emperor was accused of seeking 'to make the Kingdom of Hungarie Subject to the House of Austria'. Possibly because the Habsburgs had already undermined the position of Protestant nobles in the parts of Hungary it ruled during the 1620s–1630s, Rákóczi stressed that the Habsburgs' tyrannical policies were inimical not only to Protestants but to Catholics too: '[the Emperor] withal strives to domineer both Spiritually and Temporally over the fellow-Members of their Religion, & to keep them under'. The Protestants of Hungary, for their part, suffered because of the Habsburgs' introduction of the Jesuits, 'to the utmost ruine of the libertie & of the Protestant Religion', and because their 'lands and goods ... [had] been alienated'.[185]

The declaration went on to explain that in consideration of 'the violation of ... corporall liberties ... so as well ... the love and zeale to the Libertie of Our native Country and Nation', and having been exhorted 'by some of the Protestant [e]states and peeres ... and not lesse by some of the Roman Catholiques' to protect them, Rákóczi felt compelled to intervene 'for defence of their Liberties'.[186] In line with Just War theory, the prince stressed that his resort to the use of force was a measure of last resort. He also stressed that his goal was just, namely to protect the innocently oppressed and prevent 'the apparent ruine and perdition' of Hungary. In further elaborating his aims, Rákóczi stated:

> We have taken up Arms not for Our own profit ... nor ... out of an intention to reforme or persecute Religion, much less to extirpate the same: But that We onely intend to Erect againe the Statues and Laws of the Kingdome ... insomuch that

---

[183] Graeme Murdock, *Calvinism on the Frontier, 1600–1660. International Calvinism and the Reformed Church in Hungary and Transylvania* (Oxford, 2000), 270–90.
[184] *Declaration* in Helfferich, *Documentary History*, 228.   [185] Ibid., 229.   [186] Ibid., 230.

everyone...may professe and exercise that same wherein his conscience is appeased and thereby also safely to enjoy the corporall Liberty, because to Domineere and Rule over Consciences doth not belong to men, but to God alone.[187]

## Conclusion

The results of the last two chapters' investigation of pre-1648 international European interventions in central Europe can be summarised as follows:

Early modern rulers always felt a need to publicly justify their interventions by appealing to widely recognised norms. One such norm, which was frequently referred to by intervening powers, was that sovereign rulers had the right and responsibility to intervene against tyrannical (usually neighbouring) princes, to protect the latter's subjects from oppression. A rival norm, often appealed to by the targets of intervention, posited that rulers had the right to enjoy non-intervention and non-interference in their relations with their subjects. These two competing norms could both be supported by different theorists of the law of nations and nature. It was uncontested, however, that princes derived legitimation for their rule from fulfilling a duty of protection of their own subjects.

Such protective interventions were either characterised as punitive—the target ruler was accused of deliberate tyranny by depriving his subjects of their rights or committing atrocities against them—or as a provision of assistance when the rightful ruler had lost control of his country, and the intervening power therefore acted as a surrogate to fulfil the duty of protection which target-territory's ruler was unable to provide. An example of the former is the French intervention in the Empire in 1552; an example of the latter is the English intervention in the French wars of religion in 1562.

Thus, sovereignty was not conceived as absolute, nor did it confer a right onto princes to behave as they wished within their own polities. The sovereign rights and foreign-policy freedom of princes to take other rulers' subjects under their protection, the mutual duties and accountability among the community of Christian princes, and a shared adherence to the Law of Nations and Nature all placed limitations on rulers' treatment of their own subjects.[188]

All interventions were justified legally; not through reference to theories of writers of the Law of Nations, but by reference to positive treaty law, i.e. the violation of specific aspects of the target state's constitution and of subjects' rights for whose protection interventions were ostensibly taking place. This reflected the

---

[187] Ibid., 231.
[188] See also Wim Blockmans, 'Limitations to monarchical power', in Robert von Friedeburg (ed.), *Murder and Monarchy. Regicides in European History 1300–1800* (Basingstoke, 2004), 136–45.

highly juridified political culture of Europe, and especially the Empire. Abstract appeals to the violation of the law of nature were also occasionally made.

Subjects' religious-confessional rights were one aspect of their legal rights and were presented as such when legitimating intervention on behalf of co-religionists. The Reformation increased the propensity of princes to sympathise with persecuted co-religionist subjects under another princes' rule, and to sometimes act on this, even when it did not further their geopolitical and strategic interests, as seen, for example, by the French efforts to get the Dutch republic to tolerate the exercise of the Catholic faith among its subjects during alliance negotiations in the 1630s. Yet religious rights were components of legal-corporate liberties and expressions of political interests. Confessional solidarity and a duty of care towards oppressed co-religionists could be used as aspects of the legitimation of intervention—such as the elector-Palatine Frederick V's intervention in Bohemia (1619) and the Danish intervention in the Empire during the Thirty Years War (1625)—but such argumentation was usually overshadowed by the professed desire to uphold co-religionists' legal-constitutional and property rights. Upholding Protestant rights through intervention was also often justified as serving political aims such as staving off the emergence of Catholic universal monarchy. Opponents of such interventions did not contest the potential value of confessional solidarity in driving interventions per se—instead, they sought to discredit the intervention by asserting that the interveners' claimed desire to assist co-religionists was actually a sham and instead masked power-political, dynastic, and security motives.

Security was, however, also a key legitimation strategy to justify interventions. Most interventions discussed were presented as responses to security threats to the intervener's own state. The suppression of the rights of subjects, and the attendant general disturbances and unrest, within the target state were often argued to constitute threats to the security of the intervener. Interventions could thus be presented as defensive undertakings which made them more compatible with Just War precepts, because according to many commentators and theorists, war on behalf of another prince's subjects did not constitute a classic just cause. The various interventions in the Dutch revolt and in the Thirty Years War, for example, were justified defensively along these lines.

Linked to this was the legitimising motif of the defence of the neighbourhood. Interventions in neighbouring polities were often justified by the existence of manifold interlinkages between the peoples of both countries. The implication was that what happened in one of those countries necessarily affected the economy, commerce, and ultimately security of the other, thus justifying intervention as a self-interest. The French intervention in the Empire in 1552 and the English intervention in the Netherlands in 1585 were both justified in this manner.

The fact that security and legality featured strongly in justifications of intervention indicates that public justifications were often remarkably similar to actual motivations as reflected in the internal discussions. Nevertheless, such interventions were usually primarily motivated by geopolitical, dynastic, and security concerns, rather than an altruistic desire to protect persecuted subjects. The language of protection from persecution and violation of rights and privileges was used by the interveners as an accoutrement of a mainly strategically-motivated geopolitical intervention. Yet, the protection of foreign subjects' rights and the pursuit geopolitical advantage were by no means mutually exclusive. Instead, they reinforced one another. The Danish, Swedish, and French interveners in the Thirty Years War, for example, truly cared about German Liberties because they did not want to see their Habsburg neighbours and rivals inordinately strengthened through a constitutional balance that favoured the Emperor. Propping up the rights of rivals' territorial estates and other subjects served to protect these subjects, but also weakened their ruler. This explains why so many interventions discussed here were in part motivated and ideologically justified by a form of resistance against the threat of (mainly Spanish) Habsburg universal monarchy, which was perceived to pose the greatest geopolitical threat to all other polities. This was even the case among interveners who were only realistically concerned about Habsburg power in their own region (such as the Swedes with regard to the Baltic), yet deployed the ideology of resistance against Universal Monarchy in the hope that embedding their particular sectional interests into this wider pan-European goal would broaden support for their intervention. Supporting freedom struggles against the Habsburgs by the English in the Netherlands (1585), the Danes in northern Germany (1625–29), the Swedes across the Empire (1630–48), the French in the Netherlands, Germany, Italy, Catalonia, and Portugal (1530s–1550s, 1635–59), and by the prince of Transylvania in Hungary (1644), was justified in part as a struggle against universal monarchy, and aimed at defending the rebels in question as a medium for weakening the interveners' geopolitical rival.

This also explains why interventions occurred almost exclusively in support of subjects with socio-economic and military-political clout. Supporting the liberties of territorial estates such as the nobility, towns, and other corporate bodies, or indeed de facto quasi-'states', such as the German Imperial Estates, which were in conflict with their sovereign, promised greater geopolitical rewards for the target ruler's intervening rivals, than supporting destitute and poor subjects. Thus, the large-scale massacring of rebellious German peasants in 1524–26 never produced as much intervention by concerned neighbours as did the rebellions by noble territorial estates in the Netherlands (1560s–90s) and Bohemia (1619/20) and by princely Imperial Estates in the 1540s–50s and 1620s.

This function of intervention as a lever of geopolitical and dynastic interests can also be seen by the fact that one of the main forms of intervention—especially by the French crown—namely formal arrangements of external 'protection' (*protectio*), often became vehicles of territorial expansion by the intervener. Thus, the French king's intervention for the protection of the rebel Protestant Imperial

Estates in Germany in 1552 led to his acquisition of the towns of Metz, Toul, and Verdun, while protection treaties signed in the early 1630s with several small Alsatian Imperial Estates paved the way for France's de facto control over the Alsace before it was ceded de jure in 1648. Similarly, the French intervention in the Dutch revolt, the English and Spanish interventions during the French wars of religion, and the Spanish intervention in Catalonia all envisaged territorial annexations by the interveners. Thus, although interventions could provide genuine protection (the Alsatian princes against the Spanish army for example), this protection risked becoming an extension of territorial rule by the intervener.

More worrisome, from the perspective of the protectees on whose behalf intervention was ostensibly occurring, was the not uncommon phenomenon of the intervening protector degenerating into an external aggressor. This is what occurred during the French intervention in the Dutch revolt in 1583, while the Savoyard and French protection arrangements in southern France (1590s) and Lorraine (1630s), respectively, were also counter-productive and disadvantageous to the protectees. Similarly, although the Swedes and French were able to secure princely and Protestant rights in the Empire at the end of their intervention during the Thirty Years War, this came after they restarted an already destructive war and prolonged it by eighteen apocalyptic years, during which they often bullied the Estates, whose rights they claimed to have come to protect, into unwelcome alliances while spreading violence, disease, and destruction among those allies' populations.

Given the strategic and dynastic advantages that protective interventions could supply to the intervener, it is not surprising that there was 'protection competition' among would-be interveners in support of corporate entities and subjects of other rulers. Thus, the Dutch rebels' acceptance of French protection spurred the Queen of England to intervene in turn and provide her own protection in 1578 in this strategically vital area, so as to not fall behind the French in influence there. Similarly, the French and the Spanish competed for protection over the small Estates along the Rhine in the years preceding the outbreak of war between them in 1635. A kind of 'hegemonic protection' was also buttressed by French state propaganda and ideology, whereby one aspect of the king of France's aspired role as the 'arbiter of Christendom' was said to be to intervene and mediate in conflicts between and within other states, and if necessary, furnish protection to the weak or oppressed.

Considering the nature of protective intervention as a power-political and strategic tool, it occurred frequently as a stage of escalation between rival rulers, especially when their subjects had extensive legal rights or corporate power which the opposing prince could tap into to gain an edge over his enemies. That this trend was so pronounced is related to the fact that the distinction between the 'internal' and 'external' spheres of states was not as clear as in later periods. Corporate entities which were subject to a prince therefore often had extensive opportunities to establish links with foreign princes and to remain sought-after alliance partners. Interventionist activity thus increased in the context of civil war and inter-state war. Intervention as an aggressive act was more likely to be extended from ongoing hostilities than to be resorted to during a peaceful situation. This was because the relative escalation which intervention represented, would be much greater during peacetime, and a general norm that early modern princes wanted to be seen to adhere to, was the inherent value and desirability of peace among Christian princes. Almost all interventions considered so far either occurred in the context of civil wars, rebellions, and unrest, or themselves caused wars as a result. This general norm of aspiring to peace helps to explain why interventions as hostile acts needed to be publicly justified so carefully.

Many of the above-mentioned points explain why intervention featured heavily in central Europe, and especially in the Empire. Its structural incapacity to conduct a dynamic foreign policy as an actor in its own right correlated with its structural proneness to intervention (both from outside and within) because of its highly decentralised, polycentric constitutional form. Multiple power-centres and the extensive rights and powers of its estates (both its Imperial Estates and its territorial estates), and its mixed-confessional composition, meant that there existed numerous overlapping constellations of rivalry and conflict. This also provided numerous channels of external protection, faction-sponsoring and intervention. The density of its corpus of legal texts and treaties meant that almost any political interest or position could be justified more easily by a scrupulous intervening power.

These features also existed in other intervention-prone polities of east-central Europe, such as Poland and Hungary. But what made intervention particularly salient in the Empire was its unique position and role in the European state-system. Its vast area and position at the heart of Europe meant that it had numerous neighbours who would all be interested in developments there. Its emperorship retained a unique ideological, symbolic, and even transcendental appeal. Its elective nature would tempt ambitious princes across Europe to throw their hat in the ring and either stand for election or seek to secure the election of a proxy. Its numerous princely houses meant that most European powers were dynastically linked to the Empire, while its huge manpower reserves, economic potential, and geopolitical position meant that almost all European powers had interests there. It also ensured that the prevention of a more unified, centralised, or absolutist monarchy at the level of the Empire was a vital security interest of all European states. The struggle against Universal Monarchy—anathema to the European society of princes—would be focused on the Empire. Many princes that intervened there—such as King Henry II of France, King Christian IV of Denmark, and the Swedish government—thus declared the maintenance of its traditional constitutional balance and of its German Liberties to be a shared responsibility and core interest of all of Christendom/Europe. A norm of non-intervention in other states' affairs could therefore not apply to the Empire without posing a major joint security risk. This widespread attitude presaged the international guarantee of the Empire's internal constitution which was legally enshrined at the Peace of Westphalia in 1648 and amounted to the negation of non-interventionist sovereignty.

# 4
# Guarantees and Interventions
## European Powers and the Empire, 1645–1780

Although the interventions of foreign European powers into the Empire after the Peace of Westphalia were among the 'irregular' interventions, in the sense that they were not conducted under the judicial authority of the Emperor, the treaties of Westphalia nevertheless provided the external guarantors—France and Sweden—with the legal authority to intervene in the Empire to uphold rights stipulated by the Peace and the Imperial constitution in general, as outlined in Chapter 1. Westphalia therefore contributed to the juridification of intervention in the Reich through its innovative guarantee clauses. While Westphalia legalised certain types of intervention in the Empire, there were other cases of intervention in areas outside of the Empire during the post-1648 period, which were mainly geopolitically motivated.[1]

This chapter will begin with the congress of Westphalia (1645–48), at which, among other things, the rights of intervention were negotiated by the main belligerents of the Thirty Years War. As the guarantee formed the basis of external intervention into the post-1648 Empire, the theoretical analysis of the Westphalian guarantee and guarantees in general, by contemporary writers of the law of nations will then be discussed. This is followed by a survey of actual and discussed interventions into the Reich by the Westphalian guarantors, and other European powers.

### Negotiating Intervention in the Empire: The Congress of Westphalia, 1645–1648

The peace congress which ended the Thirty Years War was a conference which had become necessary because the Franco-Swedish side refused to conclude separate peace deals.[2] More fundamentally, the conference tried to settle the

---

[1] For a novel interpretation of the Dutch intervention in England in 1688, see Christoph Kampmann, 'Das "Westfälische System", die Glorreiche Revolution und die Interventionsproblematik', *Historisches Jahrbuch* 131 (2011), 65–92.

[2] Although they did not always see eye to eye, as demonstrated by Derek Croxton, *Peacemaking in Early Modern Europe: Cardinal Mazarin and the Congress of Westphalia, 1643–1648* (Selinsgrove, 1999).

external interventions in the Empire and the issues which had provoked intervention. It resulted in bringing external martial intervention into more regulated, legalised channels. As mentioned in the first chapter, the Peace of Westphalia increased, rather than decreased, the scope for intervention in the Empire. This was done firstly by placing the whole settlement—including the rights of princes and subject groups, and the Imperial constitution in general—under mutual and international guarantee. This gave the external guarantors the right to intervene to uphold constitutional rights of mediate and immediate Imperial subjects. Secondly, the curtailing of princes' confessional authority over their subjects, and a commensurate solidification of inhabitants' confessional rights, granted the subjects rights which could be protected by intervention. Enhanced subjects' rights therefore furnished potential interventions or intercessions with greater legal legitimacy. Thirdly, the regular Imperial-judicial 'vertical' interventions within the Empire were also equipped with a greater degree of legitimacy because of the confessional parity stipulations for the Reichshofrat and its commissions as proxy-interveners.

The fact that the internal constitution of the Empire was being renegotiated at an international congress was itself indicative of the key importance that European powers—particularly its neighbours and the interveners in the war—attached to its constitutional balance, and more broadly it also signified the Empire's own lack of sovereignty.[3] The topics of negotiation at the congress that were most relevant to the future legal capacity of intervention in the Empire, were the guarantee clauses and the individual and corporate rights of subjects, particularly their confessional rights. These were negotiated largely in parallel to the other topics, namely 'satisfaction and compensation' (territorial cessations to France and Sweden ostensibly as compensation for their efforts in defence of German Liberties, and cash payments for Sweden's army), and 'amnesty and restitution' (the restoration of rights and territories to the status quo ante bellum).[4]

The course of the negotiations on the topic of the religious terms have been covered extensively elsewhere.[5] From the perspective of capacities for intervention, it is interesting to note that the Swedes pressed for freedom of conscience among all inhabitants of the Reich, including especially those of the Habsburg hereditary lands, not least because Bohemian and Austrian Protestant rebels and exiles formed a large contingent of the Swedish army. Moreover, the Swedes were concerned about the fate of the Protestants there because their position had been

---

[3] Thus: Derek Croxton, *Westphalia. The Last Christian Peace* (Basingstoke, 2013), 361.

[4] Overview of negotiations in Siegrid Westphal, *Der Westfälische Frieden* (Munich, 2015).; For French policy: Derek Croxton, *Peacemaking in Early Modern Europe. Cardinal Mazarin and the Congress of Westphalia, 1643–1648* (Selinsgrove, 1999); Anuschka Tischer, *Französische Diplomatie und Diplomaten auf dem Westfälischen Friedenskongress* (Münster, 1999); Paul Sonnino, *Mazarin's Quest. The Congress of Westphalia and the Coming of the Fronde* (Cambridge, MA, 2008).

[5] See, inter alia, Dickmann, *Der Westfälische Frieden*, 343–73, 456–65; Karsten Ruppert. *Die kaiserliche Politik auf dem Westfälischen Friedenskongreß (1643–1648)* (Münster, 1979).

undermined most severely as a consequence of the Emperor's victories during the 1620s.[6] Seeking to maintain Protestant subjects' rights had become a matter of honour for the Swedes, as the Imperial side recognised.[7] The French were more concerned with undermining the Habsburgs by asserting the rights and liberties of the Imperial Estates—in this they were more zealous than the princes themselves who rejected the French proposal of banning Imperial elections during the lifetime of a reigning Emperor for example—and if this entailed enhanced Protestant freedom of worship, then so be it.[8] However, they did not want to promote Protestant rights for their own sake.[9] Indeed, the French chief minister, Cardinal Jules Mazarin, even viewed the promotion of the liberties of the Estates purely as a tool for weakening the Habsburgs and for permitting future intervention if the need arose, while he considered territorial gains indispensable.[10]

Over the course of the negotiations, the Protestant princes shifted their position from an emphasis on the confessional authority of all princes over their subjects (an abolition of the Ecclesiastical Reservation and an insistence on the Right of Reformation for all rulers), towards an emphasis on the confessional rights and freedom of conscience of the subject populations within the territories and therefore a limitation of the Right of Reformation and of rulers' authority over their subjects in general.[11] The religious rights of the minority of Dutch Catholics also became an issue during the Spanish–Dutch talks at Westphalia, although such terms would not be covered by the guarantee clauses of the main Peace of Westphalia, because the Spanish–Dutch war was ended by a separate treaty at Münster in January 1648. The rights of Dutch Catholic subjects at times threatened to stall the negotiations, because the Spanish wanted to secure assurances for the confessional rights of their former subjects, especially in Meierij, whereas the Dutch were reluctant to grant these.[12] The French—though allied with the Dutch and at war with Spain—had mixed views on this topic, but one of the chief plenipotentiaries at the congress, the Comte d'Avaux, was keen to see Catholic subjects' freedoms protected even though this counteracted the perceived interests of France's ally.[13]

During the negotiations, it became clear that Emperor Ferdinand III—who was at times caught between conflicting interests as the head of the Empire, defender of the Catholic faith, head of the Habsburg family, and territorial ruler of the

---

[6] APW II A, 5, no. 86, 149.     [7] Ruppert, *Kaiserliche*, 281.     [8] Croxton, *Westphalia*, 362.
[9] Brienne to d'Avaux and Servien, Paris, 30 May 1645: APW II B, 2, no. 113, 378–84 at 379.
[10] Mazarin to d'Avaux and Servien, Paris, 19 Dec. 1644: APW II B, 1, no. 331, 782–92.
[11] Croxton, *Westphalia*, 287–8; Ronald G. Asch, '"Denn es sind ja die Deutschen...ein frey Volk". Die Glaubensfreiheit als Problem der westfälischen Friedensverhandlungen', *Westfälische Zeitschrift*, 148 (1998), 113–37.
[12] Laura Manzano-Baena, *Conflicting Words. The Peace Treaty of Münster (1648) and the Political Culture of the Dutch Republic and the Spanish Monarchy* (Leuven, 2011), 192–235.
[13] Anuschka Tischer, 'Claude de Mesmes, Count d'Avaux. The perfect ambassador of the early 17th century', *International Negotiation* 13 (2008), 197–209.

hereditary lands—was less intransigent in many confessional matters than the Protestants had assumed.[14] In his secret instructions for his envoy Maximilian von Trauttmansdorff from October 1645, the Emperor had already indicated that he was quite willing to make far-reaching concessions to Protestant subjects' religious rights, even going so far as permitting a return to the conditions of 1618—as long as they were not subjects of his own hereditary lands, but only of the Imperial Estates.[15] He assumed that conceding Protestant rights in the hereditary lands could lead to frequent interventions by the Protestant princes and the foreign crowns.[16] In the end the Imperial negotiators felt obliged—because the Swedes' sense of prestige depended on it—to concede very limited rights for some Protestants in Habsburg Silesia, while also granting the Protestant princes and Sweden the right to peacefully intercede on behalf of Protestants under the Emperor's direct rule (IPO, art. V § 39–41). Ferdinand III only consented to these concessions very reluctantly and under pressure. He stressed 'that such intervention and intercession must not be anything other than peaceful in exclusion of violences and hostilities'.[17]

The catholic princes for their part were not pleased with the Emperor's plan to have them concede to Protestant rights within their princely territories, while he maintained his unfettered Right of Reformation in the Habsburg hereditary and crown lands. The end-result was that although the everyone's freedom of conscience was asserted (for Catholics, Lutherans, and Reformed), this was in effect made quasi-inoperable by simultaneously granting the princes the right to expel subjects whose religion had not existed in the territory at the time of the normative year.[18] This provision itself provided for the graded form of toleration detailed in Chapter 1, and came about after a process of 'numerical haggling'.[19] The religious rights that were granted in the Empire were all covered by the mutual guarantee and could therefore theoretically be enforced by armed intervention after a sequence of prescribed steps.

The question of how to secure and safeguard the peace through a guarantee (*assecuratio pacis*) was an important part during the congress negotiations.[20] Even before the congress was opened, it was considered by the French premiers Cardinal Richelieu and then Mazarin to be one of the most crucial elements in ensuring that French security would be preserved after the conclusion of a peace,

---

[14] See Lena Oetzel, 'Zwischen Dynastie und Reich. Rollen- und Interessenkonflikte Ferdinands III. während der Westfälischen Friedensverhandlungen', in Katrin Keller et al. (eds), *Die Habsburgermonarchie und der Dreißigjährige Krieg* (Vienna, 2020), 161–76.
[15] APW I, 1, no. 29, 440–52.
[16] Ferdinand III to Trauttmansdorff, Pressburg, 25 Mar. 1647: APW II, A, 6/1, no. 337, 662.
[17] Ferdinand III to Lamberg, Krane and Volmar, Prague 11 Apr. 1648: APW II, A, 8, no. 74, 229–35, at 235.
[18] Georg May, 'Zur Entstehung der hauptsächlichen Bestimmungen über das ius emigrandi auf dem Westfälischen Friedenskongreß', *Zeitschrift für Rechtsgeschichte, Kan.-Abt.*, 74 (1988), 436–94.
[19] Fuchs, *Medium zum Frieden*, 159–212.   [20] Dickmann, *Westfälischer Frieden*, 332–43.

because they mistrusted the Habsburgs so deeply, that they feared having to face them alone in case of the expected post-war Habsburg attempt at revanchism[21] According to an initial Swedish proposal of 1644, the guarantors would be able to immediately intervene militarily if a breach of the treaty terms was believed to have occurred, but the proposed guarantors would be limited to France, Sweden, and their allies among the German princes—which would have rendered the guarantor powers largely Protestant. France on the other hand wanted all signatories of the eventual treaties to be granted guarantor status to further the goal of a system of collective security. The Emperor found it hard to accept the French and Swedish demands that the Imperial Estates be included as guarantors.[22]

However, the Emperor was not opposed to the guarantee in principle—indeed, according to Vienna its scope did not go far enough because of the omission of Spain.[23] There was therefore not much opposition to the notion of treaty enforcement and the concomitant risk of intervention in principle; instead the actors wished to create opportunities for legally-grounded interventions by presumed allies, as they assumed that the power-political alignments of the Thirty Years War would probably persist in post-war geopolitical constellations. The guarantee was also discussed by the Imperial Estates. Interestingly, many of the German princes were hardly enthusiastic about the prospect of granting the foreign crowns a right to intervene in the Empire and were also wary about shouldering the international duties of becoming guarantors themselves. Yet, the early signalling of France that it was determined to place the treaty under a general, mutual guarantee, was crucial in persuading many of the smaller princes, especially the Protestants, that a settlement was viable, because it would help ensure that the Catholics and the Emperor would not renege on their confessional concessions.[24]

For France, conversely, the guarantee ensured that a collective effort could be launched against the Emperor if he violated the so-called 'non-assistance clause', which uncoupled the Spanish Habsburgs from their German cousins by prohibiting them from giving aid to Spain in the ongoing Franco-Spanish war. This was a clause that France was insisting on if it was to sign a treaty with the Emperor but not Spain. The Emperor had long refused to countenance such a limitation to his foreign-political freedom of action. But by late summer 1648, when Prague was in the process of being conquered by the Swedes, the Emperor finally relented and

---

[21] Fritz Dickmann, 'Rechtsgedanke und Machtpolitik bei Richelieu', in Dickmann, *Friedensrecht und Friedenssicherung* (Göttingen, 1971), 36–78; See also the main French instructions for its plenipotentiaries: APW I, 1, 58–123.
[22] Guido Braun, 'Die französische Diplomatie und das Problem der Friedenssicherung auf dem Westfälischen Friedenskongress', in Braun (ed.), *Assecuratio Pacis. Französische Konzeptionen von Friedenssicherung und Friedensgarantie 1648–1815* (Münster, 2011), 67–130.
[23] APW II, A, 9, 332.
[24] Maria-Elisabeth Brunert, 'Friedenssicherung als Beratungsthema der protestantischen Reichsstände in der Anfangsphase des westfälischen Friedenskongresses' in Guido Braun et al. (eds), *Frieden und Friedenssicherung in der Frühen Neuzeit* (Münster, 2013), 229–58.

agreed to the non-assistance clause.[25] It enjoyed greater consensus among the princes than the confessional terms, because they believed that the Emperor was delaying the conclusion of the peace simply for the sake of his Spanish relatives.[26] Both crowns viewed the legal capacity, which the mutual guarantee provided, to safeguard subjects' Westphalian rights, and the Imperial constitution in general, as essential to preventing the establishment of Habsburg absolutism in the Empire, the perceived threat of which had led to their interventions in this Imperial civil war in the first place. The adopted guarantee clauses (IPO art. 17, § 4–5; IPM § 115–16) contained stipulations prescribing the circumstances under which it could be activated: the offended or injured party would need to seek redress through amicable settlement or litigation, and to wait three years before calling upon the guarantors. This rather impractical sequence of steps ensured that the guarantee was never implemented in the manner exactly stipulated, but as we shall see, several de facto guarantor-interventions were carried out, and its deterrent effect was considerable.

## The Guarantee of the Peace of Westphalia in the Law of Nations and Nature

The guarantee and its provisions for intervention left an important imprint on international law, specifically the treaty-based positive law of nations, the *droit public de l'Europe*, and in the assessments of writers of the law of nations. For the first time, intervention in the internal affairs of another state became codified it in positive treaty law.[27] Also for the first time, the warring parties and treaty signatories themselves guaranteed their own peace treaty, including the lower-ranking Imperial Estates who lacked full sovereignty. The mutual guarantee was to some extent unevenly reciprocal, in the sense that it provided for a one-sided intervention in internal affairs affecting the Empire only. Also, France, for example, was guaranteeing the religious rights of Germans that it was denying its own subjects. Fundamentally, the external guarantee tied the constitutional law of the Empire to the law of nations, by creating an international responsibility to uphold the Imperial constitution. This is because the Westphalian treaties were simultaneously a fundamental constitutional law for the Empire, and an international peace treaty. The guarantee therefore arguably established a system of

---

[25] APW II, A, 10, No. 43, 182–203.
[26] Ruppert, *kaiserliche Politik*, 343f; Dickmann, *Frieden*, 477–88.
[27] The following sections draw on some material from Patrick Milton, 'Guarantee and intervention: the assessment of the Peace of Westphalia in international law and politics by authors of natural law and of public law, c.1650–1806', in Simone Zurbuchen (ed.), *The Law of Nations and Natural Law, 1625–1850* (Leiden, 2019), 186–226 and Milton, 'The mutual guarantee of the Peace of Westphalia in the law of nations and its impact on European diplomacy', *JHIL* 22 (2020), 101–25.

collective security for central Europe, which built on the Eternal Territorial Peace that had been established for the Empire in 1495.

How did writers of the law of nations and of German public law assess the Westphalian guarantee and, in particular, its attendant right of intervention into the Empire granted to France and Sweden? Samuel Pufendorf also discussed Franco-Swedish involvement in the Empire in his famous critique of the German constitution, *Monzambano*. Pufendorf portrayed Sweden's intervention in the Empire during the Thirty Years War in a fairly positive light as having ensured the protection of Protestants from Habsburg persecution.[28] But he argued that the princes' Westphalian right to form alliances (*ius foederum*), in combination with the guarantee weakened the unity of the Empire and exposed it to deleterious foreign machinations. Pufendorf considered it a 'pernicious Disorder...That the Princes of Germany enter into leagues, not only one with another, but with Foreign Princes too, and the more securely, because they have reserved to themselves a Liberty to do so in the Treaty of Westphalia.' He believed the *ius foederum* was dangerous because it 'not only divides the Princes of Germany into Factions', but also because it provides the guarantors, France and Sweden, with an ability to 'mould Germany to their own particular Interest and Wills'. Pufendorf therefore suggested that, while retaining Westphalia as a foundation, the members of the Empire must make provision to prevent foreign interference in its affairs and to harness common defence efforts to prevent a loss of territory to foreign conquerors.[29]

In the early 1740s, Johann-Jacob Schmauss recognised that France assigned great value to its guarantor status. He wrote that its guarantee allowed France to achieve an 'ascendancy and a higher degree of a general direction of Europe... The guarantee of the peace of Westphalia gives her a pretext to interfere in German affairs.' In general, France's use of its guarantor status shows 'that France knows well how to cunningly make use of the guarantee, to acquire direction over everything that occurs in Europe'.[30] The Guarantee was an effective instrument of French hegemony, because 'a guarantee is nothing other than a right to involve oneself in other affairs, by citing one's obligation as a guarantor, if this is deemed to further one's interests'.[31] Other assessments by German jurists and other scholars in the early to mid-eighteenth-century were similarly critical of France's use of its guarantee, without necessarily denying the theoretical value of the institution as a method to secure the peace. Like Pufendorf, Johann Köhler and Franz Häberlin viewed the *ius foederum* as dangerous, especially in combination

---

[28] Pufendorf, *Present State of Germany*, 191.
[29] Pufendorf, *Present State of Germany*, 205–6, 219–20. See also Peter Schröder, 'The constitution of the Holy Roman Empire after 1648: Samuel Pufendorf's assessment in his Monzambano', *HJ* 42 (1999), 970.
[30] Johann Jacob Schmauss, *Einleitung zu der Staats-Wissenschafft* (Leipzig, 1741), i, 630.
[31] Ibid., 631.

with the French guarantee.[32] In determining the reception of the guarantee among legal and political writers of the period, one must distinguish between assessments of the guarantee as it operated in geopolitical and diplomatic practice on the one hand, and how it was evaluated as an instrument under the law of nations on the other. When assessed in principle, the guarantee was viewed much more positively, especially in the later eighteenth century, during a period of French decline far removed from the hegemonic wars of Louis XIV. Johann Stephan Pütter, for example, lauded the guarantee as 'highly praiseworthy'.[33] The Halle professor Johann Christian Krause viewed the guarantee as beneficial in theory and in practice, as it promoted the unity of Europe by tying numerous powers into a reciprocal system of securing the peace and protecting rights.[34] Mably argued that the mutual guarantee elevated Westphalia above other peace treaties because it encompassed carefully devised mechanisms to provide long-term safeguards of the peace.[35]

Johann-Jacob Moser was one of the few jurists to write a monograph specifically on the guarantee of Westphalia.[36] It was primarily a legal exposition of the guarantee in theory, although it also served a contemporary political purpose, namely to define a set of parameters to limit the ways in which the guarantee could be applied in practice, otherwise the external guarantors could plausibly assert a right to intervene in any matter affecting the Imperial constitution.[37] Moser's aim was undoubtedly influenced by more than a century of French instrumentalisation of the guarantee for power-political ends.[38] He did this by insisting that the guarantee could be activated and implemented by armed force only if it was requested by the injured party, and only if all other internal Imperial judicial channels had been exhausted without procuring redress. Moser emphasised that the guarantee was designed to uphold not only princely rights, but also those of the 'mediate members of the Empire, territorial estates and subjects'. The guarantors 'can and must take up their cause, if they are affronted in violation of the Peace'.[39] Moser thus discussed the guarantee explicitly in terms of its potential role as a legalised form of intervention for the protection of foreign subjects, a feature which was largely implicit in other writers' works.

---

[32] Johann-David Köhler, *Kurtzgefaste und gründliche teutsche Reichs-Historie* (Frankfurt, 1736),564–6; Franz Dominicus Häberlin, *Anmerkungen über die...Frage: Ob die Crone Frankreich vor einen Erbfeind des Reichs zu achten seye?* (n.p., 1745).

[33] Johann Stephan Pütter, *Geist des Westfälischen Friedens; nach dem Buchstaben und Sinn desselbigen* (Göttingen, 1795), 543.

[34] Johann Christoph Krause, *Lehrbuch der Geschichte des Dreyßigjährigen teutschen Krieges und Westphälischen Friedens* (Halle, 1782), 130.

[35] Gabriel Bonnot de Mably, *Le droit public de l'Europe, fondé sur les traités* (Amsterdam, 1761), 8–10.

[36] Johann Jacob Moser, *Von der Garantie des Westphaelischen Fridens; nach dem Buchstaben und Sinn desselbigen* ([Stuttgart], 1767).

[37] Moser, *Garantie*, 44.    [38] Moser, *NtS* 1: 450.    [39] Moser, *Garantie*, 46.

Another author who devoted a work to the guarantee was the professor of public law Johann Christoph Steck, who penned his essay on instructions from Brandenburg-Prussia in 1757.[40] The geopolitical context was the recent activation of the guarantee by all guarantors, France, Sweden, the Emperor, and the Empire, against Prussia for having invaded and laid waste to Saxony at the outset of the Seven Years War (1756–1763). It is notable that despite the wartime interests of his employer of having this example portrayed as an alleged abuse of the guarantee, given that it was directed against Berlin, the author nevertheless highlights the benefits of the mutual guarantee in theory and when properly applied. Steck conceded that Sweden and France were authorised to defend the Imperial constitutional, to intervene on behalf of and for the protection of those subjects and princes whose Westphalian rights had been violated, 'to guard the freedom of the Imperial Estates', to interfere in Imperial business as long as called upon by the injured party, and to defend the confessional rights of all adherents of the three recognised confessions. This broad scope made the dangers of potential abuse and exploitation particularly large. Given the political aims he pursued, Steck argued that France had indeed abused the guarantee for its own self-interest, and instead submitted that Prussia was in fact defending Westphalian rights by acting defensively against a planned dismemberment.[41]

## From 'la protection' to 'la garantie'? France, Sweden, and the Rhenish Alliance, 1648–1668

It is sometimes noted by historians that the French crown's policy of *la protection* towards the Imperial Estates ended after the conclusion of the peace of Westphalia. Direct French sovereignty overtook the more nebulous rights of quasi-rule which were conferred by a protectorate when the French became guarantors of the entire Imperial constitution.[42] Formally, this is correct. Individual treaties of protection, as instruments of the law of nations that had been used by France since the later middle ages, had become largely superfluous after 1648, because the Westphalian guarantee encompassed a French duty of protection for all corporate and individual rights of mediate and immediate subjects in the Empire anyway. Yet French statesmen were still thinking in terms of protection arrangements with individual princes and estates at the congress of Westphalia and thereafter. Although they preferred sovereign gains, they also noted in 1646 that gaining territorial acquisitions from the Empire as

---

[40] Johann Christoph Steck, 'Abhandlung von den Rechten und Pflichten der hohen Garans des Westphälischen Friedens,' in *Abhandlungen aus dem deutschen Staats- und Lehnrecht* (Halle, 1757), 99–132.
[41] Steck, 'hohen Garans', 114–19.    [42] Babel, *Garde et Protection*, 304–31.

fiefs in the form of Imperial Estates (and therefore membership of the Empire) rather than cessions from the Empire, would facilitate alliances and treaties of protection with German princes in the future.[43] The French also considered offering the elector of Bavaria a traditional protection treaty in 1647.[44] There were fears among the Imperialists at various stages during the congress that France might conclude renewed protection relationships with various Imperial Estates and Imperial Kreise.[45] The Austrian envoy at Osnabrück tried to warn his colleagues in March 1646 of the potentially dangerous influence and channels of intervention which France could gain by securing the Alsace and protection over Imperial Estates. This would allow the French to 'bring armies onto German soil as often as they want' and thereby 'force [German towns and estates] to undergo protection and (as normally follows therefrom) subjection'.[46] In 1644, Mazarin felt it was necessary to parry accusations that French protection was a cover for self-aggrandisement or usurpation.[47]

The *Rheinbund*, or Rhenish alliance, was concluded in 1658 by Mainz with numerous German territories, including Cologne, the Palatinate, Braunschweig, and Hessen-Kassel, and joined by France and Sweden.[48] It was in part a continuation of the old French policy of protection and patronage.[49] Their guarantor status enabled Sweden, and more so France, to become so closely involved in Imperial politics. It was also an association which included *both* external guarantors while excluding the Emperor. It was cross-confessional, providing a platform for the assertion of princely liberties against the Habsburgs.[50] It was conceived as a collective security pact, designed to maintain peace, and to ensure that the Emperor and all estates respected the terms and stipulations of Westphalia.[51] It can therefore be seen as a 'constitutional organ' of Westphalia, a guarantor of its weaker members, and a de-escalating force in Imperial-confessional and

---

[43] Longuevilles, d'Avaux, and Serviens to Louis XIV, Münster, 9 July 1646: APW II, B, 4, no. 60, 178–89 at 189.

[44] Longuevilles and d'Avaux to Louis XIV, Münster, 17 June 1647: APW II, B, 5/2, no. 332, 1493–97 at 1496.

[45] E.g., Trauttmansdorff to Ferdinand III, Münster, 1 June 1646: APW II, A, 4, no. 146, 267; Wartenberg diary, 2 Mar. 1645: APW III, C, 3/1, 106; Wartenberg diary, 7 Mar. 1647: APW III, C, 3/2, 762–4.

[46] Session protocol of the council of princes, Osnabrück, 3/13 Mar. 1646: APW III, A, 3/3, no. 113, 281–311, at 284.

[47] Mazarin to d'Avaux, 30 Apr. 1644: APW II, B, 1, no. 80, 157–9.

[48] A detailed study from the perspective of the German princes: Joachim Brüser, *Reichsständische Libertät zwischen kaiserlichem Machtstreben und französischer Hegemonie. Der Rheinbund von 1658* (Münster, 2020). See also, from the French perspective, Roman Schnur, *Der Rheinbund von 1658* (Bonn, 1955).

[49] Tilman Haug, *Ungleiche Aussenbeziehungen*, 89–101.

[50] Martin Peters, 'Interpretationen des Rheinbundes im Wandel der Zeit', in *Der Erste Rheinbund*, https://www.historicum.net/purl/1e2/.

[51] Thus: Anuschka Tischer, 'Die Vorgeschichte des ersten Rheinbunds von 1658', in *Der Erste Rheinbund*, https://www.historicum.net/purl/1dy/.

European politics.[52] Its main architect, Johann Philipp, archbishop-elector of Mainz, viewed its cross-confessional composition as one of its strongest features.[53] The treaty text stated that the alliance was conceived as a measure to ensure the implementation of the 'guarantee as instructed by the Peace of Westphalia, for the maintenance of peace'.[54]

The geopolitical context during the mid-late 1650s is important in explaining why the two guarantors were able to align themselves with an Estates-based alliance implicitly directed against the Emperor. At this stage, the Habsburgs were perceived as a greater threat to the stability and peace of the Reich, and to princely prerogatives, than France. The princes of the western Kreise along the Rhine, with Mainz as their unofficial leader, were concerned that Austrian assistance to Spain in the ongoing Franco-Spanish war could spread disturbances and ultimately war to the Reich.[55] Such events such as the Emperor's failure to act against the occupation of Liège by the Spanish-allied duke of Lorraine in 1653 had done little to allay their suspicions. This explains why the Rhenish mutual defence alliance grounded itself so explicitly in the Peace of Westphalia, its non-assistance clause, and particularly in the guarantee clauses which were to ensure that these peace-conserving terms were adhered to and enforced with the help of the external crowns. This legitimising basis was reflected in the statements by the alliance members and its council of envoys. An oft-repeated formula in such public statements, including letters of justification sent to the Emperor, was the professed aim of preserving the 'security, tranquillity and calm' of the Reich.[56] Notes by the Mainz ministry on how to justify and present the alliance to the other Estates, partially in the hope of gaining new signatories, state that the inclusion of France as a non-Imperial Estate (with Sweden this was not an issue) was on the basis of it being a 'contracting party' and especially of its 'particular-guarantie' of Westphalia. It was argued that 'this alliance is nothing other than the implementation of...the Peace of Münster and its general and specific guarantee'. The alliance's aims were said to be prescribed by Westphalia and that the alliance was therefore argued to be 'nothing new, but merely that which all contracting parties of the Peace are in any case obliged by'.[57]

The alliance and especially the inclusion of France as a guarantor had a pacifying and stabilising effect in the West of the Reich. It isolated Spain (particularly in the Southern Netherlands) and its existence probably deterred Leopold

---

[52] Brüser, *Rheinbund*, 373–84.
[53] Johann Philipp, elector of Mainz to Bernhard Christoph von Galen, prince-bishop of Münster, 10 June 1659: HHStA, MEA, RTA, 204.
[54] HHStA, Allg.-Urkundenreihe, 1658 VIII 14.
[55] E.g., Louis XIV to duke of Saxony-Weimar and prince-bishop of Osnabrück, Paris, 24 Mar. 1656: HHStA, Staatenabteilungen, Frankreich-Varia 6(9), fols 1–14.
[56] Princes and electors of the Rhenish alliance to Emperor Leopold I, Frankfurt, 18 Jan. 1659: HHStA, MEA, Reichstag 204.
[57] Draft notes by Mainz, n.p., [early 1659]: HHStA, MEA, Reichstag 204.

I from giving the Spanish any meaningful assistance until the end of the war in 1659. The Mainz and French envoys did not tire to warn that any such assistance would have the effect of activating the guarantee clauses.[58] Here, the prospect of a guarantor intervention arguably had an effect of moderating the Emperor's conduct and keeping it within the bounds of his treaty obligations. The prestige which France as the chief guarantor enjoyed in the late 1650s and 1660s is clear from the decision of various German princes to appeal to Paris for French intervention rather than Vienna, in such cases as dynastic disputes and inter-territorial squabbles, matters which the office of the Emperorship was formally more authorised to deal with.[59] With the ending of the Fronde rebellion (1648–53—during which Spain tentatively cooperated with the rebels and Huguenots) and the approaching victory over Spain (Peace of the Pyrenees 1659), France was able to focus more on the Reich and on exercising its guarantee and the political influence this entailed.[60] Louis XIV welcomed this opportunity. He wrote in 1662: 'I am completely convinced that the princes are not demanding anything which the treaty of Münster does not grant them. I am always glad to exercise the guarantee on behalf of my friends, as indeed the treaty also obliges me to do'.[61] Louis XIV was therefore building on the earlier traditions of *protection et amitié* in French policy towards individual Imperial Estates, as a form of asymmetrical patronage and clientele relationships.

The Emperor's statesmen were aware of their relative isolation during this period. Various reports of the Imperial chancery and the privy-council bemoaned the willingness of the princes to be drawn into the orbit of the foreign crowns, with a particular resentment being reserved for Sweden, with whom the Emperor was after all, at war. One report argued that Sweden wished to use the alliance and the guarantee to 'aggrandise' itself at the expense of the Empire. It was to be feared that the Rheinbund allies would 'allow Sweden to go where it pleases in the Reich'.[62] Another report lamented that by entering into an alliance with France and Sweden, the princes were allowing themselves to be 'pulled away' from their traditional protector the Emperor.[63] Many of the leading princes for their part, welcomed France's support against the perceived overweening authority of the Emperor. As general guardians of the constitution, there was a widespread sense

---

[58] Protocol of Frankfurt Deputationstag, 19 Mar.1659: HHStA, MEA Reichstag 205.

[59] E.g., Eberhard, duke of Württemberg, to Johann Philipp, elector of Mainz, n.p., 17 June 1659: HHStA, MEA Reichstag 205. For detailed treatment of disputes, see Brüser, *Rheinbund*, 278–345.

[60] See Schnur, *Rheinbund*, 73–83. One stipulation of the Peace of the Pyrenees was that the Fronde rebel leader Condé—who had been assisted by Spain—was permitted to return to France. After this it became virtually impossible for powerful French nobles to openly seek the support of foreign powers. See also Daniel Séré, 'La réception en France de la paix de Pyrénées', Heinz Duchhardt (ed.), *Der Pyrenäenfriede 1659. Vorgeschichte, Widerhall, Rezeptionsgeschichte* (Göttingen, 2010), 59–71.

[61] Quoted in ibid., 58.   [62] HHStA, RK Vorträge 1c, report, 2 Sep. 1658.

[63] Ibid.: Reichskanzlei report, 3 Sep. 1658.

that the external guarantors were permitted, and indeed obliged, to intervene in such affairs for the preservation of princely rights.[64]

## The Wars of Louis XIV and the Discrediting of the Guarantee of Westphalia

French diplomats viewed their king's Westphalian guarantee as one of the most important jewels in his crown. They viewed the guardianship over the Imperial constitution that went with it as key to preventing the emergence of a centralised Imperial monarchy capable of external power-projection, which would have catastrophically undermined French security. It is striking that well into the eighteenth-century, French diplomats stressed the crucial importance of the guarantee both in public justifications of alliances and other policies towards Germany, and in confidential internal diplomatic correspondence.[65] For the guarantors to effectively carry out their role, however, their policies would have to respect the Imperial constitution as the guarantee applied to it above all. Under the personal rule of Louis XIV, the opportunities of the guarantee were squandered with an aggressive policy of military conquest towards the Rhine from the late 1660s. Despite French influence and prestige in the Reich during the 1660s, several princes, including *Rheinbund* members, tried to reduce French influence because they viewed it as destabilising. Various policies were already starting to instil suspicion of French aims, including French schemes to acquire parts of Lorraine and the deprivation of rights in the 'decapolis' of ten Alsatian towns, which had fallen to France in 1648. The French attack on the Spanish Netherlands during the War of Devolution in 1667/68 then sharply alienated Louis XIV from the Imperial Estates and the Rhenish alliance soon collapsed.[66]

Gottfried Wilhelm Leibniz was one of the most prominent commentators to discuss the implications of this attack for the mutual guarantee.[67] In a discussion of the best means for the Empire to achieve security in light of France's hegemonic designs, Leibniz considered means to strengthen the defence of the Empire.[68] He believed that Louis XIV did not want to directly conquer the German lands but rather, as had already occurred via the Rhenish alliance, place himself in the

---

[64] HHStA, MEA Reichstag 205, electoral-Mainz envoy Philipp Vorburg to elector Johann Philipp, Frankfurt, 26 Aug. 1659. See also Matthias Schnettger, *Der Reichsdeputationstag 1655-1663. Kaiser und Stände zwischen Westfälischem Frieden und Immerwährendem Reichstag* (Münster, 1996), 344ff.

[65] E.g., instructions for Duc de Richelieu, Marly, 28 Mar. 1725, in *Recueil des Instructions* (Paris, 1884), i, 208, and for Michel de Vilebois, 1 July 1729, in ibid, xxviii, 138–150.

[66] Haug, *Ungleiche Außenbeziehungen*, 64–7; Schnur, *Rheinbund*, 83f.

[67] Leibniz, *Sämtliche Schriften und Briefe*, IV, 1: 115–30, 141.

[68] Ibid, 133–214. See also Christoph Kampmann, *Arbiter und Friedensstiftung. Die Auseinandersetzung um den politischen Schiedsrichter im Europa der Frühen Neuzeit* (Paderborn, 2011), 220–6, and Wolfgang Burgdorf, *Reichskonstitution und Nation. Verfassungsreformprojekte für das Heilige Römische Reich im Politischen Schrifttum 1648–1806* (Mainz, 1998), 88–95.

position to be the arbiter of conflicts within the Empire and therefore indirectly dominate Germany. The princes should seek to form a broad-based alliance that was not necessarily reliant on the Emperor, modelled on the Rhenish alliance and designed to secure the Westphalian order, to harness the defensive capacity of the Empire: 'the purpose of this alliance should be nothing other than to provide each other the guarantee of the Peace of Westphalia, which all Imperial Estates are bound into anyway'. Leibniz' writings therefore embraced the concept of German collective security grounded in the Peace of Westphalia, yet—somewhat paradoxically—rejected the notion of French intervention which was arguably inherent—at least initially—in that very Westphalian system of central European collective security.[69]

The fact that during his wars against the Empire and/or its members, Louis XIV half-heartedly tried to use his guarantor status as a pretext for self-aggrandisement had a particularly deleterious effect on the reputation of the external guarantee among Germans in the late seventeenth-century.[70] About a century later, a member of the French foreign ministry reminisced: 'One no longer saw the king as a guarantor of the peace of Westphalia, but as the most dangerous enemy of German Freedom.'[71] Emperor Leopold I, on the other hand, eschewed such rapacious great-power politics within the Empire. He largely followed the traditions and precepts of Imperial law, thereby gradually establishing himself as the more reliable guarantor of Westphalia, and defender of the Imperial constitution against French aggression, which formed the basis of the revival of Imperial authority in the second half of the seventeenth and early eighteenth centuries.[72] From the 1670s, the Emperor and Louis XIV therefore switched roles in the eyes of many German princes.[73] By the early 1670s France had lost almost all support in the Empire.[74] It was especially during the Dutch War (1672–78) when both external guarantors were at war with the Empire, that the guarantee was viewed most suspiciously. Political pamphlets appeared at this time, bearing such titles as 'Considerations on how both crowns France and Sweden favour highly

---

[69] Leibniz, *Sämtliche Schriften* VI, 1: 141.

[70] *Mémoire des Raisons, qui ont oblige le Roy de France Louis XIV. À reprendre les Armes...* (Paris, 1688). See also Martin Wrede, *Das Reich und seine Feinde. Politische Feindbilder in der reichspatriotischen Publizistik zwischen Westfälischem Frieden und Siebenjährigem Krieg* (Mainz, 2004), 330–484.

[71] Quoted in Sven Externbrink, 'Staatensystem und kulturelles Gedächtnis. Frankreich, das Alte Reich und Europa', in Eva Dewes et al. (eds), *Kulturelles Gedächtnis und interkulturelle Rezeption im europäischen Kontext* (Berlin, 2008), 89–102, at 93.

[72] Volker Press, 'Die kaiserliche Stellung im Reich zwischen 1648 und 1740-Versuch einer Neubewertung', in Georg Schmidt (ed.), *Stände und Gesellschaft im Alten Reich* (Wiesbaden, 1989), 51–80.

[73] Jean Bérenger, 'Leopold I. und Ludwig XIV', in Guido Braun (ed.), *Assecuratio Pacis. Französische Konzeptionen von Friedenssicherung und Friedensgarantie 1648–1815* (Münster, 2011), 137–62.

[74] Klaus Decker, *Frankreich und die Reichsstände 1672–1675* (Bonn, 1981); Heinz Duchhardt, *Altes Reich und europäische Staatenwelt, 1648–1806* (Munich, 1990), 22.

disadvantageous things for the Empire under the pretext of the guarantee of Westphalia' (1676).[75]

## The Resurgence of the External Guarantee of Westphalia under King Charles XII of Sweden

Sweden viewed its guarantor status in the context of the two inter-related factors of Swedish security and German freedoms, in a fashion that was broadly comparable to France's assessment of its guarantee. Sweden's role as a guarantor, however, was of a different nature to that of France, chiefly because Sweden was a simultaneously an Imperial Estate and an external guarantor.[76] Sweden's power-political decline, especially after 1709, made it impossible for it to use the guarantee as part of a pretext for aggressive policies, as France had done during the late seventeenth-century.[77] France, as a Catholic power, and moreover a major power-political adversary of the Habsburgs, had to tread carefully when supporting Westphalian rights and propping up Protestants in the Empire, to avoid raising suspicions that it was merely seeking to sow discord within Germany for its own political aims of denying the Austrian ruler a strong support base as Emperor in Germany.[78] Sweden was less hampered by such suspicions in its support of Protestant rights in the Reich.

As the Peace of Westphalia was the most important foundation of Protestant rights in the Empire, its Protestants viewed Sweden, as a guarantor and as an important Protestant European power, as a natural supporter of co-religionist subjects or princes whose Westphalian confessional rights had been violated.[79] Sweden had suffered a deteriorated image since the later seventeenth century, when, for example, it failed to uphold Westphalian terms despite the Protestant princes appealing to it in 1697 against the 4th Article of the Peace of Ryswick, which upset the confessional balance in the Palatine in favour of the Catholics.[80] King Charles XII's arrival in Germany, his military prowess, and especially his

---

[75] Philalethus Archistor, *Raisonnement. Reiff-erwogenes Staats-Bedencken, wie beede Cronen Franckreich und Schweden unter dem Praetext der im Instrumento Pacis ihnen überlassenen Garantie dem Römischen Reich höchstnachtheilige Dinge favoriren* (1676), printed in *Materialien und Beyträge zur Geschichte-Stück 2*, ed., Carl Friedrich Häberlin (Erlangen, 1785), 206–31.

[76] Herbert Langer, 'Der Westfälische Frieden und Schweden', in Manfred Spieker (ed.), *Friedenssicherung* (Münster, 1989), iii, 37–56.

[77] Klaus-Richard Böhme, 'Die Grossmachtstellung bewahren - Aber wie? Die schwedische Deutschlandpolitik nach 1648', in Matthias Schnettger (ed.), *Imperium Romanum - Irregulare Corpus - Teutscher Reichs-Staat. Das Alte Reich im Verständnis der Zeitgenossen und der Historiographie* (Mainz, 2002), 77–88.

[78] This concern is expressed in instructions for Duc de Richelieu, Marly, 28 Mar. 1725, in *Recueil des Instructions* (Paris, 1884), i, 221.

[79] Wrede, *Feinde*, 301.

[80] Corpus Evangelicorum to Sweden, 31 May 1697, in Eberhard von Schauroth (ed.), *Vollständige Sammlung aller Conclusorum... des Corporis evangelicorum* (Regensburg, 1751–86), iii, 208.

intervention in Austrian Silesia in 1707 for the defence of Protestant subjects' rights there, contributed to a resurgence of the esteem in which Sweden's Westphalian guarantee was held in Protestant Germany.

Having just knocked Saxony-Poland out of the Great Northern War, Charles XII and his troops remained stationed in Saxony near Altranstädt causing anxiety among the anti-French allies of the concurrent War of the Spanish Succession (Austria, Britain, and the Netherlands), that Sweden might assault the Emperor in his hereditary lands in support of its traditional ally and sponsor France. This would have caused the two distinct European wars to merge into a general conflagration. Indeed, a series of minor insults led to a deterioration in relations between Emperor Joseph I and the Swedish King, who used the opportunity of Austria's full engagement against France in the West and against the rebels in Hungary to menace, and begin crossing, the Austrian borders of Silesia in July–August 1707. It was soon made clear to the Austrians that only a public declaration and treaty promising the full restoration of Protestant subjects' rights in Silesia, as stipulated at Westphalia, would be able to prevent a full Swedish occupation of the duchy. Under intense military pressure and moreover allied to Protestant powers, the Emperor was forced to accept the Swedish ultimatum.[81] The consequent convention of Altranstädt[82] safeguarded Protestant rights on a lasting and secure footing, with the return of churches and other provisions implemented over the course of 1707–09.

The existing literature has focussed largely on the implementation of its terms on the ground in Silesia in the following years.[83] The extent to which the guarantee of Westphalia was used as a legitimising factor by the Swedes, and the reception that this dramatic guarantor intervention had in the Reich have been less thoroughly investigated. The Swedish negotiators argued that their exercise of the guarantee was rendered legally sound by the prior appeals of the Protestant subjects of Silesia whose rights were being curtailed.[84] Indeed, the entire publicity campaign orchestrated around the intervention, by both Swedish agents and independent Protestant commentators and governments in the Reich, placed a considerable emphasis on the legality of this intervention stemming from the external guarantee. Exhortations by the Protestant princes to the Emperor to ensure the correct implementation of the convention in Silesia were printed as pamphlets and distributed at the Reichstag, where the news of the intervention was received with satisfaction among most Protestant envoys.[85]

---

[81] Joseph I to Wenzel Wratislaw, Vienna, 24 Aug. 1707: HHStA, SA-Schweden 13, fols 4–12.
[82] *EStC* 12 (1708), 107–17.
[83] Norbert Conrads, *Die Durchführung der Altranstädter Konvention in Schlesien 1707–1709* (Cologne, 1971).
[84] Ibid., 4.
[85] Reichstag-envoy Ignaz Otten to archbishop-elector of Mainz, Regensburg, 12 Sep. 1707: HHStA, MEA, Reichstag 332.

One such pamphlet noted that the Swedish king had acted 'out of the possessed guarantee of the Peace of Westphalia, and according to its instructions', adding that on the basis of the treaty of Osnabrück, 'the Swedish crown, as a guarantor, remains authorised to intervene and intercede for the freedom of religion'.[86] When communicating with the Austrian officials, Swedish envoys also stressed their master's constitutional 'obligation to intercede' in cases in which Westphalian rights were being violated.[87] The Swedish chief minister Count Piper intimated that the king was 'obliged by his conscience and by his guarantee to maintain' Protestant rights in the Empire.[88] The convention had a lasting impact, and Lutheran inhabitants who felt that its terms were being transgressed against continued to appeal to Sweden until the duchy's annexation by Brandenburg-Prussia.[89]

## Discussions of Intervention in Imperial Politics during the Early Eighteenth Century

A view on Imperial politics during the rest of the early eighteenth century can shed light on the constitutional and practical role that contemporaries ascribed to the external guarantee during numerous political, dynastic, and confessional disputes. While this period did not witness an actual guarantor intervention of the kind seen in Silesia in 1707 and against Frederick the Great fifty years later, the period is still of interest as the guarantee was discussed and debated as an ever-present possibility in the various disputes of the time. The fact that an actual exercise of the external guarantee did not occur in the 1710s and '20s, is less important for the purpose of this study, than the fact that the guarantors were often called upon to exercise their guarantee. Various politicians, diplomats, and rulers from across Germany viewed guarantor interventions for the protection of threatened rights as potential remedy for the redress of grievances against the Emperor, or against territorial rulers in cases in which the Emperor was unwilling or unable to intervene himself. This shows that the emphasis on the protection of violated rights was not just seen as an internal phenomenon within the Empire, but also extended beyond its frontiers. Given the juridification the Empire's political culture, calls for external intervention had a much greater chance of being

---

[86] *An Ihro Roem. Kayserliche...Majestät...Der Augspurgischen-Confessions-Verwandten...Stände... Fernere Intercessionales, für Ihre Glaubens=Genossen im Herzogthum Schlesien* (Regensburg, 1708), in HHStA, SA-Schweden 11, fols 115–16.

[87] Swedish envoy Strahlenheim to Imperial officials, Breslau, 27 Jan. 1708: HHStA, SA-Schweden 11, fols 117–41.

[88] Piper to Wratislaw, 10 Aug. 1707, printed in Jaroslav Goll, *Der Vertrag von Alt-Ranstaedt, 1706–1707* (Prague, 1879), 5.

[89] Reports of appeals in Otten to Lothar-Franz, Regensburg, 28 Feb. 1718: HHStA, MEA, Reichstag 373.

favourably received if they were based upon international treaty law, such as the treaties of 1648.

Various examples from the contemporary diplomatic correspondence can be cited to illustrate the fact that external guarantor intervention was readily considered as a remedy against violated rights in the Reich. During a crisis surrounding the treatment of Protestant subjects in Nassau-Siegen, the Brandenburg Reichstag envoy argued in 1711 against his king carrying out the intervention for the protection of the Protestants subjects that the *Corpus Evangelicorum* had mandated the year before, because it would be impolitic to offend the Emperor at a time when the Protestant princes were trying to favourably dispose him towards ensuring the revision of the Ryswick clause. Instead of arguing that Brandenburg-Prussia could carry out the intervention after the end of the Imperial war against France, he argued that France itself—an 'enemy' of the Reich at the time of writing—and Sweden, should be called upon to move into that direction on the basis of their guarantee of Westphalia: 'Maybe after the peace it would be more opportune if the crowns of France and Sweden could be brought to start talking about the guarantee of the Peace of Westphalia, whose execution is still lacking.'[90] The French regency government of 1715–23 continued the long-standing French foreign policy tradition of supporting the German Freedoms of the Emperor's immediate subjects out of a fear of Habsburg hegemony in the Reich.[91]

In the context of an Empire-wide confessional crisis in 1719–23, several Protestant envoys at the Reichstag appealed to the French envoy for France's support, as a guarantor of the Peace, in upholding Protestant subjects' Westphalian rights.[92] At the same time the Hanoverian envoy in Vienna warned the dowager-Empress Amalia that even though France was intolerant towards Protestants at home, it would 'nevertheless guarantee the Protestant religion in Germany, as it was a co-signatory of the Peace of Westphalia, upon which all the calm and well-being of Germany depends'.[93] The Emperor's suspension of the duke of Mecklenburg-Schwerin in May 1728 was causing excited discussions at the Reichstag and at the congress of Soissons in France between 1728 and 1729 as shall be seen. The Hanoverian envoy reported that there was talk among the opponents of the Emperor of the 'requisition of the [French and Swedish] guarantee' of Westphalia over the alleged violation of princely rights.[94] A cross-confessional princely opposition group to Emperor Charles VI discussed

---

[90] Quoted in Andreas Kalipke, *Verfahren im Konflikt. Konfessionelle Streitigkeiten und Corpus Evangelicorum im 18. Jahrhundert* (Münster, 2015), 305.

[91] Jörg Ulbert, 'Die Angst vor einer habsburgischen Hegemonie im Reich als Leitmotiv der französischen Deutschlandpolitik unter der Regentschaft Philipps von Orleans', in Thomas Höpel (ed.), *Deutschlandbilder—Frankreichbilder 1700–1850* (Leipzig, 2001), 57–74.

[92] Reported by Reichstag-envoys to Charles VI, Regensburg, 26 Dec. 1719:HHStA, RK, PK-Berichte 43b, fols 639–47.

[93] Huldenberg to George I, Vienna, 30 Dec. 1719: NHStAH, Cal.-Br. 24, 4915(4), fol. 511r.

[94] E.g., Reck to George II, n.d. [1728] Fontainebleau: NHStAH, Hann.-92, 2254, fols 43–4.

co-ordinating an appeal to the Westphalian guarantors—although apart from some letters of intercession, nothing came of it.[95]

The Emperor and his ministers rejected the notion of foreign states' interferences in internal Reich affairs, arguing that it provided opportunities for foreign power to 'cause new, and exacerbate old, differences between the head and the constituent parts of the Reich'.[96] However, this did not apply to the guarantee of Westphalia by France and Sweden, which was accepted in principle, even though its invocation was usually directed against the Emperor. In 1721, the Imperial envoy to Berlin hinted that the external guarantors of Westphalia, and not any other foreign powers, had the right to interfere in the Imperial affairs.[97] The Austrian minister Philipp Sinzendorf, who was at the congress of Soissons in 1728, wrote a report to the Emperor regarding the discussions that were being conducted at the congress of the possibility of the exercise of France's guarantee of Westphalia in the matter of the deposition of the duke of Mecklenburg. He expressed the commonly-held opinion that France indeed had the right to intervene against the Emperor on behalf of wronged parties in Germany, if *deutsche Freiheit* was really being suppressed. Naturally he did not see the removal of the duke in this light.[98] The British envoys at the congress of Soissons were also trying to get the French to carry out a Westphalian guarantor intervention against the Emperor for having violated princes' rights as stipulated in by deposing the duke of Mecklenburg. They reported with satisfaction that the French chief minister Cardinal André Hercule Fleury had said:

> ...if the Princes of the Empire...would represent to France the illegality and Grievance of this Administration, and make the proper Requisition to His Most Christian Majesty as Guaranty to the Treaty of Westphalia, France would certainly enter into the necessary Measures for their Assistance.[99]

Connected to this pervasive readiness to envisage and accept the involvement of the guarantors in German affairs—at least following Louis XIV's death in 1715— was a belief that they performed an important function in the German constitutional framework. This was the safeguarding of the existing legal framework and the protection of weaker members of the hierarchy, thereby helping to defend German Liberties and complementing the primary role of the Emperor in this regard. Many smaller Protestant rulers therefore expressed considerable

---

[95] Clemens August, archbishop-elector of Cologne to Karl Philipp, elector-Palatine, Bonn, 3 Aug. 1728: LANRW, Kurköln-VI, 1411, fol. 40r.
[96] Charles VI to Löwenstein, Vienna, 25 July 1715: HHStA, RK, PK, Weisungen 5a, fol. 59v.
[97] Vossius to Charles VI, Berlin, 1 Mar. 1721: HHStA, RK,Dipl-.Akten, Berlin-Berichte 12a.
[98] Sinzendorf to Charles VI, Fontainebleau, 6 Oct. 1728: HHStA, RK, Kl.-Reichsstände 347, fols 448–55.
[99] William Stanhope and H. Walpole to Duke of Newcastle, Paris, 30 Nov. 1728: BL, Add. MSS. 21,759, fols 244–54, at fol. 248r.

misgivings at the moves towards the expulsion of Sweden from its north German possessions by Hanover and Prussia in the later stages of the Great Northern War.[100] In 1719 a pamphlet advocated the complete expulsion of Sweden from Germany.[101] The Emperor's representatives noted that many of the Protestant Reichstag envoys disapproved of its content as they believed 'that it would give their religion a large blow, if Sweden were to be completely removed from German soil'.[102] Most Protestants believed 'that there would be no security for the weaker estates in the future, if one were to allow Sweden to be chased away from its lands and people', and that the Protestants would succumb to a Catholic supremacy in the Reich.[103]

There was a widespread belief, especially among Protestant Reichstag envoys, that Sweden—which had incriminated itself far less than France to the charge of exploiting the guarantee power-politically—had a long history of meritorious service (*Verdienst*) in the Empire. Such service included intervening in conflicts to defend weaker estates against more powerful ones, princes against excessive assertions of authority by the Emperor, and Protestants against persecution.[104] That this role was also widely seen as a *duty* is revealed in the Hanoverian and Prussian strategy of justifying its annexation of Sweden's possessions. The Prussian king argued that the Swedes had badly neglected their constitutional duties towards the Reich as a Westphalian guarantor, and could therefore justifiably be expelled from Germany.[105] A Hanoverian anti-Swedish pamphlet of 1716 also accused Sweden of having ignored its constitutional duties and of having incited general disturbances in the north of Germany, thereby betraying its protective function.[106]

Such arguments, although propagandistic, are nevertheless illuminating as they were carefully designed to strike a chord with the intended audience and would therefore have reflected prevailing norms, in this case the right and duty of an external guarantor to carry out protective and stabilising interventions in the Reich. When it suited them, the Prussians had no qualms about flipping the argument around, as in 1718, when the Hanoverian Privy-councillor Eltz went on a special mission to Berlin to gain Prussian support for measures to expel the Russians from Mecklenburg, among other things. The Prussian ministers were opposed to such an endeavour, however, as the tsar and the king of Prussia were allies. To justify their stance, the ministers told Eltz 'that without Sweden and France the religion and freedom of Germany would not have been preserved. Why

---

[100] Wrede, Feinde, 293, 311–12.  [101] *Plan projetté pour la Paix generale du Nord* (n.p., 1719).
[102] Sachsen-Zeitz and Kirchner to Charles VI, Regensburg, 28 Feb. 1719: HHStA, RK, PK, Berichte 43a, fol. 98r.
[103] Wrisberg to George I, Regensburg, 19 Mar. 1716: NHStAH, Cal.-Br. 11, 2966(3), fols 606–12r.
[104] Ibid.
[105] Frederick William I to Prussian envoy in Vienna, Berlin, 2 Apr. 1718: NHStAH, Hann.-92, 2179, fols 104–5.
[106] *Memorial, die nordische Unruhe betreffend* (n.p., 1716), in NHStAH, Cal.-Br. 11, 2968(3).

should one not use the tsar in a similar fashion henceforth?'[107] Although inconsistent with their largely concurrent arguments on the need to expel Sweden, and even though such arguments were employed to serve the Prussians' geopolitical goals at the time, the underlying assumption of the necessity and legitimacy of outside intervention for the preservation of German liberty is the same.

During this period, France also extended it rights of protection and intervention to parts of central Europe which had left the Empire at the Peace of Westphalia, namely Switzerland, through guarantees of the security and laws of its Catholic cantons. Like the Empire, Switzerland was a geopolitically diffuse zone of overlapping sovereignties and jurisdictions which lent itself to outside interference. In 1715, France signed a treaty with the Catholic cantons, which gave it a right to intervene in their internal disputes. As an 'asymmetrical relationship' between the higher-ranking French king and the quasi-sovereign republican cantons, the treaty built on earlier traditions of protection and informal patronage.[108] Similarly, France (and the cantons of Berne and Zürich) became guarantors of the constitution of the republican city-state of Geneva in 1737/38 and repeatedly intervened in its civic conflicts between rebellious burghers and the city council. Which side was supported, was dictated less by assessments of legality or justice, than be geopolitical expedients.[109]

## Implementation and Expansion of the Westphalian Guarantee: The Seven Years War (1756–1763) and the Peace of Teschen (1779)

Just as confessional politics had become power-politically instrumentalised in the context of the Austro-Prussian dualism after 1740,[110] so it was with guarantee of the Peace of Westphalia. The exercise of the guarantee against Frederick II of Prussia in 1757 during the Seven Years War, was in theory an almost textbook-case implementation.[111] It is the only example of a multilateral execution of the guarantee by *all* guarantors, France, Sweden, the Emperor, and the Empire (its Imperial Estates), against a violator of the public peace. The participation of France in the war against Prussia was justified explicitly on the basis of the

---

[107] Eltz to Bernstorff, Berlin, 28 Jan. 1718: NHStAH, Hann.-92, 2198, fol. 43r.
[108] See Andreas Affolter, '"Freye Republiquen unter frembder Protection"? Die Beziehungen der eidgenössischen Orte zur französischen Krone im 18. Jahrhundert', in Tilman Haug et al. (eds), *Protegierte und Protektoren. Asymmetrische Beziehungen zwischen Partnerschaft und Dominanz* (Cologne/Weimar/Vienna, 2016), 125–38.
[109] Fabrice Brandli, 'Der Zwerg und der Riese. Asymmetrische Beziehungen und justizielle Kooperation zwischen der Republik Genf und Frankreich im 18. Jahrhundert', in ibid., 139–57.
[110] Gabriele Haug-Moritz, *Württembergischer Ständekonflikt und deutscher Dualismus. Ein Beitrag zur Geschichte des Reichverbands in der Mitte des 18. Jahrhunderts* (Stuttgart, 1992).
[111] See Sven Externbrink, 'Frankreich und die Reichsexekution gegen Friedrich II', in Olaf Asbach et al. (eds), *Altes Reich, Frankreich und Europa* (Münster, 2001), 221–53.

guarantee of Westphalia, not the recently concluded Austro-French alliance, and Sweden also emphasised its guarantor status when justifying its intervention.[112] Both claimed to be intervening to protect not only the terms of Westphalia, but also the 'system of the Empire' in general.[113] 'German Liberties' remained as central to French security in the mid-eighteenth-century as they had in the preceding centuries. The French diplomat Louis-Augustin Blondel reiterated in 1751 that 'the Imperial constitution... is the basis of the grandeur of the King [of France] and secures the monarchy along the Rhine'.[114] In 1756 the ruler of the Habsburg Monarchy Maria Theresia formally appealed to the princes and the external guarantors, requesting their intervention and implementation of the guarantee in response to Prussia's pre-emptive attack on Saxony:

> Towards this end [halting Prussian aggression towards Saxony], and in a matter which concerns all powers that desire the preservation of the human societal bond—most of the Christian courts, and especially the crowns France and Sweden, as guarantors and defenders of the Peace of Westphalia—We appeal for assistance against such an unjust assault.[115]

The next year the Reichstag voted to carry out an 'Imperial execution' against Prussia. Sweden, and France then announced that they would join the execution, thereby exercising the guarantee.[116] Of course this was less a purposeful implementation of Imperial and treaty law, than a fortuitous convergence of the law with geopolitical interests.

The Peace of Teschen which ended the Austro-Prussian War of the Bavarian Succession in 1779, was guaranteed by France and Russia.[117] The fact that article 12 of the treaty reaffirmed the Peace of Westphalia technically extended the Westphalian guarantee to the Russian tsarina Catherine II ('the Great'). This was not an uncontested interpretation, however, and some legal expositions were published which cast doubt on whether Russia had become a fully-fledged legal guarantor of the Imperial constitution.[118] The inclusion of the tsarina was broadly reflective of Russia's ascendancy to virtual hegemony in the period after the Seven Years War.[119] This expansion of the guarantee system is indicative of the

---

[112] *Declaration du Roy Tres-Chretien de l'entrée de ses Troupes an Allemagne* (Regensburg, 1757), in *Teutsche Kriegs-Canzley* (Frankfurt, 1757), ii, 189–90; *Erklärung Sr. Königl. Majestät von Schweden* (Regensburg, 1757), in ibid., 190–2.

[113] Tischer, *Kriegsbegründungen*, 141.   [114] Quoted in Simms, *Europe*, 108.

[115] *Beantwortung des, unter dem Titul: Ursachen, welche...Preussen bewogen sich wider die Absichten des Wienerischen Hofes zu setzen, und deren Ausführungen vorzukommen, kund gewordenen Kriegs-Manifests* (Vienna, 1756).

[116] Externbrink, 'Staatensystem'.   [117] Treaty of Teschen, 13 May 1779, in *CTS* 47, 191–6.

[118] Erwin Oberländer, '"Ist die Kaiserin von Rußland Garant des Westphälischen Friedens?" Der Kurfürst von Trier, die Französische Revolution und Katharina II. 1789–1792', *Jahrbücher für Geschichte Osteuropas*, 35 (1987), 218–31.

[119] See H. M. Scott, *The Emergence of the Eastern Powers, 1756–1775* (Cambridge, 2001).

flexibility and responsiveness of this legal structure to shifting power realities, and more fundamentally of the growing ascendancy of power-based geopolitics over juridical factors. Russia had already eclipsed Sweden as the dominant east and north European power seventy years earlier, and now it also assumed the role of a Westphalian guarantor, which Sweden was no longer able to exercise effectively, although it was still formally bestowed with that status until the end of Empire in 1806.[120] However, similar to Louis XIV before her, Catherine II also squandered the considerable opportunities that the guarantee represented, not by naked expansionism, but by failing to intervene as the sponsor of the rights of the smaller princes and defender of the Imperial constitution in the context of the Austro-Prussian great-power dualism, which was eroding traditional Imperial politics. Instead she approached the Empire through the lens of *Realpolitik* by supporting her new ally since 1781, Emperor Joseph II, who had himself lost the confidence of the princes through various unconstitutional policies in Germany.[121]

## English/British Interventions in Central Europe

Apart from the guarantors of Westphalia, England/Britain was the most important power to regularly intervene for the protection of foreign subjects in central Europe after 1648. This occurred under Cromwell's English republic, and then again after the Glorious Revolution in 1688, when the defence of Protestant subjects abroad became seen by Whig parliamentarians and a broad array of commentators as inextricably linked with the security of the Protestant succession and parliamentary liberties at home.[122] The renewed Protestant succession of the Hanoverian Guelph dynasty in 1714—and the consequent creation of a personal union between Britain and the electorate of Hanover—strengthened this trend, turning the Georges' German lands into a psychological and physical launch-pad of intervention for the protection of central European Protestants.[123]

After peace was concluded in the Empire in 1648, the war between France and Spain continued. When Oliver Cromwell emerged victorious in the English civil war in 1651 and later established himself as Lord Protector, England became the

---

[120] Martin Hardstedt, 'The Westphalian Peace Congress. Understanding the consequences from a Swedish perspective', in Dorothée Goetze et al. (eds), *Warum Friedenschliessen so schwer ist. Frühneuzeitliche Friedensfindung am Beispiel des Westfälischen Friedenskongresses* (Münster, 2019), 65–73.
[121] Karl Otmar von Aretin, 'Russia as a guarantor power of the Imperial Constitution under Catherine II', *JMH* 58 (1986), 141–60.
[122] Tony Claydon, *William III and the Godly Revolution* (Cambridge, 1996); Brendan Simms, *Britain's Europe. A Thousand Years of Conflict and Cooperation* (London, 2016), 40–50.
[123] Brendan Simms et al. (eds), *The Hanoverian Dimension in British History, 1714–1837* (Cambridge, 2007).

most sought-after ally for both the French and the Spanish, who both recognised that they needed a strong ally to achieve victory and that Cromwell could determine the balance between them. Intent upon a staunchly Protestant foreign policy, he saw the Habsburgs, especially Spain, as the greatest threat to the Protestant interest, and by 1654 it was clear that Cromwell was on a path towards confronting Spain and was conducting serious negotiations with the French in 1655 for the conclusion of an Anglo-French alliance and an English entry into the war.[124] Then, in April 1655, the duke of Savoy—whose lands were a fief of the Empire—had scores of his Protestant Vaudois subjects living in Alpine mountain valleys driven from their homes, during which about 300 were killed.[125] This led to a large pro-intervention publicity campaign among Protestant authors and pamphleteers across Europe.[126]

Cognisant of the fact that Mazarin needed Cromwell's support against Spain more than vice versa, Cromwell used France's close ties with the duke of Savoy as an opportunity to extract a concession: the conclusion of the alliance would depend on Louis XIV pressurising the duke to restore the rights of the Vaudois. Beyond this indirect diplomatic intervention, Cromwell also sent embassies to the duke via Paris, had money raised to assist the Vaudois refugees, and even authorised naval action against Savoy as a potential measure of last resort. All these efforts came to fruition when the duke relented by restoring most of the Vaudois' rights at the treaty of Pinerolo in August 1655.[127] There is no reason to doubt Cromwell's personal attachment to the cause of 'poor Protestants of the Piedmont'.[128] By extracting the concession of French diplomatic intercessions on their behalf, though, Cromwell was hardly damaging his geopolitical interests, because Mazarin was desperate for the English alliance anyway. Yet Cromwell was also serious about defeating Spain—indeed his entry into the war partly decided its outcome. But by simultaneously confronting Savoy, he was damaging the chances of a potential alliance with its duke, and was thereby, in the words of one of his diplomats 'laying aside all other Reasons of State'.[129] This was because the duke's lands lay in the vicinity of the Spanish Road and whose assistance could contribute to blocking Spanish supplies reaching the theatre of war in the Low Countries.[130]

---

[124] Heinz Schilling, *Konfessionalisierung und Staatsinteressen. Internationale Beziehungen 1559-1660* (Paderborn, 2007), 554-5; Klaus Malettke, *Hegemonie - multipolares System - Gleichgewicht. Internationale Beziehungen 1648/1659-1713/1714* (Paderborn, 2012), 276-87.

[125] Gabriel Audisio, *Die Waldenser* (Munich, 1996).

[126] Christine Vogel, '"Piemontesische Ostern": Mediale Inszenierung des Waldenser-Massakers von 1655', in Vogel, *Bilder des Schreckens* (Frankfurt, 2006), 74-92.

[127] D.J.B. Trim, '"If a prince use tyrannie towards his people": interventions on behalf of foreign populations in early modern Europe', in Simms et al. (eds), *Humanitarian Intervention. A History* (Cambridge, 2011), 29-66, at 53-64.

[128] Quoted in ibid., 64. [129] Quoted in ibid., 62. [130] Simms, *Britain's Europe*, 41.

English interventionism in defence of European Protestants was paused during the restoration of the Catholic Stuarts (1660-88), but became a prominent theme again after the Glorious Revolution, not least among pamphleteers, historians and other writers of the public sphere, and Whig parliamentarians.[131] During this period, the emerging English 'fiscal-military state' was mainly geared towards sustaining an interventionist foreign policy.[132] William III—whose co-rule as king together with his wife Queen Mary II was itself a product of his own intervention as Dutch Stadholder ostensibly for the protection of Protestant liberties in England—now reversed the direction of intervention towards the continent for the protection of the same Protestant liberties in Europe. This was not accomplished by the kind of targeted intervention for the protection of small groups of foreign Protestant inhabitants that Cromwell had carried out against the duke of Savoy, for example. Instead, William III pursued a broad-based confrontation of Louis XIV to forestall the threats to the interlinked liberties of European and English Protestantism arising from aspirant French universal monarchy.[133]

William III tried to present England as the chief protector of Protestants all over Europe after 1688. Queen Anne, who was also linked by marriage to a Protestant European dynasty, continued this approach during the War of the Spanish Succession, when the Camisard Huguenots received some assistance from London. After Britain became directly linked to the content with the Hanoverian personal union in 1714, this pro-Protestant interventionist tendency increased yet further.[134] During the British diplomatic interventions in Germany and Poland during the early eighteenth century under George I, several British diplomats considered the possibility of somehow acquiring the status of an additional guarantor of the Peace of Westphalia, just as they already possessed the guarantee of the treaties of Pinerolo and Oliva, which secured Protestant rights in parts of Savoy and Poland, respectively.[135] This would have made Britain the legal guarantor of Protestant rights across a huge stretch of central Europe. Such a legally-backed position was deemed to be particularly important in the juridified political culture of central Europe which would have lent British intervention greater weight. In any case, continental Protestants in central Europe and beyond looked to England/Britain as the most promising external protector, a role that they no longer ascribed to France after the advent of Louis XIV's aggression and after the Glorious Revolution made an interventionist pro-Protestant English

---

[131] Mühling, *Religionskrieg*, 436–44; Andrew C. Thompson, *Britain, Hanover and the Protestant Interest, 1688–1756* (Woodbridge, 2006), 1–61.

[132] John Brewer, *The Sinews of Power. War, Money, and the English state, 1688–1783* (London, 1989).

[133] Christoph Kampmann, 'The English Crisis, Emperor Leopold and the origins of the Dutch intervention in 1688', *HJ* 55 (2012), 521–32.

[134] Thompson, *Britain, Hanover and the Protestant Interest*.

[135] Stanhope to Whitworth, Göhrde, 27 Oct 1719: BL, Add. MSS. 37,376, fols 163–8r, at fol. 164v. See also, Thompson, *Interest*, 74, 92, 96.

foreign policy a reality. At the same time, the other traditional foreign protectors of central European Protestants, Sweden and Denmark, were increasingly losing power-political clout while also being tied closer to the Emperor.[136] Brandenburg-Prussia at times cooperated with Britain-Hanover in challenging both Saxon leadership of the *Corpus Evangelicorum* and the Emperor's judicial and adjudicating authority in confessional matters. But the Prussian king Frederick William I also competed with his father- and brother-in-law, the king-electors George I and II, for the informal role as chief protector of central European Protestant subjects, not least to improve his standing in the Empire and Europe.[137]

Britain remained guided by the 'bigger picture' when protecting Protestantism.[138] The greatest threat to British security and to the closely interlinked Protestant liberties in Britain and on the continent was believed to come from the prospect of Catholic universal monarchy.[139] This was to be countered by Britain's active maintenance of the balance of power, through continental engagement.[140] The perceived hegemonic threat to the balance of power emanated from either the Habsburgs or the French Bourbons depending on the geopolitical constellations and the balance of power. During the 1720s, the Emperor Charles VI was believed to pose such a threat and he was therefore confronted in alliance with France. Cross-confessional anti-Catholic hegemonic alliances were moreover useful in parrying the accusation that one was conducting a religious war, which was anathema to most Europeans.[141]

This 1720s anti-Habsburg policy also helps to explain why Britain intervened so energetically in defence of Protestant rights in Germany and Poland: these endeavours also harmed the Emperor geopolitically. This does not mean, however, that George I was using the deprivation of the rights of his fellow-German co-religionists as a mere pretext for geopolitical goals. During an Empire-wide confessional crisis in late-1719 to early-1720, he sent a special envoy to the main alleged offender, the elector-Palatine, and instructed him to address the 'Violences and Severities which of late have been committed... against [the elector-Palatine's] Protestant Subjects... As the Tranquillity of Germany is herein so essentially concerned'.[142] The British envoy became convinced that a military intervention

---

[136] Mühling, *Religionskrieg*, 433–45.
[137] Renate Wieland, *Protestantischer König im Heiligen Reich. Brandenburg-preußische Reichs- und Konfessionspolitik im frühen 18. Jahrhundert* (Berlin, 2020).
[138] Brendan Simms, '"Minister of Europe": British strategic culture, 1714–1760', in Hamish Scott et al. (eds), *Cultures of Power in Europe during the Long Eighteenth-Century* (Cambridge, 2007), 110–32.
[139] Steven C.A. Pincus, *Protestantism and Patriotism. Ideologies and the Making of English Foreign Policy, 1650–1668* (Cambridge, 1996).
[140] Michael Sheehan, 'The sincerity of the British commitment to the maintenance of the balance of power, 1714–1763' *Diplomacy and Statecraft*, 15 (2004), 489–506.
[141] Mühling, *Religionskrieg*, 444–5.
[142] George I to Haldane, Herrenhausen, 22 Sep. 1719: NA, SP 44/269B.

might be necessary to counter the 'Tiranny of the Elector's Proceedings'.[143] He argued that

> the safety of all the Protestants; especially near the Rhein will depend on... that the King in conjunction with other Protestant Powers, sent Troops into the Palatinate, without any other View but to relieve the oppressed & prevent a warr; [...] all the little neighbouring Princes who follow the Elector's Example in persecuting their Protestant Subjects; would without delay submit, & put everything on the footing it ought to be.[144]

George I agreed privately that 'we cannot abandon our religious relatives in the face of such hard persecution and oppression'.[145] While intense diplomatic pressure contributed to the Emperor ordering the alleged Catholic offenders to back down, a more aggressive intervention would risk deterring the Emperor's potential participation in an anti-Russian alignment which was of greater geopolitical importance at this time than containing the Emperor's authority within the Empire.[146]

A similar geopolitical contingency determined the British course of action during the crisis surrounding the judicial killing of several Protestant townspeople in Thorn, Poland by Catholic authorities in 1724–25. At the outset of the crisis Britain intervened diplomatically and tried to encourage other neighbouring powers (chiefly Brandenburg-Prussia and Russia) to intervene militarily. George I ordered the British representative at the Reichstag to travel as a special envoy to the King of Poland in order to seek redress for the Protestants. Before his departure, the envoy gave a speech to the Protestants at the Reichstag, arguing that such cases of religious persecution, far from being of purely local relevance, had repercussions for 'the peace and tranquillity of Europe'. On a personal level, George I could not tolerate 'the death, so tragic as it is unjust, of so many innocents'. His conduct was said to be dictated by 'his conscience, by his honour, by his sentiments of humanity'.[147] Matching these sentiments, pamphlets appeared in the public sphere in Britain which argued that intervention was necessary, and that it could be justified as a defensive measure, because rulers had 'lying upon them the Care of human society', and because Protestants were 'one body or Society, united for mutual defence... whose interest is to preserve entire all its Parts, and make reprisals upon all Aggressors'.[148] During the crisis,

---

[143] Haldane to Craggs, Frankfurt a. M., 10 Oct. 1719: NA, SP 81/120.
[144] Haldane to Stanhope, Heidelberg, 14 Jan. 1720: NA, SP 81/121.
[145] Quoted in Thompson, *Britain, Hanover and the Protestant Interest*, 72.
[146] See Milton, 'German confessional crisis'.
[147] 'Discours de Monsieur Finch... aux Ministres Evangeliques, qui ont ete chez luy', 7 Feb. 1725, NHStAH, Hann. 91, Jahns 8, fol. 77–80.
[148] Quoted in Thompson, 'The Protestant interest and humanitarian intervention', 84.

the geopolitical situation suddenly shifted with the unexpected conclusion of a Spanish-Austrian alliance in the Spring of 1725 which the Franco-British entente (an unusual alliance of 1716–1731) viewed as a severe threat to the balance of power. In this context, any step which might strengthen the Austro-Spanish bloc was to be avoided. This included hostile intervention against the Poles, which 'may oblige them to fling themselves into the Emperor's hands for protection, or...give them a handle to overrun & extirpate the Protestants'.[149] Geopolitical imperatives thus dictated that plans for intervention in Poland be shelved.[150]

With the conclusion of the Austro-British alliance in 1731 and the return of France as the perceived greatest hegemonic threat, new geopolitical currents determined new approaches to protective intervention yet again. Interventions for Protestant rights in central Europe would have to be downgraded or stood down completely if they were perceived as potentially harming the new relationship with Austria. Thus, the mass expulsion in 1731 of the Protestant subjects of the prince-archbishop of Salzburg, who was closely allied with the Emperor—technically not in violation of the Peace of Westphalia—did not elicit the same kind of British intervention that the German confessional crisis of 1719/1720 had. George II and his ministers inherently sympathised with the broad-based publicity campaign which advocated the protection of the Salzburgers. Yet in their thinking, more Protestants were ultimately at risk across Europe if the Emperor's planned succession arrangements failed and France were therefore not properly contained, than were at risk by the archbishop of Salzburg's unsavoury policies.[151]

This general approach notwithstanding, isolated interventions for the protection of foreign subjects which ran counter to Britain's broader geopolitical aims did occur. Ninety years after the Cromwellian intervention for the protection of the Waldensians, George II carried out a diplomatic intervention which similarly did little to further Britain's immediate strategic aims. Despite being allied with Maria Theresia of Austria against France during the War of the Austrian Succession (1740–48), Britain intervened diplomatically[152] on behalf of the Jews who had been expelled from Prague in 1744 after being accused of conspiring with Austria's Prussian enemy.[153] This intervention—again backed by a publicity campaign—ultimately succeeded in securing the return of the Prague Jews.[154]

---

[149] Newcastle to H Walpole, Whitehall, 16 Mar. 1725, BL, Add. MSS. 32742, fols 456r–8v.

[150] Patrick Milton, 'Debates on intervention against religious persecution in the Polish-Lithuanian Commonwealth: European reactions to the Tumult of Thorn, 1724–1726', *EHQ* 47/3 (2017), 405–36.

[151] Thompson, *Protestant Interest*, 152–67; Simms, *Three Victories*, 220; Mack Walker, *The Salzburg transaction. Expulsion and Redemption in Eighteenth-Century Germany* (Ithaca, 1992).

[152] Johann Krengel, 'Die englische Intervention zu Gunsten der böhmischen Juden im Jahre 1744', *Monatsschrift für Geschichte und Wissenschaft des Judentums*, 44 (1900), 269–81.

[153] Barbara Stollberg-Rilinger, *Maria Theresia. Die Kaiserin in ihrer Zeit* (Munich, 2017), 634–44.

[154] Baruch Mevorach, 'Die Interventionsbestrebungen in Europa zur Verhinderung der Vertreibung der Juden aus Böhmen und Mähren, 1744–1745', *Jahrbuch des Instituts für deutsche Geschichte*, 9 (1980), 15–81.

## Conclusion

At the congress of Westphalia, the constitution of the Empire was renegotiated by its constituent parts (Emperor and princes) and the powers that had intervened in it during the preceding Thirty Years War. By including a broad range of subjects' rights in the treaty and placing the whole settlement under mutual guarantee, the Peace of Westphalia legalised France and Sweden's intervention in the Empire for the protection of the defined rights of its subjects and of the Imperial constitution in general. Intervention into the Empire—which had already had a long tradition and was already mainly legitimised on the grounds of legality—now became 'juridified' to a much greater degree.

This new development in international and constitutional law furnished legal thinkers with much food for thought. Among writers of the natural law tradition, there was a distinct ambivalence towards the guarantee and foreign intervention in the Empire in general, especially on the part of seventeenth-century and early-eighteenth-century scholars. The experience of the Thirty Years War had undoubtedly been traumatic, and the foreign interventions had greatly exacerbated the suffering and prolonged the war. However, such writers portrayed the risk of Habsburg monarchical hegemony over the Empire as a threat, and the confessional and princely liberties which were threatened by it could be defended only through foreign assistance. The resulting guarantee legalised this external protection of confessional and political rights, and thereby 'codified' foreign involvement in the Imperial constitution. Yet this state of affairs was at times seen as deleterious in practice, especially due to French abuse under Louis XIV, and some theorists also saw it as damaging in theory, arguing that it weakened the unity of the Empire.

Taking a longer-term perspective, it can plausibly be argued that by placing the confessional rights of religious groups under international guarantee, the Peace of Westphalia and its guarantee clauses helped to establish the principle of internationally guaranteed minority rights, potentially enforceable through intervention, as a part of the positive law of nations/international law.[155] This, together with the experience over many years of peaceful, legally regulated and guaranteed confessional co-existence within the Empire, arguably contributed to the gradual emergence of the philosophical conviction of confessional toleration as a desirable principle within states,[156] and minority rights protection as a principle in the law of nations, as based on natural law.

Very soon after its conclusion, the Peace of Westphalia and its guarantee established itself as the primary legitimating factor, guiding principle and

---

[155] Heinhard Steiger, 'Der Westfälische Frieden – Grundgesetz für Europa?,' in *Der Westfälische Friede*, ed. Heinz Duchhardt, 33–80 at 78.
[156] Christoph Kampmann: 'Der Festgeschnürte Frieden', *P.M. History*, May 2017.

constitutional reference point among all statesmen in the Reich: more evidence—if any more were needed—against the old claims of the stasis and immutability of the Imperial constitution. Actors' assessments of the guarantee, and intervention in general, were largely determined by how it affected the geopolitical position and interests of those that were commenting on it. During the 1650s–60s, there was a widespread desire for peace among the Imperial Estates after the experience of the Thirty Years War. France was perceived as the guarantor of peace and its interventions in the Empire were welcomed at this stage. This changed drastically during Louis XIV's aggression and conquest march against the Empire, under whose impression the guarantee and foreign intervention in general suffered a reputational breakdown.

However, in parallel to these developments, from the later seventeenth-century, there was a resurgence of desired protective intervention by the Empire's Protestants. This was related to a series of setbacks: the cancellation of toleration of French and Savoyard Protestants in 1685, the accession of a Catholic line in the Palatinate and the conversion of the king of England to Catholicism in the same year, and that of the elector of Saxony in 1697. That same year, the Peace of Ryswick upended Westphalian stipulations for the Palatinate to the detriment of Protestant rights. This created a growing sense of cross-border cohesion among Protestants, and a belief in international Protestant solidarity in West-Central Europe which mirrored that of the later sixteenth to early seventeenth centuries. With Sweden in decline and allied to the Emperor (except during a brief spectacular revival of its pro-Protestant interventionism in Silesia in 1707) and France under Louis XIV seen as a threat to the Protestant interest, the mantle of international Protestant protective intervention fell to England after 1688. For the new Protestant regime of England after the Glorious Revolution, one of the main founding principles and legitimating acts was intervention for the protection of foreign Protestant subjects, a policy it pursued well into the eighteenth century with a focus on central Europe.

After the end of the Spanish Succession war, France pursued a more pacific and passive policy until the 1730s and this coincided with a revival of the perceived usefulness and desirability of its potential policing and supervisory interventions in the Empire, largely as a check on overweening Habsburg power. During this period, British interventionism also persisted and there was a degree of 'protection competition' among the Emperor, France, and Britain with regard to the immediate and mediate subjects of the Empire—as was often a phenomenon surrounding protective intervention throughout the early modern period.

From the perspective of the intervening powers, intervention for the protection of foreign subjects in central Europe was usually a function of their perceived geopolitical interests as it had been prior to 1648: it served as an offensive tool against the target of the intervention, but also as a mechanism to maintain the existing constitutional balance and rights in the Empire upon which the interveners' security depended. Both before and after 1648, the great powers in Germany's vicinity tried to serve as protector of numerous clients within the Empire, in part so that these could serve as a network of dependent allies. Thus the 'protection competition' which we identified in the last chapter continued in the post-1648 period, when the Emperor's role as protector of oppressed estates and subjects continued to be challenged—or usurped—by other powers such as England/Britain, Prussia, Sweden, and Denmark. Often the geopolitical and ideological components of intervention were largely inseparable, particularly in Britain, whose post-1688 'strategic culture' was infused with the necessity of defending Protestantism abroad and at home. On occasion, though, interventions occurred which did not seem to be motived by geopolitical or strategic gain at all, but were rather pursued opportunistically and for moral-ideological reasons. Examples thereof include the English/British interventions in Savoy (1655) and Bohemia (1744/45), and the Swedish intervention in Silesia (1707). Such instances were rare, though.

The Peace of Westphalia increased *interventionism* in early modern Europe. This does not necessarily refer to the incidence of interventions (this seems to have remained relatively constant before and after 1648), but more importantly to its normative acceptance and the readiness with which it was discussed as a possible policy to be pursued or requested. The guarantee of Westphalia was crucial in this regard, while other treaty guarantees which bestowed rights of intervention soon followed that example (Pinerolo, 1655; Oliva, 1660; Swiss treaties in the 1710s–30s; Kuchuk-Kainarji, 1774). The value of the guarantee in facilitating interventions can be seen by attempts of other powers (Britain in 1719/20, Russia in the 1770s) to secure a guarantor status to be better placed to legitimate them.

# PART TWO
# INTERVENTION AS JUDICIAL EXECUTION WITHIN THE HOLY ROMAN EMPIRE

# 5
# Interventions in Defence of Mediate Subjects
## The Smallest Territories, c.1500–1780

Having examined the nature and contours of the mainly 'international' European interventions ostensibly for the protection of other rulers' subjects, we now zoom in onto Germany to consider interventions within the Empire, carried out as judicial executions. The legal-constitutional foundations pertaining to the judicial-feudal and political role of the Emperor, the Imperial judiciary, and subjects' corporate and individual rights that were detailed in Chapter 1, provided for numerous kinds of interventions, as mentioned. This chapter will outline some of the cases of regular judicial interventions, carried out mainly in the smallest and small territories of the Reich under the Emperor's authority, that were aimed at protecting Imperial Estates' subjects against their rulers, before analysing the cases of Nassau-Siegen and Mecklenburg-Schwerin in detail in the following chapters.

To avoid falling into the trap of being seduced by an excessively romanticised, rosy-tinted view of the old Empire as an unconditional protector of the liberties of the weak, one should bear in mind that, although there was indeed a basic tendency to protect subjects against illegal and violent acts, whether it would be implemented through actual interventions and if so, how forcefully, could be affected by political and strategic conditions and considerations. On the one hand, performing his protective function improved the standing of the Emperor in the Empire and therefore furthered his political interests. On the other hand, forceful interventions—inherently risky even within the judicial framework of the Empire—would need to match with pressing (geo-)political and dynastic concerns, which in turn could also inhibit protective intervention. On rare occasions, Imperial ministers were willing to consider offering more power-politically capable accused parties deals in which disadvantageous Reichshofrat verdicts would be cancelled in return for geopolitical 'equivalents'—territorial or financial. This option was secretly discussed at Vienna during the crisis over Hessen-Kassel's mandated return of the Rheinfels fortress in 1717, for example.[1] Even when geopolitical inhibitions were not present, the Reichshofrat aimed more at

---

[1] Privy Conference meeting notes, 14 Jan. 1717 and 25 Feb. 1717: HHStA, RK, Kl. Reichsstände 176.

mediating in conflicts rather than coming down definitively on one side.[2] Non-conclusive decisions permitted greater freedom of manoeuvre in their execution.[3] A reason for the increased level of legal recourse to the Reichshofrat, rather than the Reichskammergericht after 1648, might have been the necessity of the smaller territories to achieve protection against more powerful ones, which was more likely to be furnished by the Reichshofrat.[4] The kind of interventions that are examined here were far from the Reichshofrat's preferred outcome of cases; ideally the conflicting parties would reach an amicable accommodation mediated by the Reichshofrat before forceful implementation became necessary.[5]

The Reichshofrat was not only a supreme judicial tribunal which presented its recommendations to the Emperor based on considerations of law and justness, but it was also still formally a political advisory body for the Emperor. Although the privy-council and the privy-conference increasingly overshadowed the Reichshofrat in this capacity, its members still sometimes allowed assumptions of political interests to colour their judicial rulings, reflecting its nature as a 'combined judicial and governmental body'.[6] In consideration of the close dynastic and political ties between the German and Spanish branches of the Habsburg dynasty, the Reichshofrat was reluctant to issue anti-Spanish rulings in the 1590s for example, when Spanish forces encroached upon Reich territories in Westphalia and committed violence against the local population which in turn appealed to the Reichshofrat for judicial protection measures.[7] Of course the degree of judicial independence differed from case to case and over time, and between the Reichshofrat and the Reichskammergericht.[8] However, it would be remiss to claim that it was ever completely instrumentalised for Austrian great power interests.[9] Furthermore, one should remember that the Imperial judiciary also frequently supported the claims of rulers against their subjects. In the early eighteenth-century, for example, the Reichshofrat supported the claims of the

---

[2] Ulrich Rasche, 'Urteil versus Vergleich? Entscheidungspraxis und Konfliktregulierung des Reichshofrats im 17.Jahrhundert im Spiegel neuerer Aktenerschließung', in Albrecht Cordes (ed.), *Mit Freundschaft oder mit Recht? Inner- und außergerichtliche Alternativen zur kontroversen Streitentscheidung* (Cologne, 2015), 199–232.

[3] Wolfgang Sellert, *Prozessgrundsätze und Stilus Curiae am Reichshofrat im Vergleich zu den gesetzlichen Grundlagen des reichskammergerichtlichen Verfahrens* (Aalen, 1973), 341–2, 369.

[4] Milton, 'Imperial law versus geopolitical interest'.

[5] Eva Ortlieb, 'The Holy Roman Empire: the Imperial Courts' system and the Reichshofrat', in A. A. Wijffels et al. (eds), *European Supreme Courts. A Portrait through History* (London, 2013), 86–95.

[6] Ulrich Eisenhardt, 'Der Reichshofrat als kombiniertes Rechtsprechungs- und Regierungsorgan', in Jost Hausmann et al. (eds), *Zur Erhaltung guter Ordnung. Beiträge zur Geschichte von Recht und Justiz* (Cologne, 2000), 245–67.

[7] Johannes Arndt, *Das Heilige Römische Reich und die Niederlande 1566-1648. Politisch-konfessionelle Verflechtung und Publizistik im achtzigjährigen Krieg* (Cologne, 1998), 178–85.

[8] Wolfgang Sellert, 'Richterliche Unabhängigkeit am Reichskammergericht und am Reichshofrat', in Okko Behrends et al. (eds), *Gerechtigkeit und Geschichte* (Göttingen, 1996), 118–32.

[9] Thus: Friedrich von Oppeln-Bronikowski, *Der Baumeister des preußischen Staates. Leben und Wirken Friedrich Wilhelms I* (Jena, 1934), 11.

prince of East Frisia against his territorial estates.[10] Around the same time, the Reichshofrat backed the prince-bishop of Basel and the count of Hanau-Lichtenburg against the refractoriness of their subjects.[11] The court also on occasion mandated interventions for the protection of the rights of the Imperial Estates vis-à-vis their subjects, especially during rebellions.[12] One historian has pointed out that the Reichshofrat was neither dogmatically pro-estates/subjects, nor pro-rulers in principle, but that it assessed the justice and legality of each position on a case-by-case basis.[13]

One reason why the role of the Imperial judiciary and the Emperor as supervisory instances of princely conduct was so pronounced, and correspondingly why interventions were more frequent, in the smallest and the small territories of the Empire, was that these often had no intermediary instance of noble landowning estates. Instead the prince himself was the biggest landowner which greatly increased the likelihood of disputes between the ruler and peasants, mainly about taxation and foraging rights, along with the possible involvement of the Imperial authorities to whom the peasants might appeal. In the medium-sized and larger territories by contrast, aggrieved peasants would appeal to the prince against mistreatment by noble seigniorial lords in the first instance. Of course, conflicts between noble territorial estates and the princes were also frequent and could also lead to appeals to the Emperor; moreover, these had a greater chance of success because the noble estates were more organised and had greater resources at their disposal than peasants.[14] Another reason was that smaller territories did not possess many well-developed channels of judicial appeal of their own, which subjects could resort to when they had complaints. Faced with the lack of territorial courts of appeal at which they could hope to challenge the measures of the government, the Imperial courts were often the only option. Subjects' and rulers' economic distress after the Thirty Years War and again from the late seventeenth century until the early eighteenth century exacerbated tensions over taxation between princes and subjects, further contributing to appeals to the Imperial courts.[15]

The most important reason for the prevalence of Imperial interventions in smaller territories, though, was the simple fact that in cases in which the courts

---

[10] See Michael Hughes, *Law and Politics in 18th Century Germany* (Woodbridge, 1988), 67–74, 123–55.

[11] Andreas Würgler, *Unruhen und Öffentlichkeit. Städtische und ländliche Protestbewegungen im 18. Jahrhundert* (Tübingen, 1995), 70–8.

[12] E.g., Paul Nève, *Die Lütticher Revolution von 1789 vor dem Reichskammergericht* (Wetzlar, 1990).

[13] Leopold Auer, 'The role of the Imperial Aulic Council in the constitutional structure of the Holy Roman Empire', in R.J.W. Evans et al. (eds), *The Holy Roman Empire 1495–1806* (Oxford, 2011), 63–75, at 72.

[14] Winfried Schulze, *Bäuerlicher Widerstand und feudale Herrschaft in der frühen Neuzeit* (Stuttgart, 1980), 62–5.

[15] Thus: Siegrid Westphal, *Kaiserliche Rechtsprechung und herrschaftliche Stabilisierung. Reichsgerichtsbarkeit in den thüringischen Territorialstaaten 1648–1806* (Cologne, 2002), 74.

decided against larger princes, the Emperor and the commissioned interveners did not dare to execute the decisions by force. Powerful Imperial Estates such as the electors, later kings, of Brandenburg (Prussia), for example, could afford to ignore disadvantageous ruling in favour of their subjects, with impunity. Judicial executions against powerful princes *could* be executed, but this usually occurred in the context of a war that was being waged against them anyway, such as during the Thirty Years War or the Imperial execution against Frederick the Great during the Seven Years War. During peacetime, such intervention mandates would have slim chance of being executed. The Reichshofrat's mandates against king Frederick-William I of Brandenburg-Prussia during the 1720s were a case in point. On 5 January 1717 the king issued an edict which announced the unilateral transformation some of his lands which he ruled in his capacity as duke of Magdeburg, to allodial property under full ownership of the Prussian state.[16] The noble estates of Magdeburg complained about this measure to Vienna because they were now obliged to pay direct taxes.[17] As the highest feudal court of the Empire, what particularly worried the Reichshofrat, though, was that this attempted 'absolutist' streamlining of Brandenburg-Prussian administration undermined the feudal nexus and presented a threat to the hierarchical nature of the Imperial legal framework. What was perhaps equally alarming to the Reichshofrat and the Imperial authorities, however, was the concomitant prohibition of subjects—particularly the noble territorial estates—in the designated regions, from appealing to the supreme judicial tribunals of the Empire.

The Reichshofrat sent a report on the matter to the Emperor, which blended legalistic reasoning relating to feudal law with a general political assessment of the dangers posed by Brandenburg to the Imperial system and its mechanisms of protection. It recommended that a commission be appointed to investigate, but acknowledged that this had almost no chance of being implemented in practice.[18] Indeed, the king failed to comply with the Emperor's mandate instructing him to reverse the measures in February 1718. He was not intimidated by the appointment of the electors of Saxony, Trier, and the Palatinate, and the king of Sweden (as duke of Pomerania) to the commission charged with executing the judicial decision, and stated that he would rather risk war than comply with the instructions. While the Emperor's mandates did have the effect of somewhat moderating the king's stance in negotiations with his own estates—indicating the continued limitations on 'absolutism' that feudal arrangements exerted in the

---

[16] Tobias Schenk, 'Reichsjustiz im Spannungsverhältnis von oberstrichterlichem Amt und österreichischen Hausmachtinteressen. Der Reichshofrat und der Konflikt um die Allodifikation der Lehen in Brandenburg-Preußen', in Anja Amend-Traut et al. (eds), *Geld, Handel, Wirtschaft. Höchste Gerichte im Alten Reich als Spruchkörper und Institution* (Berlin, 2012), 103–219.

[17] The complaints were forwarded by the Imperial envoy at Braunschweig, Metsch to Emperor Charles VI, Braunschweig, 23 Apr. 1717: HHStA, RK-Dipl. Akten, Braunschweig-Hannover, Berichte 2c, fol. 136r.

[18] RHR-report, 27 Oct. 1717, HHStA, RHR, Vota 7(2).

eighteenth-century—the matter was dropped once the Emperor and Brandenburg-Prussia underwent a geopolitical rapprochement in 1726/28.[19]

In smaller territories, by contrast, the Reichshofrat had a better chance of acting against the illegal attempts by territorial governments to curtail their subjects' appeals against them to the Emperor. The Reichshofrat could proceed more actively in such cases, even when no appeals to it had taken place owing to its added function as an advisory council to the Emperor. From 1495 to 1555 the Reichshofrat contributed to the consolidation of the new instrument of the appeal (*Appellation*). By issuing letters of safe-conduct, the Reichshofrat secured the process of appeal, and contributed generally to the rule of law and due process. By the eighteenth century it was supervising, controlling, and censuring princes on a massive scale if they attempted to curtail appellations.[20] Interventions for the protection of the Emperor's mediate subjects had much greater chances of success in the territories that had less, or no military clout. Interventions—legitimised primarily by the office of the Emperor as overlord, usually carried out by ad hoc Imperial commissions, and not infrequently resulting in a forcefully imposed external administration by the intervening commission—occurred disproportionately often in Imperial cities and small counties and principalities which lacked military forces or powerful allies. Intervening commissions dispatched by the Reichshofrat and the Reichskammergericht were usually charged with carrying out investigations on the ground, reporting back, and mediating between the conflicting parties, but also with protecting certain groups of subjects that were at risk of victimisation by being authorised to intervene militarily. Protected subjects included high-status individuals or groups such as nobles, territorial estates, and other corporate entities such as territorial towns, or subjects such as peasants, women, people accused of witchcraft, and Jews.[21] Individuals, such as ordinary artisans or farmers, could also bring cases against their rulers and receive varying degrees of legal protection.[22] Councillors and other office-holders in

---

[19] Schenk, 'Reichsjustiz im Spannungsverhältnis', 206–9.
[20] See Jürgen Weitzel, 'Der Reichshofrat und das irreguläre Beschneiden des Rechtsmittels der Appellation', in Leopold Auer et al. (eds), *Appellation und Revision im Europa des Spätmittelalters und der Frühen Neuzeit* (Vienna, 2013), 163–74.
[21] E.g., Bernhard Diestelkamp, *Ein Kampf um Freiheit und Recht. Die prozessualen Auseinandersetzungen der Gemeinde Freienseenmit den Grafen zu Solms-Laubach* (Cologne, 2012); Matthias Bähr, *Die Sprache der Zeugen. Argumentationsstrategien bäuerlicher Gemeinden vor dem Reichskammergericht (1693–1806)* (Constance, 2012); Siegrid Westphal (ed.), *In eigener Sache. Frauen vor den höchsten Gerichten des Alten Reiches* (Cologne, 2005); Wolfgang Sellert et al., 'Hexen- und Strafprozesse am Reichskammergericht', in Ingrid Scheurmann (ed.), *Frieden durch Recht. Das Reichskammergericht von 1495 bis 1806* (Mainz, 1994), 328–35; Ronnie Po-chia Hsia, 'The Jews and the Emperors', in Charles Ingrao (ed.), *State and Society in Early Modern Austria* (West Lafayette, 1994), 71–80.
[22] E.g., Johannes Arndt, *Der Fall 'Meier Cordt contra Graf zu Lippe'. Ein Untertanenprozeß vor den Territorial- und Reichsgerichten zwischen 1680 und 1720* (Wetzlar, 1997).

territorial governments could receive protection by the high courts against unfair treatment by their princes.[23]

These interventions for the protection of their subjects could entail the formal deposition of the prince or his de facto deposition through a suspension from power. However, many, if not most, depositions of Imperial princes occurred as punishment for rebellion against the Emperor and treason against the Empire during times of war. Numerous princes were deposed for this reason during the Thirty Years War as we have seen, including the elector-Palatine (1623), the dukes of Mecklenburg (1628), and numerous smaller princes and counts, such as the count of Ysenburg in 1635. Similar depositions occurred again during the War of the Spanish Succession, when the Wittelsbach electors of Bavaria and Cologne were deposed in 1706 for allying with the Imperial enemy France, as were some princes in Imperial Italy, including the dukes of Mantua and Mirandula in 1708-09.[24] Yet, princes could also be deposed partly or mainly as a result of alleged tyranny against their own subjects.[25] Despite the enshrinement of their prerogatives at the Peace of Westphalia, most of these interventions against ruling princes occurred *after* 1648, which was therefore not a caesura in terms of making interventions in the 'internal affairs' of princes less feasible.[26]

## Interventions in Imperial Cities

Imperial cities were particularly susceptible to interventions by the Emperor— often against the wishes of its ruling city councils—because the Emperor was their overlord (*Stadtherr*), which provided him with opportunities re-arrange their civic constitutions as a result of cases at the highest Imperial judicial tribunals.[27] Many of these cases attracted considerable media attention.[28] It has been calculated that between 1648 and 1806, 44 of the 51 Imperial cities witnessed lawsuits at the

---

[23] Eva Ortlieb, 'Rechtssicherheit für Amtsträger gegen fürstliche Willkür? Die Funktion der Reichsgerichte', in Christoph Kampmann et al. (eds), *Sicherheit in der Frühen Neuzeit. Norm - Praxis - Repräsentation* (Cologne, 2013), 622-37.

[24] RHR-resolution, 4 Dec. 1709: HHStA, RHR, Prot. xviii, 18, fols 329v-30r.

[25] See Werner Troßbach, 'Power and Good Governance: The Removal of Ruling Princes in the Holy Roman Empire, 1680-1794', in J.P. Coy et al. (eds), *The Holy Roman Empire, Reconsidered* (New York, 2010), 191-209; Fabian Frommelt (ed.), *Zwangsadministrationen. Legitimierte Fremdverwaltung im historischen Vergleich* (Berlin, 2014).

[26] A chronological listing of interventions confirms this: Bernd Marquardt, 'Zur Reichsgerichtlichen Aberkennung der Herrschergewalt', at 85-9. The same point is made by Leopold Auer, 'Zwangsverwaltungen in den Territorien des Alten Reiches: Zu den reichshofrätlichen Debitkommissionen im 18. Jahrhundert', in Frommelt, *Zwangsadministrationen*, 45-62, at 45.

[27] Christopher Friedrichs, 'Urban conflicts and the Imperial Constitution in seventeenth-century Germany', *JMH* 58 (1986), 98-123.

[28] David Petry, *Konfliktbewältigung als Medienereignis. Reichsstadt und Reichshofrat in der Frühen Neuzeit* (Berlin, 2011).

supreme judicial tribunals in which citizens appealed against the often corrupt practices of the ruling city councils.[29] Cases often related to inter-communal disputes, confessional conflicts, burghers' resistance against patrician or oligarchical monopolisation of control over civic government, and complaints by Jews.[30] Charles V's interventions in various cities, rearranging their constitutions following his victory in the Schmalkaldic war of 1548, served as a model for later interventions. The interventions in Donauwörth and Aachen have already been mentioned. In Hamburg, an Imperial intervention altered the constitution of the city in 1712, increasing the civic participation of burghers in response to appeals for assistance against the ruling council.[31] Similarly, Imperial commissions dispatched to intervene in conflicts in Weil der Stadt effected a curbing of the oligarchisation of the city in 1650, 1671, and 1673. Notions of natural law also guided the Reichshofrat's dispensation of justice in many of these cases.[32]

In the early sixteenth century the Jewish community of the Imperial city of Regensburg received protection against their ruling city council from a higher court at Innsbruck after being expelled from their hometown.[33] A similar case occurred in the mid-sixteenth-century, when Emperor Ferdinand I's Reichshofrat issued a ruling to the city council of Worms proscribing their expulsion of the Jews.[34] Another notable case of Imperial intervention for the protection of urban Jewry occurred in 1612–14 in Frankfurt.[35] During a renewed conflict between burghers and government in Frankfurt in the early eighteenth century, Mainz and Hessen-Darmstadt were appointed by the Emperor to form an administration commission in 1712–32. A new constitution enacted as a result of the intervention ensured a greater degree of citizens' participation, reduced corruption and patronage influence on the distribution of offices, and introduced military reforms. These reflected the importance attached to effective contributions to the Imperial wars against France.[36]

---

[29] Thomas Lau, 'Die Reichsstädte und der Reichshofrat', in Wolfgang Sellert (ed.), *Reichshofrat und Reichskammergericht: ein Konkurrenzverhältnis* (Cologne, 1999), 129–53 at 136.

[30] E.g., Verena Kasper-Marienberg, *'vor Euer Kayserlichen Mayestät Justiz-Thron'. Die Frankfurter jüdische Gemeinde am Reichshofrat in josephinischer Zeit* (Innsbruck, 2012).

[31] Gerd Augner, *Die kaiserliche Kommission der Jahre 1708–1712. Hamburgs Beziehung zu Kaiser und* (Hamburg, 1983).

[32] Anton Schindling, 'Kaiserliche Administrationen in freien Reichsstädten im 17. Und 18. Jahrhundert', in Frommelt, *Zwangsadministrationen*, 115–41, at 130.

[33] Veronika Nickel, *Widerstand durch Recht. Der Weg der Regensburger Juden bis zu ihrer Vertreibung (1519) und der Innsburger Prozess (1516–1522)* (Wiesbaden, 2018).

[34] Hsia, 'The Jews and the Emperors', 76–7.

[35] Matthias Schnettger, 'Konfliktlösung in Krisenzeiten. Der Frankfurter Fettmilchaufstand 1612-1614 und die kaiserliche Kommission', in Irene Dingel et al. (eds), *Theatrum Belli—Theatrum Pacis. Konflikte und Konfliktregelungen im frühneuzeitlichen Europa* (Göttingen, 2018), 91–109.

[36] Würgler, *Unruhen*, 61–70.

## Interventions against Princes' Financial Policies

Interventions by the Imperial authorities against ruinous financial policies of princes also occurred via so-called 'debit commissions'. Heavily indebted princes of mainly small territories would sometimes be forced to accept the work of such commissions in their territories which would assume full control of the territory's finances until its credit improved and debts were repaid. Sometimes the indebted rulers themselves would request a debit commission, in the hope of shielding themselves against the potential forced mortgaging of their lands by their creditors.[37] Failing to retain fiscal control over one's territory often combined with other forms of bad governance such as the mistreatment of subjects, to cause interventions, as was the case in the interventions in Vaduz and in Nassau-Siegen which are analysed below.

Such interventions were often aimed at protecting subjects, because profligate princes whose finances were in disarray often extorted or violently exacted arbitrary taxes from their subjects. More generally the aim was also to protect the viability of the Empire's basic socio-political order of rule by princely dynasties. Princes forced to accept debit commissions effectively lost control over central aspects of the administration, as the commission could extend its authority over all areas of government which affected the territory's balance of payments. In exceptional cases, an imposed debit commission would formally take over the government of the territory, which occurred in the county of Montfort in 1779, for example.[38] As with almost all interventions, geopolitical considerations could also play an important role in triggering debit commissions. They often coincided with the Emperor's interest of strengthening his influence in peripheral regions of the Reich.

## Examples of Interventions against Princes for the Protection of Their Subjects, 1629–1720

Between 1629 and 1631, the Reichshofrat intervened against the illegal witchcraft trials conducted by the special tribunals of Johann Georg II Fuchs von Dornheim, prince-bishop of Bamberg in the Franconian Kreis. During the period 1626–30, 642 victims (75 per cent women) were reportedly tortured and executed following forced confessions on the mere basis of denunciations from neighbours and others. In addition, their property was confiscated, thus adding a self-perpetuating

---

[37] Auer, 'Zwangsverwaltungen', in Frommelt, *Zwangsadministrationen*, 45–62.
[38] Susanne Herrmann, 'Die Durchführung von Schuldenverfahren im Rahmen kaiserlicher Debitkommissionen im 18. Jahrhundert am Beispiel des Debitwesens der Grafen von Montfort', in Sellert, *Konkurrenzverhältnis* (Cologne, 1999), 111–27.

impetus to the persecutions.[39] Following an ordered cessation of trials and an investigation into them as a result of complaints by the victims' relatives,[40] the Reichshofrat ordered that the accused receive proper legal representation, 'so that one proceeds more gently and safely in this highly important affair, and that no one is innocently condemned'. The confiscation of property was declared illegal, as were executions themselves.[41] The Reichshofrat's intervention of 1630–31 was far more effective than that of the Reichskammergericht of 1628, as the mandates from Vienna resulted in the complete cessation of the illegal trials.[42] The case is noteworthy as it is an example of the Emperor taking an active stance against a fellow Catholic ruler on behalf of his subjects during the Thirty Years War.

The de facto deposition of Eitel Friedrich, prince of Hohenzollern-Hechingen in the Swabian Kreis, through the imposition of an imperial administration-commission in 1655 was primarily intended to restore good governance, improve the administration of finances and prevent the ruin of the princely house. But it was also hoped that the intervention would improve the lot of the subjects and reduce the corruption that they were suffering from.[43] The prince was deprived of his government as he was deemed incapable of overcoming the challenges facing the territorial administration. Although he was removed from power, he was not the target of the intervention per se: it was aimed at the preservation of the Swabian Hohenzollern dynasty as a constituent of the Empire.[44] The intervention was in line with Austrian interests of stabilising Habsburg influence in the German southwest and controlling the strategically located fortress of Hohenzollern, considerations which contributed to the decision to depose the prince.[45]

A similar case was the Reichshofrat's deposition of Count Friedrich of Wied-Neuwied in the Lower Rhenish-Westphalian Kreis, through the imposition of a Palatine sequestration-commission in 1687. The arose from a succession dispute. But it was also influenced by a desire to protect the subjects from the prince's bad governance. When the count's eldest son appealed to the Reichshofrat with claims that his father intended to circumvent the line of succession, the elector-Palatine was appointed to a sequestration-commission to administer the territory until the count's death.[46] In the Reichshofrat's protocol on this decision, the emphasis was on the abandonment of the legal succession arrangements of primogeniture. However, his deposition was justified by his general political and economic mismanagement. The protocol recorded that the count had 'deteriorated the

---

[39] Britta Gehm, *Die Hexenverfolgung im Hochstift Bamberg und das Eingreifen des Reichshofrates zu ihrer Beendigung* (Hildesheim, 2000), 118–204.
[40] RHR-resolution, 31 Jan. 1631: HHStA, RHR, Prot. Xvii, 95, fol. 28v.
[41] RHR-resolution 30 June 1631: HHStA, RHR, Prot. xvii, 95, fols 138–9r.
[42] Gehm, *Hexenverfolgung*, 270–1.   [43] Ortlieb, *Im Auftrag*, 188–237.
[44] RHR-resolution, 14 June 1655, HHStA, RHR, Prot. xvii 165, fols 228v–33r.
[45] Ortlieb, *Im Auftrag*, 237.
[46] Johann Reck, *Geschichte der fürstlichen Häuser Isenburg-Runkel-Wied* (Weimar, 1825), 215–36.

country and I people...thereby weakening the annual revenue and making it insufficient'. The notion was expressed that if the count were not stopped, further mismanagement and illegal behaviour would take its toll.[47] The decision to grant the administration of the territory to the elector-Palatine Philip William might have been affected by Austrian strategic interests. It could have been a gesture of goodwill to the new Catholic Neuburg dynasty, whose claim to the Palatinate the Emperor supported against Louis XIV of France in 1685, a few years before the Palatine and Cologne successions became a pretext for a French war against the Habsburgs.

There are numerous other examples of judicial decisions and executions against small princes for the protection of their subjects. Usually these interventions did not require the use of force, as small princes would in general obey supreme judicial verdicts passed for the protection of their subjects, even when they directly punished the government's conduct. In 1716, the Reichshofrat decided in favour of the count of Isenburg-Büdingen's subjects, who had complained about the excessive labour demands imposed on them by their ruler.[48] Although the imperial courts' dispensation of justice in the conflict between the prince of Schwarzburg-Rudolstadt and his subjects during the early eighteenth century was by no means uniformly in favour of the subjects, at various stages both the Reichskammergericht and the Reichshofrat felt obliged to warn the prince not to deprive his subjects of their customary rights and to order him to redress their grievances.[49] In another example arising from subjects' complaints, the duke of Sachsen-Meiningen was ordered by the Reichshofrat in 1720 to refrain from all further instances of denial and delay of justice at the territorial courts.[50]

## Intervention in Vaduz/Schellenberg, 1681/84

The county of Vaduz and lordship of Schellenberg (together forming present-day Liechtenstein) in the Swabian Imperial Kreis had long possessed strategic importance. At the edge of the Imperial border with the Swiss Confederation, the territory lay on the approaches to the Valtelline Alpine passes of the Grey Leagues (an 'associated' state closely allied to the Swiss Confederation) and was therefore of importance to the Spanish Road supply route during Spain's Eighty Years War with the Dutch and the remainder of the Franco-Spanish war

---

[47] RHR-resolution 28 Nov. 1687, HHStA, RHR, Prot. xvii, 281, fol. 339.
[48] Friedrich Hertz, 'Die Rechtsprechung der höchsten Reichsgerichte im römisch-deutschen Reich und ihre politische Bedeutung', *MIöG* 69 (1961), 338.
[49] Ermentrude von Ranke, *Das Fürstentum Schwarzburg-Rudolstadt zu Beginn des 18. Jahrhunderts* (Halle, 1915), 62, 96ff.
[50] Hertz, 'Rechtsprechung', 338.

(1635–59).⁵¹ The cessation of the related pensions paid by Spain to the counts of Hohenems (who had acquired Vaduz and Schellenberg in 1613) following Spain's peace with the Dutch and France in 1648/59 contributed to the counts' financial hardship. Tensions in Vaduz/Schellenberg culminated in the late 1670s and early 1680s, during the reign of Count Ferdinand Karl of Hohenems-Vaduz (1650–86).⁵²

His ruinous expenditures combined with the general reduction of revenues from the territory resulted in the count facing seemingly insurmountable debts. This, together with his scandalous personal behaviour—associating with a cabal of drunken rough men, personally committing assaults against priests and other subjects, frequent blasphemy—contributed to his relatives' belief that he was unfit to govern and represented a threat to their ruling house and to the well-being of the territory, which led to their complaint to the Reichshofrat in 1679.⁵³ In addition to the inner-dynastic conflict, the Reichshofrat also received complaints from the counts' subjects in 1681 and 1684. The first complaint by six refugees related to improperly conducted witchcraft trials from 1675, in which the property of the *c*.45 executed victims was confiscated and transferred to the government's coffers. Contrary to the portrayal in the older literature,⁵⁴ the count was not himself the main driving force behind this wave of persecution, despite being the ostensible pecuniary beneficiary. Instead a large section of the subject population itself was instigating the trials; for superstitious reasons certainly, but also because the killings and attendant confiscations of property allowed the count to service and in part repay the debt that he owed those subjects who were driving the judicial murders forward.⁵⁵ The second complaint in 1684 was issued by the political representatives of the subjects overall (including those who had instigated witchcraft trials) to the Reichshofrat. It included a catalogue of general complaints relating to the count's failure to adequately service or repay his debts, arbitrary impositions of labour duties, denials of foraging rights, and violations of their rights based on ruler-subjects treaties pertaining to the election of local officials and judges among other things.⁵⁶

---

⁵¹ Katharina Arnegger, 'Der Einfluss Spaniens auf die hohenemsischen Herrschaften Vaduz und Schellenberg', *JhVFL* 108 (2009), 183–210.

⁵² Katharina Arnegger, 'Vaduz und Schellenberg unter der Herrschaft der Reichsgrafen von Hohenems (1613–1699/1712), *JhVFL* 111 (2012), 61–79; Tilman M. Schröder, 'Die Grafen von Hohenems im 16. Und 17. Jahrhundert', in Volker et al. (eds), *Liechtenstein-Fürstliches Haus und staatliche Ordnung* (Vaduz, 1987), 163–87.

⁵³ Jacob Hannibal III to Leopold I, Vaduz, n.d. [1679]: HHStA, RHR, Den.-Rec. 261/9, fols 12r–13v.

⁵⁴ E.g., Otto Seger, 'Der letzte Akt im Drama der Hexenprozesse in der Grafschaft Vaduz und Herrschaft Schellenberg', *JhVFL* 57 (1957), 135–227.

⁵⁵ Manfred Tschaikner, '"Der Teufel und die Hexen müssen aus dem Land…" Frühneuzeitliche Hexenverfolgungen in Liechtenstein', *JhVFL* 96 (1998), 1–197. See also Manfred Tschaikner, 'Hohenemser Schreckensherrschaft in Vaduz und Schellenberg?-Graf Ferdinand Karl von Hohenems und die Hexenprozesse (1675–1685)', *Montfort* 64 (2012), 87–99.

⁵⁶ Subjects' to Leopold I, Vaduz, n.d. [late 1683]: HHStA, RHR, Denegata-Antiqua 96.

Hanging over these conflicts, and over the indebtedness of the princes and large sections of his subjects in particular, was the fact that their main creditor was the neighbouring Swiss Grey Leagues. A failure to repay or service the debt might lead to Swiss sequestrations of mortgaged lands and property in Vaduz and Schellenberg, and could under a worst-case scenario ultimately result in the Grey Leagues' annexation of the territory.[57] Additionally, the territory was increasingly encountering difficulties in paying its due taxes to the Kreis and the Empire. It was this political and strategic concern about preserving the viability of an old ruling family of Imperial counts and not losing a constituent Estate of the Reich to a foreign Protestant power which drove the Imperial intervention, in combination with the count's mismanagement of the territory's finances, his scandalous treatment of his subjects, and the clearly financially-driven campaign of judicial murder of 'witches'.[58]

The Reichshofrat appointed Rupert von Bodman, the prince-abbot of Kempten—a loyal member of the Emperor's clientele—to form a commission to investigate the complaints against the witchcraft trials, the complaints of the count's relatives, and finally the general, mainly taxation-related complaints of the subjects' representatives in 1681, 1683, and 1684, respectively. The Imperial commission's intervention did not require an armed execution. In 1683 the Reichshofrat authorised the commissioner to arrest the count if necessary and, after this occurred, commissioned him to establish an Imperial administration in the territory the following year.[59] The administration was extended after the death of Count Ferdinand Karl in 1686 and continued to administer the territory in parallel to the reign of the new count Jacob Hannibal III. He was then himself removed from government for financial mismanagement in 1692 and replaced by a new Imperial administration[60] which governed the territory until 1712 when it was sold to the House of Liechtenstein, which rules the principality to this day.[61]

Taking a closer look at the overlapping and interlinked cases against Count Ferdinand Karl—especially that of the witchcraft killings—sheds light on the political and legal norms that underpinned the Reichshofrat's intervention. Even before the first formal complaints against the witchcraft trials, the wave of persecutions was receiving comment and publicity in the southwest of the Empire. In 1679 the bishop of Chur sent a letter to the Emperor expressing his alarm at the escalating rate at which supposed witches were being sentenced to

---

[57] Fabian Frommel, 'Stabilisierung durch Verpachtung? Krise, "Admodiation" und innere Verhältnisse der Grafschaft Vaduz vor 1712', *JhVFL* 111 (2012), 81–104.
[58] Case summarised in Trossbach, 'Power and Good Governance', 191–3 and Fabian Frommelt, 'Kaiserliches Krisenmanagement in der Peripherie. Zur kaiserlichen Administration in Vaduz/Schellenberg (1684–1712)', in Frommelt, *Zwangsadministrationen*, 63–9.
[59] RHR-resolution, 11 Sep. 1684: HHStA, RHR, Prot.-res.-xvii, 274.
[60] RHR-resolution, 26 Aug. 1692: HHStA, RHR. Prot.-res.-xvii, 292.
[61] Fabian Frommelt, 'Der Kauf der Grafschaft Vaduz am 22. Februar 1712', *JhVFL* 111 (2012), 15–42.

death and executed in nearby Vaduz and Schellenberg. He wrote: 'On many occasions I have had to wistfully hear of the great tribulations of the subjects of the dominion of Vaduz, and of the inequalities that are being carried out by this ruling count Ferdinand Carl Franz.' He therefore asked the Emperor 'to graciously seek to obviate this growing inconvenience in good time'.[62]

The count's brother and heir Jacob Hannibal was also concerned about the killings and conditions more generally. He and his relatives had already complained to the Emperor in 1679 about the count's failure to pay them their customary agnates' pensions and about his profligacy and overall conduct both personally and in government. But when the Emperor appointed the count of Montfort and the prince-bishop of Constance to dispatch investigative commissions in these matters,[63] and when subjects' appeals to the Reichshofrat seemed possible, the count's brother became worried that the appalling conditions that any Imperial commission would encounter, could reflect badly on the whole house of Hohenems and have a deleterious effect on the agnates' interests and stake in the future of the territory. The mandated commissions of Constance and Montfort from 1679 were never implemented, but correspondence between the count's brother and his uncle in late 1680—at the climax of the persecution of witches and around the time a handful of subjects appealed to the Emperor for protection—sheds some light on the attitudes of the count's relatives towards the trials.

Referring to the execution by sword and fire of twenty-five persons in Vaduz that year, Jacob Hannibal noted 'this is a difficult matter, and that one has not employed reasonable and legally-trained people in this process'. He claimed that those officials and cronies to whom the count had entrusted the trials were 'carelessly inflicting injustice unto those poor people, out of envy and hate or out of interest, because they are confiscating all goods and property of the convicted'. Under such conditions, he considered appeals against the government's conduct likely: 'the priests and neighbours [neighbouring princes and clergymen] are very unhappy about these proceedings and are willing to sue at the Emperor's court, and thereafter such things could be uncovered which could be highly prejudicial against our House and against all justice'. He asked his uncle to intercede at Vienna on behalf of the interests of the count's agnates in case the count's 'misdeeds' resulted in more litigation at the Reichshofrat. But the count's brother stressed that an intervention of sorts was necessary: 'because there can be no hope of improvement with my brother, in that he behaves in such a way as to make a disgrace out of our friendship, and because no warnings will help, an

---

[62] Bishop of Chur to Leopold I, Chur, 1 June 1679: HHStA, RHR, Denegata-Antiqua 96, fol. 1.
[63] Leopold I to Johann of Montfort, Vienna, 10 Feb. 1679: HHStA, RHR, Den.-Rec. 261(9), fols 6r–7v; Leopold I to prince-bishop Franz-Johann von Altensumerau, Vienna, 17 Aug. 1679: RHR, Den.-Rec. 262(1), fols. 16r–17v.

Imperial commission must take charge'. Jacob Hannibal added that 'the bishop of Constance, the count of Montfort, and many gentlemen have warned him, but it will all be to no avail until other measures are adopted'.[64] Jacob Hannibal's uncle, Ferdinand Bonaventura von Harrach, agreed that 'naturally in such serious matters, educated, experienced, and conscionable subjects should have been employed, and sentences should not have been executed immediately'.[65]

At the same time as the count's brother was expressing concerns to his uncle in December 1680, a priest and five other subjects who had been accused of sorcery had managed to flee the territory and lodged complaints against the witchcraft trials at the Upper Austrian court chancery. This was a regional governmental body of the Habsburgs, based at Innsbruck, which was in charge of the administration of the scattered collection of Austrian territories in the Swabian region, known as Further Austria, and the Tyrol and Vorarlberg, in the vicinity of Vaduz/Schellenberg. On receipt of the complaints, the governor of Upper Austria instructed officials in one of the Further Austrian locations, Feldkirch, to investigate the matter and to send a report to Innsbruck. The report of January 1681 confirmed that a miscarriage of justice was underway in the county of Vaduz and that seemingly innocent victims were being killed to confiscate their money, but that Vaduz officials were to blame. The report recommended that an Imperial *protectorium* be issued to the subjects including those that had fled. It also suggested that an Imperial commission be dispatched to halt the trials, to seize the litigation protocols, and to restore the confiscated property to the victims' families.[66] The Upper Austrian chancery's next step was to refer the issue to the highest Imperial governmental institution at Vienna, the Reichskanzlei, whose remit included relations with the Imperial Estates. In a letter of May 1681, the Upper Austrian court chancery expressed the opinion 'that one should lend a helping hand to the complainants who have been wronged so severely contrary to all law'. It was therefore suggested that the prince-bishop of Constance should be appointed to an Imperial commission, to put a halt to the witchcraft trials.[67]

The governor of Upper Austria, duke Charles of Lorraine, had also sent a personal letter to the Emperor in February 1681. The duke argued that all reports from Vaduz indicated that the trials were conducted in an improper fashion and that torture and imprisonment was being carried out without adequate suspicion of witchcraft. Everybody subjected to this arbitrary treatment suffered the loss of all property. The decimation of the population of Vaduz/Schellenberg was also

---

[64] Jacob Hannibal to Ferdinand Bonaventura von Harrach, Vaduz, 21 Dec. 1680: ÖStA, Allg.-Verwaltungsarchiv, Familienarchiv-Harrach 252.
[65] Ferdinand Bonaventura von Harrach to Jacob Hannibal, n.p., 11 Feb. 1681: ÖStA, Allg.-Verwaltungsarchiv, Familienarchiv-Harrach 252.
[66] Feldkirch officials to Upper-Austrian chancery, Feldkirch, Jan. 1681: HHStA, Den.-Ant. 96, fols 7–11.
[67] Upper-Austrian chancery to Reichskanzlei, Innsbruck, 2 May 1681: HHStA, Den.-Ant. 96, fol. 3.

damaging the economy and commerce of the region. A 'cessation of the inquisitions' and a re-establishment of 'territorial security' was necessary. The duke therefore argued for an intervention by the Emperor, and suggested some concrete steps that ought to be taken: 'Because justice is being markedly suppressed in this very dangerous proceeding, because the committed excesses are similarly irresponsible, and because even more atrocities would occur if such proceedings were to continue and if these highly criminal acts are not halted, Your Imperial Majesty should prohibit the count from continuing the ongoing inquisitions and trials over sorcery... and should grant the supplicating subjects of Vaduz asylum in the Austrian territories, while also graciously issuing the requested safe passage.'[68]

Faced with an abundance of anecdotal evidence and appeals both from within and without the Imperial authorities, the Emperor appointed the prince-abbot of Kempten as an Imperial commissioner on 12 May 1681. He was ordered to dispatch subdelegates to Vaduz at once, in the name of the Emperor, to give the count the Emperor's orders: to cease all further trials, to confiscate all trial protocols and to forward them to a law faculty of a university of his choice for an expert legal opinion. This was then to be sent to the Reichshofrat at Vienna, for a final decision.[69] On the same day the Emperor sent a strongly worded letter to the count, in which he was warned that he was in no way authorised to carry out such proceedings and in which he was ordered to cease all trials and to surrender the trial papers to the Imperial commission's appointed subdelegates. He was given two months to submit his own report on the matter to the Reichshofrat.[70] Having dispatched subdelegates to the territory for investigations, the commissioner sent his first main report to the Reichshofrat in November 1681. The witch trial protocols were submitted to the abbot of Kempten's subdelegates and sent to the law faculty of the university of Salzburg. The prince-abbot himself judged the commission to be absolutely necessary for the 'complete remedy and settlement of this crucial business', not least because the trials had ceased when the commission was appointed. The new sense of legal security which came with the arrival of the Imperial commission, and the enforcement of the Reich's hierarchical structure of authority is reflected in the statement of a saved defendant's brother, who was reported to have exclaimed 'It is good, that there exist those that are higher than the count and his officials!'[71]

The Salzburg law faculty completed its weighty report on the witchcraft trials in October 1682, and it was sent to the Reichshofrat after having been received by the

---

[68] Charles V Leopold to Leopold I, 8 Feb. 1681: HHStA, Den.-Ant. 96, fols 4–6.
[69] Leopold I to prince-abbot of Kempten, Vienna, 12 May 1681: HHStA, Den.-Ant. 96, fols 16–17r.
[70] Leopold I to Ferdinand Karl, count of Hohenems, Vienna, 12 May 1681: HHStA, Den.-Ant. 96, fol. 14.
[71] Rupert, prince-abbot of Kempten to Leopold I, Kempten, 11 Nov. 1681: HHStA, Den.-Ant. 96, fols 20–6.

commissioner.[72] The report declared every single witchcraft trial that was examined from Hohenems-Vaduz to have been conducted sloppily and improperly. In its summary section, the report stated that the trials were 'instituted contrary to the prescribed judicial form... the use of the special inquisition [torture] was implemented much too unscrupulously, in that it was resorted to with insufficient grounds,... the Vaduz government even confiscated the property of those accused, who had escaped because of the gruesome and irregular procedures, without determining whether they are guilty'.[73] The Reichshofrat resolution on receipt of the Salzburg report was delayed, possibly by the Ottoman siege of Vienna the following year. When the Reichshofrat finally got round to drafting a response to be approved by the Emperor, numerous new complaints against the count by his brother and the bishop of Chur had arrived. The Imperial commissioner was authorised to place the count under arrest if necessary and to investigate other complaints, including the state of his regime and the dispute with his relatives.[74] Because of his obstructionism, the count was arrested by the commissioner's men in late March 1684 and a formal prosecution for a miscarriage of justice in the witchcraft cases was initiated two months later by the Reichshofrat's public prosecutor Franz Karl Sartorius.[75]

In it the de facto invalidation of all witch trials was approved and the count was threatened with being deprived of the actual and nominal control of the territorial judiciary, although this had in fact already occurred with his arrest and transportation to Further Austria. The prosecutor cited the sixteenth-century dictum by the jurist Andreas Gail ('that a prince may be deprived of his jurisdiction and rule on account of great and dreadful encumbrances and tyranny... also that a prince's fief may be withdrawn and he may be deposed because of the abuse of his jurisdiction or power').[76] The return of confiscated property to the victims or their families was announced. The count was accused of having 'tried and dared to justify the illegal, severe procedures and the numerous indefensible measures against life and honour, in front of God and [the Emperor]'. It was noted that one of the purposes of the measures against the count was to bring his subjects under the 'protection and shield' of the Imperial authorities.[77] In September 1684 the count was additionally charged with blasphemy.[78]

A report was sent by the Imperial commissioner in July 1684, more than four months after his subdelegates had assumed control of the administration of the territory after the imprisonment of Ferdinand Karl. It sheds further light on the

---

[72] Report *Rechtliche Gedencken über den... Criminal Process* in HHStA, Den.-Ant. 96.
[73] *Gedencken*, fols 4v–5r.
[74] Leopold I to Rupert von Bodman, Vienna, 11 June 1683: HHStA, Den.-Ant. 96.
[75] Gernot Obersteiner, 'Das Reichshoffiskalat 1596 bis 1806', in Anette Baumann et al. (eds), *Reichspersonal. Funktionsträger für Kaiser und Reich* (Cologne/Weimar/Vienna, 2003), 89–164.
[76] RHR-prosecutor Franz Karl Sartorius report, [June 1684]: HHStA, RHR, Decisa 2025(9).
[77] RHR-prosecution notice, Vienna, 22 June 1684, HHStA, Den.-Ant. 96, fols 113–115r at fol. 114r.
[78] RHR-prosecution notice, Vienna, 20 Sep. 1684: HHStA, RHR, Den.-Rec. 261(12), 77–82.

impetus behind the persecutions and relations between the territorial ruler and the subjects in general, prior to the intervention. There had long been disputes between the count and his subjects over how the burden of Imperial taxes should be shared, and the commissioner found that the territorial finances were in an 'exceedingly poor state'. The subjects also complained that the count had imposed forced labour on the subjects and had forcibly recruited young men into the armed forces without pay, to come up with the contingent he owed to the Imperial army. The commissioner also had some interesting insights into the purpose of the intervention. For although the first commission was dispatched to investigate the witchcraft trials, protecting the subjects from such perversions of justice was not the only goal. At least as important was the intention to put a halt to the count's bad governance and thereby 'save the whole countship's dynastic house from total ruin'. Deposing Ferdinand Karl—albeit provisionally—was necessary to ensure that the territory could be re-established as a well-run and tax-paying Imperial Estate, 'because apart from this [the count's suspension], there is not a single method which can ensure that the county of Vaduz's owed Imperial and Kreis contributions can be financed, in light of the prevailing poor conditions [in the territory] and of the desperate distress of the valued fatherland'.[79]

This mention of the 'distress of the fatherland' was a reference to the ongoing Great Turkish War (1683–99). The implication was that a true collective effort by the Imperial Estates would only be possible if there existed a harmonious and balanced relationship between ruler and subjects within each of them; one that was free from persecutions and the resulting costly litigation, and in which each side respected the other's rights. In other words, there could be no trade-off between the Empire's external security and the liberties of territorial subjects within the legal framework of the Reich. The following year, the Imperial commissioner added another geopolitical incentive behind the intervention and resulting Imperial administration: it would help to improve the territory's finances and debt management, which was important given the risk that the main creditor, the Swiss-affiliated Grey Leagues, might 'detach the county from the Empire'.[80]

Although the Imperial administration had already existed de facto since the count's arrest in March 1684, it was only officially announced in the Reichshofrat's protocols on 11 September 1684. The announcement placed greater emphasis on improved governance than on any punishment for the witchcraft killings, and the count was never formally deposed. In it the prince-abbot of Kempten was instructed 'to sequestrate the lordships and to place them under due care on the basis of this sequestration, to administer them in such a way as best ...

---

[79] Rupert von Bodman to Leopold I, Kempten 26 July 1684: HHStA, RHR, Den.-Ant. 96, fols 156–60.
[80] Rupert von Bodman to Leopold I, Kempten, n.d. [1685]: HHStA, RHR, Den.-Rec. 261(9) fols 65–7.

ensures the servicing and repaying of debts'.[81] There was no protest among the count's fellow-princes in the Empire, despite the fact that he had been effectively deposed and was even imprisoned. Perhaps this was related to the fact that he was only provisionally suspended from government and not officially placed under the ban, which had remained a controversial measure since the Thirty Years War. More important in explaining the lack of an outcry in the Empire was probably the fact that he was a distasteful minor count, whose small territory was very much in the Habsburgs' back yard, as opposed to a major prince far from the Habsburg sphere of direct control, such as the duke of Mecklenburg, whose similarly provisional suspension in 1728 did cause an outrage among princes and neighbouring powers.

Following the death of Count Friedrich Karl in custody and the succession of his brother Jacob Hannibal III in 1684, the administration commission remained in force in an uneasy and legally imprecise dual government, whereby the subjects had to swear their oath of loyalty to both the new count and the Imperial commission. The new count did not fare much better than his predecessor. Although innocents were not being murdered *en masse* under the pretext of an alleged pact with the devil, Count Jacob Hannibal was almost as incapable of managing his finances as his brother had been. This brought him into conflict with his relatives over the family assets.[82] The subjects similarly resented his extortionate taxes and his failure to comply with the ordered restitution of confiscated property from the executed 'witches', and violations of contracts he had conclude with their representatives of the *Landschaft*,[83] leading to the submission of complaints to the Reichshofrat. As a result, the Reichshofrat issued a resolution in which Jacob Hannibal was removed from government and the entire administration was taken over by a new joint Imperial commission. This consisted of the existing commissioner Rupert von Bodman, abbot of Kempten, and the newly-appointed prince-bishop of Constance Marquard Rudolf von Rodt.[84]

The intervention was successful in the sense that the violent excesses during the witchcraft persecutions ceased and the risk of a potential annexation of the territory by the Grey Leagues (or their heightened influence in Vaduz) was averted. Furthermore, the possible implosion of a noble house of Imperial counts was arguably forestalled, which was certainly in the political interests of the Emperor, the counts forming part of his core clientele network in the Empire, particularly in the southwest.[85] The administration also facilitated the purchase of the territory by the Liechtenstein family who were loyal to the Emperor and

---

[81] RHR-resolution, 11 Sep. 1684: HHStA, RHR, Prot.-res.-xvii 274.
[82] Summary in RHR-protocol, 26 Jan. 1688: HHStA, RHR, Prot.-res.-xvii 282.
[83] *Landschaft* to Leopold I, Vaduz, n.d.: HHStA, RHR, Den-Rec. 261(14), fols 3–5, 27–9.
[84] RHR-protocol, 26 Aug. 1692: HHStA, RHR, Prot.-res-xvii 294.
[85] Volker Press, 'Reichsgrafenstand und Reich', in Volker Press (ed.), *Adel im Alten Reich* (Tübingen, 1998), 113–38.

entered the Reichstag and Swabian Kreis diet as part of the pro-Habsburg party.[86] Yet the intervention was painfully slow—years passed between the receipt of complaints and the dispatch of commissions—and conditions did not drastically improve under the Imperial administration. The commission was accused of nepotism through patronage and of curbing subjects' rights to appeal against the administration-commission's measures. The deposed count continued to attempt to interfere in government and rejected the legitimacy of the Imperial administration, while the subject population seemed to be divided in its stance towards the Imperial administration. Ultimately the commission sought to be relieved of its administration duties.[87]

## Intervention in Bentheim, 1722

The intervention in Vaduz/Schellenberg in the 1680s has some parallels with the case of Bentheim in the 1720s. Both cases concerned low-ranking, heavily indebted, and mentally unstable counts who ruled small but geo-strategically important territories on the Empire's external frontiers. They both bordered foreign Protestant powers which were not on friendly terms with the Habsburgs and which had both received formal recognition of their independence at the Peace of Westphalia in 1648: the Swiss-associated state in the case of Vaduz, and the Dutch republic in the case of Bentheim. In both cases, the counts were deposed from power de facto following litigation at the Reichshofrat, and their lands entrusted to an Imperial commission. Both cases were driven in part by the geopolitical aim to prevent the counties' sequestration and possible annexation by their main creditors, the Dutch in Bentheim and the Grey Leagues in Vaduz.

Interventions in the governance of territories which were ruled by seemingly mentally ill princes usually arose from a genuine desire to improve the governance, finances, and administration of justice of the constituent parts of the Empire. The possibility of such measures was recognised by legal scholars as a clear advantage of the system of rule in Germany, where the territorial princes, as semi-independent rulers lacking full sovereignty, could be removed from power if they failed to meet certain standards.[88] However, as Troßbach has pointed out in reference to the deposition of the count of Wied-Neuwied in the late eighteenth century, such depositions of princes could have a hidden agenda and would often be pursued with greater vigour if they were politically advantageous.[89] The Bentheim case demonstrates how the primary goal of improving the administration of a territory, in which corruption, economic mismanagement, and other abuses were endemic under the rule of a mentally ill prince, was reinforced by a

---

[86] Frommelt, 'Krisenmanagement', 77.  [87] Ibid., 82–90.  [88] Moser, *NtS* 13, 284–5.
[89] Troßbach, 'Fürstenabsetzungen', 451.

politico-strategic consideration, resulting in the deposition of a ruling count of the Empire by the Reichshofrat.

The prince in question was Hermann Friedrich, count of Bentheim-Bentheim in the Lower Rhenish-Westphalian Kreis.[90] The small county was wedged between the Dutch republic and the prince-bishopric of Münster. The Reichshofrat sent the Emperor a report in 1722, in which they recommended that the count be removed from power and the territory administered by an Imperial commission.[91] Following a complaint over the general state of the territorial government by the subjects' representatives of the territorial estates of Bentheim, the Emperor had appointed the prince-bishop of Münster (simultaneously the archbishop-elector of Cologne) as an investigative-commissioner in Bentheim to determine the extent of the count's 'physical and spiritual weakness, and hence inability to govern'. The report of the commissioner's subdelegate indicated that the count was indeed mentally ill and virtually catatonic.

The subjects' representatives were complaining of bad governance and poor administration of justice. Assemblies of the territorial estates—*Landtage* or territorial diets—were not being summoned according to the territorial custom. The estates' complaints to the territorial government about the stagnation of governmental activity and the arbitrary decisions to which they were subjected were left unanswered. The commissioner reported that the finances of the territory were in a state of chaos, and that the count's soldiers had committed acts of violence to plunder from the subjects who refused to be arbitrarily taxed. Furthermore, bogus territorial diets were called to which the estates were not invited and which were designed to give the count's court officials unchecked control of the treasury, which was supposed to be under the co-management of the estates according to the territorial constitution. In light of the state of the administration of the territory, the Reichshofrat urged the imposition of an Imperial administration-commission and the de-facto deposition of the count: 'the elector of Trier ought to be entrusted with the administration of the county...because as long as the currently ruling count of Bentheim's physical and mental incapacitation may last, he will by consequence be incapable of adequately heading the said county, while his consort and the servants taken into her service are by no means to be entrusted with the government and administration, in light of the account of their dreadful handling of the administration.'

Addressing the strategic threat of a sequestration of at least part of the county by the neighbouring United Provinces, to whom the count was heavily indebted, the Reichshofrat urged speedy intervention, 'as thereby the resolution of the States-General regarding the intended execution, potentially aimed at seizing and sequestrating the lower county, could be prevented'. Such a sequestration would certainly not be in the Emperor's interests, both as head of the Empire and

---

[90] The case is mentioned in Moser, *NtS* 11, 383.
[91] The following is based on RHR-report, 8 Oct. 1722: HHStA, RHR Vota 4.

as the head of house of Habsburg, and therefore needed to be pre-empted. Relations with the Dutch were fraught over a continuing confessional crisis in the Empire, and commercial rivalry.

The Imperial Ostend Company—intended in part to rival Dutch commercial dominance in the Low Countries—was chartered in the month following the Emperor's confirmation of the Reichshofrat's report on Bentheim.[92] Instead of the elector of Trier, whom the Reichshofrat had suggested, the Emperor appointed the bishop of Münster, who had carried out the investigative-commission and who became elector of Cologne in 1723, to administer the territory under Imperial authority. This was also in the geopolitical interests of the elector of Cologne as proxy-intervener and Imperial commissioner, because Cologne had its own history of disputes with the Dutch.[93] The administration by the elector of Cologne continued after the death of the count in 1731 because his successor was a minor, and lasted until 1751 when Bentheim was mortgaged to Hanover.[94]

## Examples of Interventions in the Later Eighteenth Century

Despite the successive legal restrictions on the Emperor's capacity to depose ruling princes after 1711 and 1742, that the electors had imposed on the Emperors in their capitulations of election, measures were still being undertaken after these dates which resulted in some princes' de facto loss of governmental powers as a consequence of their mistreatment of subjects.[95] This was possible if serious criminal charges such as murder were brought against a ruler, in which case the Reichshofrat had the sole jurisdiction.[96]

Numerous minor rulers were deposed under the emperorship of Joseph II (r. 1765–90) who took an activist—or even revolutionary—approach to Imperial politics compared to his predecessors.[97] In 1770, the Reichshofrat had count Friedrich of Leiningen-Güntersblum in the Upper-Rhenish Kreis placed under house arrest, and appointed the next agnate as the administrator of the territory. The main report of the Reichshofrat gives an indication of the willingness to intervene against a small ruler's tyrannical treatment of his subjects, even in the absence of any strategic imperatives, apart of course from the general political interest of the Emperor to maintain the viability to the Imperial counts.[98] The report recounted how the convening princes of the Kreis, the electors of Mainz and the Palatinate, had found it necessary to report 'the cruelly

---

[92] Derek McKay and H.M. Scott, *The Rise of the Great Powers, 1648–1815* (London, 1983), 123.
[93] Various reports from the Hanoverian envoy to the Reichstag deal with disputes between the Dutch and Cologne: NHStA, Cal.-Brief 11, 2966(ii) (Jan.–Apr. 1716).
[94] Josef Greiwing, *Der Übergang der Grafschaft Bentheim an Hannover* (Münster, 1934), 21.
[95] Werner Troßbach, 'Fürstenabsetzungen', 443.   [96] Gschließer, *Reichshofrat*, 25.
[97] Karl Otmar von Aretin, *Das Alte Reich, 1648–1806* (Stuttgart, 1993–2000), iii, 113–236, 299–354.
[98] The following is based on RHR-report, 13 Aug. 1770: HHStA, RHR, Vota 29.

troublesome and no longer tolerable conduct of one of their fellow Estates of the Kreis...who dishonours the dignity of his status...and who abuses the advantages of the territorial-governing powers entrusted to him in a more than tyrannical fashion, through the public injuring and intimidating of innocent subjects'. The count's 'transgressions and the abuse of the administration of the county's lands and subjects' were of such a magnitude that it 'requires an inexorable provisional remedy' through the implementation of 'speedy remedial action'. The convening princes' appeal for an intervention at the Reichshofrat had detailed various crimes committed by the count, including 'attempted murder, sorcery, bigamy, lèse-majesté, the extortion of his subjects, and impermissible mistreatments of foreign persons, including clerics'. They argued that such crimes required them, as the heads of the Kreis, to initiate investigations and report them to Vienna to 'secure servants, subjects and the public against tyrannical mistreatments'. The Reichshofrat agreed that the misdeeds which the count was accused of were undoubtedly 'Crimina publica' for which an ordinary criminal trial would be well-suited, 'which the Imperial laws explicitly permit Your Imperial Majesty to prosecute against immediate Imperial Estates'. The Reichshofrat suggested that the count be placed under house arrest while an investigation was under way.

The report expressed some doubt about the impartiality of the convening Kreis princes as they were both involved in disputes with the count, but as they would initially only be appointed to an investigatory commission, with final decisions resting with the Reichshofrat and Emperor, this was not deemed to be too problematic. What presented a greater difficulty was the convening princes' suggestion of having the count deposed and replaced by the next agnate as an administrator of the territory, in light of the Emperor's promise in his capitulation of election not to depose ruling princes without the consent of the Reichstag, be it in a provisional or indeed any other fashion. Nevertheless, the Reichshofrat indicated that this was likely to be the only viable option in this urgent case, and that the special circumstances made such a move legally defensible, given that the count was subjected to criminal proceedings and that the territory would continue to be governed in his name. A comparison was made to the deposition of insane rulers which was also seen to be permissible despite the restrictions imposed in the capitulation. The solution adopted was that the count was incarcerated while the next male agnate, the prince of Leiningen-Hartenburg, was installed as administrator under Imperial authority. While the Imperial administration retained actual control, edicts were still to be issued in the name of the imprisoned count, presumably as a loophole to bypass the stipulations of the Emperor's 1742 electoral capitulation.[99] In any case the scandalous behaviour of

---

[99] Werner Trossbach, 'Power and Good Governance', 199.

this petty despot ensured that he received little to no sympathy among his fellow-counts in the Empire, and certainly not from higher ranking princes.

A slightly different reaction occurred during the similar case of the deposition of the count Karl Magnus of Rheingrafenstein and Grehweiler in the Upper Rhenish Kreis in 1775, on whose behalf some neighbouring minor counts did write a letter of intercession.[100] He had been sentenced to ten years' imprisonment on account of 'shameful fraud ... irresponsible abuse of the territorial governmental powers, and manifold forgeries'.[101] His 'unheard-of procedures' included the illegal production of counterfeit currency to maintain his exorbitant spending. He also took large sums of money from several of his subjects, seemingly without any intention of repaying them and without spending the money in the agreed manner. He was also accused of having caused a 'disrupted administration of justice'.[102] As a result of the investigation it was decided that he should be 'kept under close physical arrest in a fortress situated in the Roman Empire for ten years, and completely deprived of the competencies he has hitherto enjoyed'.[103]

Other examples include the two-year prison sentence handed by the Reichshofrat to Count Gebhard Xaver of Waldburg-Wolfegg-Waldsee in the Swabian Kreis in 1778. He was convicted of theft from fellow-noblemen, extortion, and harassment of his own subjects. The count was already undergoing bankruptcy proceedings at the time he was charged.[104] The Reichskammergericht also authorised depositions, such as in 1790 when it approved the request of the subjects and relatives of Count Leopold of Lippe-Detmold to remove him from power and entrust the territory's administration to the territorial estates during his mental illness.[105] Similarly, the Reichskammergericht authorised the deposition of prince Carl Friedrich of Wied-Neuwied in 1793 on the grounds of mental illness, although political intrigue and a conflict with his subjects also played important roles in securing the verdict.[106] The interventions of the courts in princely affairs did not normally result in their removal from power, though, nor did they necessarily involve criminal prosecutions of the target princes. In most cases in which the supreme courts censured princes' treatment of their subjects, resolutions were issued which mainly confirmed the appealing subjects' complaints and instructed their prince to desist from the offending behaviour. In various Reichskammergericht resolutions issued in 1787–94, for example, the count of Sayn-Hachenburg in the Lower-Rhenish Westphalian Kreis was ordered to cease imposing arbitrary fees, taxes and fines onto the complainants, his peasant

---

[100] HHStA, RK, Kl.-Reichsstände 538.   [101] RHR-report, 28 Sep. 1775: HHStA, RHR, Vota 65.
[102] RHR-report, 19 May 1775: HHStA, RHR, Vota 65.
[103] RHR-report, 28 Sep. 1775: HHStA, RHR, Vota 65.
[104] RHR-report, n.d. [1778]: HHStA, RHR, Vota 61.
[105] Johannes Arndt, 'Kabale und Liebe in Detmold. Zur Geschichte einer Hofintrige und einer Fürstenabsetzung in Lippe', *Lippische Mitteilungen*, 60 (1991), 27–74.
[106] Troßbach, 'Fürstenabsetzungen', at 444–53.

subjects.[107] Criminal proceedings against ruling princes and other immediate subjects of the Emperor seemed to have been a relatively regular occurrence, which caused occasional comment among the princely envoys at Vienna.[108]

## Conclusion

Interventions by the Imperial authorities in the territories of the smallest Imperial Estates occurred occasionally throughout the early modern period. The dispatching of intervening Imperial commissions into the territories of the Imperial Estates was relatively uncontroversial among the political elite of the Empire. What was more controversial was the removal of ruling princes from power. The smallest and least powerful princes were the most susceptible to being deposed during such interventions—this appears to have occurred relatively often in the Empire, largely owing to their lack of power-political capabilities, and of sovereignty and to legal precepts which the Reichshofrat could cite in support of such measures.

The position of the small counts and prelates at the lower end of the Imperial hierarchy among the Imperial Estates (as reflected in their collective sharing of votes at the Reichstag and Kreis diets) contributed to the fact that their removal from power following interventions was far less controversial than the deposition of higher ranking Imperial Estates.

In the sixteenth and early seventeenth centuries, princes targeted with Imperial intervention were usually placed under the ban by the Emperor and then driven out of their territories and dispossessed by princely forces allied to the Emperor. After the Imperial Estates successfully wrested control over the Imperial ban from the Emperor during the late seventeenth century and more definitively in 1711/42,[109] small princes could still be deposed on the basis of legally vague provisional suspensions from power or criminal convictions:[110] the legal mechanisms and justifications of the most intrusive form of intervention therefore evolved over the course of the early modern period.

Yet the norms underpinning such Imperial-judicial interventions against the princes remained relatively constant. They related to the necessity of upholding territorial and Imperial law and feudal hierarchies in general, the responsibility of protecting subjects in their rights and thereby curtailing tyranny, preventing the setting of a bad example and thereby serving as a warning to other princes, rectifying financial crises and 'bad governance' in what today would be termed failed states, and protecting the viability of the territory and its ruling dynasty

---

[107] Hertz, 'Rechtsprechung', 338.
[108] E.g., Huldenberg to George I, Vienna, 20 Sep. 1719, NStAH, Cal.-Brief 24, 4915(iii), fol. 234r.
[109] Christoph Kampmann, '"Der Leib des Römischen Reichs ist der Stände Eigentum und nicht des Kaisers": Zur Entstehung der Konkurrenz zwischen Kaiserhof und Reichstag beim Achtverfahren', in Sellert, *Konkurrenzverhältnis*, 169–98.
[110] Frommelt, 'Krisenmanagement', 72; Ortlieb, *Im Auftrag*, 230–43.

from a violent, profligate, or mentally ill, incumbent. As opposed to intervening against one side and in support of the other side during a dispute, the Reichshofrat usually preferred to intervene by mediating between conflicting parties in a constitutional conflict, especially in the Imperial cities. The office of the Emperor as the political head of the hierarchy, feudal overlord and highest judge legitimised the act of intervening. Moral arguments were also often added by the Reichshofrat and its proxy interveners to further bolster the legitimation. Such interventions were always justified before the public and other political stakeholders; but because these cases received less publicity and media coverage than interventions against more powerful princes, there was less incentive to orchestrate a coordinated publicity campaign.

In the smallest territories, these underlying normative attitudes could be sufficient to incentivise the implantation of interventions. But if they were reinforced by geopolitical-strategic or dynastic interests, the intervention would certainly be pursued more energetically, as seen in the examples of Vaduz and Bentheim. In any case, such considerations tended to merge because by stabilising crisis situations, protecting corporate entities in the Empire and its territories (including subjects), and fostering good governance by carrying out interventions, the Emperor was able to maintain and enhance his political standing among the various clientele and support networks in the Empire, while perpetuating the system over which he presided.

Interventions in the smallest territories were the most straightforward. They usually did not require the application of military force, the existence of powerful proxy-interveners, or a laborious and delicate building-up of a regional or international diplomatic consensus, which interventions against more powerful and connected princes—such as Duke Carl Leopold of Mecklenburg-Schwerin—seemed to demand. These benefits notwithstanding, interventions in the smallest territories were still slow and sometimes ineffective, with complaints continuing against the target prince and/or the Imperial commission, and the intervention itself often taking years to be implemented after the beginning of the litigation. And as with the larger territories, the intervening commissions needed to establish a working relationship and partnership with many of the old regime's stakeholders and local officials and subjects' representatives.

But by drawing such representatives into a process of consultation and governing participation, the judicial interventions often enhanced the level of corporate representation in the territories and cities in question, which contributed to the stabilisation of local crises and the curtailment of violence.[111] By placing clear limitations on the capacity of the target princes to rule, the interventions often imposed a system of restraint on the princes, which helped to forestall excessive arbitrariness and bad governance.[112]

---

[111] See also: Wilson, *Empire*, 636.
[112] For this concept of restraint, see James Allen Vann, 'New directions for the study of the Old Reich', *JMH* 58 (1986), 3–22 at 12.

# 6
# Intervention in Small Principalities
## The Case of Nassau-Siegen, 1699–c.1724

In 1707, the current affairs journal *Europäische Fama* reported on the entry of some troops of the archbishopric-electorate of Cologne and the Lower-Rhenish-Westphalian Kreis into the principality of Nassau-Siegen, and on the subsequent flight of the ruling prince. It was argued that the intervention had been necessary as the costs of the prince's extravagant court was causing excessive hardship among the subjects of his small territory.[1] That this inner-German political-legal intervention received coverage in a journal chiefly dedicated to international European affairs is noteworthy. This issue mainly dealt with developments in the War of the Spanish Succession and the Great Northern War. Although the journal did not discuss this, the two concurrent momentous European conflicts indirectly influenced the course of intervention, and indeed non-intervention, in the Nassau-Siegen case. Yet although reinforcing politico-strategic imperatives were not as important for interventions against weak princes as they were for interventions against more powerful princes, such considerations were always present and important, even in cases of intervention against princes with virtually no power-political clout such as Prince William Hyacinth of Nassau-Siegen. But because a strategic and geopolitical rationale was less central in such cases, they can potentially shed more light on contemporary normative views on the treatment of subjects and their protection through external interventions.

The conflict in Nassau-Siegen played out on several levels of the Imperial hierarchy, including local and trans-regional networks of patronage and clientele and the Imperial Kreis at the lower and intermediary levels, and the Emperor at his Reichshofrat and the party of Protestant princes represented at the Reichstag at the higher level. That the conflict was conducted along this multitude of levels and instances is reflective of the complex hybrid nature of the conflict. It was an inner-dynastic conflict of sorts, between the different branches of the princely house of Nassau, and a marital dispute also played a part in the first Imperial intervention. It was related to a succession conflict over the Orange inheritance. It was also a ruler-subjects conflict over excessive taxation and violent, arbitrary rule between the prince and his subjects of both confessions. It was simultaneously a

---

[1] *Europäische Fama* 66 (1707), 434.

confessional conflict between the Catholic prince William Hyacinth during the early stages of the conflict, followed by the Catholic-dominated Imperial and Kreis administrations during its later stages, on the one hand, and the Protestant subjects of Catholic Nassau-Siegen, the Protestant prince of Nassau-Siegen and his supporters among the Protestant princes of the Empire, primarily Brandenburg-Prussia, on the other hand. Additionally, there was a three-way rivalry over competencies of intervention and capacities of enforced external administration, between the Kreis, the Emperor and his Reichshofrat, and the Protestant princes of the *Corpus Evangelicorum*.

Nassau-Siegen is a good case-study, because in addition to the vertical interventions of the 'regular' Imperial channels, there also occurred actual and discussed armed horizontal interventions and administrations by other authorities in the Imperial structure, with the same professed intention of protecting the subjects of Nassau-Siegen. The existing literature does not adequately treat the interventions and administrations in Nassau-Siegen during the early eighteenth-century. Older local and regional histories of the *Landesgeschichte* tradition which address the case, are biographical essays on Hyacinth (focusing largely on his pursuit of the Orange inheritance),[2] histories of Siegen town,[3] and treatments of the religious dimension of the conflict, in which confessionally biased accounts skew the analysis.[4] Most works suffer from fundamental factual errors and do not sufficiently address the ruler–subjects conflict and the attendant interventions. A useful article examines the involvement of the Kreis in Siegen during the eighteenth century, although the breadth of its timeframe necessarily results in a rather thin treatment of the interventions at the beginning of the period.[5] One aspect of the case—the confessional conflict and the involvement of the *Corpus Evangelicorum* and the media coverage of the confessional strife—has been expertly analysed in detail in the modern German scholarship.[6] However, this was only one aspect of many that characterised the Nassau-Siegen case, and furthermore, it was not the main driving force behind the two main military interventions of 1706 and 1707.

This chapter will therefore focus on the actual military interventions of 1705–1707 and thereby offer the first comprehensive account of the interventions and the subsequent external administrations. It is based on a detailed analysis

---

[2] Ernst Keller, 'Fürst Wilhelm Hyacinth', *Annalen des Vereins für Nassauische Alterthumskunde und Geschichtsforschung* 9 (1868), 49–122.
[3] Heinrich Achenbach, *Geschichte der Stadt Siegen* (Siegen, 1894).
[4] Protestant account: Friedrich Cuno, *Geschichte der Stadt Siegen* (Dillenburg, 1872). Catholic perspective: Franz Höynck, *Geschichte des Dekanats Siegen* (Paderborn, 1904).
[5] Hans-Joachim Behr, '"Zu rettung deren hart getruckten Nassaw-Siegischen Unterthanen". Der Niederrheinisch-Westfälische Kreis und Siegen im 18. Jahrhundert', *JwK* 85 (1991), 159–84.
[6] Andreas Kalipke, *Verfahren im Konflikt. Konfessionelle Streitigkeiten und Corpus Evangelicorum im 18. Jahrhundert* (Münster, 2015), 275–352; Johannes Arndt, *Herrschaftskontrolle durch Öffentlichkeit. Die publizistische Darstellung politischer Konflikte im Heiligen Römischen Reich 1648–1750* (Göttingen, 2013), 395–429.

of the Reichshofrat case records of all three interventions used in conjunction with the holdings of the archive of the Lower Rhenish Westphalian Kreis. Researching the manuscript material of the Reichshofrat together with that of the regional authorities—the Kreis and selected territorial rulers—is crucial as it permits insights into the various levels of the Imperial framework (Emperor/Reichshofrat—Kreis—territory) through which interventions were carried out, influenced, assessed, and commented upon. Analysing the intervening Imperial commissions in this way is apposite, because they resulted from an interaction between the different levels of the Imperial hierarchy. After providing some background information on the territory and the main actors in the conflict, and a brief outline of events, the chapter will proceed to address the conditions under the rule of Prince Hyacinth, before the main analysis focuses on the interventions against the government and the subsequent administrations.

## Summary of Events

The Catholic prince William Hyacinth succeeded to the government of Nassau-Siegen at the end of 1699. 1702 marked the beginning of a drastic rise in the level of taxation imposed on his subjects and the beginning of 'state' violence against the population. This date was no coincidence—it was related to the broader international context. The War of the Spanish succession began in 1701, but it was in the following year that the fighting got underway and that the Empire's fiscal demands on the Imperial Estates, via the Kreis, correspondingly increased.[7] 1702 was also the year of the death of the childless sovereign prince of Orange, King William III of England. As part of pursuing his not implausible claim to the continental Orange inheritance which included the small eponymous principality in southern France and various lands in the Low Countries, Hyacinth overreached himself, by initiating a ruinously costly campaign. The increased levels of 'extraordinary' taxes that the princes were allowed to impose on their subjects in time of war—as stipulated in §180 of the latest Imperial Recess of 1654—provided Hyacinth with a pretext to financially exploit his subjects, albeit in pursuit of his dynastic succession ambitions.

These new policies from 1702 led to a conflict with his chancellor Hermann Jung and with the Reformed prince of Nassau-Siegen, Hyacinth's cousin Friedrich Wilhelm Adolf. When it became increasingly clear over 1702 that the Orange inheritance would be divided between the prince of Nassau-Diez, Brandenburg-Prussia, and France, Hyacinth accused his chancellor of having conspired with

---

[7] Peter H. Wilson, 'Financing the War of the Spanish Succession in the Holy Roman Empire', in Matthias Pohlig et al. (eds.), *The War of the Spanish Succession: New Perspectives* (Oxford, 2018), 267–97.

Brandenburg. The prince's mistreatment of Jung and his Protestant subjects also steered Hyacinth into a confrontation course with the Prussian king, who had issued the chancellor with a letter of protection. It resulted in a brief occupation of Catholic Nassau-Siegen by Brandenburg forces in 1705.[8] Following complaints by his wife, Hyacinth was again subjected to an external intervention the following year, this time in the form of an Imperial intervention carried out by an armed Palatine investigation-commission. The same year, Hyacinth's subjects lodged a complaint against him at the Reichshofrat, which appointed the cathedral chapter of Cologne to carry out a *Protectorium* and set up a commission in the territory. The Cologne cathedral chapter, assisted by supplementary forces from the Kreis, invaded Nassau-Siegen in 1707. Hyacinth's flight necessitated the de facto administration of the territory by the commission, which was retrospectively approved by the Reichshofrat.

In a 1709 resolution by the Reichstag (*Reichsgutachten*), the Imperial Estates requested that a Kreis-run commission replace the Cologne commission in Nassau-Siegen (because electoral Cologne was not part of the same Kreis as Nassau-Siegen) but Emperor Joseph I refused to ratify the resolution. After Joseph's death in 1711, the elector-Palatine, as Imperial vicar, implemented the Reichstag's resolution by appointing himself along with his Kreis co-directors to the administration, while Hyacinth was partially restored to government under the supervision of the Kreis. The Kreis administration, which had never attained explicit Imperial approval by the next Emperor Charles VI, was finally abolished by him in 1722 and the administration passed to a regular Imperial commission under the elector of Cologne in 1724, with Hyacinth losing his nominal partial restoration to power. Henceforth, Hyacinth never returned to power in Nassau-Siegen.

## Conditions under the Rule of Prince William Hyacinth, 1699–1707

Living conditions under Hyacinth's regime were almost universally affected by government policy. For the prince, his ancestral territory was little more than a stepping-stone to the Orange inheritance, a source of funding for the pursuit of his succession claims.[9] In pursuit of this goal, Prince Hyacinth was determined to plunder as much wealth as he could from his subjects in Nassau-Siegen, even to the point of risking the complete ruin of the principality by crippling economic activity and driving its subjects abroad. Naturally, the consequences for the

---

[8] Arndt erroneously states that this intervention was authorised by the Kreis: Arndt, *Herrschaftskontrolle*, 399.

[9] Hyacinth to Leopold I, Siegen, 29 June 1701: HHStA, RK, Kl.-Reichsstände 373, fols 414–21.

subjects were far reaching. There were three main effects: the deprivation of their legal security; the arbitrary imposition of exorbitant taxes and fines; and the infliction of actual and threatened violence by governmental authorities.

Princely policies towards the subjects amounted to a denial of their rights, and while these rights were not buttressed by concrete treaties in Nassau-Siegen, their basis in customary law was equally valid.[10] It was this basic conventional right of not being taxed far in excess of the ordinary and agreed rates (except in times of real crisis) that Hyacinth was denying them, and replacing with a new conception of an unlimited prerogative to collect taxes arbitrarily.[11] Thereby the subjects lost the element of legal certainty which had been provided by an adherence to traditional custom. The situation was worsened when Hyacinth's dismantling of the territorial judicial system removed the subjects' ability to lodge legal complaints against their treatment by the authorities. This was done by the prince's refusal to appoint councillors to the communal chancery in Siegen, thereby rendering it defunct and depriving the subjects of the territory's highest court of appeal.[12] A final step in the effort to expose the inhabitants to a truly arbitrary regime of financial exploitation was the attempt to prevent them from appealing to the Reichshofrat, by prohibiting the collection of funds for the lawsuit at Vienna, and threatening those that were organising the appeal.[13]

The taxes and contributions imposed on the subjects were by all accounts crushingly high, and at a level unprecedented in Nassau-Siegen. While it is impossible to verify the exact amount of taxes raised, as estimates were possibly exaggerated, there are several estimates of the total losses suffered by all the subjects during the seven years of Hyacinth's rule.[14] More tellingly, after thorough investigations, the Imperial commission of 1707 came to the conclusion that the subjects' complaints were well-founded,[15] and this conclusion was seconded by the Reichshofrat.[16] Moreover, it was an fact accepted by all involved parties (other than Hyacinth himself) during the years after the prince's removal from power, that the punishing levels of taxes imposed by the government had undoubtedly led to the territorial conflict in the first place.[17]

The subjects always maintained, and this was accepted by the Reichshofrat and its commission,[18] that they had never resisted paying the 'ordinary' taxes, in other

---

[10] Joseph I to Cologne cathedral chapter, Vienna, 21 Feb. 1707: LANRW, NW Kreis, I N 15, 46, fol. 14r.

[11] For Hyacinth's conception of his prerogatives: *Facti Species, In Nassau=Siegenischer Rebellions=Sache* (1709), in *Electa Juris Publici* 1 (1709), 658–67.

[12] Siegen town-council protocol, 21 Apr. 1705: HHStA, RHR, Den.-Rec. 828, fol. 100v.

[13] RHR-resolution 14 Apr. 1707: HHStA, RHR, Prot.-xviii, 17, fol. 238v.

[14] E.g., Notarised account of interview of subjects, June 1705: LANRW, NW Kreis, VIII, 34, fols 515–17r.

[15] Report, Cologne, 1 Mar. 1708: *EStC* 13, 73–9, at 74–5.

[16] RHR-report 21 June 1707: HHStA, RHR, Vota 40, fol. 7r-v.

[17] E.g., Palmer to Elector-Palatine, Siegen, 5 Mar. 1712: LANRW, NW Kreis, I N 15, 48, fol. 58r.

[18] RHR-report, 21 June 1707: HHStA, RHR, Vota 40, fol. 7v.

words, the long-established, customary rates for the maintenance of the princely court, servants, garrison troops, and territorial services.[19] What they objected to was the government's excessive imposition of 'extraordinary' taxes: the special contributions[20] designed to deliver extra money to the Kreis and the Empire during times of war and crisis. While agreeing to supply Imperial and Kreis taxes in principle, the subjects argued that despite huge amounts of money being raised under the spurious pretext of such contributions (ten times the usual amount), they were not being used for their designated purpose,[21] a claim which was confirmed by the Kreis authorities.[22] At the same time Hyacinth asked the Emperor to be exempted from Imperial dues.[23] While the ordinary taxes and the official level of extraordinary contributions could possibly have been manageable, the fact that a whole range of arbitrary seizures, fines, and fees were also imposed, made the subjects' position unbearable. New fees were imposed for the use of communal grazing land while the entire iron industry was forcibly shut down until lump sums were received. Furthermore, the government demanded large sums of money as special loans which were not repaid.[24] With all economic activity stifled in this way, it is not surprising that many subjects fled to other territories.[25] All property owned by those that had fled was confiscated.[26] In addition to these hardships endured by all the subjects, the Reformed communities were additionally burdened with special confessional restrictions and fines.[27] Given that a sizeable proportion of the population (if not the majority) was Protestant, these restrictions constituted a widespread grievance.

Considering the sheer scale of the taxes and the number of fines and restrictions imposed on the subjects, it is unsurprising that a high degree of actual and threatened governmental violence was necessary to enforce these measures. Random searches of homes occurred frequently. Those subjects who put up resistance had their homes billeted until they paid the required sums. If local communities resisted, leading members were imprisoned and often mistreated until the whole community had paid the required sum.[28] Subjects who complained or were perceived to be organising resistance were imprisoned without trial in the castle's dungeon, often receiving severe beatings and being threatened with death.[29] Kidnappings were carried out for ransoms.[30] A princely edict of

[19] This amounted to 20,000 Fl. (13,333 Rtlr): LANRW, NW Kreis, I N 15, 64ii, fol. 469r.
[20] Taxes were usually in units of 600 Rtlr. The market value of a cow was c.10 Rtlr.
[21] Subjects to Joseph I, presented 19 Jan. 1707: LANRW, NW Kreis, I N 15, 64ii, fol. 510r-v.
[22] Kreis-diet protocol, 15 May 1705: LANRW, NW Kreis, VIII, 34, fol. 494.
[23] Hyacinth to Leopold I, 6 Apr. 1705: HHStA, RHR, Den.-Rec. 828(12).
[24] Reformed prince of Nassau-Siegen to Joseph I, 15 Apr. 1707: HHStA, RHR, Den.-Rec. 829.
[25] Subjects to Joseph I, 30 August 1706: LANRW, NW Kreis, I N 15, 64ii, fol. 479r.
[26] Notarised account, Cologne, 7 Nov. 1706: LANRW, NW Kreis, I N 15, 64ii, fol. 500r.
[27] List of Protestant grievances, 21 May 1707: EStC, 12 (1708), 144–5.
[28] Petition by 392 subjects, 21 Jan. 1707: LANRW, NW Kreis, I N 15, 64ii, fol. 442v.
[29] Ibid., fols 442v–3r.
[30] Subjects of Nassau-Siegen to commission-subdelegates, April 1707: ibid., fol. 463r.

November 1706 threatened those subjects who were able to pay contributions but refused to do so with death.[31] Numerous inhabitants who protested against violent plundering raids were shot dead, while there were reports of some being beaten to death in their homes.[32] This violent and arbitrary treatment was not limited to the ordinary subjects; princely councillors and military officers who expressed doubts about policies or were reluctant to help organise exactions were themselves liable to imprisonment and ill-treatment.[33] It was such an instance which contributed to the first intervention against Hyacinth's rule.

## Intervention against the Princely Government I: Brandenburg-Prussia's 'Horizontal' Intervention (1705). The Case 'Nassau-Siegen Catholic vs Protestant prince'

Brandenburg-Prussia's brief occupation of the Catholic territory resulted in a round of litigation at the Reichshofrat between the two princes of Nassau-Siegen, which sheds light on the preceding intervention. Hyacinth complained against Prussian measures, and also accused the Reformed prince of complicity in the Prussian expedition. In August 1705, the Reformed prince Friedrich Wilhelm Adolf submitted a notarised account detailing Hyacinth's treatment of the former chancellor of the Catholic government, Hermann Jung, which the Reformed prince considered one of the main causes of the Prussian intervention.[34]

Following his dismissal on account of doubts expressed over the violent policies towards the subjects, Jung was repeatedly imprisoned and beaten. He was accused of having conspired with Brandenburg to undermine Hyacinth's chances in the Orange inheritance. The protection afforded him by the Reformed prince enraged Hyacinth and caused him to erect a separation wall through Siegen and to construct bulwarks and towers with cannons trained on the Reformed prince's castle.[35] Threats and violence against the Reformed prince's personnel, communal town officials and Jung continued over the course of 1702–04, despite Brandenburg-Prussia's repeated warnings to refrain from such actions. Jung had been issued with a royal Prussian letter of protection and Brandenburg-Prussia was offended by the imposition of increasingly severe confessional restrictions on the Reformed citizens of Siegen during the escalation of tensions with the Reformed prince.[36]

---

[31] Notarised account by Heinrich Lippsius, Siegen, 30 Nov. 1706: ibid., fols 502v–4r.
[32] Commission-protocol, 23 Apr. 1707: ibid., fol. 434r.
[33] E.g., Commission-protocol, 21 Apr. 1707: ibid., fol. 427r.
[34] HHStA, RHR, Den.-Rec. 828(9), fols 36–46.
[35] Reformed prince's RHR-agent to Joseph I, 20 Aug. 1705: HHStA, RHR, Den.-Rec. 828(9), fols 18–35, 113–20r.
[36] Siegen town-council protocol, 21 Apr. 1705: ibid., fols 99–107; Frederick I to William-Hyacinth, Berlin, 24 Oct. 1704: HHStA, RHR, Den.-Rec. 828(13).

On 18 January 1705 several hundred Prussian troops invaded Catholic Nassau-Siegen. They released prisoners and dismantled the new offensive structures. The princely forces did not put up any resistance and the prince himself fled to Vienna to complain about Prussia's actions. After imposing a settlement on the two governments of Siegen whereby each prince was not to tax the town more than 105 Rtlr. per month, the Prussians left Siegen and occupied the countryside.[37] The litigation at the Reichshofrat began before the departure of the Prussians on 24 February 1705. Hyacinth's exhibit (submission) condemned the Prussian king as an 'arrogated overlord and chastiser', who was unauthorised to issue orders to the prince as a territorial ruler in his own lands.[38]

Hyacinth sued the Reformed prince, accusing him of having called in the Prussians, and emphasised the violation of the Emperor's supreme judicial office and overlordship of the Empire that this represented. He also highlighted the suffering and damage to his own subjects.[39] Given that the Brandenburg-Prussian use of force had not been mandated by the Emperor, the Reichshofrat was receptive to this line of argument. It therefore condemned the unauthorised Prussian intervention, and the Reformed prince was blamed for having caused it. The relevant passages of the 1495 Eternal Territorial Peace prohibiting princes from using force against one another on their own initiative were quoted. The Prussian measures were said to have been carried out 'as if there were no more overlordship, no more head of the Empire, neither secular nor divine law'. Instead of calling in the Prussians, the Reformed prince should have sought 'appropriate legal redress' against Hyacinth's alleged aggression and his Reformed subjects' grievances.[40]

The Reichshofrat likely desisted from issuing mandates against Brandenburg-Prussia directly as its support in the War of the Spanish Succession was a strategic priority at the time. Friedrich Wilhelm Adolf was understandably displeased at having to shoulder the entire blame for the Prussian intervention. He denied the accusation of having called upon the Prussians to invade and therefore of having committed an infraction of the Public Peace. The Prussians were argued to have intervened on their own accord on the basis of insupportable insults against the king, and the persecution of the territory's Reformed subjects and of Jung.[41] The Prussians' destruction of Hyacinth's newly erected offensive structures was defended as justified, given that they violated the condominium agreements and were designed to threaten the Reformed prince and the subjects. Hyacinth was moreover accused of seeking to stir up confessional tensions in the region in the

---

[37] Reformed prince to RHR, 2 May 1705: HHStA, RHR, Den.-Rec. 828(9): fols 68–79; Hyacinth's lawyer Klerff to RHR, 2 Feb. 1705: ibid.
[38] Klerff to RHR, 2 Feb. 1705: HHStA, RHR, Den.-Rec. 828(9).
[39] Ibid. See also, Cath. Nassau-Siegen to elector-Palatine, Siegen, 11 Feb. 1705: LANRW, NW Kreis, I N 15, 46, fol. 3.
[40] Imperial *Citation*, 6 Mar. 1705: HHStA, RHR, Den.-Rec. 828(9).
[41] Reformed prince to Joseph I, 20 Aug. 1705: ibid., fols 18–22.

hope of gaining the support of other Catholic princes, by spuriously presenting himself as a victim of a Protestant conspiracy. The exhibit argued that this was an invidious tactic, as it was well known that Hyacinth was oppressing his Catholic subjects to a degree that was almost as severe as that suffered by the Protestants. Furthermore, Hyacinth's 'quite laughable' claim that he had felt compelled to travel to Vienna to protest on behalf of his suffering subjects at the Prussian occupation was argued to be disingenuous and hypocritical.[42]

The passages in the Reformed prince's exhibits which seek to defend his position by means of a general critique of Hyacinth's regime reflect a similar normative basis to the points made in Hyacinth's exhibit and the statements from the Reichshofrat, despite the Reformed prince's accusation that Hyacinth was being dishonest and deceitful in making such points. Whether or not this was true (it almost certainly was), the normative basis is the same and the conflicting parties seemed to have realised that their arguments needed to be framed along its guidelines in order for them to achieve acceptance. The norms that can be discerned include the need to alleviate the suffering of subjects and the importance of the Imperial office in maintaining order and the protection of rights in the Reich. Hyacinth and the Reichshofrat argued that the Prussian intervention was unacceptable as it disregarded the supreme Imperial office and as it augmented the tax burden on the subjects. According to the Reformed prince, on the other hand, Hyacinth's rule itself was causing the greatest suffering to the subjects and that his aggression internally (towards the subjects) and externally (towards himself and Prussia), constituted an affront to the Imperial overlordship and jurisdiction. He argued 'that the Catholic prince... has hitherto ignored [the Emperor] in a highly criminal fashion, by seeking to be his own judge in this affair... and has acted contrary to all divine and secular rights and against Imperial fundamental laws'.[43] The Reichshofrat was not swayed by these arguments as it could not have left an actual horizontal military intervention pass uncensured without surrendering its authority and claim (together with the Reichskammergericht) of a monopoly on legally authorised violence between Imperial Estates. The fact that an unauthorised use of force had occurred, and that Hyacinth was complaining against it, forced the Reichshofrat to take his side in this case.

## Intervention against the Princely Government II: Imperial 'Vertical' Intervention in the Case 'Nassau-Siegen Princess vs Columba', 1706

A year and a half after Brandenburg-Prussia's occupation of Nassau-Siegen, another military intervention occurred, although on this occasion it was carried out under the

[42] Reformed prince to RHR, 2 May 1705: ibid., fol. 75.   [43] Ibid.

authority of the Emperor by a Reichshofrat-appointed investigation-commission. The accused was Carlo Columba, the leading figure in Hyacinth's entourage. Although the Palatine commission resulted from a complaint by Hyacinth's wife, and was related to a marital dispute, the focus of attention during the subsequent investigations of Columba's actions soon shifted to the nature of the princely government, and the role of Columba within it. The litigation dragged on for many years as its emerging focus, the governmental treatment of the subjects, soon became the *de jure* focus of another new case 'Nassau-Siegen subjects vs. prince'.

Prince Hyacinth, like many of the petty tyrants targeted for Imperial intervention—indeed this was also true of Duke Carl Leopold who features in the next chapter—seemed to experience severe marital problems. In her initial submission to the Reichshofrat in April 1706, Princess Anna Maria Josepha claimed that Columba was sowing discord between her and Hyacinth to such an extent that their marital relations suffered a complete break-down. She also accused Columba of mistreating the subjects and extorting money from them for his personal enrichment.[44] The Reichshofrat decided that the Kreis's co-director, the elector-Palatine, should be appointed to set up a commission authorised to enter Nassau-Siegen in force and to seize Columba for interrogation.[45] A week before the commission was executed Hyacinth's lawyer lodged a complaint against the planned measures at the Reichshofrat. It argued that it was impermissible that the prince's servants be 'dragged away through clandestine force' and his princely authority supplanted by 'external judges'.[46] This came dangerously close to denying the Emperor's supreme judicial authority, although it was not explicitly stated.[47]

The Palatine commission troops entered the territory on 15 July 1706, released political prisoners and arrested Columba.[48] After interrogating the suspect and interviewing witnesses, it emerged that Columba had indeed sought to discredit the princess in the eyes of Hyacinth. But in addition to the marital dispute, the interviews revealed much about the mismanagement of territorial affairs and the mistreatment of subjects in general. Witnesses testified that Columba had 'taken many thousands [Rtlr] out of the territory'.[49] The elector-Palatine sent a preliminary report to the Reichshofrat in which he explained that although the case technically concerned the marital dispute, many credible indicators were emerging that Hyacinth himself was conducting a highly questionable form of government. It certainly appeared that Columba had organised several 'harsh persecutions' in the territory, and it seemed plausible that these were directly

---

[44] Anna Maria Josepha to Joseph I, Frankfurt, 14 Apr. 1706: HHStA, Ob.-Reg. 793.
[45] RHR-resolution, 17 June 1706: RHR, Prot.-xviii 14, fols 338v–9r; Joseph I to elector-Palatine, Vienna, 17 June 1706: HHStA, Ob.-Reg. 793.
[46] Klerff to Joseph I, 9 July 1706: ibid.
[47] RHR's response: RHR-resolution, 17 Sep. 1706: RHR, Prot.-xviii, 16, fols 204v–5r.
[48] Nassau-Siegen governmental protocol, Siegen, 15 July 1706: *EStC* 13 (1709), 54–8.
[49] Protz to Elector-Palatine, Jülich, 31 Aug. 1706: HHStA, RHR, Ob.-Reg. 793.

ordered by Hyacinth.[50] In September 1706 Hyacinth personally sent a letter of complaint to the Emperor, in terms stronger than the previous complaint written by his lawyer. It shows that the prince was very reluctant to accept any Imperial authority in the internal affairs of his territory. He argued that the 'committed excesses' of the Palatine troops 'could not have been carried out through a commission that is constitutionally recognised', and he expressed regret that he had only been unable to resist the intervention on account of a lack of hard power. He complained that by prying into his domestic territorial affairs, the commission was perpetrating a 'terrible and abominable persecution'. He even asked the Emperor not to listen to the reports of the commission which the Emperor himself had appointed.[51]

In November 1706, the subdelegate reported to the Reichshofrat that Columba was believed to have strengthened Hyacinth's resolve to continue and exacerbate the exploitations, by 'burdening the subjects with disproportionate imposts, and executing these in such an unchristian manner that the subjects have been devastatingly impoverished and ruined'. The exacted money was not spent for the good of the territory or for the Empire's war effort, but was wasted 'as is generally known, for the process of the Orange succession'. The administration of the territory itself was being 'neglected, or at least run poorly',[52] and Columba had been given a free hand to employ 'all kinds of fantastical means to extort money from the subjects'.[53] The Palatine privy-council's final report confirmed the accuracy of the accusations against Columba. In addition to discrediting and threatening the princess, his central role in the oppression of the subjects through 'inadmissible monetary exactions' was obvious. The privy-council recommended a harsh punishment, given that he had violated 'life and limb' of the subjects.[54] In its final verdict, the Reichshofrat found Columba guilty and sentenced him to banishment from the Empire.[55]

## Intervention against the Princely Government III: Imperial 'Vertical' Intervention in 1707 in the Case 'Nassau-Siegen Subjects vs Prince'

By the time it received the first complaint from the subjects of Nassau-Siegen against their prince, the Reichshofrat would already have been aware of the kind of

---

[50] Preliminary report by elector-Palatine to RHR, [mid-1706]: ibid.
[51] William-Hyacinth to Joseph I, Aachen, 21 Sep. 1706: ibid.
[52] Commission-subdelegate Brügge to RHR, 10 Nov. 1706: ibid.
[53] Brügge to the RHR, Frankfurt, 13 Nov. 1706: ibid.
[54] Privy-council to elector-Palatine, Düsseldorf, 23 Feb. 1709: ibid.
[55] RHR-verdict, 20 Dec. 1710: ibid. This was one of the rare occasions in which the Reichshofrat reached a final, definitive verdict in a case. For the rarity of verdicts, see Wolfgang Sellert, *Prozessgrundsätze und Stilus Curiae am Reichshofrat im Vergleich mit den gesetzlichen Grundlagen des Reichskammergerichtlichen Verfahrens* (Aalen, 1973), 341–2.

allegations that they were about to read. Worrying indicators of the abuse of governmental authority had become apparent in the context of the above two cases. Shortly before the subjects' first exhibit was presented in Vienna, the Reformed prince lodged another complaint against his cousin. Hyacinth's repeated infractions of the condominium arrangements in Siegen were detailed, such as the unilateral imposition of tolls on the passage of coal through the town and restrictions imposed on the communal chancery. But the statement also criticised Hyacinth's treatment of his own subjects and the communal subjects of Siegen, in particular the imposition of unusual fines and the use of widespread arrests. It was argued that the Emperor ought to act to uphold not only law, 'but also natural justness'. The Reformed prince therefore requested that the Emperor issue 'inhibitory' mandates which would invalidate the 'unjustifiable assaults', and thereby prevent 'an irreparable damage to the subjects'.[56]

The subjects' first complaint was presented on 30 August 1706. It was organised from Cologne by Jung, while fundraising in Nassau-Siegen was conducted by the leading members of the subjects' opposition, including Johann Schutte, Johann-Jacob Flender, and others. The exhibit detailed the infractions of the customary tax regime and the violent methods used to exact the contributions, and emphasising that all attempts at judicial recourse and appeal to the prince had been futile.[57] Notarised accounts of acts of violence demonstrated that princely policies and threats were spreading 'fear and terror'.[58] It was argued that there existed an acute danger in delaying any remedial action (*summum in mora periculum*), and that therefore harm should 'rapidly be forestalled with a strong hand'. Furthermore, 'such harsh procedures of a territorial ruler against his subjects, especially those like us who are not serfs...are in no way judicially justifiable'.[59] As a consequence of the Reichshofrat's resolution[60] on the exhibit, an Imperial rescript was sent to Hyacinth, in which he was ordered to report on the allegations and to release any political prisoners.[61] In late 1706, the Reichshofrat received additional submissions from the subjects, along with notarised accounts attesting to the continued use of force and intimidation in the exacting of contributions. The subjects requested a formal *Protectorium* to be passed to the elector-Palatine.[62]

The territorial conflict reached a climax on 6 December 1706, when hundreds of subjects marched towards Hyacinth's castle in Siegen to demonstrate against the arrest and threatened execution of the community leader of Weidenau, who

---

[56] Reformed prince's lawyer Praun to RHR, 27 Aug. 1706: HHStA, RHR, Ob.-Reg. 797.
[57] Subjects to Joseph I, 30 Aug. 1706: ibid., fols 477–82.
[58] Notarised subjects' statements, Cologne, 10 Aug. 1706: ibid., fols 485–6r.
[59] RHR exhibit, 30 Aug. 1706: ibid., fols 479v–80r.
[60] RHR resolution, 3 Sep. 1706: HHStA, RHR, Prot.-xviii, 16, fol. 186v.
[61] Joseph I to William-Hyacinth, Vienna, 3 Sep. 1706: LANRW, NW Kreis, I N 15, 64ii, fol. 476.
[62] Subjects' RHR-exhibit, n.d. [Oct. 1706]: ibid., fol. 488–91.

had been seized after he told princely raiding squads that his community could not pay the demanded contributions. Several accounts of the march on Siegen exist, but all indicate that shots were fired into the crowd of unarmed subjects from the princely castle, resulting in several casualties. The government version was received at Vienna first, and it requested an investigation-commission to be passed to the Cologne cathedral chapter, in the hope of having the allegations of a subjects' revolt confirmed.[63]

Thus, it appears that the commission which eventually deposed Hyacinth was initially requested by the prince himself. However, the records of the interrogation of the princely councillor Weller by the commission in April 1707 indicate that, according to Weller, the Reichshofrat-agent Klerff had acted on his own initiative in requesting the investigation-commission. Weller stated that Hyacinth, once he heard of the request and the actual appointment of the commission, tried to have the decision reversed by formally revoking the request, as he would have much preferred 'to retain a free hand against the subjects'.[64] The resolution to the princely exhibit appeared quite advantageous to Hyacinth. The cathedral chapter was appointed to form a commission to investigate the events, and it was instructed to communicate Imperial orders to the subjects 'to desist from any further forceful acts, on pain of corporal, capital and property punishment, and not to evade Imperial and Kreis taxes or other customary Imperial dues in any way'.[65]

With hindsight, Klerff's request for a commission was of course a miscalculation. The commission mandate, which was initially slanted towards Hyacinth's position, was soon amended to give it a remit of protecting the subjects, by force if necessary, as new and reliable evidence against Hyacinth arrived. It is plausible, however, that the seemingly pro-government stance is misleading. The Reichshofrat was aware of the violent and illegal conduct of the government from numerous, legally sound pieces of evidence submitted from various parties, and of the fact that the prince had until then failed to refute, or even to address, the allegations made by the subjects since August 1706. In December matters seemed to be rapidly coming to a head with mass protests and an escalation of violence. It seems likely that the sharply worded warning issued publicly to the subjects did not reflect any sympathy for Hyacinth's position, but was instead aimed at preventing further social unrest and demonstrations, and thereby to prevent more bloodshed and a further escalation of the territorial conflict.

Exhibits detailing the events of 6 December by the subjects and the Reformed prince were received in December 1706 and early January 1707 respectively. They largely corroborated each other. The Reformed prince's exhibit argued that the subjects protested unarmed and peacefully. The shooting from the castle was an

---

[63] RHR-report, 22 Dec. 1706: HHStA, RHR, Prot. xviii 16, fol. 403r-v.
[64] Commission-protocol, 25 Apr. 1707: LANRW, NW Kreis, I N 15, 64ii, fol. 436r.
[65] RHR-resolution, 22 Dec. 1706: HHStA, RHR, Prot. xviii, 16, fol. 403v.

unprovoked attack. Hyacinth's policies constituted an affront to the condominium as he had unilaterally resorted to violence, thereby increasing the risk of 'disorder, riot, and fire' in the communal town. It was argued that the actions of Hyacinth were insupportable as they posed a real danger of igniting a full-scale armed rebellion. The exhibit concluded that 'the whole town and many innocent persons could suffer irreversible damage, if the accused [i.e. the subjects who had been sued by Hyacinth in this instance] are not provided with immediate legal help'.[66] This implicit appeal for Imperial intervention echoed that of the subjects in their exhibit of December 1706, in which they stated:

> These gruesome procedures are not supported by any rights. Monetary extortion... in excess of ancient custom must not be allowed to be extracted through threats, actual imprisonments, bondage, branding, hanging, beheading, shooting, wounding, expulsions, and the confiscation of goods.[67]

The exhibit therefore argued that it was the Emperor's duty to intervene against such tyrannical conduct, both on the basis of Imperial law and his position as Imperial overlord, especially when victims were being subjected to extrajudicial killings without trial:

> regarding the well-known right that no innocent person may be killed without being heard and without a verdict and legal procedure: when a government acts contrary to this principle, Your Imperial Majesty is clearly authorised and obliged to protect the innocent, to contain the acts of violence and similar tyrannical procedures... owing to the highest Imperial office and also by virtue of the laws and constitutions of the Empire.[68]

The new exhibits did not yet effect a change in course on the part of the Reichshofrat. The maintenance of calm seems to have remained a priority.[69] New exhibits and notarised accounts from the subjects in January and February 1707[70] led the Reichshofrat to amend the initial commission order to Cologne on 21 February.[71] Its emphasis shifted towards ensuring the safety of the subjects. The Cologne cathedral chapter was instructed to move into Nassau-Siegen and to release prisoners and to investigate all tax-related complaints.[72] But by the time

---

[66] Friedrich Wilhelm Adolf to Joseph I, 7 Jan. 1707: HHStA, RHR, Den.-Rec. 829.
[67] Subjects to Joseph I, [Dec. 1706]: LANRW, NW Kreis, I N 15, 64ii, fols 493v–8v, at fol. 497r-v.
[68] Ibid. at fols 497v–8r.
[69] RHR-resolution, 13 Jan. 1707: HHStA, RHR, Prot. xviii, 17, fols 25v–6r.
[70] Subjects' lawyer Kistler to RHR, 19 Jan. 1707: LANRW, NW Kreis, I N 15, 64ii, fols 508v–12v; Petition of 392 subjects, 21 Jan. 1707: ibid., fols 441–50.
[71] RHR-resolution, 21 Feb. 1707: HHStA, RHR, Prot.-xviii, 17, fols 116v–17r.
[72] Joseph I to Cologne cathedral chapter, Vienna, 21 Feb. 1707: LANRW, NW Kreis, I N 15, 64ii, fols 507v–8v.

the amended commission-rescript was announced, a second act of violence which gained some notoriety in the Nassau region had occurred in the village of Obernau on 15 February 1707. An armed plundering raid resulted in several subjects being shot and beaten to death.[73] The resulting subjects' exhibit argued that

> it would in no small measure be contrary to Your highest Imperial authority and the Imperial Constitution... if it were permitted that suppressed subjects are being attacked in such a manner by Imperial Estates... in an attempt to forcefully deter them from humbly requesting the administration of justice and protection against unjust violence.[74]

The exhibit argued that the economic restrictions that were imposed on the iron industry were resulting in 'irreversible damage and total ruin of the country'. This also represented a loss for the Reich as a whole, as the territory would be unable to pay its Imperial and Kreis dues during the ongoing war against France.[75] The subjects' lawyer issued another request for a formal *Protectorium*, which would permit a more forceful military intervention against the prince.[76] The Reichshofrat decided to retain the formal status of an investigation-commission,[77] but the commission was nevertheless instructed 'to ensure all due security for the subjects'.[78]

Another exhibit of late March 1707 resulted in an Imperial rescript being directly addressed to the commander and garrison soldiers of Siegen castle, ordering them 'not to allow themselves to be used for acts of violence against the subjects, on pain of corporal and capital punishment'.[79] These orders arrived too late. For by the time the Reichshofrat-resolution was issued, Hyacinth had already committed a provocative violent act which accelerated the execution of the commission, bringing about the end of his rule in Nassau-Siegen. Hyacinth had had an arrested associate of the opposition leaders, Friedrich Flender, beheaded without trial.[80] According to the Reichshofrat's public protocol summarising the subjects' exhibit, the execution was 'unheard-of, without legal procedure... and without proof of any crime, but solely because he had been among the group of subjects which had the territory's complaints presented here [Vienna]'.[81] This extra-judicial killing as an attempt to intimidate the subjects resulted in a further upgrading of the commission on 14 April 1707, with a formal *Protectorium* finally

---

[73] Subjects to Joseph I, 3 Mar. 1707: ibid., fols 520v–6r.
[74] RHR-exhibit, 3 Mar. 1707: ibid., fols 521–3 at 522r-v.      [75] Ibid.
[76] Kistler to RHR, 17 Mar. 1707: ibid., fols 527–8.
[77] RHR-resolution, 22 Mar. 1707: HHStA, RHR, Prot.-xviii, 17, fols 183v–4r.
[78] Joseph I to Cologne cathedral chapter, Vienna, 22 Mar. 1707: LANRW, NW Kreis, I N 15, 64ii, fols 526–7r.
[79] RHR-resolution, 1 Apr. 1707: HHStA, RHR, Prot. xviii, 17, fols 209v–10r.
[80] Helmut Busch, 'Gewerke Friedrich Flender vor der Haardt. Opfer fürstlicher Willkür', *Siegerland* 84(2007), 9–18.
[81] RHR-resolution, 14 Apr. 1707: ibid., fol. 238v. Records of the subsequent investigation: 25 April 1707: LANRW, NW Kreis, I N 15, 64ii, fols 434r–7v.

being issued to the cathedral chapter. It provided legal authorisation for immediate military action.[82]

A day after the announcement of the *Protectorium*, a lengthy exhibit was presented by the Reformed prince's lawyer, which corroborated many of the allegations made by the subjects. The Reformed prince professed his duty to intercede on behalf of the persecuted subjects of the Catholic territory, on account of the 'new, unauthorised and highly prejudicial procedures' inflicted on them. Flender's execution was confirmed and recounted, as was the raid in Obernau. The prince of Nassau-Hadamar was also criticised for supplying troops to Hyacinth. A large part of the exhibit bemoaned the broader detrimental effects of Hyacinth's oppression during the territorial conflict. His measures were causing a flight of skilled labour out of both Nassau-Siegen principalities. The Reformed prince also asked the Emperor to transfer the appointed commission to the agnates of the house of Nassau, in accordance with the Nassau family pacts which stipulated that internal Nassau disputes should be attempted to be settled among the agnates first.[83] The Reichshofrat dismissed the requested transfer.[84]

The subjects' representatives not only pressed Vienna for a speedy intervention, but also implored the appointed commissioner to execute its mandate. Shortly after Flender's execution, the Cologne cathedral chapter received a list of grievances.[85] The accompanying letter referred to the 'hastily, furiously and unchristianly decapitated and murdered... Friedrich Flender' as having been killed in a fashion that was patently illegal, because the imposition of the death penalty without a trial violated the *Constitutio Criminalis Carolina* of 1532. These and other examples of arbitrary violence demonstrated that there existed *summum periculum in mora*, that the remaining prisoners would remain at risk of being killed 'if the Imperial commission is not accompanied by a strong military hand to Siegen'.[86] Beyond appealing to the Emperor and the Reichshofrat's appointed commissioner, the subjects (and the Reformed prince on their behalf) cast their net wider in the quest for external protectors. Addressing the Prussian king Frederick I as their 'protector and patron', the subjects sent a request for help against their prince to the traditional sponsor of Protestant rights in the Kreis (especially in Jülich-Berg, a territory which he coveted).[87] This appeal was backed by the Reformed prince who also appealed to the Prussian king in late March 1707 and requested that he sent some troops into the territory again, as he had already done in 1705.[88] In addition to broader considerations, the king was probably

---

[82] RHR-resolution, 1 Apr. 1707: HHStA, RHR, Prot.-xviii, 17, fol. 239r.
[83] Lawyer of Friedrich Wilhelm Adolf to Joseph I, 15 Apr. 1707: HHStA, RHR, Den-Rec. 829.
[84] RHR-resolution, 19 Apr. 1707: HHStA, RHR, Prot.-xviii, 17, fols 256v–7r.
[85] LANRW, NW Kreis, I N 15, 64ii, fols 469–73.
[86] Subjects to Cologne cathedral chapter, [Apr. 1707]: ibid., fols. 475r.
[87] Subjects to Frederick I: GStAPK, I HA GR, Rep. 11: Ausw.-Bez. 185/34.
[88] Reformed prince to Frederick I, 31 Mar. 1707: ibid.

deterred from doing so by the fact that litigation in the case was already at an advanced stage at Vienna, with an intervener having already been commissioned. Instead of intervening again, Frederick I sent a message to Hyacinth's ally and fellow-Catholic prince of Nassau-Hadamar, in which he called upon him to withdraw the soldiers that he had lent Hyacinth and which had been used during the shootings at Siegen castle.[89]

\*

Even before their commission was upgraded to a more robust *Protectorium*, the Cologne cathedral chapter began paving the way for a smooth execution of the intervention at the regional level of the Kreis. The commission's subdelegates Johann Solemacher and J.J. Maes sent a letter of notification and request for assistance to the Kreis. They argued that situation demanded that one 'apply the strong hand, and to this end order a sizeable number of men on horse and foot over there'. The subdelegates had already spoken to the Kreis general about the possibility of the Kreis providing military assistance to the Cologne cathedral chapter's commission troops. Now the subdelegates expressed the hope that the Kreis diet envoys would 'be inclined to agree thereto by themselves, as a result of their possessed equanimity, for the salvation of the hard-pressed subjects of Nassau-Siegen, and to prevent the shedding of innocent blood, and not least for the promotion of laudable justice'.[90]

Two days after the statement was presented at the Kreis diet, the Palatine directorial-envoy Gerhard Büllingen forwarded it to his master along with a covering letter.[91] Here Büllingen argued that it could not be ignored that the Kreis was bypassed by the Reichshofrat in the appointment of the commission, given that 'according to the fundamental laws of the Empire, such commissions should not be appointed outside of the Kreis in which the accused party is located'.[92] He conjectured that the directorate was probably bypassed because the Prussian and Palatine co-directors would not meet the standards of impartiality in the case, as Hyacinth had issued numerous, albeit unjustified, complaints against both of them at the Reichshofrat and the Reichstag in the context of the Prussian intervention of 1705, and the ongoing Palatine commission in the Columba case. Büllingen nevertheless recommended that the 'extra-circular' commission's request be approved:

> As the raging procedures and the shedding of innocent blood without judicial sentence, as if there were no head and no law in the Empire, are continually

---

[89] Frederick I to Franz-Alexander of Nassau-Hadamar, 9 Apr. 1707: ibid.
[90] Solemacher and Maes to Kreistag, Cologne, 11 April 1707: LANRW, NW Kreis, I N 15, 46, fol. 18.
[91] The Directorial-envoy was the envoy to the Kreis-diet (*Kreistag*).
[92] Büllingen to Johann Wilhelm, Elector-Palatine, Cologne, 13 Apr. 1707: ibid., fol. 13r-v.

increasing, the Klevian [i.e. Prussian envoy] and I are of the humble opinion that the cathedral chapter's petition... should be agreed to.[93]

The elector replied that he had already decided to furnish the commission with the requested Kreis forces, 'for the highly necessary, most rapid stifling of such raging, unjust procedures', after having received a letter from the Kreis general.[94]

The decision to appoint the cathedral chapter and not the Kreis directors has received some comment in the literature, where it is suggested that confessional-political interests had probably played a role in the Reichshofrat's decision. This is related to the notion that the cathedral chapter of Cologne was directly controlled by Vienna during the absence of the banned elector and that electoral Cologne was the only substantial Catholic territory in the region, while the pre-eminent directorial estate Münster was still in an interregnum.[95] In the Reichshofrat's internal papers, however, there is little to suggest that it was guided in any degree by confessional considerations at this early stage of the case. Moreover, although it is correct that the cathedral chapter was under a high degree of Vienna's influence,[96] an Imperial commission was in theory the instrument of the Reichshofrat anyway. The Reichshofrat's main report of 21 June 1707, in which the case history and the rationale behind the decisions were explained, contains no indication that such confessional-political considerations played a part in the appointment of the Cologne commission. Instead, the decision to amend the commission mandate into one that would protect the subjects from their prince, and the formal issuing of a *Protectorium*, comes across in that report as a natural and convenient step given that an investigation-commission had already been appointed to Cologne on the request of Hyacinth in the case, in the aftermath of the march on Siegen.[97] A subsequent Reichshofrat report explained that the cathedral chapter had been appointed due to electoral Cologne's proximity to Nassau-Siegen.[98]

On 20 April 1707 the commission troops along with the supplementary Kreis forces (over 1,000 troops in total) invaded the territory, once again without encountering resistance.[99] It was by far the largest invasion of the three external interventions in Nassau-Siegen between 1705 and 1707, and it was to have the greatest impact on the future of the territory. The broad strokes of the commission protocol papers covering the initial activities of the commission are largely in line with the princely version of events.[100] The commission forces occupied most of the territory, released the political prisoners and took over Siegen castle. Before fleeing his territory, the performative-ritual aspect of Imperial interventions

---

[93] Ibid. [94] Johann-Wilhelm to Büllingen, Düsseldorf, 14/4/1707: ibid., fol. 23r-v.
[95] Behr, 'Zu rettung', 162–3.
[96] See Eduard Hegel, *Geschichte des Erzbistums Köln* (Cologne, 1979) iv, 77–9.
[97] RHR-report, 21 June 1707: HHStA, RHR, Vota 40, fols 5v–6v.
[98] RHR-report, 12 Apr. 1713: ibid.  [99] Account in *EStC*13 (1709), 63.
[100] The princely account: ibid, 61–4.

occurred with the handing over of the Emperor's commission-mandate document by the representatives of the appointed commissioner to the accused party.[101] During this exchange, Hyacinth had reportedly indicated 'that he would not recognise any commission as he was an absolute lord in his land'. He said that the troops sent to invade his territory would have been much better employed fighting the Hungarians, whose anti-Habsburg rebellion was ongoing at that time.[102] He was clearly frustrated that he was targeted with hostile Imperial action despite not posing a direct strategic threat to the Emperor. He seems not to have appreciated that the protection of persecuted mediate subjects was an integral element of the Emperor's judicial-political authority and that it was in his interest to exercise this role.

## Imperial Administration by the Cologne Cathedral Chapter Commission, 1707–1711

The fact that the commission occupied Nassau-Siegen with such a large force of troops, and the fact that the prince and many of his councillors had fled the territory, meant that the commission henceforth constituted the de facto government of the territory. Governmental measures it undertook almost immediately included the annulment of princely edicts that were contrary to previous Imperial rescripts, the release of prisoners, the drastic lowering of tax rates, the disbanding of the princely militia, and the instruction of the local judges and leaders.[103] Having received several reports from the commission, the Reichshofrat decided to address a report to the Emperor to seek his approval for such far reaching changes in the government of a territory.[104]

The report of 21 June 1707 recounted that the commission's investigations came to the preliminary conclusion that the subjects' allegations were largely true.[105] The Reichshofrat approvingly referred to the commission's overall assessment of the situation, namely that neither the prince nor his councillors could be entrusted with a continued unchecked regime, because this would constitute a mortal threat to most subjects:

> ...harsh executive measures have been visited upon the helpless subjects, after their appeals to the territorial ruler failed to be heard. [...] In case the prince's

---

[101] For ritual aspects of the supreme courts: Barbara Stollberg-Rilinger, 'Die Würde des Gerichts. Spielten symbolisch-zeremonielle Formen an den höchsten Reichsgerichten eine Rolle?', in Peter Oestmann (ed.), *Zwischen Formstrenge und Billigkeit. Forschungen Zum Vormodernen Zivilprozess* (Cologne, 2009), 191–216.
[102] LANRW, NW Kreis, I N 15, 64ii, fol. 425r.
[103] Siegen town-council conference, 24 Nov. 1707: LANRW, NW Kreis, I N 15, 46, fols 29–32r.
[104] RHR-report, 21 June 1707: HHStA, RHR, Vota 40, fols 3–14.   [105] Ibid., fols 6v–8r.

unchecked domination is not contained, or even if the principal governmental servants were to assume the direction of government, then the most extreme ruin would be brought unto the subjects, and the majority of them would be exposed to a risk of injury and death.[106]

The commission's specific recommendations were then listed. The territory's Kreis taxes should be paid by the subjects' chosen representatives to the Kreis authorities directly, to avoid embezzlement by governmental officials. Provisions should be made to pay an allowance to the princess and to settle the debts amassed by Hyacinth. Princely servants guilty of crimes against the subjects should be punished. The continued presence of commission troops was strongly recommended, to ensure 'the protection of the territory of Catholic Siegen'. Given the damaging after-effects of government exactions, the commission suggested the possibility of granting the territory a 50 per cent reduction in Imperial taxes and a cancellation of two or three months' Kreis tax arrears.[107] The Reichshofrat recommended that the Kreis's requested transfer of the commission to its own directorate was to be rejected in light of the Cologne cathedral chapter's diligent work, and because the constitution did not prescribe such a move to the Emperor.[108]

The most far-reaching of the Reichshofrat's recommendations related to the installation of an Imperial administration, whereby the commission should 'establish the government until the time when the prince comes to his senses... besides, to implement everything beneficially for the prevention of further harm and oppression of the subjects'. Thus Nassau-Siegen should be placed 'under the highest authority of Your Imp. Majesty'. Moreover, the cathedral chapter should remain ready to send more troops into Nassau-Siegen if necessary.[109] Finally, the report presented the Emperor with a choice over whether he wished to initiate a criminal prosecution against Hyacinth on account of his insulting statements. The Emperor resolved to give the prince another chance by issuing a sharp rescript instead of prosecuting him.[110] By granting the report Imperial approval, the de facto administration of the territory by the commission was placed on a firmer legal footing. The confirmation of the report's recommendations therefore amounted to a de facto deposition of the prince after which his readmission to government would be legally impossible without explicit Imperial mandates.[111]

The official instructions for the commission were not dispatched to Siegen and Cologne until September 1707.[112] A challenge faced by the commission was how

---

[106] Ibid., fols 7v–8r.   [107] Ibid., fols 8r–11r.   [108] Ibid., fols 11r–12v.
[109] Ibid., fols 13r–v, 8v.   [110] Ibid., fols 13v–14v.
[111] There was no formal deposition decree, as stated by Keller 'Fürst', 77, nor was the territory sequestrated by the Emperor as claimed by Karl Otmar von Aretin, *Das Alte Reich*, (vol. i, Stuttgart, 1993), 95–6.
[112] Emperor to Cologne cathedral chapter, Vienna, 19 Sep. 1707: LANRW, NW Kreis, I N 15, 46, fols 39–41.

to deal with many of the princely councillors, who had at different stages been both Hyacinth's accomplices and victims. One of the most important steps of the commission was to overturn the territory's tax regime, as it constituted the main grievance of the subjects. The exorbitant extraordinary taxes were abolished and the former dissident Schutte was appointed as the commission's tax collector after being nominated by the local communities. The commission-subdelegates ordered all officials in the territory not to deliver any taxes to Hyacinth or his servants.[113] Thereby the prince was deprived of his *ius collectandi*, while the subjects were assuaged by the appointment of a leading member of the former opposition movement as the chief tax official.

Empowered by the Imperial rescript of September 1707, the cathedral chapter commission decided to send its subdelegates on a second trip to Siegen in November 1707 together with additional Cologne troops, which were intended to replace the 80 Münster Kreis troops that had remained garrisoned in Siegen castle.[114] The subdelegates received the new tax collector Schutte, along with the officials of each district court, and various representatives of the local communities. They gave a speech in which they indicated that the Emperor had decided to take the subjects of Nassau-Siegen under his 'protection and shield' via the Imperial commission, which was now mandated to assume 'the complete administration of the princely lands of Catholic Siegen'.[115] Although the local representatives were not explicitly relieved of their oath of obedience to their prince, it was stressed that they were bound to the Emperor as their highest duty.[116]

The subdelegates proceeded to assure their audience that the commission would respect and restore the territory's customary practice. Liaison officers were elected from the local communities to interact with the commission in Cologne.[117] It was agreed that princely officials accused of excesses should be dismissed and punished whereas the others could remain in office. As a consequence of subjects' petitions, some princely officials were dismissed and their jobs provisionally added to the remit of the newly appointed administration-councillors Ley and Henrothe.[118] Shortly before the departure of the subdelegates, a constitutionally significant step was taken. The commission decided that the communal (dual princely) chancery in Siegen would be replaced by the office of the administration-councillors.[119] This was not only a reflection of Hyacinth's removal from power. It also had implications for the Reformed prince's condominium in Siegen which was thereby effectively removed.

---

[113] *EStC*13 (1709), 70–1.
[114] Solemacher to Cologne cathedral chapter, Siegen, 14 Nov. 1707: LANRW, NW Kreis, I N 15, 46, fol. 26.
[115] Commission-protocol, 14 Nov. 1707: LANRW, NW Kreis, I N 15, 64ii, fols 455v–6r.
[116] Ibid., fols 456r-v.   [117] Ibid., fols 456v–7v.
[118] Commission-protocol, 21 Nov. 1707: ibid., fols 459v–60v, 467r.
[119] Maes to Nassau-Siegen Reformed government, Siegen, 26 Nov. 1707: LANRW, NW Kreis, I N 15, 46, fol. 27r.

Over the next years, attempts were made by the Reichshofrat and the commission to incrementally strengthen their control over the territory. In March 1708, the Cologne cathedral chapter announced its intention to appoint the envoy of Catholic Nassau-Siegen to the Lower-Rhenish-Westphalian Kreis diet.[120] In May, the Reichshofrat sent a rescript to the commission instructing it to withhold the Kreis diet appointment for the time being, in the hope that a full submission by Hyacinth could permit his restoration. Apart from this, the commission's work received full approval, and its subdelegates' freedom to appoint and dismiss officials was confirmed.[121] In August 1708, the commission's administration was formally extended to the town of Siegen, although after its assumption of control over the communal chancery the Reichshofrat was merely providing official legal cover for existing facts.[122]

Apart from the Reformed subjects complaining about continuing restrictions to their confessional rights under the new administration, a problem that the commission faced for the duration of its administration was that Hyacinth's former officials and councillors tried to obstruct the work of the commission and to undermine its authority.[123] That Hyacinth was able to continue exerting influence is not surprising given that there was no indication that the informal deposition was to be permanent, and that Imperial commissions usually left their assigned territories before long, and in any case they lapsed at the death of the Emperor or the commissioner. By the later years of the administration the cathedral chapter was growing increasingly wary of its commission, because it soured its relationship with the Kreis among other reasons.[124] However, they were unwilling to give it up without explicit orders from the Emperor.[125]

## Reactions and Assessments

There was a broad consensus among all parties (other than Hyacinth himself, of course, and one or two of his fellow-princes of the house of Nassau) that an armed intervention against the prince's rule had been necessary. The subjects demanded external protection, while the Emperor and his Reichshofrat, the Cologne cathedral chapter as the designated intervener, the Reformed prince of Nassau-Siegen, and the Kreis directors all agreed that Hyacinth's regime needed to be curtailed militarily and to thereby ensure sustainable fiscal policies, and the protection of

---

[120] Statement 7 Mar. 1708: ibid., fol. 45.
[121] Joseph I to Cologne cathedral chapter, Vienna, 30 May 1708: LANRW, NW Kreis, I N 15, 53, fols 415–17r.
[122] RHR-resolution, 5 Aug. 1708: HHStA, RHR, Prot.-xviii, 21, fols 211r-v.
[123] RHR-resolution, 10 Dec. 1708: ibid., fols 336v–7r.
[124] Kreis directors' conference, Cologne, 21 Mar. 1711: LANRW, NW Kreis, I N 15, 47, fols 105–7.
[125] Palmer to elector Palatine, Cologne, 25 Mar. 1711: ibid., fol. 101r.

his subjects. The documentary evidence does not indicate that the intervening powers were motivated primarily by their own short-term political or strategic interests or by any expansionary motives. It was, however, in the long-term political interest of the Emperor to preserve and exercise his protective jurisdiction and authority as the highest judge. Similarly, the designated commissioner would have placed itself at a political disadvantage in terms of its relations with Vienna had it refused the commission mandate. Yet it was also acutely aware that executing the commission could potentially cause problems closer to home with the Kreis. Münster, Brandenburg-Prussia, and the Palatinate felt that their rights as Kreis directors had been violated when they were bypassed in the appointment of the commission. Nevertheless, they all contributed towards an intervention which was at best imperfect from the point of view of their immediate self-interest. Similarly, the Reformed prince continued to press for an intervention for the protection of his cousin's subjects, even after Cologne was appointed as the commissioner, and it had therefore already become apparent that the intervention would not be carried out by the agnates as he was demanding on the basis of the family pacts. Outrage at the prince's acts of violence and pretended sovereignty is frequently attested in the private correspondence of the actors, and this, along with a desire to prevent further bloodshed and protect the persecuted subjects, is what drove the involved parties to advocate and participate in an intervention that was not obviously in their short-term political or strategic interests.

Yet once the intervention had occurred and the immediate threat to the lives of the subjects had been removed, the political self-interest of the involved parties started to assert itself, particularly in reaction to the prince's deposition and the imposition of a long-term Imperial administration. This was especially true for the Kreis directors and the agnates. The assessments of the Emperor and his Reichshofrat on the one hand, and Hyacinth on the other hand, as the instigator and target, respectively, of the intervention, remained constant. In a series of rescripts and statements the Reichshofrat continually approved the commission's actions and praised its conduct, frequently noting that its work was being carried out expeditiously in the face of considerable costs and not insignificant adverse circumstances.[126] The Reichshofrat might have been inclined to highlight the good work of its chosen commission to strengthen its position against criticism by the Kreis. However, the positive assessment of the cathedral chapter's administration was not merely made in public statements of the Reichshofrat's protocol, but also in its internal reports which were for the eyes of the Emperor and his privy-conference only.[127]

\*

---

[126] Joseph I to Cologne cathedral chapter, Vienna, 19 Sep. 1707: LANRW, NW Kreis, I N 15, 46, fols 39–41.
[127] RHR-report, 12 Apr. 1713: HHStA, RHR, Vota 40.

Hyacinth fled Nassau-Siegen after the intervention and remained in self-imposed exile for the duration of the Imperial administration-commission. He tirelessly criticised and sought to undermine the commission, while also denying the right of the Empire to intervene in his internal affairs. He repeatedly issued formal requests to the Reichshofrat for his readmission to government, all of which were rejected.[128] Hyacinth's strongly-worded criticisms of the Imperial commission, including the accusation that the commission was stirring up his subjects against him,[129] led to the Emperor sending him several sharp warnings.[130]

Hyacinth's denial of the central Imperial authorities' right to intervene in any manner on behalf of mediate subjects is striking, and he thereby set himself apart from normative consensus in Germany. One princely pamphlet argued that ruler-subjects conflicts were not under the purview of the Imperial tribunals. The Cologne commission was accused of having despoiled him of his lands, thereby committing a breach of the territorial peace. The office of the Emperor 'as head and protector of the Empire' was acknowledged, but it was argued that this function needed to be exercised for the protection of the prince's rights, as the cathedral chapter had not been authorised to depose him.[131] The jurisdiction of the Reichshofrat in domestic territorial affairs of the German princes was denied.[132] It was argued that there needed to be a formal criminal trial for a deposition to take place, in which the prince in question was found guilty and convicted, of notorious crimes namely treason, and that the Emperor and the Reichstag had to agree on the step.[133]

\*

The subjects of Nassau-Siegen were naturally relieved to see the armed intervention against their prince implemented, as they had been litigating towards this goal for months. The subjects' representatives expressed gratitude to the subdelegates after the entry of the commission, and told them that any further delay would have spelt the ruin of the territory and its inhabitants.[134] The subjects also acknowledged that the removal of Hyacinth resulted in a drastic reduction of the tax burden that they were exposed to.[135] By 1709, the Protestant subjects seemed to have changed their mind as indicated by a petition addressed to the Kreis directorate. It was stated (probably hyperbolically) that although the tax pressure had subsided in the aftermath of the intervention, taxes were gradually raised again, to the extent that the levels imposed even exceeded the official rates under

---

[128] E.g., RHR-resolution, 12 Jan. 1708: HHStA, RHR, Prot. xviii, 19, fol. 299.
[129] William Hyacinth to Joseph I, Münster, 14 Oct. 1707: HHStA, RHR, Ob.-Reg. 796, fols 153–4.
[130] E.g., Joseph I to William Hyacinth, Vienna, 19 Sep. 1708: *EStC* 13 (1709), 92–4.
[131] *Memoire Raisonnée... pour le Prince de Nassau Siegen et d'Orange*, LANRW, NW Kreis, I N 15, No. 14, fols 1–11r.
[132] Ibid., fol. 6r.     [133] Ibid., fols 2v–3r, 11r.
[134] Commission-protocol, 17 Nov. 1707: LANRW, NW Kreis, I N 15, 64ii, fol. 459r.
[135] Subjects to Kreis-diet, 26 May 1707: LANRW, NW Kreis, VIII, 35, fols 273–4.

Hyacinth's rule.[136] The main grievance detailed in the petition concerned confessional restrictions, however.[137]

The subjects' retrospective assessment of the period 1707–11 is perhaps more telling. They clearly remained terrified of the prospect of a return to the conditions of 1700–07 long after the end of the cathedral chapter's administration, especially when rumours were circulating of a possible readmission of Hyacinth to government.[138] In 1716, after the replacement of the Imperial administration by a Kreis administration, the subjects appealed to the directorate against the partial restoration of Hyacinth and asked it to seek the status of a fully-fledged Imperial administration, sanctioned by the Emperor and the Reichshofrat, 'so that the Catholic territory of Nassau-Siegen may be mildly and justly governed under the Emperor's highest protection as occurred from 1707 until 1712'.[139]

The Reformed prince deemed his condominium rights in Siegen usurped by the imposed administration. Worried that the Catholic part of the territory might be annexed, he asked the Reichshofrat not to agree to the formal sequestration of the territory as previously requested by the subjects.[140] After the announcement of the Imperial administration, he addressed a letter to the Kreis directorate, in which he expressed alarm at the extent to which Hyacinth had been removed from power. Although Hyacinth's subjects had undeniably required protection and an intervention through an Imperial commission had been necessary, this should have been passed to the agnates or at least to the Lower-Rhenish-Westphalian Kreis. He claimed that the effective abolition of the communal chancery was infringing upon his rights of condominium in Siegen. He argued that it would be of dangerous consequence for the interests of all princes, if it were accepted that they 'could be made completely incapable of their territorial government and if the Imperial court were given the power and authority to transfer their governmental administrations to others according to its whim'.[141]

\*

After participating in the intervention militarily in April 1707 and retaining a small number of troops in the territory until the announcement of the administration in November, the directorate of the Lower-Rhenish-Westphalian Kreis monitored the developments in Nassau-Siegen closely. Once the morally pressing task of helping the 'hard-pressed subjects' had been accomplished, considerations

---

[136] Protestant subjects to Kreis-directorate, Siegen, Feb. 1709: LANRW, NW Kreis, I N 15, 46, fols 95r-v.
[137] Ibid., fols 95v–6v.
[138] Kreis directorial-envoys to Emperor Charles VI, Cologne, 23 May 1715: LANRW, NW Kreis, I N 15, 49, fol. 205v.
[139] Subjects to Kreis-directorate, 28 Nov. 1716: LANRW, NW Kreis, I N 15, 63, fol. 182v.
[140] Ibid., 17, fol. 323v.
[141] Friedrich Wilhelm Adolf to Kreis-directors, Siegen, n.d.: LANRW, NW Kreis, I N 15, 46, fols 33–6r.

of *Realpolitik* came to the fore again. Although the directorate presented a united front in pursuit of a commission it felt entitled to, there was a great deal of mutual suspicion and jealousy among the three co-directors behind the scenes, which even included the two Catholic directors coming close to considering the use of force against their Brandenburg-Prussian co-director in 1711.

At a directors' conference in May 1707, the Münster envoy Ernst Kochenheim suggested that a request should be made for a formal transfer of the commission to the Kreis directors, as the execution had already been carried out with the participation of directorial troops, and 100 Kreis troops remained in Siegen. The other two directorial-envoys agreed that a request should be sent to the Emperor.[142] In the letter to the Emperor, the directorate stressed that although they agreed to provide military assistance to 'external hands', in other words to a power that was not part of the Kreis, this was only done as the urgency of the situation in Nassau-Siegen required immediate action, but under the condition that directorial rights would not be permanently undermined. Therefore, the transfer of the commission to the Kreis was requested as stipulated in Imperial law and custom, given Nassau-Siegen's undeniable membership of the Lower-Rhenish-Westphalian Kreis. It was argued that it was necessary for the Kreis's troops to remain in the territory to adequately ensure 'the safeguarding of the subjects'.[143] In effect, the Kreis directorate was thereby competing with the Emperor for the protection of the territory's subjects. The commission transfer request was frequently repeated[144] and repeatedly rejected by the Reichshofrat.[145]

Being denied the commission transfer by the Reichshofrat, the directors considered other ways to assert their rights. One step taken in March 1708 was to refuse acceptance of the credentials of the commission-appointed Kreis diet envoy for Nassau-Siegen.[146] The elector-Palatine and prince-bishop of Münster tentatively agreed to second the general complaints of the Reformed prince against the administration-commission as another way of pressurising it, despite misgivings about his own personal ambitions for the commission appointment.[147] While the prince-bishop of Münster resented the fact that the directorate's commission-transfer suit was 'highly mischievously thrown out' by the Reichshofrat, he expressed misgivings about supporting the Reformed prince's complaints against the administration-commission. He explained that the directorate should not be seen to claim a judicial mediating power over disputes between another territorial prince and an Imperial commission, as such an assertion would be seen as injurious

---

[142] Directorial-conference, Cologne, 23 May 1707: LANRW, NW Kreis, VIII, 35, fols 217–18.
[143] Kreis directorial-envoys to Joseph I, Cologne, 23 May 1707: LANRW, NW Kreis, VIII, 35, fols 225–6.
[144] Kreis directorial-envoys to Joseph I, Cologne, 16 Apr. 1708 and 26 Mar. 1711: LANRW, NW Kreis, I N 15, 46, fols 53–4 and no. 47 fols 45–6.
[145] E.g., RHR resolution, 30 May 1708: HHStA, RHR, Prot. xviii, 20a, fol. 233v.
[146] Elector-Palatine to Büllingen, Düsseldorf, 21 Mar. 1708: LANRW, NW Kreis, I N 15, 46, fol. 51.
[147] Elector Palatine to prince-bishop of Münster, Düsseldorf, 14 Aug. 1708: ibid., fol. 61.

to the Emperor's supreme judicial office.[148] Addressing the elector-Palatine, he did, however, stress that it would be unwise to withdraw assurances of support from the Reformed prince, as this might allow him to be sucked deeper into the orbit of the *Corpus Evangelicorum*, in particular Brandenburg and Hessen-Kassel.[149]

During a directors' conference in early 1709, the Brandenburg-Prussian envoy Reinhard Diest spoke out forcefully for a more robust stance against the administration-commission. He stated that allowing the cathedral chapter to retain the commission was setting a bad precedent, to the detriment of the Kreis directorate. He believed the cathedral chapter could be pressurised into requesting its own dismissal from the commission. He regretted the lack of vigour on the part of the directorate and launched a scathing criticism of Münster which he accused of neglecting directorial rights as the senior co-director. Brandenburg was particularly disappointed at Münster's unilateral withdrawal of the remaining Kreis troops from Siegen castle at the behest of the commission in November 1707, without prior communication with the other co-directors. This step had allowed Cologne to virtually take over a territory which the directorate should be governing. If the commission transfer could not be effected by a combination of requests at Vienna and of applying pressure on the canons of the cathedral chapter in Cologne, then the directors should consider 'applying the strong hand', in other words, seizing the administration by force. The Palatine envoy Büllingen expressed agreement.[150] Later in 1709, the Brandenburger Diest argued that the chances of getting the Cologne cathedral chapter to request its dismissal had improved, especially after the recent draft resolution of the Reichstag. He recounted a conversation he had had with the cathedral chapter's commission-subdelegate Solemacher, during which he had found him to be 'very reasonable' in this regard.[151]

By late 1710, with no progress in sight, the directors seemed to have shifted back towards trying to pressurise the cathedral chapter. The Palatine privy-council sent a letter to the Cologne cathedral chapter indicating that they would press hard for the commission-transfer at the Kreis diet. Interestingly, the main thrust of the letter was a complaint about the administration-commission's treatment of the Protestant subjects of the Catholic territory, with regard to the alleged violation of their confessional rights.[152]

During March 1711, shortly before the extinguishment of the Imperial administration-commission through the death of Emperor Joseph I, a renewed Brandenburg-Prussian drive towards the use of force against the commission almost led to an open breach between the co-directors. Here confessional and

---

[148] Prince-bishop of Münster to Elector-Palatine, Ahaus, 7 Sep. 1708: ibid., fols 63–4.
[149] Ibid., Münster, 16 July 1709: ibid., fol. 84.
[150] Directorial conference, Cologne, 21 Jan. 1709: ibid., fols 67–9.
[151] Diest to Palatine ministry, Cologne, 10 July 1709: ibid., fols 109–10.
[152] Palatine privy council to Cologne cathedral chapter, Düsseldorf, 1 Dec. 1710: ibid., fols 136–7r.

geopolitical concerns and the involvement of the *Corpus Evangelicorum* played an important role. In early March, the Palatine directorial-envoy J. H. Palmer expressed concerns in a report to his master over the obvious Brandenburg-Prussian willingness to see the Reformed prince take over the administration-commission. Under this scenario, according to Palmer, there would be 'no small concern about the threat to religion'. However, the threat to the Catholic interest would not be very big, if the commission were passed to the directorate collectively, as the Catholic co-directors constituted the majority. The Brandenburger Diest was reportedly suggesting that Kreis troops could simply move into Siegen, after which the directorate could present the Reichshofrat with a fait accompli. The Münster envoy Kochenheim, the Palatine envoy Palmer and the Palatine ministry believed further appeals should be sent to the Emperor first.[153]

The bishop of Münster obviously shared the Palatinate's misgivings about the effects of Prussia's influence on the confessional conditions in the territory, and by extension on the broader confessional balance in the Reich, expressing the hope that the commission could be passed to Münster and the Palatinate alone.[154] Palmer and Kochenheim were alarmed by reports that the two princes of Nassau-Siegen were considering selling the succession rights to their territories to Prussia. Palmer argued that this would not only pose a threat to the confessional balance in the Kreis, but that it would also pose a danger to the nearby Palatine duchy of Berg, which Brandenburg-Prussia coveted. Palmer and Kochenheim were told by members of the cathedral chapter that Prussian and Hessen-Kassel troop movements had been observed near Nassau-Siegen with the apparent aim of threatening the administration-commission. Palmer expressed amazement that Prussia was threatening force so openly, and the two Catholic envoys decided to advise the cathedral chapter on possible defensive measures.[155] The Catholic directorial-envoys were thus coming close to working directly against their Prussian co-director colleague when it seemed that Prussia was planning to use force unilaterally without acting under collective Kreis auspices. They found it increasingly difficult to reconcile their distaste at *Corpus Evangelicorum* threats against the cathedral chapter with their own opposition to the administration-commission. Although the reports of an amassing of Prussian troops soon turned out to be false,[156] the initial reaction of Palmer and Kochenheim was indicative of the diverging interests of the members of the Kreis directorate.

Thus, there existed considerable infighting and differences in the strategies and considerations of the three co-directors in the context of the pursuit of the commission. While the Palatinate and especially Brandenburg-Prussia were in

---

[153] Palmer to electorPalatine, Cologne, 8 Mar. 1711: LANRW, NW Kreis, I N 15, 47, fols 99–100.
[154] Bishop of Münster to Kochenheim, Neuhaus, 20 Mar. 1711: ibid., fol. 102r.
[155] Palmer to elector-Palatine, Cologne, 20 Mar. 1711: ibid., fols 109, 111r.
[156] Ibid., 22 Mar. 1711: ibid., fol. 104.

favour of a more vigorous assertion of perceived directorial rights, even to the point of considering the use of force, Münster was much more cautious and reluctant to confront the commission and by implication, the Emperor. At the same time, however, Münster and the Palatinate were wary of Prussian involvement and the possible expansion of its influence in the Kreis through the Nassau-Siegen administration dispute. They worked closely together in an attempt to limit Prussian influence, and thereby further the Catholic interest. Among the Catholic co-directors there was a constant fear of a powerful Protestant nexus consisting of Brandenburg-Prussia, the Reformed prince of Nassau-Siegen, and the other leading *Corpus Evangelicorum* members, Hessen-Kassel and Hanover.

Therefore, from the point of view of Münster and the Palatinate, pressing for directorial rights in conjunction with Brandenburg-Prussia and the Reformed prince was a double-edged sword: there undoubtedly existed a community of interests among the three co-directors and, to a lesser extent, the Reformed prince in opposing the Cologne administration. But on the other hand, this had to be weighed up against the possible danger of thereby facilitating a Protestant take-over of the territory. The perceived risk appeared real, as the *Corpus Evangelicorum* was calling for its members to carry out an intervention against the Imperial administration from 1708.[157] On balance, however, the desire of the Catholic co-directors to achieve the transfer of the administration-commission to the Kreis directorate collectively outweighed its misgivings over possible Prussian machinations, presumably because Prussia's influence in this Kreis was relatively limited.

\*

The case was not only discussed at the intermediary, regional level of the Kreis diet, but also at the central assembly of the Reichstag. The Reichstag was probably more reflective of a principled princely interest and interpretation of the case, and of Imperial law in general, than the Kreis because most Reichstag members were not as geopolitically involved in the case as the Kreis estates. Hyacinth had a series of pamphlets informally distributed among Reichstag envoys.[158] One complained against both the Palatine commission in the Columba case and the Cologne cathedral chapter commission. It requested the assembled envoys to pass a favourable resolution asking for the appointment of a different commission which would investigate the disputes impartially and ensure the return of Siegen castle and the control of government to the prince, rather than illegitimately administering the territory itself.[159] In March 1708, the cathedral chapter distributed its own counter-arguments in pamphlets at Regensburg. They detailed

---

[157] Ibid., 25 Feb. 1711: ibid., fol. 93r.
[158] Austrian Reichstag-envoy Jodoci to Joseph I, Regensburg, 3 May 1709: HHStA, SK, Regensburg, Österr.-Ges.-Berichte 29, fol. 246.
[159] *EStC* 13 (1709), 49–53.

princely exactions and the oppressive nature of Hyacinth's government to discredit him and his critique of the administration-commission. It was stressed that the commission's work and its administration had received the explicit approval of the Emperor as the highest judge.[160]

The Nassau-Siegen case was discussed formally at the Reichstag in mid-1709, in a process which culminated in the Reichstag draft resolution (*Reichsgutachten*) of June 1709. In April 1709, the archbishop-elector of Mainz's 'directorial envoy' Otten (in charge of permitting or denying the dictation of statements, a prerequisite for the official deliberation on a topic) reported that many princely envoys believed that Hyacinth's situation was prejudicial to the princely rank in general.[161] The reply of the elector of Mainz gives an indication of his attitudes to the events in Nassau-Siegen. Lothar Franz was not averse, in principle, to the discussion of the case, nor to the prince's readmission to government, as long as the princess (Lothar Franz's niece) could be assured of an allowance befitting her rank. However, Lothar Franz believed that Hyacinth's removal from power was his own fault. He would have 'done Well by duly submitting to His Imp. Maj. immediately, by offering to lead a different, more Christian kind of government in future, and letting the Imperial commission in the disputes with his subject run its course'.[162]

The draft resolution called for the Emperor to 'redress the complaints through the speedy appointment of a different commission, in conformity with the Imperial constitution'. In other words, the appointment of the Kreis directorate was requested, as its previous bypassing had been, according to the princely interpretation, unconstitutional. Hyacinth should be readmitted to government. At the same time, however, the Emperor and the new Imperial commission should ensure that 'the Imperial laws are meticulously observed, and the subjects secured and mildly governed'. The new commission was to allocate a sufficient allowance not only to the prince, but also to his wife.[163] Both Jodoci[164] and Lothar Franz[165] seriously doubted whether the prince would be satisfied with this resolution. Although it called for his restoration, it also requested a supervisory Imperial commission to be stationed in his territory, which would protect his subjects and ensure the payment of an allowance to his estranged wife, caveats which were incompatible with Hyacinth's conception of his prerogatives. The following month the Reichshofrat announced, without providing any explanation, that the

---

[160] *Information, von einem Hochwürdigen Domb=Capitul zu Cölln*, 30 Mar. 1708: *EStC* 13 (1709), 73–9.
[161] Otten to Lothar Franz, Regensburg, 11 Apr. 1709: HHStA, MEA, Reichstag 339.
[162] Lothar Franz to Otten, Bankenfeld, 14 Apr. 1709.
[163] *Reichsreport*, 19 June 1709: HHStA, MEA, Reichstag 340.
[164] Jodoci to Joseph I, Regensburg, 21 June 1709: HHStA, SK, Regensburg, Österr.-Ges.-Berichte 29, fols 510, 523.
[165] Lothar Franz to Otten, Aschaffenburg, 24 June 1709: HHStA, MEA, Reichstag 340.

Emperor had decided against ratifying the draft resolution.[166] It therefore never attained the status of Imperial law.

\*

The Nassau-Siegen case did not receive much comment in the Empire's news and comment media (because it was a relatively small and politically low-ranking territory and because no newspapers were published in Siegen), and when it was mentioned in journals and newspapers, it mainly dealt with the confessional conflict.[167] This does not mean that the case was not present in the public sphere; as during most political conflicts in the Empire, the main protagonists published and distributed numerous printed pamphlets defending their positions and legal interpretations.[168] These were often reprinted years later in historical and legal compendia aimed mainly at academic audiences, but which also served as reference works for political actors.[169] Such pamphlets were primarily addressed to the Reichstag and to other princes—constituting a kind of 'inter-governmental public discourse' that was aimed at securing political support.[170] Although most of the media coverage focussed on the aspect of the confessional conflict, the early interventions against the prince by the Reichshofrat and the ruler-subjects conflict did receive some comment. In terms of the confessional grievances of the Reformed subjects of the Catholic territory against the various Imperial and Kreis administrations, the media commentary was largely sympathetic towards the subjects and critical of the administrations.[171]

Yet the attitude among authors and editors of print media towards the initial interventions was uniformly positive. Although they were critical of the work of the administrations, there was no question that limiting or removing Hyacinth's governmental powers had been necessary. The author of the journal *Europäische Fama*, for example, commented in 1707 that 'the princely agnates *had to* support the oppressed subjects by appealing to the proper instances for a cessation of the confused fiscal policies, because this small principality cannot afford the upkeep of such a large number of servants'.[172] The Imperial intervention of 1706 was reported in a matter-of-factly way by other journals, including the *Monatlicher Staats-Spiegel* and the *Curieuses Bücher-Cabinet*.[173] Clippings from newspapers, which generally contained less comment and appeared more frequently than

---

[166] RHR-resolution, 15 July 1709: HHStA, RHR, Prot.-xviii, 23, fol. 31r.

[167] Arndt, *Herrschaftskontrolle*, 406–22.

[168] Ulrich Rosseaux, 'Flugschriften und Flugblätter im Mediensystem des Alten Reiches', in Johannes Arndt et al. (eds), *Das Mediensystem im Alten Reich der Frühen Neuzeit (1600–1750)* (Göttingen, 2010), 99–114.

[169] Arndt, *Herrschaftskontrolle*, 126–39.

[170] Wolfgang Burgdorf, 'Der intergouvernementale publizistische Diskurs', in Arndt et al. (eds), *Mediensystem*, 75–98.

[171] Arndt, *Herrschaftskontrolle*, 427.     [172] *Europäische Fama* 66 (1707), 434.

[173] *Monatlicher Staats-Spiegel* (1706) 65; *Curieuses Bücher-Cabinet* 1 (1711), 906–8.

journals, and pamphlets were often collected by diplomats and statesmen involved in the case and sometimes attached to reports to give an indication of attitudes in the public sphere.[174] The *Wöchentliche Relation* newspaper commented favourably on the 1707 intervention against the prince.[175]

\*

Apart from the Emperor and the Reichshofrat, the assessments by the involved contemporaries of the Imperial administration by the Cologne cathedral chapter commission were negative. However, this did not generally reflect a rejection of the principle of protective intervention itself. Apart from Hyacinth, those actors that were unfavourably disposed to the Imperial administration had clearly recognised the necessity of intervening against the prince's brutal regime, and advocated the intervention largely independently of immediate politico-strategic considerations (apart from the importance of maintaining general good governance and finances in order not to endanger the funding of the war against France). After the removal of the threat to the subjects and the establishment of the Imperial administration, sceptics started to criticise the post-intervention arrangements, not the execution of the commission itself. The Nassau agnates were alarmed at the complete dispossession of one of their relatives and would have liked to see the family pacts respected through an arrangement in which they themselves were appointed to the commission. While the Kreis directors were less concerned by the transformation of the investigation-commission into an administration-commission, along with the concomitant deposition of the prince, they did start to raise vociferous objections to the fact that the administration was not carried out by them, as they believed Imperial law prescribed.

While political self-interest started to predominate such considerations after the intervention itself, the continued need to protect the subjects was ostensibly recognised by all external actors. While it was certainly not in the corporate interest of the Imperial Estates to allow a precedent to be set whereby a ruling prince could be removed from power by Imperial authorities without the consent of the other Imperial Estates, the Reichstag did not simply issue a straightforward critique of the deposition. By calling for a continuation of a protective commission in Nassau-Siegen, the princes effectively expressed their approval of the concept of protective intervention. The principled opposition of the princely rank as a whole to the deposition, which is apparent in the 1709 draft resolution at the Reichstag, was less visible at the Kreis level, presumably because the directors were tempted by the prospect of themselves gaining administrative control over the territory in their vicinity. At the Reichstag, most represented rulers were unaffected by considerations specific to the Lower-Rhenish-Westphalian Kreis. The Reichstag-

---

[174] Several are in LANRW, NW Kreis, I N 15, 29, 145.
[175] *Wöchentliche Relation* 24, 13 June 1711.

resolution that resulted was therefore an attempt to harmonise the norm of upholding the rights of mediate subjects with need to respect the corporate rights of princes.

## The Involvement of the Corpus Evangelicorum

The first appeal that was received by the *Corpus* in 1707 detailed the range of confessional persecution suffered by the Protestants: physical attacks, the confiscation of property, fines for Protestant worship, the seizure of chapels, and the removal of Protestant school masters. The appeal stated that Hyacinth's measures 'run directly contrary to law and justice, the Peace of Westphalia, Christian love itself'.[176] Reports were indicating that confessional restrictions were resuming under the administration commission which was installed later in 1707.[177] The resulting *Corpus* resolution in 1709 instructed 'all neighbouring Protestant Estates...to lend a helping hand' in ensuring that the subjects were restored to their Westphalian rights, but it also unhelpfully requested that the power-politically weak Protestant Nassau princes take the first step.[178]

New subjects' appeals continued to be forwarded to the *Corpus* in 1709.[179] The Reformed prince of Nassau-Siegen called for a more active intervention by the *Corpus*, stressing that the 'entire Protestant well being' depended upon 'clear and settled' Westphalian rights being respected everywhere.[180] With appeals to the *Corpus Catholicorum* for the matter to be settled by direct negotiation being unsuccessful, the *Corpus* addressed the Emperor with requests for redress.[181] The *Corpus* then resorted to a more robust mandate in 1710, namely requesting Brandenburg-Prussia, Hanover and Hessen-Kassel, to carry out a (potentially military) intervention.[182] The circle diet envoys of the three designated interveners threatened the cathedral chapter in Cologne in the hope of effecting redress, causing a degree of apprehension among the local Catholic princes.[183]

Confessional grievances continued during the subsequent administration by the circle directors, despite the fact that Brandenburg was a junior co-administrator.[184] Violent confrontations in Siegen in 1712 and 1716 in which several Protestants were killed by Palatine and Münster administration troops led

---

[176] *Gravamina*, 15 Feb. 1707, in *EStC* 13 (1709), 38–40.
[177] *Memorial*, 8 Sep. 1708, in *EStC* 13 (1709), 46–8.    [178] *Corpus*-resolution, ibid., 48–9.
[179] Appeal by Reformed subjects, 14 Apr. 1709: ibid., 19–21.
[180] Julius Zinckgraf to *Corpus*, Regensburg, 27 Apr. 1709: ibid., 1–9.
[181] *Corpus*-resolution, 22 Nov. 1709, ibid., 35–6; *Corporus* to Emperor, Regensburg, 28 Dec.1709: ibid., 94–6.
[182] *Corpus*-resolution, 18 Oct 1710: LANRW, NW Kreis, I N 15, 47, fol. 87.
[183] Lower-Rhenish-Westphalian circle envoys to Cologne cathedral chapter, 28 Jan. 1711: ibid., fols 89–9.
[184] Numerous confessional grievances of reformed subjects against the circle-administration, 1715–21: HHStA, RHR, Ob.-Reg. 796(4).

to a flurry of *Corpus* activism.[185] The elector of Brandenburg (as circle codirector) criticised the actions of his fellow administrators' troops as 'highly criminal acts of violence which cannot be justified before God and humans'.[186] Although not part of the administration, George I of Britain-Hanover pointed out that 'this matter is of far too great a consequence as to not attract Our attention and that of the other Protestant Estates...and to not lead them to sympathize with their highly oppressed coreligionists'.[187]

After the 1716 killings, Frederick William I of Brandenburg-Prussia informed his Reichstag envoy, Ernst Metternich, that he had ordered a contingent of troops into Nassau-Siegen to protect the Reformed subjects against further mistreatment, 'as directed by the... *Corpus Evangelicorum*'. Metternich was instructed to ascertain whether Hanover and Hessen-Kassel wished to send troops into Nassau-Siegen as well, in accordance with the 1710 *Corpus* resolution.[188] In July the Hanoverian envoy Rudolf Wrisberg reported that Metternich had told him 'His Majesty of Prussia hoped that he would not be expected to settle this business alone. He had done his part and would have to lower his fists if he were not seconded.'[189] A Prussian memo distributed at the Reichstag argued that Protestant princes could not be blamed for 'assisting their suppressed and innocently persecuted coreligionists against all contrary [to Westphalia] acts of violence.' Not to intervene would be 'unjustifiable before God and the world'.[190]

Apart from Brandenburg increasing its military presence in Nassau-Siegen by about thirty men, the *Corpus*' intercessions remained ineffectual. Although the *Corpus* implicitly claimed a right to independently authorise external interventions, the regular channel of intervention authorised by the Emperor and the Reichshofrat held more traction. Similar Reichshofrat mandates to intervene had, after all, been promptly executed by electoral Cologne and the circle in 1706 and 1707. The Protestant princes' claimed right of intervention was only in an incipient stage during this conflict. It is noteworthy that Frederick William justified his decision to dispatch more troops on the basis of the previous *Corpus* resolution, instead of his existing circle-mandated co-administration of the territory. Therefore, for some Protestant powers at least, the perceived legitimising power of the *Corpus* seemed to be greater than that of the circle, when it came to justifying interventions, at least to fellow-Protestant princes. The involvement of the *Corpus* in this case helped to consolidate it, both as a platform for

---

[185] See material in LANRW, NW Kreis, I N 15, 155.
[186] Frederick William I to co-directors, Berlin, 24 Mar. 1716: LANRW, NW Kreis, I N 15, 64(i), fols 355-6.
[187] George I to elector-Palatine, St James, 1 May 1716: ibid., fols 406-8r.
[188] Frederick William I to Metternich (copy), Berlin, 12 May 1716: NHStH, Cal.-Br. 11, 2967(3), fol. 421.
[189] Wrisberg to George I, Regensburg, 6 July 1716: NHStH, Cal.-Br. 11, 2968(i), fol. 29.
[190] Prussian memorandum, 4 Nov. 1716: LANRW, NW Kreis, I N 15, 64(i), fols 271-2.

common Protestant action, and as a new, alternative, channel of appeal against perceived transgressions by Catholic rulers—an informal tribunal which operated in parallel to the courts, and represented a new variety of the juridification of religious conflict.

Despite personal sympathies with the Protestant subjects, the leading princes of the *Corpus* were geopolitically disinclined to intervene without the Emperor's authority, as this would have been seen as an affront to the Emperor, and this failure of moral sentiment to match with their political interests inhibited intervention in this case.[191] The formal head of the *Corpus*, the elector of Saxony, and the most powerful *Corpus* members Hanover and Brandenburg, all owed—to varying degrees—their respective rank elevations of 1697, 1692, and 1701 to the Emperor. They were all involved in the Great Northern War and did not welcome the prospect of a military distraction in the far west of the Reich. More important was the fact that the War of the Spanish Succession was ongoing, and the revision of the Ryswick clause was deemed to be of greater importance. To achieve this would require not only a victory over France, but also a sympathetic attitude towards this question by the Emperor during the peace negotiations, which the leading *Corpus* princes did not wish to squander by carrying out an unauthorised 'horizontal' intervention.[192] Thus the Brandenburg envoy at the Reichstag noted in 1711 that 'excessive force [in Nassau-Siegen] could be more detrimental than advantageous during the current political trends, because unity and a good understanding is so necessary in the Empire'.[193]

Political interests relating to less grand schemes also inhibited Protestant intervention: Frederick William I's chief foreign political goal was the acquisition of Jülich-Berg, for which the Emperor's support and ultimately enfeoffment would be necessary. The king-elector of Britain-Hanover George I was geopolitically closely aligned with the Emperor until well into the year 1719 and was therefore similarly disinclined towards carrying out a rogue military intervention which would offend the Emperor. It was only after the conclusion of the Spanish Succession war that the Prussian king was willing to take a token step.[194] Apart from this very limited engagement, the three main *Corpus* princes remained trapped in a 'vicious circle of inaction',[195] in which each summoned the others to intervene collectively, but refused to take the action first.

---

[191] For the following, see also Kalipke, *Verfahren*, 287–352.
[192] Thus: Peter Wilson, 'Prussia and the Holy Roman Empire 1700–40', *German Historical Institute London Bulletin* 36 (2014), 3–48, at 29.
[193] Envoy Henniges to Frederick I, Regensburg, 21 May 1711, quoted in Kalipke, *Verfahren*, 305.
[194] Frederick-William I to Metternich, Berlin, 12 May 1716: NHStH, Cal.-Br. 2967(iii), fol. 421.
[195] Kalipke, *Verfahren*, 329.

## Conclusion

The case reflects the high degree to which the different overlapping levels of the Imperial system (locality, territory, Kreis, Reichstag and *Corpus Evangelicorm*, Emperor and Reichshofrat) were interlocked and needed to be taken into account by each other.

The diplomacy, litigation, and commentary surrounding the interventions and external administrations in Nassau-Siegen also reveal the importance contemporaries attached to norms of governmental conduct and the treatment of subjects. These related not only to legal precepts but also to concepts of 'Christian', civilised behaviour. It was because Prince Hyacinth defied such norms and behaved as if he could act within his own territory in a sovereign manner that an intervention was deemed necessary. Protecting the prince's subjects therefore became a necessary assertion and defence of the Emperor's authority, overlordship, and jurisdiction in the eyes of the Reichshofrat.

Strategic and political considerations played a role in a broad sense, particularly the context of the ongoing Imperial war against France. It largely explains the non-intervention of the leading *Corpus* members against the administration. The war also provided Hyacinth with a spurious pretext to financially exploit his subjects for his own dynastic goals. It also possibly contributed to Vienna's desire to intervene against the prince to act as a deterrent against other princes who failed to contribute to Imperial defence yet used the context of the war as a pretext to exploit their subjects. The banning of the elector of Cologne and the passage of the commission to Cologne's interim-government, the cathedral chapter, also affected the choice of who was to be appointed to the administration.

Yet geopolitical interests did not need to be as pressing as in more substantial territories to reinforce a desire to furnish protection in a territory of the size and political weight of Catholic Nassau-Siegen. Instead the extent of the violation of norms allowed an intervention to take place in a large part thanks to notions of a duty to defend persecuted subjects. Corporate and political considerations of self-interest certainly took centre stage immediately after the intervention of 1707 and from the time of the external administrations, but all the while the discourse of a necessity of ensuring subjects' security was at the forefront of arguments used. Indeed, for many actors at different levels (the Emperor, the Kreis and factions therein, individual princes, the *Corpus*), putting oneself in a position to be able to protect subjects more effectively entailed an improved power-political position.

While there was general agreement that Hyacinth's rule and perceived violations of subjects' rights (both before and after his deposition) necessitated intervention, the course of the Nassau-Siegen case reflects two very different, and in theory at least, incompatible approaches to the provision of external protection. The Emperor, the Reichshofrat, and some of the leading princes espoused the notion that only 'vertical' intervention was legally defensible and compatible with the authority and rights of the Emperor as the head of the Imperial hierarchy and as the highest judge. According to the *Corpus* and, to a much lesser extent, the Lower Rhenish-Westphalian Kreis, 'horizontal' intervention was also permissible. Given the extent of the juridification of German political culture, all arguments had to be framed primarily in legal terms.

As was often the custom during such conflicts in the multi-layered sociopolitical and confessional fabric of the Empire, those seeking protection had a wide array of potential protectors to appeal to. While appeals to the Kreis and Imperial Estates, and the Emperor, implored the recipient to intervene by making emotive references to great suffering and injustice, appeals to the Reichshofrat always sought to underline the head of the Empire's authority and duty to intervene and protect, on the basis of his overlordship and supreme judicial office. Appeals to the Protestant princes and the Kreis, on the other hand, tended to emphasise the crucial importance of Westphalian rights being upheld, and the estates-based prerogatives of the office of the Kreis directors. Despite the disagreement over vertical versus horizontal intervention (in which the former remained the more authoritative), the underlying normative emphasis on the limitations of princely powers and the unacceptability of arbitrary violence against subjects and fellow princes, and the belief that infractions of these norms called for intervention, was the same on both sides.

# 7
# Intervention in Medium-Sized Principalities
## The Case of Mecklenburg-Schwerin, 1713–1730

In contrast to the Nassau-Siegen case, which was more peripherally affected by geopolitical and strategic considerations, the intervention in Mecklenburg was an altogether more complex affair. While the personality, claimed rights and persecutory measures of the rulers in both cases were similar, the Mecklenburg ruler-estates conflict in the Lower-Saxon Kreis gained a degree of diplomatic and politico-strategic salience that was absent from the smaller-scale conflict in Nassau-Siegen. This was largely due to the broader context of the Northern War, the related alliance between the duke of Mecklenburg and Russia, and the rivalry of Hanover and Brandenburg-Prussia in northern Germany. The Emperor's political stance towards developments in the north also affected Vienna's approach to the crisis and added a further set of relationships which influenced the case. On the other hand, the confessional dimension which played a part in Nassau-Siegen was largely absent in the Mecklenburg intervention.

The Mecklenburg case has received more coverage in the secondary literature than the Nassau-Siegen and Vaduz/Schellenberg cases examined above, although many of the works are dated.[1] A detailed monograph provided an analysis of the role of Mecklenburg in the strategic assessments and policies of Russia and Hanover during the Northern War, but neglected the Imperial constitutional context.[2] This gap was filled by Hughes, whose book assessed the case at the Reichshofrat, providing a valuable contribution by charting the litigation process and analysing the case in terms of structures and processes.[3] More recently, Arndt has examined the coverage of the duke's suspension from power in 1728 in the contemporary Germany print media.[4] The aim of the present investigation is

---

[1] Peter Wick, *Versuchezur Errichtung des Territorialabsolutismus in Mecklenburg in der ersten Hälfte des 18. Jahrhunderts* (East Berlin, 1964); Otto Vitense, *Geschichte von Mecklenburg* (Gotha, 1920), 255.

[2] Walther Mediger, *Mecklenburg, Rußland und England-Hannover 1706–21. Ein Beitrag zur Geschichte des Nordischen Krieges* (2 vols., Hildesheim, 1967).

[3] Michael Hughes, *Law and Politics in 18th Century Germany. The Imperial Aulic Council in the Reign of Charles VI* (Woodbridge, 1988).

[4] Johannes Arndt, *Herrschaftskontrolle durch Öffentlichkeit. Die publizistische Darstellung politischer Konflikte im Heiligen Römischen Reich 1648–1750* (Göttingen, 2013), 448–503.

different. Instead of providing another detailed account of the course of the crisis or its attendant litigation, this chapter will seek to discern the normative basis of the motivations, aims, perceptions, and reactions of the involved and uninvolved parties in the case.

The duchy of Mecklenburg on the Baltic coast has traditionally been regarded as one of the most socially backward territories of the Old Reich, with a large number of aristocratic landowning 'Junkers' who lorded over toiling indentured peasant-serfs.[5] Duke Carl Leopold (r.1713–28)[6] had inherited a long-standing conflict between estates and dukes in which the latter sought to gain greater taxation rights and alter the constitutional balance in the territory in their favour.[7] Where Carl Leopold set himself apart from his predecessors was in his willingness to resort to violence against both his noble subjects and his own officials, and in his readiness to challenge the Emperor's authority while also scheming with foreign powers.[8] The estates conflict began soon after Carl Leopold's accession in 1713 and revolved around the question of taxation, the duke's attempts to set up a large standing army, and his determination to replace the customary territorial constitution founded on limited, estates-based government with an absolutist regime.[9] The ducal government's use of force against both the landed nobility and the city officials of Rostock, and forceful exactions of the demanded taxes, led to a string of appeals to the Reichshofrat[10] and other Imperial Estates.[11] In April 1716 Carl Leopold staked his fortunes on an alliance with Tsar Peter of Russia, whose niece he married.[12] The resulting large-scale introduction of Russian troops on aristocratic lands in Mecklenburg not only exacerbated the hardships and complaints of the nobility, but also alarmed neighbouring Hanover, the Emperor and other rulers. The Reichshofrat had consistently condemned the duke's actions from 1714 onwards.[13]

The Guelph rulers George I of Britain-Hanover and August Wilhelm, duke of Braunschweig-Wolfenbüttel were appointed by the Reichshofrat to a commission

---

[5] E.g., Wick, *Versuche*, 13–33.

[6] Gerhard Heitz, 'Herzog Carl Leopold von Mecklenburg-Schwerin', in Rolf Straubel et al. (eds), *Kaiser-König-Kardinal. Deutsche Fürsten 1500–1800* (Leipzig, 1991), 303–10.

[7] Sigrid Jahns, '"Mecklenburgisches Wesen" oder absolutistisches Regiment? Mecklenburgischer Ständekonflikt und neue kaiserliche Reichspolitik (1658–1755)', in Paul-Joachim Heinig et al. (eds), *Reich, Regionen und Europa in Mittlealter und Neuzeit* (Berlin, 2000), 323–51.

[8] Previous dukes had long sought external support for their domestic aims: Sebastian Joost, *Zwischen Hoffnung und Ohnmacht: Auswärtige Politik als Mittel zur Durchsetzung landesherrlicher Macht in Mecklenburg (1648–1695)* (Münster, 2009).

[9] Mediger, *Mecklenburg*, 367.

[10] E.g., Nobility's RHR-agent Daniel Praun to Charles VI, 14 Feb. 1716: HHStA, RHR, Den.-Rec. 696(4).

[11] E.g., territorial estates' core committee (*engerer Ausschuss*) to George I, Ratzeburg, 22 Sep. 1716: NHStAH, Cal. Br. 24, 3866, fols 34–8.

[12] Original copy: LHAS, Ausw.-Bez 2.11–2/1, 1043.

[13] RHR-report 24 Dec. 1714: HHStA, RHR, Vota 34.

to execute a *Conservatorium* over Rostock in 1716,[14] and over the combined estates in 1717.[15] The execution was carried out in February–March 1719 and the investigation-commission was set up soon afterwards.[16] Duke Carl Leopold's refusal to acknowledge the authority of the commission, and the killing of alleged traitors in the two towns he still controlled (Dömitz and Schwerin) in 1722,[17] forced the Reichshofrat and the neighbouring princes to continue dealing with the case. Over the years following the 1719 intervention, relations between the commission and Vienna generally deteriorated, mirroring the relationship between George I and the Emperor.[18] Following the former's death in 1727 and the consequent lapsing of the commission, the Emperor issued several decrees on 11 May 1728. These stipulated the replacement of the Hanoverian-led commission by an Imperial administration under the duke's brother Christian Ludwig as administrator, the suspension of Carl Leopold from government, and the extension to Brandenburg-Prussia of the former commissioners' continuing *Conservatorium* over the estates.[19] The decreed Imperial administration was never implemented on the ground, due to strong opposition by the former commissioners and Imperial Estates throughout Germany. In this context an intervention against the Emperor and his new Prussian ally by the external guarantors of Westphalia was discussed.

## Ducal Strategies and Arguments

This section and the next addresses the range of strategies and arguments that were used by the duke and the nobles in the contest over support and approval, a contest which took place at the Empire's main platforms for publicity, the Reichstag and the Imperial court. While the protagonists represented differing interpretations of Imperial law and the validity of Imperial intervention, both sides argued legalistically, revealing a limited degree of common ground on the basis of constitutional law. In addition to arguing his case publicly, the duke sought to curtail his opponents' appeals to the Reichshofrat as these had given rise to disadvantageous litigation and negative publicity. The duke used a combination of violence and threats against the nobility and the city officials of Rostock in the hope of cowing them into submission and deterring further appeals to Vienna.[20]

---

[14] Charles VI to George I and August Wilhelm, Vienna, 21 Aug. 1716: NHStAH, Cal. Br. 24, 3866, fols. 4–7r.
[15] Ibid., 22 Oct. 1717: NHStAH, Cal. Br. 11, 1613.
[16] Hanoverian account: NHStAH, Hann.-92, 2204, fols 67–71.
[17] RHR-report 26 Nov. 1723: HHStA, RHR, Vota 35.
[18] Jeremy Black, 'When "Natural Allies" fall out: Anglo-Austrian relations, 1725–40', *MöStA* 36 (1983), 120–49.
[19] RHR-resolution 11 May 1728: Moser, *Merckwürdige RHR-Conclusa*, vi, 869–88.
[20] Reported in Metsch to Charles VI, Braunschweig, 26 July 1718: HHStA, RK, Dipl.-Akten, Braunschweig-Hannover, 2c(1), fols 234–5.

Treaties of submission were forcibly extracted from Rostock[21] and then presented at Vienna[22] and Hanover[23] in the hope of thereby stalling Imperial protective measures. Once the leading nobles had fled to Hanoverian territory, the government proceeded to initiate criminal prosecutions against them.[24]

While the ducal government initially litigated energetically at the Reichshofrat, it soon shifted its focus to other methods.[25] Letters continued to be sent to the Emperor and the commissioners-designate, but these were simultaneously published, and were primarily designed to influence princely opinion.[26] The duke hoped to take advantage of Mecklenburg's strategic location in the context of the Northern War so as to gain support against his domestic opposition. The centrepiece of his foreign policy was the alliance with Russia.[27] Apart from relying on the hoped for Russian military assistance against the execution,[28] ducal policy was also aimed at rallying the support of fellow princes. Carl Leopold's envoy to Vienna, Johann Eichholtz, stressed the importance of conducting a good publicity campaign.[29] Being denied the official dictation of ducal statements at the Reichstag by Mainz, the Mecklenburg envoy resorted to informally distributing large numbers of pamphlets among the envoys.[30] In addition to the indirect channel of the Reichstag, the duke also sent hand-written circular letters to various princes.[31] Some of the duke's diplomats found their government's conduct unpalatable, admissions which were made informally to fellow envoys.[32] After the execution, the duke tried hard to obstruct the commission's work by organising disruptive measures from his remaining towns of Dömitz and Schwerin.[33] His basic arguments remained the same and were repeated tirelessly in the hope of a full restoration.[34] Because of his lack of imagination, his pamphlets missed out on potentially effective arguments, such as portraying the noble estates not primarily

---

[21] Treaty and Imperial invalidation in Moser, *Merckwürdige RHR-Conclusa*, ii, 158–9.
[22] Johann Eichholtz to Carl Leopold, Vienna, 5 Dec. 1716: LHAS, Ausw.-Bez. 2.11-2/1, 1601, fols 82–5r, at fol. 82v.
[23] Carl Leopold to George I, Rostock, 7 Oct. 1716: NHStAH, Cal. Br. 24, 3866, fols 80–1.
[24] Metsch to Charles VI, Braunschweig, 15 July 1718: HHStA, RK, Dipl.-Akten, Braunschweig-Hannover-Berichte 2c(2), fols 224, 227.
[25] Hughes, *Law*, 156–7.
[26] E.g., *Justifications-Schreiben an Ihro Kayserl.-Majestät*: EstC 32 (1719), 144–50; *Copia Wieder-Antwort*: ibid., 187–98.
[27] Mediger, *Mecklenburg*, 87–121, 176–220.
[28] Eichholtz to Carl Leopold, Vienna, 27 Nov. 1717: LHAS, Ausw.-Bez. 2.11-2/1, 1602, fols 151–4.
[29] Eichholtz to Wolffradt, Vienna, 5 Mar. 1718: LHAS, Ausw.-Bez. 2.11-2/1, 1603, fols 22–4.
[30] Otten to Lothar Franz, archbishop-elector of Mainz, Regensburg, 16 May 1718: HHStA, MEA, Reichstag 374.
[31] E.g., Carl Leopold to archbishop-elector of Cologne, Rostock, 17 Dec. 1717: LANRW, Kurköln-VI, 1411, fols 1–4. Such letters were soon printed, e.g., EstC 32, 68–9, 140–3.
[32] Wrisberg to George I, Regensburg, 23 Nov. 1716: NHStAH, Cal. Br. 11, 2968(iv), fols 769–71r, at fol. 769v.
[33] Commission subdelegates' memorandum, Rostock, 21 Mar. 1721: NHStAH, Hann.-9g, 19, fols 18–24.
[34] E.g., Carl Leopold to Charles VI, Danzig, 15 Dec. 1728: Klüver (ed.), *Beschreibung* (Hamburg, 1740), v, 654–60.

as disobedient subjects, but as selfish exploiters of the territory and the majority of its poor inhabitants which harmed the common good.[35]

The ducal government argued—not unreasonably—that neutral Mecklenburg had fallen victim to occupying and traversing troops during the Northern War.[36] Appeals for Imperial assistance had been ineffective and therefore the duchy needed to provide for its own security through a standing army and strengthened fortifications. The security imperative also explained the alliance with Russia. The princely right of concluding alliances and maintaining armies enshrined in the Peace of Westphalia IPO Art. VIII §2, together with §180 Last Imperial Recess (1654) which stipulated the duty of territorial estates to contribute financially to the upkeep of territorial defences, formed the twin legal foundations of the duke's arguments.[37] These were inalienable princely prerogatives that were argued not to be liable to any limitations by ancient treaties concluded between the estates and his predecessors. These territorial arrangements could only be considered valid as long as they did not infringe upon princely rights as enshrined in fundamental Imperial laws.[38] As the princely rights of providing for defences of the territory and taxing subjects for this purpose were definitively guaranteed, it was argued that these 'taxation and territorial defence matters are no longer subject to any judicial consent', in other words, the jurisdiction of the Imperial courts was denied when it came to appeals against such rights.[39] While the duke stressed that he had no intention of questioning the Emperor's supreme overlordship,[40] he did emphasise that he was determined to enforce his rights vis-à-vis his subjects 'at whatever cost'.[41] In an open letter, Carl Leopold appealed to the principle of 'not interfering in the domestic affairs and government of fellow Estates'.[42]

## The Territorial Estates

The strategy of the estates was wholeheartedly focused on the attainment of Imperial intervention in the form of a *Conservatorium* preferably executed militarily by Hanover. An energetic campaign of lobbying the Imperial court was launched which manifested itself primarily in a well-run lawsuit at the Reichshofrat. The litigating efforts of the nobility were impressive, and they documented the

---

[35] Arndt, *Herrschaftskontrolle*, 502.
[36] For the following: *Hochgemüßigte Anzeige* (Rostock, 1717), *EStC* 32, 74–107.
[37] Also: *Ersuch-Schreiben des Hertzogs zu Mecklenburg-Schwerin*: ibid., 151–6.
[38] *Wahrhaffte Benachrichtigung des...Hertzogen Carl Leopolds...* (1718): ibid., 157–78.
[39] Carl Leopold to Reichstag-envoy Hagen, Rostock, 15 Jan. 1718: NHStAH, Cal. Br. 11, 2971, i, fols 218–21.
[40] *Justifications-Schreiben...des Hertzogs zu Mecklenburg-Schwerin*: *EStC* 32, 144–50.
[41] *Nachdrückliche Declaration...* (1717): ibid., 51–61.
[42] *Ausführlichen Wieder-Antwort...* (1718): *EStC* 32, 187–98.

whole range of ducal excesses through detailed notarised accounts.[43] In addition to submissions to the Reichshofrat by their Reichshofrat-agent Daniel Praun, the nobles also sent direct appeals to the Emperor and George I, which were often simultaneously published.[44] The nobles were adept at using their extensive network of supporters (many Mecklenburg nobles had found employment at various German and European courts) to favourably influence policy towards the estates conflict.[45] Thanks to their considerable resources, the nobles also employed envoys who travelled to Vienna, Regensburg, Braunschweig, and London. Before the Reichshofrat mandated the comprehensive *Conservatorium* in October 1717, the nobles' main efforts were directed at Vienna towards the issuing of such a resolution.[46] Once this goal was achieved, they shifted their focus to encourage the commissioners-designate to promptly carry out the decreed intervention, and to favourably dispose other princes towards such measures.[47] After the intervention was carried out, the estates focused their energies on preventing any relaxation of the commission or a return of the duke to full governmental powers.[48]

A vital corollary of their litigation efforts was the nobility's tireless and efficient publicity campaign. It was designed not only to create a generally favourable attitude towards their cause among the informed public in the Empire but also to support their lawsuit at Vienna. Given the nobles' lack of hard power, their media campaign has aptly been described as an eighteenth-century form of asymmetrical warfare.[49] The arguments used by the nobles in their private and public representations reveal an emphasis on Imperial law that was quite different from Carl Leopold's. The estates' arguments were in the tradition of positivist constitutional law.[50] This was predicated upon a belief that in addition to the overarching framework of fundamental Imperial laws, each territory had its own territorial constitution based on local treaties and/or custom. While the former regulated relations between and within each level of the Imperial hierarchy and safeguarding certain basic corporate and individual rights, the diverse territorial constitutions specified the particular rights, duties and privileges of rulers, subjects and territorial estates within any given territory. It was the duty of each territorial ruler to respect these customary constitutional arrangements, and of the Emperor to act against princes transgressing this norm. The duke's determination to throw all

---

[43] E.g., Praun to Charles VI, n.d. HHStA, RHR, Den.-Rec. 694(5).
[44] E.g., Behr to Charles VI, Vienna, 21 July 1716: HHStA, RK, Kl.-Reichsstände 347, fol. 159; *Abdruck an I. Kayserl.-Majestät Geschehenen... Vorstellung* (n.p., 1717): LHAS, Ausw.-Bez. 2.11–2/1, 1600.
[45] Hughes, *Law*, 64.
[46] E.g., Behr to Charles VI, Vienna, 4 May 1717: HHStA, RK, Kl.-Reichsstände 347, fols 213–26.
[47] *Abdruck des/an die/von Kayserl-Majestät... Verordnete Conservatores...* (1718): LANRW, Kurköln-VI, 1409, fols 33–8.
[48] RHR-Report 20 Mar. 1719 and 21 Apr. 1719: HHStA, RHR, Vota 35.
[49] Arndt, *Herrschaftskontrolle*, 500.   [50] Pečar, 'Am Rande', 214.

customary and treaty rights of the estates overboard constituted the illegality of his government and necessitated Imperial intervention.

The most important pamphlet published by the nobility accused Carl Leopold of undermining the rule of law and of 'completely ignoring salutary justice, which ought to be the highest law of each ruler, and... seeking to introduce an arbitrary government through military might'.[51] The pamphlet proceeded to posit five specific arguments: Firstly, the ducal armaments programme was excessive and unnecessary: 'territorial defence serves as a pretext for territorial destruction'; in other words, the complete suppression of the nobility. The demanded contributions vastly exceeded what was constitutionally permitted under the 1701 recess. The forces being built up were both too small and too large: too small to constitute an effective defence against European great power, yet too large given the resources available in the duchy. Secondly, the *ius foederum* (right to conclude alliances) cannot be used as an excuse to billet thousands of Russian troops on noble lands and have them carry out brutal exactions, in contravention of Imperial resolutions. It was argued that the Russian alliance failed to meet the conditions stipulated for the exercise of the *ius foederum*, because the Russian presence was undermining Kreis and Reich security. Thirdly, the duke's conduct was excessive and illegal, even from the sole point of view of Imperial fundamental laws. The Imperial laws recognised the validity of territorial constitutional arrangements and this constituted a crucial 'piece of the German Freedom'. Even JRA§180 only authorised subjects' financial contributions to the upkeep of fortresses and garrisons that were deemed 'necessary'. If no agreement could be reached on the definition thereof, the adjudicating authority of the Emperor as the highest judge needed to be respected, which the duke was refusing to do as the Emperor had decided in favour of the subjects. The fourth point stressed the validity of each of the territorial treaties. The final and most important argument concerned the Reichshofrat's supreme judicial authority in the Reich and the Emperor as highest judge. To underline the legality of Imperial interventions in territorial conflicts, the pamphlets mentioned the East Frisian and Nassau-Siegen cases as precedents. Reference was also made to notions of civilised governmental behaviour and it was argued that the ducal government was displaying 'harshness never known in Christendom'.[52] Similarly, another pamphlet accused the government of seeking to establish an 'arbitrary domination otherwise unheard of in Christendom'.[53]

---

[51] *Gegründete Wiederlegung/Einer Höchstgemüßigten Anzeige*... (n.p., 1718): NHStAH, Cal. Br. 11, 2971(ii), fols 264–81.
[52] *Abdruck des/an die/von Kayserl-Majestät... Verordnete Conservatores*... LANRW, Kurköln-VI, 1409, fols 33–8.
[53] *Abermahlig=höchstnöthige Vorstellung*, in *EstC* 32, 225–34.

## The Emperor's Court at Vienna

On the political side of court, the Austrian court-chancery (Hofkanzlei) and the Imperial chancery (Reichskanzlei) were primarily involved in the case.[54] The Reichskanzlei was run by the Imperial vice-chancellor Friedrich Karl von Schönborn (a nephew of Lothar Franz von Schönborn, archbishop-elector of Mainz and arch-chancellor of Germany), who was at the centre of the 'Imperial faction' in Vienna.[55] Leading members of the rival Austrian faction that worked on the case included the court chancellor Philipp von Sinzendorf, Prince Eugene of Savoy, and Gundaker Starhemberg. Schönborn's virtual outsider status among the Austrian ministers and Reichshofrat-members was to some extent mirrored in their attitudes towards Duke Carl Leopold, with Schönborn being the only leading figure somewhat sympathetic towards him.[56] The leading ministers of both factions and the Reichshofrat-president were all members of the privy conference, presided over by Prince Eugene.[57]

### (i) The Reichshofrat[58]

On examination of the Reichshofrat's reports and public statements and the reported private statements of Reichshofrat-members before the execution of the protective *Conservatorium* in February–March 1719, five principal arguments emerge. These relate chiefly to the reasons why Imperial intervention against the Mecklenburg government was deemed necessary. Firstly, the duke's conduct was deemed to be illegal and a violation of the territorial constitution and the Imperial fundamental laws. Compounding the unconstitutionality of his regime was its

---

[54] For their rivalry: Lothar Gross, 'Der Kampf zwischen Reichskanzlei und österreichischer Hofkanzlei um die Führung der auswärtigen Geschäfte', *Historische Vierteljahresschrift* 22 (1924/25), 279–312.

[55] Hugo Hantsch, *Reichsvizekanzler Friedrich Karl von Schönborn (1674–1746). Einige Kapitel zur politischen Geschichte Kaiser Josefs I. und Karls VI* (Augsburg, 1929), 169, 209.

[56] Eichholtz to Wolffradt, Vienna, 28 Oct. 1716: LHAS, Ausw.-Bez. 2.11–2/1, 1601, fols 21–3.

[57] McKay, *Prince Eugene*, 154–5.

[58] Hughes' work provides a step-by-step account of the Reichshofrat-litigation in the Mecklenburg case while omitting an overall analysis of the main principles of the dispensation of justice in the case and in particular with regard to the question of intervention. This is what will be attempted here. Hughes' main argument that the Reichshofrat was not under much pressure by the political branches of the court to reach verdicts in line with Habsburg interests will not be disputed here (Hughes, *Law*, 60–2). However, the present study utilises a range of reports on the informal statements and conversations of various ministers and Reichshofrat-members, which, when used in conjunction with the formal reports that form the basis of Hughes' study, reveal a less stark divide between the supposedly purely legal considerations of the Reichshofrat and the politico-strategic concerns of the ministers. Contrary to Hughes' claim (ibid., 43) that the Reichshofrat was only concerned with the questions of legality or illegality, it is argued here that it did in fact argue along the lines of justness, right and wrong, Christian duty and civilisation, in addition to the primary emphasis on legality/illegality, although these considerations often merged. Conversely, leading ministers also stressed the importance of legality and were not solely concerned with political considerations.

inherent injustice and its tyrannically violent arbitrariness. Secondly, there was an urgent necessity to intervene to save the nobles and other subjects from ruin. Thirdly, action was necessary to salvage and enforce the Emperor's authority as highest judge and Imperial overlord, given that the duke decided to ignore Imperial mandates ordering a cessation of measures against his subjects. Fourthly, putting a halt to the duke's oppressive and insubordinate policies by protecting the estates was necessary to serve as an example and a warning to other princes. Finally, the Reichshofrat also considered geopolitical factors.

1. The Reichshofrat consistently maintained from 1714 that the duke's actions were illegal according to the territorial and Imperial constitutions, and that therefore the estates' complaints were entirely justified. A 1714 report stressed that 'the introduction of unusual imposts and the violent exaction of contributions is totally unjustified'. According to the territorial treaties the duke was permitted 'at no time...to demand more from the territorial estates...than the annual 120,000 Rtlr'. The duke's application of Imperial laws, particularly the Last Imperial Recess of 1654, was spurious, because 'no Imperial Estate can have the right to self-servingly impose taxes on the subjects for the upkeep of a perpetual standing army, under the pretext of necessary maintenance'.[59] The *ius armorum et foederum* was also being misinterpreted by the duke, for the 'exercise of this right requires considerable causes, above all the good of the subjects...also that no danger results to the Reich'.[60] The illegitimate goal of the duke's measures was clear: he intended to impose an 'arbitrary power...and domination' on his subjects, totally devoid of any 'Christian compassion'.[61] In general, he had 'acted in a manner almost unheard-of under German Freedom,[62] [...] completely illegally'.[63] Following the arrival of the Russians, the Reichshofrat expressed the 'strong suspicion...that the undertaken Russian arrests and exactions have largely been instigated by the ducal Mecklenburg court...without any right or authorisation', in contravention of the 1555 Imperial Ordinances of Execution.[64] Reichshofrat-members expressed themselves similarly in private. In 1718, the Reichshofrat-president Ernst von Windischgrätz told the Hanoverian envoy to Vienna, Daniel Huldenberg, that the duke 'would not avoid just punishment, and God would ensure that his tyranny can be punished'.[65] Reichshofrat-members told the ducal envoy Eichholtz that although princely alliances with foreign powers had been authorised at Westphalia, for them to be legal, they must

---

[59] RHR-Report, 24 Dec. 1714: HHStA, RHR, Vota 34.    [60] RHR-Report, 2 Oct. 1717: ibid.
[61] RHR-Report, 24 Dec. 1714: HHStA, RHR, Vota 34.
[62] Charles VI to Carl Leopold, Vienna, 26 July 1715: ibid.    [63] RHR-Report, 9 Mar. 1715: ibid.
[64] RHR-Report, 31 Aug. 1716: HHStA, RHR, Vota 34.
[65] Huldenberg to George I, Vienna, 12 Mar. 1718: NHStAH, Cal. Br. 24, 4912(i)/1, fols 178–81, at fol. 179r.

present 'no obvious danger to the Empire', which was not the case with the Russia-Mecklenburg pact.[66]

2. There was a sense among the Reichshofrat-members of an urgency of swift protective measures for the nobles and other subjects. The Reichshofrat-reports frequently emphasised the 'impending downfall of the nobility'.[67] In consequence, it was deemed 'urgently necessary that all...legal, powerful means be resorted to, to save the highly oppressed Mecklenburg lands'.[68] The Reichshofrat clearly recognised that as long as ducal and Russian militia continued to be at the duke's disposal, 'complete security cannot be achieved'. Partly in reaction to the case's delay, the Reichshofrat took the unusual step of recommending that the technically required two-month prior notification of the *Conservatorium* to the duke be skipped. It was hoped to thereby 'forestall many worrying, irreversible calamities...as this highly important conflict, which is entangled in many dangerous circumstances, does not tolerate delay'.[69] During informal conversations, the urgency of a quick intervention was stated even more strongly by Windischgrätz. He said that providing Carl Leopold with an advance warning of the planned intervention 'could expose the public to danger, also the country could suffer irreparable damage'. The intervention-order was said to have been repeated, 'because...the executions against the territorial estates are continuing in the most barbaric manner...and His Imperial Majesty would consider it highly irresponsible if there were no judicial recourse against such terrible savagery'. He urged Hanover to 'proceed with the execution without further loss of time...to finally end the misery there'.[70]

3. While the illegality of ducal policies and the subjects' urgent requirement of protection led the Reichshofrat to press for an intervention in the first place, it was the authority of the Emperor as highest judge and head of the Empire that was frequently cited by Reichshofrat-members as the legitimating factor behind the Imperial intervention they were advocating. Furthermore, continuing ducal persecution became seen by the Reichshofrat as an increasingly insufferable affront and challenge to Charles VI's judicial authority and protective role, therefore the element of Imperial authority simultaneously became another important reason why intervention against the duke was deemed crucial, possibly surpassing the importance of protection per se. Even before he started to ignore direct mandates ordering a halt to persecution, the Reichshofrat argued that his practice of punishing subjects for their appeals to the Imperial high courts constituted 'a dangerous principle, which challenges Imperial authority'.[71] According to the

---

[66] Eichholtz to Carl Leopold, Vienna, 24 Oct. 1716: LHAS, Ausw.-Bez. 2.11–2/1, 1601, fols 10–17r, at fol. 13v.
[67] RHR-Report, 5 Aug. 1718: HHStA, RHR, Vota 34.     [68] RHR-Report, 31 Aug. 1716: ibid.
[69] RHR-Report, 2 Oct. 1717: ibid.
[70] Huldenberg to geh.-Räte, Vienna, 11 Jan. 1718: NHStAH, Cal. Br. 24, 4912(i)/1, fols 33–6.
[71] RHR-Report, 24 Dec. 1714: HHStA, RHR, Vota 34.

Reichshofrat, the role of the Emperor as the highest protector of persecuted (im)mediate subjects was integral to the Imperial office. The nobles' judicial appeals for protection were therefore approvingly presented as recourse 'to ... the supreme overlord and highest judge'.[72] When warning Carl Leopold to cease persecutions, a mandate referred to 'those protective measures, which We as Roman Emperor, are obliged to provide the oppressed with'.[73] Similarly, another letter warned the duke that 'on the basis of Our highest Imperial office, We ... cannot tolerate mediate estates of the Empire being harmed'.[74]

The Reichshofrat argued that Carl Leopold's refutation of the validity of Imperially-confirmed territorial treaties constituted 'an undeniable encroachment on Imperial jurisdiction'.[75] Once the duke began ignoring Imperial mandates, his actions became equated with a publicly defiant disregard of Imperial authority. By committing 'new violence', the duke was not only harming his subjects, but also adding 'insult to Our Imperial judicial authority'.[76] In private conversation, Windischgrätz reportedly explained that the Emperor was determined to see the intervention executed because the duke wanted to 'insult him, and not least because of his compassion with the nobility'.[77] When Eichholtz complained that the duke was being victimised on account of mere 'private Mecklenburg *Junkers*', he was told that it was now 'more a matter of Imperial authority being at stake, than the interests of the nobility', and that the Emperor viewed the case as a point of honour.[78] In short: defending the subjects of Mecklenburg had become synonymous with a defence of the Emperor's authority as highest feudal overlord, judge and protector.

4. Closely related to the necessity of upholding Imperial authority was the Reichshofrat's argument that the intervention was necessary to safeguard the existing system of rule in the Empire, based on mutual checks and balances, the protection of the rights of the weak, and the primacy of legality over power-politics, which were all predicated upon the judicial and protective role of the Emperor at the head of a hierarchical feudal structure. If the duke were to be allowed to get away with defying the Emperor's authority by committing crimes against his own subjects, other princes might be tempted to emulate him in pursuit of absolutist pretensions and the whole Imperial system would unravel. By averting the setting of a bad precedent, the Emperor would defend the existing Imperial hierarchical structure, along with his own apex position therein, and its system of protecting the weak against possible predation of the strong. The

---

[72] RHR-Report, 31 Aug. 1716: ibid.  [73] Charles VI to Carl Leopold, Vienna, 26 July 1715: ibid.
[74] Charles VI to Carl Leopold, Vienna, 20 Oct. 1716, in Mauelshagen, 'Freiheiten', 86.
[75] RHR-Report, 26/11/1715: HHStA, RHR, Vota 54.
[76] Charles VI to George I and August-Wilhelm, Vienna, 21 Aug. 1716: NHStAH, Cal. Br. 24, 3866, fols 4–7r, at fol. 5v.
[77] Huldenberg to George I, Vienna, 7 Jan. 1719: ibid., fol. 5.
[78] Eichholtz to Wolffradt, Vienna, 12 Feb. 1718: LHAS, Ausw.-Bez. 2.11–2/1, 1602, fols 271–2.

point can be illustrated by a Reichshofrat-report which was written for the estates' conflict with Carl Leopold's predecessor. Windischgrätz said that the Reichshofrat's stance in that case was being used as a guideline now.[79] The report argued that 'if innovations in the form of government were allowed to remain subjected to arbitrariness, it would cause much of a sensation among all the others, and it could easily be introduced by all territorial rulers... Wherever such principles would be established, the mediate estates' future would look very bleak, and consequently they would all be trampled underfoot.'[80] In the case under discussion, the Reichshofrat warned against the 'utterly dangerous consequences which would arise in the Empire, if an estate, instead of displaying obedience, as required by renowned Imperial laws, were to continue with arrogated, unjust violence'.[81] In conversation, Windischgrätz mentioned that the ordered intervention would serve other princes as a 'good lesson'.[82] He argued that if the Empire's system of protection were to collapse, 'the strong would suppress the small, and all estates would descend into mutual war'.[83]

5. The Reichshofrat concerned itself primarily with questions of legality, justice, and Imperial authority, regularly providing its legal opinion while noting that the question of how or if judicial decisions were to be executed had to be left to the Emperor and his ministers in consideration of political circumstances.[84] Nevertheless, the Reichshofrat did include geopolitical factors when considering how to deal with Carl Leopold, and when justifying recommendations. This was probably because it was hard to isolate the purely legalistic arguments from expositions of the geopolitical impact of his policies. Furthermore, Reichshofrat-president Windischgrätz attended the grand strategy meetings of the privy conference. By making some political and strategic points in the context of legal arguments, the urgency of intervening would become more apparent and improve the chances of decisions being executed. This could be done especially in more informal settings. But even in the official reports, references were made to the high risk of ducal oppression 'resulting in dangerous [political] conjunctures'.[85] The Reichshofrat consistently criticised the duke's actions towards his subjects, and from 1714 had called for an intervention through a *Conservatorium*, long before large Russian armies started assisting the duke, introducing a clear geopolitical threat to the Reich and the Habsburgs.[86] However, following the large-scale incursion of foreign troops with the consent of the duke, it had to be noted that

---

[79] Huldenberg to George I, Vienna, 4 Oct. 1717: NHStAH, Cal. Br. 24, 4911(ii) 2, fols 185v–6r.
[80] RHR-report, 9 Sep. 1708, HHStA, RHR, Den.-Rec. 694(4).
[81] RHR-Report, 10 Mar. 1716: HHStA, RHR, Vota 54.
[82] Huldenberg to George I, Vienna, 23 Oct. 1717: NHStAH, Cal. Br. 24, 4911(ii) 2, fols 243–5.
[83] Huldenberg to George I, Vienna, 27 Nov. 1717: ibid., fols 295–302, at fol. 297r.
[84] Hughes, *Law*, 104–6.   [85] RHR-Report, 2 Oct. 1717: HHStA, RHR, Vota 34.
[86] See RHR-Report, 24 Dec. 1714: ibid; Charles VI to Carl Leopold, Vienna, 26 May 1715: ibid.

given such a foreign-political track record, the duke was capable of 'setting in motion numerous dangerous developments in the future'.[87]

Considering the broader context of the Northern War, Windischgrätz reportedly said that the duke

> is hiding behind the king in Prussia and the tsar, and is envisaging very dangerous designs; a separate peace might be concluded with Sweden, and a Swedish army then brought back into Germany by the tsar, the duke of Schwerin and others... Because the duke's intrigues and his retained Russian troops pose a threat to the public... it is highly necessary to rapidly and abruptly interrupt the dangerous plans.[88]

The duke's reliance on foreign allies not only worsened domestic oppression; it emboldened him to continue defying Imperial authority, thus magnifying the overall threat of his policies. Huldenberg reported that Reichshofrat-members considered ducal policies very much in the context of the strong Russian presence in Poland, the leverage which the tsar thereby possessed over Augustus II of Saxony-Poland, and the military-financial capabilities of Russia's and Mecklenburg's ally, Brandenburg-Prussia. A treaty of friendship between Russia, Prussia, and France, concluded in August 1717,[89] heightened the sense of insecurity.[90] News of an imminent renewal of a Prussian-Mecklenburg treaty[91] caused Windischgrätz further concern.[92] He also stressed that one of the goals of the intervention would be for the conservator-commissioners to take control of Rostock and to prevent it from being opened up by the duke as a potential Russian seaborne entry-point and bridgehead.[93] He even contemplated the commission's preventive occupation of Swedish Wismar as it was feared that the duke might occupy it and grant access to Russia or Sweden.[94]

A traumatic historical awareness of the devastating Swedish intervention against the Emperor in the Thirty Years War, which started with a Swedish protection agreement and garrisoning of Wismar, might have played a role here. Geopolitical considerations thus clearly played a role in the Reichshofrat's rationale of the necessity of action against the duke, arguably the most important role. Eichholtz thus reported that some Reichshofrat-members had said that 'the tsarist procedures and manifold harsh threats gave the greatest occasion to the sharp and

---

[87] RHR-Report, 2 Oct. 1717: ibid.
[88] Huldenberg to George I, Vienna, 4 Oct. 1717: NHStAH, Cal. Br. 24,4911(ii) 2, fols 179–86, at fols 179–80r.
[89] J.F. Chance, *George I and the Northern War 1709–1721* (London, 1909), 223.
[90] Huldenberg to George I, Vienna, 4 Oct. 1717: NHStAH, Cal. Br. 24, 4911(ii) 2, fols 179–80.
[91] Mediger, *Mecklenburg*, 370–1.
[92] Huldenberg to George I, Vienna, 20 Nov. 1717: NHStAH, Cal. Br. 24, 4911(ii) 2, fols 281–5r.
[93] Huldenberg to George I, Vienna, 4 Oct. 1717: ibid., fols 182–3.
[94] Huldenberg to George I, Vienna, 2 July 1718: NHStAH, Cal. Br. 24, 4912(i) 2, fol. 484.

extreme mandates'.[95] Windischgrätz wished the intervention against the duke could have taken place before the Russian alliance when the conflict remained localised without external involvement.[96] Huldenberg summarised his assessment of Vienna's motivation in mandating the intervention:

> [The Emperor] adopted such vigorous resolutions against the duke, not merely because of the great injustice and hardships he inflicts on his territorial estates, but also *especially* because of the consequences of his excessively far-reaching schemes and links with foreign powers, which could result in great misfortune for the whole Empire.[97]

The stance of Brandenburg-Prussia was another political issue which the Reichshofrat felt obliged to tackle head-on. Brandenburg initially opposed the intervention, but following the Austrian victory over the Ottomans in July 1718, it started to tenaciously demand inclusion in the conservatorial-commission, which, as Kreis co-director, Brandenburg-Prussia felt entitled to. Its request presented the Reichshofrat with a dilemma, as Windischgrätz explained to Huldenberg, for both Prussia's inclusion and exclusion would be dangerous. Brandenburg-Prussia was allied to the duke and therefore not impartial.[98] Windischgrätz had previously been extremely hostile towards Prussian inclusion, arguing that 'the territory would suffer the greatest injustice...if one were to give such a wolf access to the sheep as their shepherd, because Prussia aims at the introduction of the greatest slavery and despotism, for it to be able to inherit the territory in such a condition'.[99] However, the Reichshofrat recognised that it was 'to be feared that he might obstruct, at least indirectly, and thereby debilitate the commission' were he to remain excluded. To prevent the main protective aim of the execution from being potentially sabotaged in such a way, the Reichshofrat surprisingly amended its recommendations in September 1718 and suggested that Prussia should be included. This shows that the principal concern of the Reichshofrat was that the duke's subjects received help, and it therefore recommended options known to be contrary to Habsburg geopolitical interests to achieve that goal, 'because the most urgent necessity demands that the Mecklenburg nobility, which is oppressed to the highest degree, receives actual Imperial rescue without further delay'. The recommendation was rejected.[100]

\*

Following the successful intervention and the installation of the commission in March 1719, the Reichshofrat continued to play the active role in Vienna's policy

---

[95] Eichholtz to Carl Leopold, Vienna, 9 Apr. 1718: LHAS, Ausw.-Bez. 2.11–2/1, 1603, fols 88–9.
[96] Huldenberg to George I, Vienna, 4 Oct. 1717: NHStAH, Cal. Br. 24, 4911(ii) 2, fols 184–5.
[97] Huldenberg to George I, Vienna, 30 Oct. 1717: ibid., fols 247–8r. (Emphasis added.)
[98] Ibid., 7 Sep. 1718: NHStAH, Cal. Br. 24,4912(ii) 1, fols 138–41.
[99] Ibid., 4 Oct. 1717: NHStAH, Cal. Br. 24, 4911(ii) 2, fol. 185v.
[100] RHR-Report, 7 Sep. 1718: HHStA, RHR, Vota 34.

towards Mecklenburg. In the following years, four main objectives of the Reichshofrat can be identified:

1. It aimed to take an active role in the direction of the administration of the duchy, as its commission had become the de facto governing body.[101] A corollary of this was the perceived necessity of controlling the Hanoverian commission as it was increasingly felt to be acting too independently.[102]

2. It aimed at ensuring that one of the original purposes of the intervention—the protection of the subjects—was implemented, by reducing the burdens on the population and taking measures against continuing isolated instances of persecution.[103] When discussing the possible deposition of the duke, the need to provide security to the subjects was identified by a Reichshofrat-dominated special deputation as the 'principal purpose' of further measures.[104]

3. Closely related to this was the major priority of the Reichshofrat in this period, namely dealing with the duke's continued contumacy and defiance against Imperial authority.[105] The Reichshofrat described several of his actions as 'criminal atrocities'.[106] Ducal soldiers' physical assaults against commission personnel was an 'enormous barbarity... even contrary to the customary treatment of declared enemies by civilised peoples'. In general, the duke's conduct was governed by 'principles that run contrary to natural reason, and to the universally-renowned rights of all peoples, heathen and Christian'.[107] Following a prompt by the Emperor,[108] the special deputation advised that the duke should be suspended from power and replaced by his brother Christian Ludwig as Imperial administrator because of 'the appalling excesses committed against [the Emperor], the Imperial commission, and the inhabitants of Mecklenburg'.[109]

4. A peripheral goal was to minimise criticism of its dispensation of justice among the princes.[110]

## (ii) The Emperor's Ministers and Diplomats

While the Austro-Imperial ministers assessed the Mecklenburg case primarily from the angle of how it affected the Emperor's geopolitical standing and his authority in the Empire, some of their private and public statements reflect a

---

[101] E.g., Patent to Mecklenburg officials, 14 May 1723: HHStA, RHR, Den.-Rec. 699(7).
[102] RHR-Resolution, 31 May 1719: HHStA, RHR, Prot.-xviii, 46, fols 381–3.
[103] RHR-Report, 26 Nov. 1723: HHStA, RHR, Vota 35.
[104] Deputation report, 30 Mar. 1724: HHStA, RHR, Vota 35.
[105] RHR-Report, 5 Nov. 1727: HHStA, RHR, Vota 36.
[106] RHR-Report, 3 Nov. 1722: HHStA, RHR, Vota 34.   [107] Ibid.
[108] Charles VI to RHR, 14 Feb. 1724: HHStA, RHR, Vota 35.
[109] Deputation report, 30 Mar. 1724: HHStA, RHR, Vota 35. Nassau-Siegen was cited as a precedent.
[110] RHR-Report, 26 Nov. 1723 and 3 Nov. 1728: HHStA, RHR, Vota 36; RHR statement, 11 July 1729: HHStA, RHR, Den.-Rec. 699(7).

moral emphasis on the duties of ruling princes towards their subjects and the obligation of intervention to curtail perceived tyranny. The diplomats of the Imperial chancery frequently commented upon the illegality and injustice of the duke's measures, and also made reference to the necessity of helping the nobility. Michael Kirchner (at the Reichstag) dismissed the interpretation of Imperial law as expounded in ducal pamphlets as erroneous,[111] while Metsch (at the congress of Braunschweig) expressed sympathy for the nobles' plight.[112] In numerous reports, he referred to the 'ruthless'[113] nature of the ducal government's 'insufferable exactions',[114] while also emphasising that protection was required to prevent their downfall.[115] He argued that the duke's 'unjust cause' consisted of gaining a *'carte blanche* to deal with his territorial estates freely and despotically'.[116] The Austrian court-chancery's envoys at Regensburg[117] also strongly criticised the illegality and immorality of Carl Leopold's government, describing the duke's actions as 'running contrary to all reason and justness'.[118]

Various Austro-Imperial ministers also commented on the unjust nature of the duke's policies during private conversations. *Obersthofmeister* Johann Trautson reportedly said that the duke had no right to throw the territorial constitution overboard. Even the Emperor himself, despite being sovereign, was equally bound to the customary practice of his hereditary lands.[119] Sinzendorf said that the Reichshofrat had 'sufficient cause to undercut the evil intentions of the duke'.[120] Among the Imperial ministers, Prince Eugene was most hostile towards Carl Leopold's 'rage and tyranny'.[121] He told the British resident in Vienna, St.-Saphorin, that Carl Leopold was 'evil and insane'.[122] Eugene told Huldenberg that he was 'outraged at ... how far he abuses his alliance with the tsar'.[123] Eugene viewed Carl Leopold's 'conduct towards the nobility as the most atrocious tyranny, which could not even be perpetrated by a despotic prince against his serfs

---

[111] Kirchner to Charles VI, Regensburg, 18 Mar. 1718: HHStA, RK, Prinzipalkommission-Berichte, 42(1), fols 148–52.
[112] Metsch to Charles VI, Braunschweig, 13 Aug. 1717: HHStA, RK, Dipl.-Akten, Braunschweig-Hannover, Berichte 2c, fol. 318.
[113] Metsch to Charles VI, Braunschweig, 8 Oct. 1717: ibid., fol. 412.
[114] Metsch to Charles VI, Braunschweig, 29 Oct. 1717: ibid., fols 442–50.
[115] Metsch to Charles VI, Braunschweig, 2 Dec. 1718: ibid., fol. 407.
[116] Metsch to Charles VI, Braunschweig, 11 Jan. 1718: ibid., fols 9–10.
[117] Philipp Friedrich Jodoci, Franz-Philipp Zech, and the count Starhemberg.
[118] Austrian envoys to Charles VI, Regensburg, 24 June 1718: HHStA, SK, Regensburg, Österr-Ges-Berichte 45, fols 402–4.
[119] Seger to Carl Leopold, Vienna, 9 Oct. 1717: LHAS, Ausw.-Bez. 2.11–2/1, 1602, fols 93–5, at fol. 93v.
[120] Huldenberg to George I, Vienna, 25 Sep. 1717: NHStAH, Cal. Br. 24, 4911(ii) 1, fols 164–6, at fol. 164v.
[121] Huldenberg to George I, Vienna, 13 Apr. 1718: NHStAH, Cal. Br. 24, 4912(i) 2, fols 268–9r, at fol. 268v.
[122] St.-Saphorin to George I, Vienna, n.d. [May 1719]: NHStAH, Hann.-92, 1099, fols 14–19r, at fol. 14v.
[123] Huldenberg to George I, Vienna, 23 Oct. 1717: NHStAH, Cal. Br. 24, 4911(ii) 2, fols 243–5.

and slaves, without provoking the horror of the respectable world'.[124] Starhemberg criticised Brandenburg-Prussia's seeming willingness 'to support such an unjust cause' as that of Carl Leopold.[125] The war minister Thierheim emphasised the Emperor's determination to see the intervention effected, 'even if this should result in a proper war'.[126] Over the course of 1718, vice-chancellor Schönborn seems to have lost patience with Carl Leopold. He reportedly told the Emperor, 'that this duke has lost all reason and has become a complete tyrant; therefore he would have to be stopped'.[127]

As was the case with the Reichshofrat, the Emperor's ministers and diplomats also assessed the intervention in Mecklenburg according to the necessity of vindicating Imperial authority over immediate subjects and of safeguarding the prevailing order of the Imperial framework. Metsch was acutely aware of the broader significance of the conflict for the Imperial system and the Emperor's authority. He commented that the duke

> wishes to do as he pleases and to rule despotically over his vassals and subjects. If he were to succeed in this, it would result in consequences which are extremely disadvantageous to Imperial authority... If he were forced to submit with the required severity... it could serve as a good lesson for others who might already secretly harbour similar intentions.[128]

Metsch's patron in Vienna, Schönborn, wondered whether Carl Leopold wanted to be 'completely sovereign'.[129] In August 1718 he told Eichholtz that it was no longer only a matter regarding the rights of the subjects, but the authority of the Emperor.[130] Similar criticism was expressed by court-chancery statesmen. The Austrian envoys at Regensburg wrote that the latest ducal pamphlet was unacceptable, as it 'aimed at destroying the jurisdiction of the Reichshofrat'.[131] Eugene deplored the hesitancy of Hanover in implementing of the *Conservatorium*, arguing that the delay was causing 'great damage, not only to the country of Mecklenburg, but also to the whole Reich and its system'.[132]

---

[124] Huldenberg to George I, Vienna, 2 Apr. 1718: NHStAH, Cal. Br. 24, 4912(i) 1, fol. 247.
[125] Huldenberg to George I, Vienna, 26 Jan. 1718: ibid., fols 78–9.
[126] Huldenberg to George I, Vienna, 7 Dec. 1718: NHStAH, Cal. Br. 24, 4912(ii) 2 fols 343–50, at fols 347v–8r.
[127] Huldenberg to George I, Vienna, 10 Dec. 1718: ibid., fols 361–4, at fol. 364r.
[128] Metsch to Charles VI, Braunschweig, 11 Feb. 1718: HHStA, RK, Dipl.-Akten, Braunschweig-Hannover, Berichte 2c(2), fols 39–42, at fols 41v–42r.
[129] Eichholtz to Carl Leopold, Vienna, 21 Dec. 1718: LHAS, Ausw.-Bez. 2.11–2/1, 1604, fols 185–6, at fol. 185r.
[130] Eichholtz to Carl Leopold, Vienna, 17 Aug. 1718: ibid., fols 290–6.
[131] Austrian envoys to Charles VI, Regensburg, 17 May 1718: HHStA, SK, Regensburg, Österr-Ges-Berichte 45, fol. 506.
[132] Huldenberg to George I, Vienna, 23 Feb. 1718: NHStAH, Cal. Br. 24, 4912(i)1, fols 147–9.

The same arguments which were uttered in private, were also expressed in the public statement produced by the Emperor's embassy at the Reichstag, the *Kommissionsdekret* of November 1717. This document would have been written with the aim of achieving a maximum level of approval by the target-audience— the princely public sphere—in the hope of receiving a favourable resolution by the princes in response. The document referred to the 'harsh personal arrests' and other violent methods aimed at 'forcing [the subjects] into an arbitrary subjection'. It was stated that the Emperor found himself obliged to act upon 'his supreme Imperial office, which is founded upon the administration of justice and the protection of irresponsibly oppressed subjects in the Reich'. Accordingly, it was announced that the decision had been made 'to counter these ducal measures—unheard-of conduct by a territorial prince against his subjects— through constitutional means of execution'. The internal policies of the duke, unacceptable in themselves, acquired a broader strategic dimension through the risk entailed by them, of 'creating dangerous commotion and unrest within the Empire, and also of attracting such disturbances from outside'.[133]

This points to the most important factor considered by Austro-Imperial statesmen, although, as the *Kommissionsdekret* indicated, the geopolitical dimension was closely intertwined with the other assessments of Carl Leopold's policies. Imperial authority and general outrage demanded putting a halt to Carl Leopold's suppression of the nobility. But the geopolitical dangers associated with his policies meant that an intervention against his regime was also in line with the Emperor's interests beyond those of salvaging Imperial authority. In general, the Austro-Imperial ministers were wary of the strengthening of the Emperor's power-political rivals in the north of the Empire, Hanover and Brandenburg-Prussia. Keeping them divided was in Vienna's interest.[134] Austria also sought to prevent, or limit, the incursion of external powers into this region, primarily Russia and Sweden. There was concern about the unilateral seizures of the Swedish territories of Bremen-Verden and Stettin by Hanover and Prussia, respectively, especially in light of the elector of Hanover's recent acquisition of the British crown.[135] However, relations with George I were good on the whole, as British support was needed in the Mediterranean against Charles' arch-rival Philip V of Spain and, to a lesser extent, in the north against Russia. An Austro-British defensive alliance was signed in June 1716.[136] Spanish enmity was uncompromising and its foreign policy was directed at the conquest of former Spanish territories in Italy which had fallen to Austria when the former Spanish empire was partitioned at the Peace of Utrecht-Rastatt between Charles VI and

---

[133] Kommissionsdekret, 17 Nov. 1717: Pachner (ed.), *Vollständige Sammlung*, iii, 740–1.
[134] Privy Conference report 6 June 1719: HHStA, RK, Vorträge 6c, fols 115–19.
[135] Huldenberg to George I, Vienna, 19 Feb. 1716: NHStAH, Cal. Br. 24, 4910(i), fols 164–7r.
[136] Simms, *Three Victories*, 116.

Philip V (1713/14).[137] On news of a new Franco-British entente in 1716, the privy conference stressed the importance of complying with its wishes for an Austro-Spanish compromise settlement, as otherwise the Emperor could not hope for Franco-British support against any Spanish aggression.[138] Indeed, once the Spanish assault against Habsburg possessions in Italy began in August 1717, Vienna found itself forced to accept the British secretary of state James Stanhope's peace plan for southern Europe, and in return France and especially Britain helped defeat Spanish forces.[139]

The war against Spain in Italy came at a time when the Emperor was already at war with the Ottomans in the Balkans. The Emperor was reportedly piqued when Austrian overtures for common action against Turkey were brusquely rebuffed by the tsar.[140] However, it was the Russo-Mecklenburg alliance which provoked Vienna's intense hostility against both the tsar and the duke,[141] as the duke was seen to flout Imperial mandates while the Russians violated the Empire's borders and ignored the Emperor's authority. In the north, the interests of the Emperor, Hanover and Britain intersected as they shared an opposition to Russia's military presence in Mecklenburg. Brandenburg-Prussia's willingness to support Russia was perceived as a threat in Vienna and made the Russian presence in Mecklenburg appear more ominous.[142] Sinzendorf stressed the importance of maintaining good relations with George I to deal with emerging Russian/Prussian threats particularly in Mecklenburg.[143] In May 1717, Austria's privy conference warned of the dangerous military rise of Russia and Brandenburg-Prussia and recommended a close alignment with Hanover in northern affairs. It was hoped that thereby 'one could win over England for Your Imperial Majesty's aims elsewhere, and strengthen the connection to that court by granting certain advantages [to George I]'.[144] The value of British naval power to Austrian interests was made obvious when Admiral Byng destroyed the Spanish Mediterranean fleet off Cape Passaro in August 1718, effectively ending the Spanish threat to Habsburg Italy. Already in 1716 the hope was expressed that the British fleet in the Baltic could prevent the Russians from returning to Mecklenburg following the cancellation of the invasion of Scania.[145] The Emperor's anger and embarrassment at the Russian occupation of Mecklenburg[146] receded slightly once

---

[137] Heinz Duchhardt and Martin Espenhorst (eds), *Utrecht-Rastatt-Baden 1712–1714. Ein europäisches Friedenswerk am Ende des Zeitalters Ludwigs XIV* (Göttingen, 2013).
[138] Privy conference report, 9 Jan. 1717: HHStA, SK, Vorträge 22(1), fols 7–34.
[139] Ottokar Weber, *Die Quadrupelallianzvom Jahre 1718* (Vienna, 1887).
[140] Huldenberg to George I, Vienna, 23 May 1716: NHStAH, Cal. Br. 24, 4910 (ii), fols 395–8r.
[141] Huldenberg to George I, Vienna, 13 May 1716: ibid., fols 383–4.
[142] Chance, *George I*, 147–50.
[143] Huldenberg to George I, Vienna, 30 Dec.1716: NHStAH, Cal. Br. 24, 4910 (iii), fols 337–9.
[144] Privy Conference report, 19 May 1717: HHStA, SK, Vorträge 22, fols 129–42.
[145] Huldenberg to George I, Vienna, 21 Oct. 1716: NHStAH, Cal. Br. 24, 4910 (iii), fols 233–40.
[146] Charles VI to Reichstag-representative Sachsen-Zeitz, Vienna, 10 June 1717: HHStA, RK, PK-Weisungen 5a, fols 258–66.

the majority of Russian forces withdrew in the late summer of 1717,[147] but a determination to counter the duke's dangerous willingness to pander to foreign powers for his own tyrannical domestic aims[148] and to prevent a return of Russian forces remained.[149]

In light of the international context, the privy conference was happy to see that the Reichshofrat had recommended George I as Hanoverian elector as the chief-executor of the *Conservatorium* against Carl Leopold. Charles VI's resolution to the Reichshofrat-report of October 1717 stated that an intervention against the duke was indeed necessary given that his policies 'could lead to dangerous disturbances and consequences, not only in the Lower-Saxon and neighbouring Kreise, but in the whole Empire'.[150] Nevertheless, the appointment of George I as proxy-intervener did coincide with Austrian geopolitical interests, as did the toppling of Carl Leopold's unpredictable regime. Starhemberg regretted that the Emperor was tied up in the Balkans, otherwise he could take firmer measures against Prussia.[151] While Prince Eugene and the Austrian ministers agreed that the execution had to take place, they recognised that a tactical delay was necessary, until sufficient Austrian troops became freed up in the Balkans.[152]

A privy conference meeting in September 1718 addressed the dangers of the alignment between Russia, Prussia, and the duke of Mecklenburg. It was argued that their treaties and large armaments reflected 'a secret agreement to carry out sinister plans... Your Imperial Majesty's hereditary lands are all the more susceptible to be engulfed and involved by these because the Russians are masters over Poland.'[153] Given the diplomatic situation in the north, Prussia's offer to participate in the Mecklenburg commission, although laudable in principle, had to be turned down, unless it could give firm assurances that it would help to repel any Russian and/or Swedish incursions into Mecklenburg or other parts of the Empire.[154] The threat of a Russian attack against the execution of the *Conservatorium* via Poland was the main concern behind the conclusion of a treaty at Vienna between the Emperor, Hanover, and Saxony in January 1719, which provided for common action in case of Russian/Prussian counter-measures in Poland and the Reich.[155] The war minister Thierheim underlined the geopolitical security considerations underlying the necessity of an intervention against the duke. He said that the duke was willing to keep his ports open to the Russians

---

[147] Huldenberg to George I, Vienna, 1 Sep. 1717: NHStAH, Cal. Br. 24, 4911(ii) 1, fols 101–3.
[148] Ibid., 24 Mar. 1717: NHStAH, Cal. Br. 24, 4911(i) 1, fols 149–51.
[149] Ibid., 25 Sep. 1717: NHStAH, Cal. Br. 24, 4911(ii) 1, fols 164–6.
[150] RHR-Report, 2 Oct. 1717: HHStA, RHR, Vota 34.
[151] Huldenberg to George I, Vienna, 26 Jan. 1718: ibid., fols 78–9.
[152] Huldenberg to George I, Vienna, 2 Apr. 1718: ibid., fols 247.
[153] Privy conference report, 1 Sep. 1718: HHStA, RK, Vorträge 6c, fols 89–95, at fol. 90r-v.
[154] Ibid, fols 94–5.
[155] Original in NHStAH, Hann.-10, 168. See also L.R. Lewitter, 'Poland, Russia and the Treaty of Vienna of 5 January 1719', *HJ* 13 (1970), 3–30.

and/or Swedes, thereby giving their forces access to Germany, and that hence he must be stopped.[156] The risk was compounded by secretive Russian–Swedish negotiations for a possible separate peace.[157]

Soon after the intervention, Vienna's relations with George I deteriorated. The emergence of the two hostile alliances of Vienna and Hanover pitted Charles VI and George I against one another at the helm of two armed camps which at times came close to war. Rival alliance diplomacy, especially in the Empire, meant that enticing Brandenburg-Prussia to defect from the Alliance of Hanover was a high priority for Austria's foreign policy, an aim which was achieved in October 1726.[158] Soon afterwards, Vienna became considerably more amenable to its new Prussian ally's requests for an appointment to the Mecklenburg commission. In December 1726, a deputation of ministers and Reichshofrat-members recommended Brandenburg-Prussia's inclusion.[159] Following the lapsing of the commission and the decreed Imperial administration (along with the suspension of Carl Leopold), the ministers worked hard to justify the step before the Reich and Europe to undermine the Hanover allies' attempts at using the issue to provoke hostility towards the Emperor.[160] The Emperor instructed his embassy at the Reichstag to specifically stress the suffering of the subjects and the need to protect them against the duke's continuing pernicious influence when defending the 1728 decrees.[161]

## Britain-Hanover

The intervention in Mecklenburg also coincided with the geopolitical interests of the chief proxy-intervener, George I. As the Reichshofrat-appointed commissioner and executor of the *Conservatorium*, George was acting as elector of Hanover only, although the intervention was also arguably in George's interests as British king. Nevertheless, Hanover was set to gain the main strategic advantages from the intervention. In addition to his primary loyalty to Hanover, Hanoverian chief minister Andreas Gottlieb von Bernstorff, a Mecklenburg nobleman, was also effectively the leader of the estates' opposition to Carl Leopold.[162] While in theory there was a clear division between Hanoverian

---

[156] Huldenberg to George I, Vienna, 16 Nov. 1718: NHStAH, Cal. Br. 24, 4912(ii) 2, fols 296–9.
[157] Chance, *George*, 268–71.  [158] Chance, *Alliance*, 418–21.
[159] Deputation report, Vienna, 8 Dec. 1726: HHStA, RK, Vorträge 6c, fols 290–307.
[160] E.g., Sinzendorf to Charles VI, Fontainebleau, 6 Oct. 1728: HHStA, RK, Kl.-Reichsstände 347, fols 448–55.
[161] Charles VI to Reichstag-representative, Vienna, 3 Apr. 1729: HHStA, RK, Kl.-Reichsstände 348, fols 209–10.
[162] Hartwig Bernstorff, *Andreas Gottlieb von Bernstorff 1649–1726. Staatsmann, Junker, Patriarch: Zwischen deutschem Partikularismus und europäischer Politik* (Bochum, 1999), 9.

and British personnel, in practice the personal union resulted in a degree of overlap.[163]

The Hanoverian justifications for intervening against Carl Leopold reveal a similar normative argumentation as that which is evinced from statements from Vienna. In a published propagandistic letter to the duke, George I admonished his uncivilised treatment of the nobles, his irresponsible introduction of Russian forces, his disregarding of territorial custom, Imperial law and the Emperor's mandates, and his attempts to cut off his subjects from the Empire's protective channels. Such behaviour could not possibly find approval in the 'impartial world', among 'Reich-loving, and Christian-minded' people.[164] George expressed himself similarly in confidential letters. In a letter to the Privy-councillor Philipp Eltz, George wrote that he had felt compelled to accept the execution-commission because 'such atrocities are being committed in Mecklenburg, which are still increasing rather than decreasing, and which are unheard-of among Turks and barbarians, let alone among Christians'.[165] In a rescript to Huldenberg, George wrote that the mandated intervention was 'so just and laudable, because of the cruelties which are being committed against the innocent Mecklenburg nobility, that helping to implement such mandates can justly be regarded as a Christian duty'.[166] Hanoverian statesmen expressed themselves in similar tones. During the delay to the intervention, the Hanoverian *Oberappellationsrat* Marquard expressed sympathy with the nobility, writing to the Mecklenburg nobles' agent Burghard Behr that 'it is a misfortune that the exercise of justice must yield to political circumstances'.[167]

While geopolitical factors caused the execution of the *Conservatorium* to be delayed by George I, such considerations also contributed towards Hanover advocating the intervention in the first place and then carrying it out. Hanover joined the Northern War against Sweden with the objective of gaining Bremen-Verden to enhance Hanoverian security by preventing the encroachment of Denmark, a potential rival in northern Germany, into its vicinity.[168] In pursuit of this aim, and to influence the Hanoverian-Prussian-Danish anti-Swedish alignment in Hanover's favour, Bernstorff was willing to do business with Russia by concluding the treaty of Greifswald in October 1715 and drawing Russian troops into Pomerania during the early stages of George's involvement in the war.[169] Brandenburg-Prussia was still considered the greatest potential threat to Hanover's security. Although George expressed some concern about the effects

---

[163] Janet Hartley, *Charles Whitworth. Diplomat in the Age of Peter the Great* (Aldershot, 2002), 165.
[164] George I to Carl Leopold, Kensington, 17 May 1718: *EStC* 32, 182–6.
[165] George I to Eltz, London, 31 Dec. 1717: NHStAH, Cal. Br. 24, 709, fols 10–11.
[166] George I to Huldenberg, London, 15 Feb. 1718: NHStAH, Hann.-9g, 16, fols 21–4, at fol. 21.
[167] Marquard to Behr, 12 Dec. 1717: LHAS, Meckl.-Landstände, 3.1-1, III-1.
[168] Walther Mediger, 'Die Gewinnung Bremens und Verdensdurch Hannover im Nordischen Kriege', *Niedersächsisches Jahrbuch für Landesgeschichte* 43 (1971), 37–56.
[169] Chance, *George I*, 99–100.

of the rise of Russia on the Baltic balance in the summer of 1715, the Jacobite rebellion in Scotland later that year improved relations with Russia. George and Peter's common adversary Sweden was believed to support the Jacobite Pretender, and Sweden's invasion of Norway was seen as a threat in connection with an expected invasion of Scotland in support of the rebellion.[170] George and Bernstorff had always been highly sensitive about external influence in Mecklenburg given its immediate proximity to Hanover.[171] Thus in the context of the siege of Wismar, news of an imminent Russo-Mecklenburg marriage alliance caused fears that the tsar might try to grant nominal possession of the fortress to Carl Leopold, while Russia and/or Prussia assumed actual control over it.[172] Concern turned to alarm when large Russian armies arrived in Mecklenburg on conclusion of its alliance with the duke in April 1716.[173]

This proved to be a turning point in George's northern policy. From then on Russia was perceived as the main threat to Hanoverian security, and to a slightly lesser extent, British interests in the Baltic. Countering the acute geopolitical threat of Russia via Duke Carl Leopold neatly coincided with the secondary goal of protecting the nobility, a cause which was close to Bernstorff's heart anyway. The cancellation of the invasion of Scania and the subsequent return of the Russians to Mecklenburg in late 1716 was the final straw in the collapse of the anti-Swedish coalition, and Russo-Hanoverian relations in particular.[174] From the time of the Russian occupation, Hanover pressed for stronger measures against the duke and the Russians at Vienna.[175] Such representations were often combined with reminders that Charles VI needed George I more than vice-versa, especially in terms of support against Spanish aggression in the Mediterranean, and that if Charles were more forthcoming to George as elector, this would make him more inclined to support the Emperor as king.[176]

However, Russia's presence in Mecklenburg also alarmed many British statesmen. The British resident in Berlin, Charles Whitworth, reported with trepidation about the presence and actions of the Russians across the border in both Mecklenburg and Poland.[177] He noted that the tsar's 'intention of assisting the duke of Mecklenburg against his Nobility' was 'an injustice in itself', in addition to

---

[170] Mediger, *Mecklenburg*, 260-1, 266-7.
[171] Geh.-Räte to George I, Hanover, 16 Oct. 1714: NHStAH, Hann.-92, 2184.
[172] George I to geh.-Räte, London, 17 Mar. 1716, quoted in Mediger, *Mecklenburg*, 278.
[173] Ibid., 282-3.
[174] George I to Wrisberg, 11 Nov. 1716: NHStAH, Hann.-92, 2191, fols 47-9; See also John Murray, 'Scania and the end of the Northern Alliance', *JMH* 16 (1944), 81-92.
[175] George I to Charles VI, Hanover, 6 Oct. 1716: NHStAH, Cal. Br. 24, 3866, fol. 58.
[176] Huldenberg to George I, Vienna, 22 Sep. 1717: NHStAH, Cal. Br. 24, 4911(ii) 1, fols 160-3. This was also related to the Hanoverian desire for the Imperial investitures with Bremen-Verden: St.-Saphorin to George I, Vienna, 6 July 1718: NHStAH, Hann.-92, 1092, fols 14-18.
[177] Whitworth to Townshend, Berlin, 15 and 29 Aug. 1716: BL, Add. MSS. 37,363, fols 14-17r, 50-5r.

a security threat to George I.[178] He criticised Russia's 'arbitrary Proceedings' in Mecklenburg, and stressed the dangers of its potential hegemony in the Baltic, as this would make it 'master of all the naval stores' in this crucial region.[179] The Russo-Prussian alliance of November 1716 caused additional anxiety, with Whitworth commenting that Berlin was pursuing 'a very odd Politick' and that 'the Suppression of the Nobility of Mecklenburgh' was an unjust cause to support.[180] On hearing of the cancellation of the Scania descent, the British secretary of state for the Northern Department (northern Europe) Charles Townshend requested more information on the 'clouds that gather so much in the North... and... seem to threaten a Storm'.[181] The British secretary of state Stanhope wrote to Whitworth that George was very concerned about the return of the Russians to Mecklenburg, and criticised Frederick William I for being a 'tame spectator of the mischief done to his neighbours'.[182] Ultimately the Russian threat made a settlement with France more urgent, thus contributing to the conclusion of Anglo-French alliance of November 1716.[183]

A divergence in British and Hanoverian aims did emerge regarding the policy towards Brandenburg-Prussia. From the point of view of the Hanoverians, Prussia was almost as dangerous as Russia. While most of the Russians left Mecklenburg during the summer of 1717, Prussia seemingly remained firmly aligned with Carl Leopold—a renewed Prusso-Mecklenburg treaty was signed in December—and opposed to the execution. This exacerbated already deep-seated tensions.[184] The Russian threat still remained, however (especially in Poland), and in general both Prussia and Russia were regarded with deep suspicion.[185] Therefore, much of Hanover's pre-execution diplomacy revolved around the creation of a safety-net against feared Prussian and/or Russian military assistance to Carl Leopold.[186] Privy-councillor Eltz was sent on a special mission to Berlin in December 1717 to ascertain the risk of Prussian counter-intervention.[187] When his assessment turned out more troubling than expected,[188] Hanover focussed its diplomatic efforts on the Emperor and Denmark. In the latter case, the Hanoverian envoy Friedrich Bothmer was instructed to solicit Danish military assistance for the intervention.[189] He was informed of the geopolitical aims of the intervention,

---

[178] Whitworth to Townshend, Berlin, 20 Oct. 1716: ibid., fol. 125.
[179] Whitworth to Townshend, Berlin, 14 Nov. 1716: BL, Add. MSS. 37,363, fols 166-20, at 167-8.
[180] Whitworth to Townshend, Berlin, 17 Nov. 1716: ibid., fols 175-7, at fol. 177r.
[181] Townshend to Whitworth, Hampton Court, 28 Sep. 1716 OS: ibid., fol. 100.
[182] Stanhope to Whitworth, Göhrde, 15/10/1716: ibid., fols 102-3.
[183] Ragnhild Hatton, *George I. Elector and King* (London, 1978), 190-1. On the alliance: Jeremy Black, 'The Anglo-French alliance 1716-1731', *Francia* 13 (1986), 295-310.
[184] George I to Heusch, Hampton Court, 12 Oct. 1717: NHStAH, Hann.-92, 2172, fols 27-8r.
[185] George I to Huldenberg, London, 8 Nov. 1718: NHStAH, Hann.-9g, 16, fols 44-7r.
[186] E.g., George I to privy council, London, 29 June 1717: ibid., fols 2-3.
[187] George I to Eltz, London, 31 Dec. 1717: NHStAH, Cal. Br. 24,709, fols 10-11.
[188] Eltz to George I, Berlin, 21 Jan. 1718: NHStAH, Cal. Br. 24, 709, fols 32-3r.
[189] Bothmer to George I, Copenhagen, 2 Nov. 1717: NHStAH, Hann.-92,2200, fols 246-9.

which were accorded central importance. It was important 'to prevent the Russians and Swedes from returning to Mecklenburg in good time. For this it would be necessary above all to occupy Rostock, and here the Imperial commission mandated to Us would provide a good occasion.'[190]

At Vienna, Huldenberg was to get the Emperor to accept delaying the execution until the expected Austrian victory over Turkey, and at securing large Austrian armies to back the execution in Bohemia and Silesia by menacing the Prussian borders there.[191] With these demands accepted in early 1718,[192] the British resident at Vienna, St.-Saphorin, was charged with the distinctly Hanoverian task of forging an Austro-Saxon-Hanoverian alliance as a further safety-measure to forestall and Prussian and/or Russian obstruction of the intervention. An important reason why the British ministers refused their counter-signature to the resulting treaty of Vienna, apart from the promise of British naval backing for a Hanoverian operation, was probably its perceived anti-Prussian orientation and the fact that it failed to assign any role to France, Britain's ally, in the settlement of northern affairs.[193] Indeed, British policy now aimed at isolating Russia by enticing Prussia to ally with Britain,[194] in an integrated approach to European politics which sought to liberate George's northern policy from the perceived narrow Hanoverian agenda of Bernstorff.[195] By the time George sided with the British ministers against Bernstorff's anti-Prussian policy in July 1719,[196] and the subsequent conclusion of British/Hanoverian-Prussian alliances in August,[197] the execution in Mecklenburg had already occurred, realising one of Bernstorff's chief aims. While Hanoverians were pleased by their successful occupation of the duchy,[198] British statesmen also expressed satisfaction at the turn of events in the southern Baltic and their effects on Britain's European position. John Stair wrote from Paris that the execution in Mecklenburg was poised to effect 'a considerable and very advantageous change with regard to northern affairs'.[199] Whitworth noted 'we no longer have anything to fear from those quarters'.[200]

The Hanoverian commission acted very forcefully on arrival in Mecklenburg, arresting numerous ducal officials and ministers,[201] impounding ducal revenues,

---

[190] George I to Bothmer, Hampton Court, 30 Sep. 1718, quoted in Mediger, *Mecklenburg*, 409.
[191] George I to Huldenberg, 15 Feb. 1718: NHStAH, Hann.-9g, 16, fols 20–4v.
[192] Huldenberg to George I, Vienna, 9 Mar. 1718: NHStAH, Cal. Br. 24, 4912(i) 1, fols 170–3.
[193] Derek McKay, 'The struggle for control of George I's northern policy, 1718–19', *JMH* 45 (1973), 367–86, at 379.
[194] Stanhope to Sunderland, n.p., [1719]: Coxe, *Walpole*, i, 321–3.
[195] Simms, *Three Victories*, 138.  [196] McKay, 'The Struggle', 383–4.
[197] Whitworth to Stanhope, Berlin, 2 Sep. 1719: BL, Add. MSS. 37,375, fols 11–13r.
[198] E.g., Huldenberg to George I, Vienna, 12 Apr. 1719, NHStAH, Cal. Br. 24, 4915(i), fols 146–50.
[199] Stair to minister James Craggs, Paris, 2 Apr. 1719: NA, SP 78/163, fols 261–70.
[200] Whitworth to Bothmer, The Hague, 28 Mar. 1719: ibid., fols 53–4.
[201] Metsch to Charles VI, Braunschweig, 7 Apr. 1719: HHStA, RK, Dipl.-Akten, Braunschweig-Hannover 3a, fol. 96.

and disbanding the duke's army.[202] The heavy-handed approach in Mecklenburg, in which the commission exceeded its initial mandate, caused some acrimonious exchanges between Hanover/London and Vienna in which Hanover tried to justify its conduct in the duchy.[203] George only reluctantly agreed to the May 1719 order of reducing commission troops in February 1720.[204] Attempts were also made to assuage the tsar's anger at the execution against his former client-prince Carl Leopold.[205] Despite the robust Hanoverian assertion of control in Mecklenburg, it is untrue that George wished to annex any part of the duchy.[206] In November 1719 Huldenberg apologised to George for mentioning to Reichshofrat-member Berger that Hanover should be allowed to annex Boitzenburg. On hearing this, George I reprimanded Huldenberg and repudiated any expansionary ambitions.[207] It also appears that George did not even intend to economically exploit Mecklenburg, because commission-troops were ordered not to live off the land as they were being supplied from Hanover.[208] In a letter to the privy-council in 1721, George wrote that the Russian threat via Mecklenburg had not served as a pretext to take permanent control of the duchy.[209]

Fears of a renewed Russian invasion of Mecklenburg as a first step of an anticipated revenge-attack against Hanover existed from the time of the execution.[210] Hanoverian anxiety increased at the time of Peter's successful conclusion of peace with Sweden at Nystad. Before this, the privy-council warned George that Russia might invade Mecklenburg as soon as it had defeated Sweden. They recommended preventively sending a large army into the duchy to reinforce the existing forces there to avert or delay the expected Russian landing.[211] George rejected the recommendation arguing that this could itself provoke the Russian invasion, and that illegally surpassing the commission's permitted military strength would cost Hanover the Reich's support in the resulting war.[212] Bernstorff sent another letter in late 1721 to re-emphasise the case for an

---

[202] Commission financial-director Georg Werpup to George I, Ratzeburg, 4 May 1719: NHStAH, Hann.-92, 2205, fol. 12.
[203] George I to Huldenberg, n.p., 5 May 1719: NHStAH, Hann.-9g, 17, fols 82–4r.
[204] George I to Huldenberg, 23 Feb. 1720: ibid., fols 27–34. But the fact that he complied with this order shows that he did not only obey instructions from Vienna that corresponded to his wishes, as claimed by Arndt, *Herrschaftkontrolle*, 442.
[205] Message for Peter the Great: 'Memoire pour Monsieur de Campredon' [1722]: NA, SP 100/52.
[206] E.g. asserted in Johann-Gustav Droysen, *Geschichte der Preußischen Politik* 4/2 (Leipzig, 1869), 156, 261.
[207] Huldenberg to George I, Vienna, 1 Nov. 1719: NHStAH, Cal. Br. 24, 4915, iv, fols 346–51. Kerstin Rahn, '"Die Weide des Weissen Rosses von Braunschweig bis an die Ostseeerweitern..."? Kurhannover und Mecklenburg in der ersten Hälfte des 18.Jahrhunderts', in Matthias Manke and E. Munch (eds), *Verfassung und Lebenswirklichkeit. Der landgrundgesetzliche Erbvergleich von 1755 in seiner Zeit* (Lübeck, 2006), 335–49, at 347 also argues against expansionary Hanoverian motives.
[208] George I to Field marshal von Bülow, London, 28 Mar. 1719: NHStAH, Hann.-9g, 26.
[209] George I to privy council, London, 20 June 1721: NHStAH, Hann.-92, 2166.
[210] Privy council to Bülow, Hanover, 5 Apr. 1719: NHStAH, Hann.-92,2204, fol. 27.
[211] Privy council to George I, Hanover, 16 May 1721: NHStAH, Hann.-92, 2166, fols 2–3.
[212] George I to privy council, London, 27 May 1721: ibid.

occupation of Mecklenburg by 17,000 troops to deprive the tsar of a bridgehead. It was argued that this should be not justified on the basis of the Imperial commission and the *Conservatorium*, but on the grounds of self-defence in the face of an imminent threat. He therefore viewed the Law of Nations as being more applicable in justifying such a move than Imperial constitutional law.[213] Privy-councillor Johann Alvensleben disagreed. He argued that a preventive, large-scale occupation of Mecklenburg in the face of Prussian hostility would be too risky. It would likely be a self-fulfilling prophesy with regard to the Russian invasion and unviable according to principles of self-defence and pre-emption, given the absence of any imminent attack. He asserted the primacy of Imperial law in this case by arguing that for any such measure, Imperial approval was necessary, as it would otherwise result in a possible cancellation of the commission, and the hostility of many princes. Instead, Hanover should be strengthened internally and externally through broad-based sets of alliances and a system of collective security founded on Imperial authority and mutual defence.[214] Mecklenburg was thus still regarded very much through the lens of Hanoverian security.

With the deterioration of relations between Britain-Hanover and the Emperor in the years following 1719, and their break-down from 1725 until 1731, the Hanoverian and British attitude towards the Mecklenburg case also changed in line with the shifting diplomatic constellation. Nevertheless, an underlying normative emphasis on the necessity of protecting subjects from oppression continued to be used as an argument to bolster political aims. Tensions with the Emperor continued into the reign of George II. There was mounting concern over the seemingly overweening ambition of the Emperor in Germany.[215] St.-Saphorin, who in 1719 had expressed his confidence in the Reichshofrat's handling of the Mecklenburg case,[216] offered a different interpretation in 1727, which was undoubtedly coloured by the 'cold war' between Britain-Hanover and Austria, along with their respective allies, that had emerged in the meantime.[217] St.-Saphorin subjected Austria's Reichs-policy to a stringent critique, arguing that its *Leitmotiv* was an augmentation of the Emperor's power and influence, especially at the expense of the Protestant princes.

Thus, the Emperor's practice 'of intervening in the disputes which this or that prince has with his subjects' was exploited in furtherance of his power-political aims. He claimed that the subjects of the Emperor's princely rivals received preferential judicial treatment, and that the protective function of the Imperial office was cynically exploited for political ends. St.-Saphorin argued that during the time when Carl Leopold's conversion to Catholicism was seen as a possibility,

---

[213] Bernstorff to George I, Hanover, 23 Dec. 1721: ibid., fols 13–18, at fols 14v–15r.
[214] Report of Alvensleben, Hanover, n.d. [1721]: ibid., fols 32–45.
[215] Charles Delafaye to Walpole, n.p., 8 Aug. 1727: NA, SP 78/187.
[216] St.-Saphorin to George I, Vienna, n.d. [May 1719]: NHStAH, Hann.-92, 1099, fols 14–19r.
[217] St.-Saphorin, 'Relation sur les affaires du Mecklenbourg', NA, SP 80/61.

'Vienna was no longer responsive to all the...appeals of the nobility of Mecklenburg'. Instead, George I was portrayed as the one who was 'strongly interested in the cause of this nobility', and whose 'compassion for these nobles, who truly were very oppressed' had ensured their rescue. Apart from the immediate objective in 1725–26 of enticing the defection of Prussia, the long-term strategy of the Emperor's policy in northern Germany was to sow discord between Brandenburg-Prussia and Hanover, thereby preventing a united front of Protestant princes and ensuring his own supremacy in Germany. In this context, St.-Saphorin saw the planned extension of the *Conservatorium* to Prussia as a means of 'increasingly making it an enemy of the King[George]'. He therefore recommended a reconciliation with Brandenburg-Prussia to thwart the Emperor's plans.[218]

George II expressed deep resentment at his decreed ejection from Mecklenburg in May 1728, but argued legalistically that the simultaneous suspension of the duke from power violated Charles VI's capitulation of election (art. 20). He affirmed his recognition of the Imperial supreme judicial office but stressed that princely rights, equally safeguarded by Imperial law, must not be surrendered to spurious claims of Imperial authority.[219] Already in August 1727, the Hanoverian privy-councillors had identified the upcoming Congress of Soissons as a platform at which to publicise grievances against Charles VI in the Empire.[220] The Hanoverian diplomat Johann Reck was later dispatched and kept his British colleagues abreast of the Mecklenburg crisis. He told them that 'this effectively amounts to a ban' and therefore required the consent of the Reichstag, which the Emperor was illegally bypassing.[221] The Hanoverian privy-council hoped that France could use its influence with the Catholic electors to provoke hostility towards the Emperor's policies.[222]

The British plenipotentiaries William Stanhope and Horatio Walpole conducted the main deliberations with the French Cardinal-premier Fleury on the possibility of invoking the French guarantee of the Peace of Westphalia and thereby effecting an external intervention against the perceived 'violent and arbitrary Proceeding of the Imperial Court'. They argued that 'the weakness of the Princes...in not daring to unite together to demand the protection of the Powers that are Guarantys, would at last make the Emperor absolute Master of their Privileges'.[223] Stanhope and Walpole argued that the decision to replace the Hanoverian commission by an Imperial administration was taken 'purely on

---

[218] Ibid.
[219] George II to Frederick William I, St. James, 2/5/1729: Klüver (ed.), *Beschreibung*, v, 714–19.
[220] Thompson, *Interest*, 135–41.
[221] Reck to George II, n.p., n.d.: NHStAH, Hann.-92, 2254, fols 15–16.
[222] Memorandum by the Hanoverian privy council, n.p., n.d.: LANRW, Kurköln-VI, 1420, fol. 5.
[223] H. Walpole and Stanhope to Newcastle, Paris, 7 Dec. 1728: BL, Add. MSS. 32,759, fols 295–300, at fol. 295r.

account of His Majesty's having entered into the [1725] Hanover Treaty'. They impressed upon Fleury the dangers of allowing the Emperor to set a precedent by deposing territorial rulers arbitrarily. The measure could not be justified according to the duty of protecting the subjects as 'it would by no means answer the End first proposed, of securing the Nobility of Mecklenburg against Oppression...no provision being effectually made in this Mandate for that Purpose'.[224] Stanhope and Walpole told Fleury that the fact that princely rights were being violated 'obliges France to seriously involve itself in this affair'.[225] They argued that if an attempt were made to militarily execute the May 1728 decree, 'His Most Christian Majesty will be obliged, on the basis of the undertakings of the treaty of Westphalia, to oppose by force the execution of the said decree'.[226] Fleury was also warned that a failure to exercise the guarantee would damage France's credibility in Germany: if 'the Allys of France could not depend upon its Assistance, it would have a very ill-Effect; and the Princes, instead of being ready to make Union with France, would be discouraged from it'.[227]

Britain-Hanover changed its tune from an emphasis on protecting the Mecklenburg nobles to that of stressing the necessity of upholding princely rights because of shifting geopolitical interests. But opposition to the deposition of Carl Leopold did by no means translate into support for the duke himself. The commissioners made this clear when they assured the Emperor, 'that we by no means intend to advocate the cause of Carl Leopold'.[228] Indeed, George II's hostility towards the measure was not directed against the ducal suspension component of the decree, but the ending of the commission and the imposition of a Prussian-backed Imperial administration. The emphasis on the illegality of the suspension reflects the high degree of juridification of German political culture. The continuation of a propagandistic strategy of appealing to a protective duty towards subjects demonstrates the normative weight that such notions held in the Empire. According to Britain-Hanover, supporting the initial intervention against the duke and opposing his deposition was no contradiction. The two stances could be presented as reflecting a similar necessity of upholding the legal rights of corporate groups in the Empire, the Mecklenburg territorial estates in the first case, and the rights of the Imperial Estates in the second. The 1728 decree did not, according to this argument, improve the position of the former, but it certainly harmed the collective rights of the latter. The fact that Carl Leopold was guilty of tyranny and illegal conduct should not justify similarly illegal moves on the part of the Emperor, especially when the duke had already been effectively neutralised and his subjects shielded from him in 1719. This legitimised the

---

[224] H. Walpole and Stanhope to Newcastle, Paris, 30 Nov. 1728: ibid., fols 244–54, at fols 247v, 248v.
[225] H. Walpole and Stanhope to Fleury, Paris, 2 Dec. 1728, fol. 303v.
[226] Statement by British plenipotentiaries, n.p., 22 Dec. 1728, fol. 423.
[227] Stanhope and H. Walpole to Newcastle, Paris, 30 Nov. 1728, fols 244–254, at fol. 249r.
[228] George II and August-Wilhelm to Charles VI, n.p., n.d.: Klüver (ed.), *Beschreibung*, v, 705–13.

requested intervention in the form of the Westphalian guarantee, which was the only legal option available when the offending party was the Emperor himself.

## Brandenburg-Prussia

The centrality of geopolitical considerations which many of the actors displayed in connection with their assessments of the Mecklenburg case comes across particularly strongly in the case of Brandenburg-Prussia.[229] Mecklenburg was a vital site of geopolitical competition between Brandenburg and Hanover, the largely evenly balanced rivals in north Germany. During the period of Hanover's appointment to the commission, relations were particularly strained.[230] It was therefore natural for Brandenburg to oppose Hanover's mandate to militarily occupy large parts of Mecklenburg and disarm the duke, a Prussian ally, in order to prop up Hanover's own partners, the nobles. However, regardless of the basic geopolitical goal of denying Hanover control over Mecklenburg, the language used in the statements of the Prussians shows the basic normative validity of intervention, regardless of whether such expressions were sincere.

An important factor in Berlin's approach to the crisis was its sense of vulnerability in the face of the large Russian military presence in its vicinity during the Northern War. East Prussia was especially geopolitically exposed to the surrounding Russian forces in Poland.[231] While Hanover decided to confront Russia in partnership with the Emperor, Frederick William I opted to 'bandwagon' with the tsar to influence and, hopefully, limit Russian aggression. Whitworth reported from Berlin in late 1716 that 'this Court was resolved to make no stop which might any ways displease the Czar'. The Prussian minister Dönhoff explained that Prussia was 'lying most expos'd to the Czar's attempts' to establish an ascendancy in the region and that therefore Frederick William 'could not concern himself in [Russia's incursions into Mecklenburg] so properly as might be done by [George I] and the Emperor'.[232] During an audience, Frederick William agreed with Whitworth's argument that if Hanover and Brandenburg were seen to be lacking vigour in opposing Russian atrocities in Mecklenburg, this would increase the Emperor's disinclination to grant the investitures (enfeoffments) for

---

[229] For the centrality of geopolitics in Frederick William I's thinking: Instructions to his successor, Potsdam, 17 Feb, 1722: Richard Dietrich (ed.), *Die politischen Testamente der Hohenzollern* (Cologne, 1986), 237–8; Christopher Clark, *Iron Kingdom. The Rise and Downfall of Prussia, 1600–1947* (London, 2006), 101.

[230] E.g., Metsch to Charles VI, Braunschweig, 5 Jan. 1717: HHStA, RK, Dipl.-Akten, Braunschweig-Hannover 2c(1), fols 5–12.

[231] Martin Schulze-Wessel, *Russlands Blick auf Preussen 1697–1947. Die polnische Frage in der Diplomatie und der politischen Öffentlichkeit des Zarenreiches und des Sowjetstaates 1697–1947* (Stuttgart, 1995), 43–9.

[232] Whitworth to Townshend, Berlin, 17 Oct. 1716: BL, Add. MSS. 37,363, fols 104–8.

Bremen-Verden and Stettin which they had conquered from Sweden. But the king explained that 'his Dominions...were more expos'd to the Czar than those of [Hanover] or England, and therefore he was obliged to have a greater consideration for him'.[233] The Prussian chief-minister Heinrich Ilgen attempted to defend Russian actions in Mecklenburg arguing that the duke had a right to conclude external alliances. Ilgen admitted that his king 'could not be sorry to see that Nobility moderated because of the distant expectance He had of that Succession'. According to Ilgen, it was a shame that 'private Gentlemen' were suffering, but that it would be 'more dangerous to embroil the publick affairs on that account'.[234]

Brandenburg-Prussia's apparent willingness to accept the duke's conduct correlated with the amount of confidence it had in Russia's good will. Around the time of the conclusion of the Prusso-Russian Havelberg convention of November 1716, Ilgen tried to ascertain how George would react if Brandenburg were forced to support the duke against his enemies.[235] Ilgen indicated that although the tsar's assistance of Carl Leopold was questionable, Prussia felt compelled to accommodate Russian wishes.[236] Whitworth believed Prussia's was completely under the tsar's thumb.[237] Frederick William's statements were correspondingly bellicose. He said 'the Mecklenburgers ought to be left to their own destiny' and that the Emperor's 'Papers & Mandates' were useless unless backed up by force.[238] A report by Whitworth from April 1717 indicates the resentment felt by Frederick William against George. Hanover's attempt to divert Russian forces from Mecklenburg to Prussian Pomerania after the Scania cancellation was singled out as an instance of particularly bad faith, 'as if the Interests of a few Nobility were to be preferr'd to his who was a Son-in-Law'.[239]

However, over the course of 1717–18, cracks began to appear in Prussia's pro-Russian/ducal-Mecklenburg position, in a process which culminated in the signing of treaties with Britain-Hanover in August 1719. A more ambivalent stance towards the Mecklenburg conflict was a result. The Prussian envoy at Hanover, Friedrich Knyphausen, noted that both the duke and his estates were in the wrong.[240] The Hanoverian envoy to Berlin, Johann Heusch, reported in October 1717 that the Prussians were in favour of joint Prusso-Hanoverian mediation in the estates conflict.[241] They hoped to thereby prevent being excluded from an Imperial-Hanoverian settlement of the conflict which the Reichshofrat and

---

[233] Whitworth to Townshend, Berlin, 20 Oct. 1716: ibid., fols 113–22.
[234] Whitworth to Townshend, Berlin, 20 Oct. 1716: ibid., fol. 119.
[235] Whitworth to Townshend, Berlin, 31 Oct. 1716: ibid., fols 140–4.
[236] Whitworth to Townshend, Berlin, 31 Oct. 1716: ibid., fols 145–6r.
[237] Whitworth to Townshend, Berlin, 1 and 5 Dec. 1716: ibid., fols 195–7, 200–2.
[238] Whitworth to Townshend, Berlin, 24 Nov. 1716: ibid., fols 181–4r, at fol. 181v.
[239] Whitworth to Stanhope, Amsterdam, 15 Apr. 1717: BL, Add. MSS. 37,364, fols 22–6r, at fol. 22r. George I was Frederick William I's father-in-law.
[240] Metsch to Charles VI, Braunschweig, 1 Jan. 1717: HHStA, RK, Dipl.-Akten, Braunschweig-Hannover-Berichte 2c(1), fols 1–4.
[241] Heusch to unknown, Berlin, 3 Oct. 1717: ibid., fols 23–6.

Hanover were already preparing for. Persuading Hanover and Vienna that Prussia would not protect the duke was possibly considered a means towards preventing Prussia's exclusion from the settlement. Prussia's resident in London, Louis-Frédéric Bonet, presented memoranda to George arguing for joint mediation in Mecklenburg.[242] Once the decreed *Conservatorium* became known in late 1717, an effort was made by Berlin to publicise Prussian efforts to bring the duke to reason.[243] Huldenberg surmised that this increasing Prussian coolness towards the duke was related to the birth of his nephew, which made the prospect of a Prussian succession more distant.[244]

When the Hanoverian commission failed to be implemented during the rest of 1717, Frederick William seems to have returned to a pro-ducal/Russian position which lasted for the first half of 1718. During his mission to Berlin, the Hanoverian Privy-councillor Eltz found the Prussians to have considerably hardened their attitude towards the Mecklenburg estates again. Frederick William said that he 'had an alliance with the duke, one therefore could not blame him'. He argued that it would be wrong to strengthen subjects' resistance against their legitimate ruler.[245] The ministers reaffirmed their reliance on Russia and their belief that Peter would not abandon them.[246] Eltz reported that the Prussians still feared the Russians but that their stance towards Mecklenburg depended on the outcome of the Austro-Turkish war which was being followed closely. The Prussians told Eltz 'in the heat of the conversation, that they regarded the duke's rights as their own and that they would have the country sooner or later'. When Eltz retorted 'that it is highly dangerous and irresponsible to draw a foreign power into the Reich and involve it in its affairs', he was told foreign powers such as the Westphalian guarantors Sweden and France had contributed greatly to the protection of religion and liberty in German, and that Russia could henceforth also serve such a purpose.[247] This argument was probably used cynically and disingenuously to defend their alignment with Russia and oppose Hanover's stance towards Mecklenburg. Nevertheless, it reflects a normative acceptance of the principle of intervention, although in this case more with regard to the external guarantors safeguarding princely rights against the Emperor, than to Imperial intervention for the protection of mediate subjects against their princes.

During the spring and summer of 1718, Brandenburg-Prussia repeatedly reaffirmed that it was not committed to aid the duke,[248] but it simultaneously sought to rally support for his cause among the princes, through activism at the

---

[242] E.g., NHStAH, Hann.-92, 2157, fols 8–10.
[243] Huldenberg to George I, Vienna, 25 Dec. 1717: NHStAH, Cal. Br. 24,4911 (ii) 2, fols 375–9r.
[244] Huldenberg to George I, Vienna, 13 Dec. 1717: NHStAH, Cal. Br. 24, 4911(ii) 2, fols 354–5r.
[245] Eltz to George I, Berlin, 21 Jan. 1718: NHStAH, Cal. Br. 24, 709, fols 32–3r, at fol. 32v.
[246] Eltz to George I, Berlin, 23 Jan. 1718: NHStAH, Hann.-92, 2198, fols 46–58.
[247] Eltz to Bernstorff, 28 Jan. 1718: NHStAH, Hann.-92, 2198, fols 42r–3v.
[248] Heusch to George I, Berlin [April/May1718]: NHStAH, Hann.-92, 2179, fols 107–8r.

Reichstag[249] and circulars to the German courts appealing to princely solidarity,[250] in the hope of deterring the execution. Prussia's stance changed again over the summer of 1718, when it became increasingly clear that the execution would take place as Austria emerged victorious in the Balkans.[251] Prussia now offered to participate in the execution against its nominal ally, in the hope of preventing sole Hanoverian dominance in Mecklenburg.[252] Prussian diplomats lobbied for the inclusion in the commission.[253] In this context axioms of the external protective duty towards subjects and the unacceptability of the duke's arbitrary, tyrannical rule were drawn upon in published statements. In one such letter, it was stated that 'the notion... that he can proceed according to his own whim in the dispute with his nobility, and is answerable to no one in such matters, is wrong; and the fundamental Imperial laws, the customary observance and countless examples in the Empire prove the opposite'.[254] At the same time, Prussia's efforts at brokering a settlement between the duke and the nobility were publicised, presumably to bolster Frederick William's mediating credentials as a potential commissioner.[255]

By the time the conclusion of the seemingly anti-Prussian Hanoverian-Saxon-Austrian alliance was known to be imminent, Prussia probably realised that its efforts at preventing the Hanoverian commission had failed.[256] Carl Leopold's flight to Brandenburg did not help optically.[257] In the aftermath of the execution, Prussia repeatedly complained at Vienna that Hanover had effectively taken over Mecklenburg, deposed the duke and exceeded its commission-mandate.[258] Part of this strategy aimed at reducing Hanover's dominance in Mecklenburg was to intercede on behalf of the duke, with claims that Prussia had moved him to adequately submit to Imperial authority in the hope of seeing his control restored and that of Hanover reduced.[259] When the Emperor ordered a reduction of Hanover's military presence in May 1719, Berlin was predictably content.[260] The conclusion of the British/Hanoverian—Prussian treaties in August 1719 inaugurated a period of rapprochement which lasted until 1726, and during this period Mecklenburg no longer caused tensions between George and Frederick William.[261] Once Prussia defected from the Franco-British-led Hanover alliance

---

[249] Kirchner to Charles VI, Regensburg, 31 May 1718: HHStA, RK, PK-Berichte-42(1), fols 309–28.
[250] Berlin, 5 Mar. 1718: *EStC*32, 203–5.
[251] Huldenberg to George I, Vienna, 27 Aug. 1718: NHStAH, Cal. Br. 24, 4912(ii)1, fols 112–16.
[252] Frederick William I to George I, Berlin, 16 Aug. 1718: NHStAH, Hann.-9g, 16, fol. 33.
[253] Numerous reports Metsch to Charles VI, Braunschweig, Aug.–Sept. 1718: HHStA, RK, Dipl.-Akten, Braunschweig-Hannover-Berichte 2c(2), fols 295–310; Huldenberg to George I, Vienna, 7 Sep. 1718: NHStAH, Cal. Br. 24, 4912(ii)1, fols 138–41.
[254] Frederick William I to Carl Leopold, 4 Oct. 1718: [Moser (ed.)] *Reichs-Fama*, iv, 515–19.
[255] Prussian statement, 28 Oct. 1718: *EStC* 32, 243–6.
[256] Huldenberg to George I, Vienna, 24 Dec. 1718: NHStAH, Cal. Br. 24, 4912(ii) 2, fols 399–400.
[257] Heusch to George I, Berlin, 28 Mar. 1719: NHStAH, Hann.-92, 2203, fols 86–8.
[258] Frederick William I to Charles VI, 31 May 1719: NHStAH, Cal. Br. 24, 4915, ii, fols 416–18.
[259] St.-Saphorin to George I, Vienna, 5 Apr. 1719: NHStAH, Hann.-92, 2140.
[260] Whitworth to Stanhope, Berlin, 10 June 1719: NA, SP 90/8.
[261] E.g., Whitworth to Townshend, Berlin, 8 Nov. 1721: NA, SP 90/15.

and was rewarded with the extended *Conservatorium* on 11 May 1728,[262] Mecklenburg once again became a flashpoint in British/Hanoverian-Prussian relations. The fear that Prussia might execute the decreed Imperial administration in Mecklenburg by force was compounded by a Prusso-Hanoverian war-scare in 1729.[263]

Frederick William's 'natural irresolution' has often been commented upon.[264] However, Brandenburg-Prussia's policy in the Mecklenburg crisis displays a consistent aim of maintaining influence in this strategically vital area, and of denying Hanover sole control over it—expedient temporary alignments with Hanover notwithstanding. The shifting attitudes and statements regarding the duke and his policies were tailored to this basic aim. Thus, attempts were made to rally support for the duke in 1718, while in 1729 Prussia essentially supported his deposition, because it was linked to Prussia's inclusion in the Mecklenburg administration.[265] In this context lip service was at times paid to norms of princely duties and the necessity of protective intervention. That such strategies of argumentation were calculated to be effective is nevertheless indicative of the normative framework within which German politics was conducted.

## Other Imperial Estates and the Reichstag

The Mecklenburg case received considerable attention among the Imperial Estates, not least because it related to a perceived external threat to the Empire. Furthermore, the fact that a middling territory with powerful allies was the executee caused comment. Many princes expressed their opinions in response to the duke's and estates' rival publicity campaigns. As a centre of communication and information exchange, the Reichstag was a forum in which general princely opinion can be gauged.[266] The Reichstag first came to deal with the case indirectly by addressing the dangers of the Russian presence in Mecklenburg.[267] There was a growing realisation that the duke shared responsibility for Russian actions.[268] In December 1717, the electoral-Cologne envoy Neuhaus reported on the attitudes towards the Mecklenburg case. Most envoys disapproved of the duke's conduct, his excessive taxation regime and the violence used to enforce it. There was a belief

---

[262] Frederick William I to Charles VI, Berlin, 9 Nov. 1728: HHStA, RK, Kl.-Reichsstände 347, fols 444–7.
[263] Seckendorff to Fürstenberg, Berlin, 3 Aug. 1729: HHStA, RHR, Den.-Rec. 701.
[264] Whitworth to Stanhope, Berlin, 17 Sep. 1719: BL, Add. MSS. 37,375, fols 213–15, at fol. 213v.
[265] Frederick William I to Carl Leopold, Berlin, 20 Aug. 1729: Klüver (ed.), *Beschreibung*, v, 747–9.
[266] Susanne Friedrich, *Drehscheibe Regensburg. Das Informations- und Kommunikationssystem des Reichstags um 1700* (Berlin, 2007).
[267] Neuhaus to Josef-Clemens, Regensburg, 28 May 1716: LANRW, Kurköln-VI, 530, fol. 58.
[268] Mecklenburg agent Christiani to Eichholtz, Regensburg, 24 Nov. 1716: LHAS, Ausw.-Bez. 2.11–2/1, 1601, fol. 76.

that he was not authorised to act with such harshness.[269] Eichholtz reported with concern that the nobility's envoy Behr was said to be gaining 'a strong following' at Regensburg.[270] The Hanoverian envoy Wrisberg reported that most envoys disagreed with the ducal position of not being bound by the treaty obligations.[271] Most were convinced of the 'great injustice of the court of Schwerin'.[272] In mid-1718 Wrisberg reported that the continued failure of George to carry out the execution was causing comment, rather than the legitimacy of the mandated intervention itself, and when it finally took place, it did not receive much mention at the Reichstag.[273]

A similar mood was reported from other centres of princely public opinion. Metsch reported from the congress of Braunschweig in mid-1717 that most envoys blamed the duke for the presence of the Russians.[274] Eight months later, Metsch reported that most envoys 'in all ways disapprove' of the duke's treatment of his estates.[275] A further nine months later, he reported that many commentators at Braunschweig were astonished at the duke's contumacy and that there was a general opinion that intervention was necessary to prevent larger territories being encouraged to flout Imperial judicial authority.[276] At Vienna, where numerous princes kept resident envoys, the duke's envoy reported that the nobility's representations were receiving more credence than his own, and that the nobles were being actively supported by many envoys.[277]

The archbishop-elector of Mainz, Lothar Franz, was involved with the case primarily through his directorate of the Reichstag, an office which gave him the choice over the dictation of statements to the plenum. Lothar Franz approved of his directorial-envoy Otten's suggestion that the dictation of the duke's statements be denied, given that it was a judicial matter already treated at the Reichshofrat.[278] Mainz was very much in favour of the intervention in Mecklenburg.[279] Lothar Franz's influence in the Reich—his dignity of arch-chancellor being second only to that of the Emperor in the Imperial hierarchy—derived solely from the legal and protective framework of the Reich, which granted him a status incomparable to the limited power-political potential of his modest territory.[280] He therefore

---

[269] Neuhaus to Josef-Clemens, Regensburg, n.d. [December 1717]: LANRW, Kurköln-VI, 1419, fols 1–4.
[270] Eichholtz to Wolffradt, Vienna, 2 Mar. 1718: LHAS, Ausw.-Bez. 2.11–2/1, 1603, fols 19–21.
[271] Wrisberg to George I, Regensburg, 17 Mar. 1718: NHStAH, Cal. Br. 11, 2971 (i), fol. 217.
[272] Wrisberg to George I, Regensburg, 8 Aug. 1718: NHStAH, Cal. Br. 11, 2972, fol. 45.
[273] Wrisberg to George I, Regensburg, 8 June 1718: NHStAH, Cal. Br. 11, 2971 (ii), fols 523–4v.
[274] Metsch to Charles VI, Braunschweig, 7 May 1717: HHStA, RK, Dipl.-Akten, Braunschweig-Hannover-Berichte 2c (1), fols 150–1.
[275] Metsch to Charles VI, Braunschweig, 14 Jan. 1718: HHStA, RK, Dipl.-Akten, Braunschweig-Hannover, Berichte 2c (2), fols 11–16.
[276] Metsch to Charles VI, Braunschweig, 6 Sep. 1718: ibid., fols 313, 318.
[277] Eichholtz to Carl Leopold, Vienna, 27 Feb. 1717: LHAS, Ausw.-Bez. 2.11–2/1, 1601, fols 206–7.
[278] Lothar Franz to Otten, Mainz, 8 Jan. 1718: HHStA, MEA, Reichstag 373.
[279] Lothar Franz to Otten, Mainz, 23 Nov. 1717: HHStA, MEA, Reichstag 372.
[280] On Mainz: T.C.W. Blanning, *Reform and Revolution in Mainz, 1743–1803* (Cambridge, 1974), 46–69.

usually supported Imperial judicial measures designed to uphold the existing politico-legal framework.[281] In a letter to the elector of Cologne, Lothar Franz defended the measures against Carl Leopold, arguing that if one were to allow Imperial jurisdiction to decay, the whole Imperial system would collapse and 'minor powers would lose out every time'.[282] At times Mainz also considered politico-strategic factors, such as in 1720 when the archbishop-elector explained that his reluctance to join other princes in complaining about the Hanoverian commission was due to an unwillingness to provoke a further deterioration of relations with Hanover. He specifically feared a possible Hanoverian attack on his exclave territory of Eichsfeld along the southern border of Hanover.[283]

In an example of cross-confessional princely solidarity, the archbishop-elector of Cologne, Joseph Clemens, was sympathetic to the duke's position.[284] This was possibly related to the fact that he was also involved in conflict with his territorial estates, and that he had similarly been penalised by the Emperor's judicial authority when he was placed under the ban and suspended from power in 1706. Cologne's privy-council noted that siding with Carl Leopold was inadvisable as it risked alienating Vienna.[285] If Cologne were the first elector to support him, this might 'cause an odd impression in various places'.[286] Despite these misgivings Cologne resolved to ask for an end to the execution.[287] In 1723 Joseph Clemens indicated he would follow the lead of his brother, the elector of Bavaria, in matters relating to Mecklenburg.[288] Bavaria had been similarly proscribed with the Imperial ban, and was also unwilling to criticise Carl Leopold.[289]

The duke of Mecklenburg-Strelitz sought to publicise the fact that the nobles were not Carl Leopold's only victims, but that his rights were being violated by him as well.[290] He therefore supported the mandated *Conservatorium* against his fellow duke and requested that it be extended to cover his own duchy.[291] As the appointed junior conservator-commissioner, the duke of Braunschweig-Wolfenbüttel naturally supported the intervention in which he was going to participate, despite Braunschweig-Wolfenbüttel's tradition of rivalry with Hanover and its troubled historical relationship with Vienna.[292] He sent a

---

[281] Alfred Schröcker, 'Die Amtsauffassung des Mainzer Kurfürsten Lothar Franz von Schönborn', *MöStA* 33 (1980), 106–26.
[282] Lothar Franz to Joseph Clemens, Mainz, 22 Mar. 1718: LANRW, Kurköln-VI, 1409, fols 43–4r.
[283] Lothar Franz to Otten, Mainz, 21 May 1720: HHStA, MEA, Reichstag 381.
[284] Joseph Clemens to Carl Leopold, Bonn, 18 Aug. 1718: LANRW, Kurköln-VI, 1411, fol. 18.
[285] Cologne privy council to Joseph Clemens, Bonn, 9 Mar. 1719: ibid., fols 17–18r.
[286] Cologne privy council to Joseph Clemens, Bonn, 14 Mar. 1719: ibid., fols 21–2r.
[287] Cologne privy council to Klingstedt, Bonn, 14 Mar. 1719: ibid., fol. 23.
[288] Joseph Clemens to Max-Emanuel, Bonn, 3 Aug. 1723: LANRW, Kurköln-VI, 1419, fol. 10.
[289] Max Emanuel to Carl Leopold, Munich, 9 Jan. 1718: EStC 32 (1719), 73.
[290] Wrisberg to George I, Regensburg, 15 Aug. 1718: NHStAH, Cal. Br. 21, 2972, fol. 86.
[291] Adolf Friedrich to George I, Strelitz, 18 Aug. 1718: NHStAH, Hann.-92, 2204, fols 14–15r.
[292] Christof Römer, 'Der Kaiser und die welfischen Staaten 1679–1755', in Harm Klueting et al. (eds), *Das Reich und seine Territorialstaaten im 17. und 18. Jahrhundert* (Münster, 2004), 43–66, at 47–8.

published letter to Carl Leopold in 1718, in which he warned him 'not to proceed so strongly against your nobility'.[293]

Princes which were not directly affected by the case also voiced objections to the duke's behaviour. The privy-council of the Protestant prince-bishop of Osnabrück informed their Hanoverian colleagues in 1718 that Carl Leopold's request for support was refused.[294] In 1717, Eichholtz had singled out the prince-bishop of Würzburg as a promising candidate for supporting the duke's cause as he was in conflict with his estates too.[295] Nevertheless, in 1723 the prince-bishop wrote to the Imperial vice-chancellor Schönborn, that he would not support Carl Leopold.[296] The Palatine Reichstag-envoy announced that his master would have nothing to do the duke's schemes.[297] The landgrave of Hessen-Kassel offered his troops for a possible intervention in Mecklenburg in 1716.[298] At the court of the prince-bishop of Hildesheim there was reportedly a feeling of astonishment at the severity of Carl Leopold's measures.[299] The duke of Sachsen-Gotha's Reichstag envoy frequently expressed himself critically about the injustice of Carl Leopold's methods, despite also representing the latter at the Reichstag.[300] Saxony's approving attitude towards the intervention is clear from numerous statements and from its adherence to the Treaty of Vienna of January 1719, which included provisions for the Mecklenburg execution.[301] In 1721 Augustus II wrote a published letter to the duke criticising his conduct.[302]

While there was a broad consensus behind the necessity of intervening against the duke and executing the *Conservatorium* of 1717, there was strong opposition among the princes against the decrees of 11 May 1728. One hundred years after Emperor Ferdinand II had provoked consternation among princes during the Thirty Years War, by deposing the native dukes of Mecklenburg in 1628, Charles VI adopted a similarly bold measure as his Habsburg ancestor in the same duchy.[303] The new elector of Cologne, Clemens August, was active in opposing the 1728 measure at the Reichstag, together with the other Wittelsbach electors. In 1728, he wrote to the elector-Palatine that he hoped the princes would collectively protest the decree.[304] In reply, Karl Philipp referred to the 'sensation' that it had

---

[293] August Wilhelm to Carl Leopold, Braunschweig, 23 June 1718: *EStC* 32 (1719), 201–2.
[294] Osnabrück, 10 Jan. 1718: NHStAH, Cal. Br. 24, 3874, fol. 1.
[295] Eichholtz to Wolffradt, Vienna, 11 Dec. 1717: LHAS, Ausw.-Bez. 2.11–2/1, 1602, fols 171–2.
[296] Johann Philipp Franz von Schönborn to Friedrich Karl von Schönborn, Würzburg, 19 Nov. 1723: HHStA, RK, Kl.-Reichsstände 347, fols 381–9.
[297] Wrisberg to George I, Regensburg, 8 June 1718: NHStAH, Cal. Br. 11, 2971, ii, fols 523–4v.
[298] Wrisberg to George I, Regensburg, 23 Nov. 1716: NHStAH, Cal. Br. 11, 2968, iv, fols 769–71r.
[299] Twickel to Joseph Clemens, Hildesheim, 20 Dec. 1717: LANRW, Kurköln-VII, 130/2, fols 159–60r.
[300] Wrisberg to George I, Regensburg, 23 Nov. 1716: NHStAH, Cal. Br. 11, 2968, iv, fols 769–71r.
[301] Huldenberg to George I, 11 Dec. 1717: NHStAH, Cal. Br. 24, 4911 (ii) 2, fols 332–5.
[302] Augustus II to Carl Leopold, Dresden, 18 Oct. 1721: *EStC* 39, 773–5.
[303] Christoph Kampmann, *Reichsrebellion und kaiserliche Acht. Politische Strafjustiz im Dreissigjährigen Krieg und das Verfahren gegen Wallenstein, 1634* (Münster, 1993), 90–8.
[304] Clemens August to Karl Philipp, Bonn, 3 Aug. 1728: LANRW, Kurköln-VI, 1411, fol. 40r.

caused. He stressed that he had no intention of denying the Imperial supreme judicial authority, but it was important that princely rights were equally respected.[305]

In 1728, one Hanoverian diplomat was pessimistic about the prospect of widespread princely opposition to the decree at Regensburg.[306] However, opposition became more vociferous following the dictation of the Emperor's *Kommissionsdekret* statement which sought to justify the measures. The Emperor's representative at the Reichstag reported that opposition was especially strong among Protestant envoys. There was a belief that any deposition must occur through formal ban proceedings.[307] The envoy Plettenberg reported to Clemens August that opposition to the measure was being driven with increasing 'seriousness and fervour'.[308] Plettenberg summarised the general attitude: the 1717/19 intervention had been just and legal, but the suspension-decree constituted a violation of princely rights. Opposing the measure was important for its own sake, even though the Hanover-allies were hostile for power-political reasons. The fact that there had not been much opposition to the Nassau-Siegen deposition did not justify the current suspension.[309] The elector of Bavaria was also strongly opposed to the suspension.[310]

Princely opposition to the 1728 decree was not unanimous, however. Apart from Prussia, Sachsen-Gotha also supported the decreed administration.[311] Mainz's position was ambivalent, but overall the archbishop-elector tended towards Vienna's side. As in 1717–19, Lothar Franz was refusing the dictation of the duke's protests against the 1728 decree at the Reichstag.[312] Wary of the dilemma between the importance of staying on good terms with the Emperor and avoiding the hostility of the other princes, Lothar Franz recommended that the decree not be brought before the Reichstag for official debate.[313] His successor wrote to Cologne advising a more cautious approach as it was important for the Catholic electors to retain the Emperor's favour, especially in the context of resurgent confessional tensions. Therefore it would be unwise for the Catholics to align themselves so closely with the Hanover allies in the Mecklenburg case.[314] By 1730 Franz Ludwig seemed to have come down on the Emperor's side as he tried to persuade his fellow electors that the interests of the princes lay not in a

---

[305] Karl Philipp to Clemens August, Schwetzingen, 22 July 1728: ibid., fol. 41r.
[306] Reck to George II, n.p., n.d. [1728]: NHStAH, Hann.-92, 2254, fols 49–50.
[307] Fürstenberg to Charles VI, Regensburg, 21 June 1729: HHStA, RHR, Den.-Rec. 700(6).
[308] Plettenberg to Clemens August, Regensburg, 2 June 1729: LANRW, Kurköln-VI, 1419, fols 18–19.
[309] Plettenberg to Clemens August, Regensburg, 5 Sep. 1729: ibid., fols 307–13.
[310] Karl Albrecht to Plettenberg, Munich, 16 July 1729: Kurköln-VI, 1419, fols 156–8r.
[311] Seckendorff to Fürstenberg, Berlin, 3 Aug. 1729: HHStA, RHR, Den.-Rec. 701.
[312] Lothar Franz to Friedrich Karl von Schönborn, Mainz, 24 July 1728: HHStA, RK, Kl.-Reichsstände 348, fols 22–39.
[313] Lothar Franz to Charles VI, Mainz, 12 Oct. 1728: HHStA, RK, Kl.-Reichsstände 347, fols 456–7.
[314] Franz Ludwig to Clemens August, Mainz, 9 July 1729: LANRW, Kurköln-VI, 1419, fols 143–6.

narrow-minded assertion of their rights against the Emperor, but primarily in a good working relationship with the Emperor.[315]

## European Powers

Apart from Britain, several other European powers also commented upon the Mecklenburg case. The general mood among European diplomats at the Hague was reportedly critical of the duke in late 1717.[316] For Tsar Peter, Mecklenburg was destined to be a crucial conduit for an envisaged global commercial empire and the marriage-alliance with the duke was designed to enable that goal, and to more immediate Russian strategic aims in the war against Sweden.[317] An unintended side-effect of Peter's Mecklenburg policy was the hostility it provoked from within the Empire. Peter blamed Bernstorff personally for the deterioration of his relations with Hanover and Vienna.[318] Several Russian diplomats and statesmen privately regretted the support given to the duke as it was believed to be causing unnecessary problems.[319] The Hanoverian resident in Russia, Friedrich Weber, was told that although the tsar regretted the alliance with the duke, they could not abandon him now.[320] Until Peter's death the intervention against the duke remained one of the main obstacles towards a re-establishment of good relations between George I and the tsar.[321]

Denmark was very sympathetic to the cause of protecting the Mecklenburg estates. Many of its leading statesmen were Mecklenburg noblemen themselves.[322] The Danish envoy in Vienna frequently interceded on the nobility's behalf with the Emperor.[323] The ducal envoy Eichholtz reported that the court at Copenhagen was influenced by the 'Bernstorff spirit'.[324] Nevertheless, Danish support for the nobility reached its limit at diplomatic intercessions. When Hanover solicited military support against Carl Leopold for the upcoming intervention, it was politely turned down.[325] Although Carl Leopold admired Charles XII of Sweden, and there were widespread fears that the duke was conspiring not only with

---

[315] Franz Ludwig to Karl Philipp, Mainz, 2 Jan. 1730: ibid., fol. 3.
[316] Sande to Carl Leopold, The Hague, 14 Sep. 1717: LHAS, Ausw.-Bez. 2.11–2/1, 4069, fols 171–3.
[317] Mediger, *Mecklenburg*, 122ff.
[318] Metsch to Charles VI, Braunschweig, 5 Feb. 1717: HHStA, RK, Dipl.-Akten, Braunschweig-Hannover-Berichte 2c(1), fols 51–4r.
[319] Reported in Metsch to Charles VI, Braunschweig, 20 Apr. 1717: ibid., fols 132–3.
[320] Weber to George I, Moscow, 21 Mar. 1718: NHStAH, Hann.-92, 1360, fols 398–407.
[321] Russian statement to George I, 17 Oct. 1720: NA, SP 100/52; Tsar Peter to Charles VI [1721]: *EstC* 39, 777–8.
[322] Mediger, *Mecklenburg*, 13–14.
[323] Reck to George I, Vienna, 29 Aug. 1716: NHStAH, Cal. Br. 24, 4910(iii), fols 91–2r.
[324] Eichholtz to Carl Leopold, Vienna, 9 Jan. 1717: LHAS, Ausw.-Bez. 2.11–2/1, 1601, fols 129–31.
[325] Bothmer to George I, Copenhagen, 2 Nov. 1717: NHStAH, Hann.-92, 2200, fols 246–9.

Russian but with Sweden as well,[326] the Swedish envoy in Vienna emphatically denied that Sweden supported Carl Leopold.[327] At the congress of Soissons in 1728, Sweden expressed itself favourably to the prospect of invoking the guarantee of Westphalia over the duke's suspension.[328] The Imperial envoy in Stockholm reported that the Swedes were largely convinced by Britain's anti-Austrian representations, and that they would follow Britain-Hanover's lead against Vienna, in line with Sweden's membership of the anti-Austro-Spanish Alliance of Hanover.[329]

The duke made futile attempts to forge alliances with both Sweden and France on the basis of their Westphalian guarantee.[330] The fact that France—the archrival of the Habsburgs—made no serious attempt to rouse the princes against the 1719 intervention is instructive. It reflected in part the normative approval of the initial intervention in the Reich which was seen by most as just and legal. The French leadership saw the 1728 suspension decree, by contrast, as an opportunity to provoke hostility towards the Emperor. In addition to differing normative assessments of the 1719 execution on the one hand and the 1728 deposition on the other hand among potential French partners in the Reich, the broader geopolitical context was probably more important in explaining the contrasting French reactions. In the period after the Peace of Utrecht (1713), France, under the leadership of the regent d'Orléans and his chief minister Cardinal Dubois, was allied with Britain in an unusual *entente*.[331]

Dubois worked closely together with British secretary of State James Stanhope to maintain the Utrecht peace settlement and expand their cooperation to encompass other powers, notably Spain and Austria, which were still on bad terms following the conclusion of the War of the Spanish Succession. While Emperor Charles VI reluctantly agreed to be co-opted into the planned Anglo-French 'Quadruple Alliance' because he was under Spanish attack in the Mediterranean, Philip V of Spain and his wife Elisabeth Farnese needed to be coerced into stopping their aggressive revanchism.[332] Thus, during the 1719 Mecklenburg intervention, the normally axiomatic Franco-Habsburg rivalry had been temporary put on hold and this explains why France did not make more noise about the armed dispossession of a German prince on the Emperor's orders. Moreover, the intervention had been carried out by France's closest ally, the king of Great Britain George I in his capacity as Hanoverian elector. Had France not been on such

---

[326] See Huldenberg to George I, Vienna, 13 Apr. 1718: NHStAH, Cal. Br. 24, 4912(i) 2, at 268v.
[327] Huldenberg to George I, Vienna, 2 July 1718: ibid., fol. 484.
[328] Schleinitz to duke of Braunschweig-Wolfenbüttel (copy), Paris, 4 Dec. 1728: BL, Add. MSS. 32,759, fols 307–8.
[329] Envoy to Charles VI, Stockholm, 30 June 1729: HHStA, RK, Kl.-Reichsstände 348, fols 20–1.
[330] Negotiations in LHAS, Ausw.-Bez.-2.11–2/1, 418, 5338, 5340.
[331] Black, 'The Anglo-French alliance 1716–1731'.
[332] Frederik Dhondt, *Balance of Power and Norm Hierarchy: Franco-British Diplomacy after the Peace of Utrecht* (Leiden, 2015), 41–252; Derek McKay and H.M. Scott, *The Rise of the Great Powers, 1648–1815* (London, 1983), 101–18.

unusually good terms with both Britain and Austria, it is highly probable that statesmen in Paris would have considered the de facto deposition of the duke of Mecklenburg as a good opportunity to stir up trouble for the Habsburgs.

By contrast, at the time of the 1728 deposition decree, the geopolitical context was far more amenable to the traditional French policy of being a thorn in the Emperor's side when he strayed, or was perceived to have strayed, from a strict reading of Imperial law in Germany with regard to the Imperial Estates' rights. Paris was still aligned with Britain, however the Habsburgs were now seen as the enemy again. France was at this time already engaged in a diplomatic drive in the Empire to win over princes to the Hanover Alliance.[333] During the congress of Soissons, Cardinal-premier Fleury told the British plenipotentiaries that French military intervention against the Emperor on the basis of the Westphalian guarantee could be provided if this were requested by the princes. He later elaborated that France would consider intervening even without a unanimous Reichstag requisition.[334] How serious the French were is hard to determine. They did not go further than offering words of support. Contrary to what he had told the British, Fleury explained to the Braunschweig-Wolfenbüttel envoy that the requisition would indeed have to be unanimous.[335] When Fleury brought up the Mecklenburg issue with the Austrian envoy Sinzendorf, he did so somewhat diffidently.[336] Nonetheless, the following year the French envoy to Mainz was instructed to dispose the archbishop-elector towards opposing the May 1728 decree as it was contrary to the terms of Westphalia and to the interests of the German princes. It was argued that allowing the Reichshofrat to depose rulers at a whim could greatly increase the power and authority of the Emperor, to the detriment of France.[337]

## The Public Sphere[338]

As has been shown, various rulers and actors involved in the Mecklenburg case attached considerable importance to the public presentation of their policies, through the publication of pamphlets and pieces of correspondence, to highlight

---

[333] Jean Dureng, *Mission de Théodorre Chevignard de Chavignyen Allemagne, 1726–1731* (Paris, 1912).
[334] H. Walpole and Stanhope to Newcastle, Paris, 7 Dec. 1728: BL, Add. MSS. 32,759, fols 295–300, at fol. 296v.
[335] Schleinitz to duke of Braunschweig-Wolfenbüttel, Paris, 4 Dec. 1728: BL, Add. MSS. 32,759, fols 307–8, at 308r.
[336] Sinzendorf to Charles VI, Fontainebleau, 6 Oct. 1728: HHStA, RK, Kl.-Reichsstände 347, fols 448–55.
[337] Instructions for Michel de Vilebois, Paris, 1 July 1729: *Recueil des instructions* (Paris, 1962), xxviii, 138–50, at 144–8.
[338] See also Arndt, *Herrschaftskontrolle*, 448–99.

the injustice of an opponent or stress the correctness of one's own stance.[339] A related aim was to present and justify policy to the other princes in the hope of favourably influencing their policies and stances.[340] In addition to governmental publications, the Mecklenburg case was also covered in the independent press. Although journalists were generally more inclined towards governments (*Obrigkeit*) in their coverage of ruler-subjects conflicts,[341] the independent media's treatment of the Mecklenburg estates and Imperial measures against the duke was largely favourable. The public newspapers covered the Mecklenburg intervention extensively, thus reflecting public interest in the case, although with varying degrees of accuracy.[342] One article referred to the 'imposed heavy contributions' and 'such strong recruitment' in the duchy, which indicated that the duke was determined 'to resist the execution' with an army of 18,000. Anecdotes of personal experiences in the duchy indicate sympathy the author had for the suffering of the subjects.[343]

The leading political journal in early eighteenth-century Germany, the *Europäische Fama*, was critical of the duke's conduct, which is noticeable from the language used to describe ducal policies ('severe recruitments...which have been continued with great zeal').[344] The nobility's pamphlets were reported to be 'far stronger' than the ducal ones.[345] The dangers of developments in Mecklenburg were underlined and it was stated that they could lead to 'vaster consequences'. The author commented that sharp warnings from Vienna failed to bring the duke to reason, and that he was continuing his armaments programme as if preparing for an expected war.[346] The first report after the execution expressed great relief that the crisis had been overcome without the outbreak of a general war.[347] The initial report on the 1728 suspension decree was favourable. The suspension was argued to have been forced upon the Emperor because of the duke's intransigence and refusal to submit to Imperial authority.[348] Subsequent reports became more critical of the decree as the debate surrounding it gained momentum. In 1729 strong doubts were expressed regarding the legality of the measure.[349] The question over the decree was now argued to be one of the most important matters being debated in the Reich, 'both with regard to its current condition, and with regard to the consequences which are feared as a result of it'.[350]

---

[339] For public presentation of policy in general: Andreas Gestrich, *Absolutismus und Öffentlichkeit. Politische Kommunikation in Deutschland zu Beginn des 18. Jahrhunderts* (Göttingen, 1994), 26–7.
[340] Wolfgang Burgdorf, 'Der intergouvernementale publizistische Diskurs', in Arndt et al. (eds), *Mediensystem*, 75–98.
[341] Gestrich, *Absolutismus*, 175.
[342] Eichholtz to Wolffradt, Vienna, 9 Dec. 1716: LHAS, Ausw.-Bez. 2.11–2/1, 1601, fols 92–5.
[343] *Mit Kays. Majest. Privilegiis Journal*, 7 (1718), 25/1/1718.
[344] *Europäische Fama*, 206 (1717), 164–74.      [345] Ibid., 239 (1720), 1006–8.
[346] Ibid., 216 (1718), 1050–64.      [347] Ibid., 222 (1719), 220–49.      [348] Ibid., 316 (1728), 320.
[349] Ibid., 322 (1729), 843–66.      [350] Ibid., 324 (1729), 1019.

Other journals also criticised Carl Leopold's regime. Moser's *Reichs-Fama* was highly critical of ducal policies and largely seconded his opponents' arguments. Imperial measures against the duke were portrayed as a necessary intervention.[351] Moser commented: 'under the pretext of the administration of justice, the nobility was tormented and curtailed in innumerable ways'.[352] The historical-political journal *Jubilæum Theatri Europæi* made reference to the 'dreadful harshness' of ducal oppression which led to Imperial mandates being issued.[353] The *Historischer Mercurius* reported on the Mecklenburg case largely in the context of the Northern War but the duke's internal policies were also described and characterised as unjust.[354] The author argued that the aim of the duke's policy of 'bleeding [the nobles] dry' was to attain 'complete sovereignty'.[355] The intervention was praised for being aimed at 'restoring old privileges and freedoms to the Mecklenburg aristocracy'.[356]

The *Gespräche in dem Reiche derer Todten* was a journal in which the author, David Fassmann, wrote imaginary conversations between recently deceased famous individuals and historical figures.[357] In the conversation between George I and Charles IX of Sweden, Fassmann had George comment on the Mecklenburg intervention as an important aspect of his reign. The mandated intervention was portrayed as a measure designed to save the nobles: 'the nobility would without a doubt have been completely ruined, if the Emperor had not taken up the case rather forcefully'. The execution was also explained as a necessary measure to defuse a dangerous situation in the north.[358]

Several other periodicals functioned as source collections, regularly reprinting the official governmental publications and pamphlets that appeared. The most important of these, *Europäische Staats-Cantzley* included extensive material on Mecklenburg. In a volume from 1719, 210 out of 770 pages were devoted to the case.[359]

## Conclusion

Whether the intervention in Mecklenburg can be described as a success-story is doubtful. The territorial estates eventually received the protection which the intervention was designed to furnish; yet the nobles were a selfish group of landlords who were entirely committed to defending their own sectional interests.

---

[351] *Reichs-Fama*, 3 (1728), 150–75.   [352] *Reichs-Fama*, 4 (1729), 498–529.
[353] *Jubilæum Theatri Europæi*, 21 (Frankfurt, 1738), 140.
[354] *Historischer Mercurius* (Augsburg, 1712–18), vol. 61, 95–6; vol. 72, 541–4; vol. 65, 423–5; vol. 67, 89–92; vol. 74, 155–7.
[355] Ibid., 77 (May, 1718).   [356] Ibid., 80 (August, 1718), 113–16.
[357] David Fassmann (ed.), *Gespräche in dem Reiche derer Todten* (Leipzig, 1720–37).
[358] Fassmann (ed.), *Gespräche*, 123 (1728), 1171–2.   [359] *EStC* 32 (1719).

The intervention process itself was agonisingly slow. The Reichshofrat first issued mandates against the duke in 1714 and then issued the first 'conservatorial' order in 1716, but it was only in 1719 that the executors could bring themselves to carry out the intervention due to complicated execution regulations and long-winded diplomatic preparations. Even after the intervention, the duke was still able to carry out atrocities under legal authority as late as 1722.

The geopolitical result of the intervention was that this medium-sized territory shifted from being under the sway of Russia to Hanover during the 1720s and then finally fell under a de facto condominium of its Hanoverian and Brandenburg-Prussian neighbours during the 1730s and early 1740s.

Despite the intervention being mainly geopolitically-driven, the case was also assessed according to a set of norms pertaining to acceptable princely rule and the duty of intervention because of serious infractions of those standards. These norms included an emphasis on legality and the obligation to respect basic rights of recognised groups and mediate subjects. Additionally, the sheer brutality of Carl Leopold's regime gave rise to a related set of assessments which were reflective of more abstract notions of civilised conduct and Christian duties. Accusations of barbarism and uncivilised behaviour were not just applied to Turks and other foreign enemies but could also be levelled against German princes.

This basic underlying normative outlook was evinced from a range of involved and uninvolved actors and commentators throughout the Empire. While the Reichshofrat primarily approached the case according to principles of legality and justness, for the political wing of the court at Vienna, and the proxy-intervener Hanover and its rival Brandenburg-Prussia, geopolitical considerations were paramount. Given the fact that the oppression of Carl Leopold's domestic opponents became inextricably linked to an acute geopolitical threat and the complex diplomatic constellations of the Northern War, it is understandable that the involved rulers were guided by power-political imperatives. For some of these powers, the underlying normative emphasis on the duty to protect and to salvage the law coincided with their geopolitical interests and this is what made the intervention compelling for the Emperor and George I. Most neutral, uninvolved actors and commentators approved of the intervention against the duke's regime and his foreign-political machinations is indicative of the general normative validity of the arguments employed by the interveners.

The rapidly shifting European and German diplomatic landscape during the 1720s ensured that most actors reassessed their attitude towards the Mecklenburg case in the context of the 1728 suspension decree. Opponents of Vienna and many neutral princes shifted the emphasis from a necessity of protecting the subjects of Mecklenburg to a necessity of safeguarding the legal rights of the Emperor's immediate subjects. In this context they mooted a potential intervention by the Westphalian guarantors.

# Epilogue
## Intervention through the Ages

Over the course of the period c.1500–1780, there were both continuities and changes in the phenomenon of intervention. Many of the norms and values implicit in interventions, and those explicitly stated, remained relatively constant over the period. As today, there was a divide among legal thinkers between those arguing for the legality of 'international' interventions in some cases (Bodin, Gentili, Grotius), and those largely denying it (Hobbes, Vattel, Suarez). A discourse against tyrannical, arbitrary rule and a perceived responsibility to protect one's own—and to a lesser extent, other rulers'—subjects persisted throughout the early modern period, and was by no means a new development in the nineteenth century, let alone the twentieth or twenty-first century. Notions of a duty to protect thus placed limitations on princely prerogatives and state sovereignty. The inbuilt tension between the two also persisted throughout the period and was never fully resolved. The tension remained less stark within the hierarchical structure of the Empire, although even here numerous rival laws, precepts, and concepts could be cited by jurists and advocates either to undergird a strong concept of princely rights and the territorial rule of the Imperial Estates or to justify robust means to disrupt, punish, or, if necessary, depose the latter if it was guilty of major offences against Imperial law and prevailing norms.

The other main constant was the blend of different motivations in interventions, which has existed from the sixteenth-century until today. Usually considerations of security, geopolitics, and grand strategy were central in driving considerations and implementations of interventions. Cases with limited matching geopolitical goals, such as the English intervention in defence of the Waldensians of Savoy in 1655, the British diplomatic intervention in support of the Prague Jews of 1744, or the British intervention in Sierra Leone in 2000, were and are exceedingly rare. Nevertheless, geopolitical factors were sometimes inseparable from more ideological considerations such as confessional and other corporate political rights. Realist and other theories of IR neglect this nuance in their largely ahistorical generalisations. When these elements were not inseparable, however, geopolitical factors usually—but not always—prevailed. This was true especially in the 'international' European interventions, but also in Imperial interventions within the Empire. Geopolitical imperatives, however, were far less important in interventions carried out in its smallest territories. In the Empire,

*Intervention and State Sovereignty in Central Europe, 1500–1780.* Patrick Milton, Oxford University Press.
© Patrick Milton 2022. DOI: 10.1093/oso/9780192871183.003.0009

measures of judicial protective intervention could be an end in itself (which also reinforced the political objective of enhancing the Emperor's standing), whereas in the case of the European interventions, interventions were usually simply a means to a geopolitical and/or dynastic end.

It was also because of the primacy of geopolitics that states were never consistently pro or anti-interventionist in principle. In the eighteenth century, Brandenburg-Prussia shielded neighbouring petty client-tyrants from intervention while referring to principles of non-intervention, while simultaneously intervening in other states' domestic affairs in pursuit of power-political interests. Similarly, today, China and Russia regularly profess the inviolability of the principle of non-intervention in other states' domestic affairs, while often intervening themselves in other states to further their own interests.[1]

Early modern central Europe can be viewed as a 'condensed intervention zone', in the sense that interventions were inherent to the system of political co-existence itself and were—at least in its judicial variety—less controversial than the European 'international' interventions. The various case-studies from the Empire indicate that there were mechanisms in place for the protection of corporate and individual rights at all levels of the hierarchy of the Empire. A guiding principle and normative emphasis of the Reich's political culture was that existing rights, whether based on explicit laws and treaties or on customary practice, were to be safeguarded and that the existing political plurality of the Empire needed to be preserved. The survival of this old plurality depended on the prevention, and if necessary, the undercutting of, absolute rule at any level of the hierarchy at which an authority ruled over subjects. Therefore, in theory, the territorial rulers were expected to respect the rights of their subjects, just as the Emperor had to respect the rights of his immediate subjects, the territorial rulers. The following words of Moser astutely sum up the—heavily idealised—notion of a system based on the mutual protection of the various rights, privileges, and liberties of the different groups of the Empire:

> That the Emperor should respect the rights of the Estates; that the strong shall not oppress the weak and no territorial ruler shall oppress his subjects, but that the Emperor shall protect them against this. This freedom is a common good, it represents the bond of unity between the constituent parts of our unique Imperial constitution... and it is a matter which is in the mutual interest of the Emperor and all immediate and mediate members of the Reich.[2]

The system of rule in the Reich was such that there were manifold opportunities for interventions in different directions and on different levels of the hierarchy.

---

[1] Zheng Chen and Hang Yin, 'China and Russia in R2P debates at the UN Security Council', *International Affairs* 96/3 (2020), 787–805.

[2] *Gedanken über das neu-erfundene vernünftige Staats-Recht* (np, 1767), 32.

Rulers (the Emperor and the princes) could be targeted for intervention by different authorities (Westphalian guarantors, the Emperor, the princes), and subjects (both mediate and immediate) could thereby receive support from many different sources. Yet the highly juridified political culture and the detailed litigation procedures stipulated to deal with conflicts also meant that the system was seemingly designed to *prevent* military intervention, in other words to deter the target from continued intransigence which might necessitate a military execution of judicial decisions as a measure of last resort. The prevailing culture of potential intervention engendered a high degree of mutual inspection of domestic affairs, especially regarding the question of the observance or non-observance of subjects' rights. Thus, the Reich has aptly been characterised as a 'geopolitical panopticon' whereby it was in everyone's interest to ensure that corporate rights at all levels of the hierarchy were respected, because the position of every recognized group was dependent upon their legal status and liberties being respected by others within the broader system.[3] When it coincided with princes' and/or the Emperor's political interests, this willingness to sponsor the complaints of subjects facilitated energetic interventions. As the Reich was a hierarchical legal-political order, rather than an anarchic state system, interventions to safeguard rights were in the long-term political interests of all members of the Empire who were intent upon the survival of the existing rule of law, the decentralised diffusion of geopolitical power, and the mutual and reciprocal rights of all corporate groups.

That interventions did not always take place as theorised and were not always carried out smoothly or effectively is indicative of another continuity across the period and across both the Empire and Europe: they only sometimes 'worked'. Some interventions were able to achieve the interveners' geopolitical and legal goals, and the intended protectees were sometimes successfully defended. But this outcome was very much hit and miss. Just as often, the interventions were grotesquely slow, ineffective, or catastrophically counter-productive. Interventions in support of local resistance have always carried the risk that the situation on the ground comes to be so overwhelmed with the interests and goals of the intervening external actors. They therefore resulted in chaos and fragmentation more often than not, then as today. The empowerment of one group of foreign subjects through intervention often resulted in the disempowerment of other groups, who would then in turn sometimes rebel and/or seek foreign protection. The Reichshofrat was less inefficient than has previously been thought, but it is undeniable that a large proportion of sometimes urgent cases languished there for years.

One thing that could be relied upon, was that the outcomes and consequences of interventions—except in the smallest Imperial territories—were always unpredictable, sometimes dramatically so. This was especially true of the irregular

---

[3] Simms, *Europe*, 104.

military interventions conducted outside the channels of the Imperial judiciary. Few people could have predicted, for example, that by intervening in support of the Bohemian rebels in 1619, the elector-Palatine would unleash a cascading avalanche of numerous further destructive interventions which would kill about a fifth of the inhabitants of the Empire and result in the socio-political elimination of the Protestant Bohemian estates whom he was claiming to protect.[4] The same unpredictability of interventions' outcomes has been one their defining features ever since, and remains true to this day. The NATO-led intervention in Libya in 2011—the first to be carried out explicitly with reference to R2P—was aimed at protecting rebelling Libyan civilians from imminent danger posed by their ruler. While it was arguably successful in preventing a bloodbath in the short term, the intervention contributed to further interventions and the fragmentation of that state and ultimately to its implosion into civil war. In the period investigated in this book, as today, interventions in civil conflicts (apart from Imperial judicial interventions) greatly enhanced the probability of additional interventions which often cancelled each other out while increasing overall levels of violence.

While intervention was a structural feature of European international and German Imperial politics, there were changes in the phenomenon between the beginning of the sixteenth and the end of the eighteenth-century. In both cases there was an increasing juridification of intervention, especially with the Peace of Westphalia. The rights that were to be protected through intervention, such as religious/confessional rights, also underwent juridification: religious solidarity needed to be backed up by concrete political-legal rights attached to confessional status. The Imperial constitution and law were continually evolving and undergoing reform. While the catalogue of subjects' rights and the mechanisms by which they could be protected through intervention were increasingly honed and optimised, the rights of rulers to not be deposed and 'banned' were similarly buttressed. The norms to be defended by intervention also underwent adjustment. Over the course of the eighteenth-century, Enlightenment thinkers changed their attitudes towards the rights that were enshrined at Westphalia, with many concluding that it had resulted in an inadequate separation of church and state, and an excessively limited and circumscribed tolerance. Thus, intervention was discussed in cases such as the Salzburg expulsions in the 1730s, on grounds that would have seemed alien one or two hundred years earlier.

While there was never a complete separation of the 'internal' from the 'external' spheres in early modern statehood, there was a trend towards a growing distinction between the two over the course of our period. Territorial estates' freedom and ability to operate internationally and their perceived and recognised rights of rebellion, for example, were rapidly declining over the course of the later sixteenth

---

[4] Wilson, *Tragedy*, 786–9.

and first half of the seventeenth-centuries. This made interventions increasingly appear as a tangible separate category of an interference in a normally inviolable area of princely or sovereign control. At the beginning of our period, by contrast, they would have appeared as less of a distinct phenomenon, and instead simply as a stage of escalation in conflict. Yet despite this trend, interventions continued unabated; the difference was that they needed to be justified and legitimised more carefully. Simple references to 'tyranny' would no longer suffice, although such accusations were still levelled in severe cases. The resulting increase in the juridification of intervention and of international politics in general resulted in a lowering of the level of violence inherent in interventions, which were increasingly merely threatened on the basis of legal stipulations (both constitutional and international) in the hope of securing the protection of legal rights.

How did early modern interventions compare to the subsequent nineteenth-century examples during what Klose termed the classical 'century of humanitarian intervention'?[5] The application of intervention as a global phenomenon which occurred across vast distances first occurred in the nineteenth-century, while in the earlier period it was almost always a regional affair. While early modern international interventions were usually unilateral endeavours, in the nineteenth century they were mostly collective undertakings carried out by the Concert of European great powers. In both periods, consideration of geopolitics, security and grand strategy remained a crucial component of the mix of motivations. This explains some cases of non-intervention against the Ottomans in the nineteenth century despite humanitarian outrage in the Eastern Question, for example. Similar to some of the cases we have encountered in this book, nineteenth-century interventions stemming from a professed desire to protect foreign subjects could segue into conquest and foreign rule by the intervener, as occurred in the Philippines following the US intervention against the Spanish empire in 1898. A key transition in the nature of intervention during the nineteenth century was arguably 'the departure from the early modern concept of protection on the grounds of religious affinity to the practice of defending humanitarian norms for all individuals regardless of their religious affiliation and on the basis of an evolving notion of a common humanity'.[6] There is some truth to this. Many of the international interventions and also several of the interventions within the Empire were driven largely by confessional solidarity. Instead of individual human rights, the language deployed to justify early modern interventions overwhelmingly emphasised corporate rights based on groups' legal status, rather than individual humanity.

---

[5] Fabian Klose, *'In the cause of humanity'. Eine Geschichte der humanitären Intervention im langen 19. Jahrhundert* (Göttingen, 2019), 15.
[6] Fabian Klose, 'The emergence of humanitarian intervention. Three centuries of "enforcing humanity"', in Klose (ed.), *The Emergence of Humanitarian Intervention. Ideas and Practice from the Nineteenth Century to the Present* (Cambridge, 2016), 1–27, at 20.

However, as we have seen, early modern interventions were not only carried out for the protection of co-religionists. Nor was the language of humanity—and references to 'atrocities' as being contrary to it—totally absent in discussions and legitimations of interventions. When used to justify or advocate intervention, it suggested the incipient existence of a vaguely defined norm of protection that transcended confession or even legal status, although it did not yet supplant these. Within the Empire, while there was certainly an emphasis on corporate rights, there were also several core *individual* rights which were explicitly codified and could be referred to when justifying Imperial interventions. Although there was an increasing level of juridification of the justifications and mechanisms of interventions over the course of the early modern period, as mentioned, this receded again during the nineteenth century. The abstract language of humanity and humanitarian outrage—as evinced in terminology such as 'massacre' and 'extermination'—began to overshadow references to numerous laws and privileges which had mainly underpinned early modern intervention. This trend has continued into the twentieth and twenty-first centuries when intervention is hard to justify without the existence of 'mass atrocity crimes', while in the early modern period these (if they occurred) would be cited in the same breath along with violations of the minutiae of specific corporate privileges and laws in order to strengthen an impression of arbitrary rule. In this sense, the bar for intervention for the defence of foreign subjects was lower in early modern Europe, than today.[7]

---

[7] Christoph Kampmann, 'Kein Schutz fremder Untertanen nach 1648? Zur Akzeptanz einer "responsibility to protect" in der Frühen Neuzeit', in Haug et al. (eds), *Protegierte und Protektoren*, 201–16 at 216.

# Bibliography

## 1 Primary sources

### 1.1 Unpublished Archival (Manuscript) Sources

Österreichisches Staatsarchiv, Abteilung Haus-, Hof- und Staatsarchiv, Vienna
- Allgemeine Urkundenreihe 1600–1699.
- Reichshofrat, Relationes 105.
- Reichshofrat, Vota 4, 7, 29, 34–36, 40, 54, 57, 61, 65.
- Reichshofrat, Denegata-Recentiora, 261–2, 694–6, 699–701, 828–9.
- Reichshofrat, Denegata-Antiqua, 96.
- Reichshofrat, Decisa 2025.
- Reichshofrat, Obere-Registratur, 786–8, 793, 796–7.
- Reichshofrat, Protocolla-rer.-res.-saec. xvii, 95, 165–6, 274, 280–1, 292, 294.
- Reichshofrat, Protocolla-rer.-res., saec. xviii, 14, 16–19, 20a, 21–4, 26–7, 38–42, 45–9, 51–3, 55–8, 60–2, 64–6, 68–71, 73.
- Reichskanzlei, Vorträge 1c, 6b, 6c.
- Reichskanzlei, Diplomatische-Akten, Berichte aus dem Reich 20.
- Reichskanzlei, Diplomatische-Akten, Braunschweig-Hannover, Berichte 2c, 3a.
- Reichskanzlei, Diplomatische-Akten, Berlin, Berichte 11a, 11b, 12a.
- Reichskanzlei, Regensburg, Kurböhmische-Gesandtschaft, Weisungen 1.
- Reichskanzlei, Kleinere Reichsstände 176, 347–8, 367, 373–4, 538.
- Reichskanzlei, Notenwechsel 3, 4.
- Reichskanzlei, Prinzipalkommission, Berichte 36–7, 41b, 42, 43a, 43b, 44a, 44b, 44c, 53a.
- Reichskanzlei, Prinzipalkommission, Weisungen 4b, 5a, 5b.
- Reichskanzlei, Prinzipalkommission, Instruktionen 1.
- Staatskanzlei, Vorträge 12, 22–4.
- Staatskanzlei, Regensburg, Österreichische-Gesandtschaft, Berichte 1a, 29, 44–6.
- Staatskanzlei, Regensburg, Österreichische-Gesandtschaft, Weisungen 1.
- Staatskanzlei, Geheimregistratur österr-Staatskanzlei, Rep. N, 3
- Mainzer Erzkanzlerarchiv, Friedensakten 60–3.
- Mainzer Erzkanzlerarchiv, Reichstagsakten 70, 192, 201, 204–9, 312, 328, 332, 339–40, 371–81.
- Mainzer Erzkanzlerarchiv, Kommissionsakten 7.
- Mainzer Erzkanzlerarchiv, Reichshofratsakten 8b.
- Staatenabteilung, Deutsche Staaten, Palatina, 34; Moguntina 2–3.
- Staatenabteilungen, Frankreich, Dipl.-Korr. 23 (Berichte 1618–1659), Frankreich-Varia 6; Schweden 2, 11, 13.

Niedersächsisches Landesarchiv—Hauptstaatsarchiv Hannover
- Hannover 9g (Mecklenburgische Exekution): 16–22, 26.
- Hannover 10 (State treaties): 168.

- Hannover 91 (Nachläße): von Bernstorff 4.
- Hannover 92 (Deutsche Kanzlei, London): 1092, 1094, 1099, 1100, 1360, 2140, 2157-8, 2166, 2172, 2177-9, 2184, 2191, 2198, 2200, 2202-5, 2254.
- Calenberg Brief 11 (Holy Roman Empire): 1613, 1620, 1637, 1736, 2966 (ii–iii), 2967 (i–iii), 2968 (i–iv), 2969 (i–ii), 2970 (i–iii), 2971 (i–ii), 2972-3, 3025.
- Calenberg Brief 24 (Foreign Affairs): 709, 1535, 2490, 3866, 3871, 3874, 4119, 4910 (i–iv), 4911 (i: 1-2; ii: 1-2), 4912 (i: 1-2; ii: 1-2), 4913, 1415 (i–iv).

### Landesarchiv Nordrhein-Westfalen, Abteilung Rheinland, Standort Düsseldorf

- Kurköln II (Erzstift), 5045, 5663.
- Kurköln VI (Reichs-und Reichstagshandlungen), 530, 556, 1166, 1188, 1409–11, 1413, 1419-20, 1481-82.
- Kurköln VII (Kriegssachen), 130/2, 107/2.
- Niederrheinisch-Westfälisches-Kreisarchiv, I N 15 (Nassau-Siegen), 1–5, 14, 29, 46–55, 55a, 56, 59, 62, 63, 64i–ii, 65, 80, 81.
- Niederrheinisch-Westfälisches-Kreisarchiv, VIII (Kreishandlungen), 34, 34½, 35.

### Landeshauptarchiv, Schwerin

- Auswärtige-Beziehungen 2.11–2/1, 1043, 1599–1604, 4069, 4071.
- Mecklenburgische-Landstände, 3.1–1, III-1.

### National Archives, Kew, London

- SP 43/6 (Regencies)
- SP 44/269B (Entry books)
- SP 78/163, 187, 190 (France)
- SP 80/41, 61 (Austria)
- SP 81/120-1 (Hessen-Kassel)
- SP 90/9, 15, 18–19 (Prussia)
- SP 91/9–10 (Russia)
- SP 100/52 (Foreign ministers)
- SP 104/42 (Letterbooks)

### British Library Manuscripts, London

- Add. MSS. 32759, 32770 (Newcastle papers), 37363-4, 37366, 37371-2, 37375-8 (Whitworth papers), 48982 (Townshend papers).

### Universitätsbibliothek, Rostock

- Mss. Meckl. B 703 (5), B 707.[a]
- Mk. 10662

## 1.2. Printed (edited source collections, treatises, and pamphlets)

*A General Collection of Treatys, Manifesto's... and other Publick Papers 1495–1712* (London, 1732).

*Acta Pacis Westphalicae* [APW]. Ed., Konrad Repgen (Münster, 1962–present).
  Serie I: Instruktionen.
    1. *Frankreich-Schweden-Kaiser*. Ed., Fritz Dickmann et al. (1962).
  Serie II: Korrespondenzen.
    Abteilung A: Die kaiserlichen Korrespondenzen
      4. *1646*. Ed., Hubert Salm et al. (2001).
      5. *1646–1647*. Ed., Antje Ochsmann (1993).
      6/1. *March–July 1647*. Ed., Antje Ochsmann *et al.* (2011).
      8. *February–May 1648*. Ed., Sebastian Schmitt (2008).
      9. *May–August 1648*. Ed., Stefanie Fraedrich-Nowag (2013).
      10. *1648–1649*. Ed., Dorothée Goetze (2015).
    Abteilung B: Die französischen Korrespondenzen
      1. *1644*. Ed., Ursula Irsigler (1979).
      2. *1645*. Ed., Franz Bosbach (1986).
      4. *1646*. Ed., Clivia Kelch-Rade/Anuschka Tischer (1999).
      5/2. *1647*. Ed., Guido Braun (2002).
  Serie III: Protokolle, Verhandlungsakten-Diaren-Varia.
    Abteilung A: Protokolle
      3/3. *Fürstenrat in Osnabrück, 1646*. Ed., Maria-Elisabeth Brunert (2001).
    Abteilung C: Diarien
      3/1. *Diarium Wartenberg 1644–46*. Ed., Joachim Foerster (1987).
      3/2. *Diarium Wartenberg 1647–48*. Ed. Joachim Foerster (1988).

Althusius, Johannes, *Politica Methodice* (Herborn, 1614).
*Apologie of Prince William of Orange* (1581).
Aquinas, St. Thomas, *Summa Theologiae* ([1265–74] Cambridge, 2006).
Archistor, Philalethus, *Raisonnement. Reiff-erwogenes Staats-Bedencken, wie beede Cronen Franckreich und Schweden unter dem Praetext der im Instrumento Pacis ihnen überlassenen Garantie dem Römischen Reich höchstnachtheilige Dinge favoriren* (1676).
*Augspurgische Ordinari=Post=Zeitung.*
de Ayala, Balthasar, *De Jure et Officiis bellicis et disciplina militari* ([1582] Washington, 1912).
*Beantwortung des, unter dem Titul: Ursachen, welche... Preussen bewogen sich wider die Absichten des Wienerischen Hofes zu setzen, und deren Ausführungen vorzukommen, kund gewordenen Kriegs-Manifests* (Vienna, 1756).
Bodin, Jean, *The Six Bookes of a Commonweale* ([1576] London, 1606).
Böhmer, Justus, *Introductio in ius publicum universale* (Magdeburg, 1710).
Brechenmacher, Caspar (ed.), *Historischer Mercurius* (Augsburg, 1712–1718).
[Brutus, Stephanius Jurius], *Vindiciae, contra tyranos*. Ed. George Garnett ([1579] Cambridge, 1994).
Cobbett, William, *Parliamentary History of England. From the Norman Conquest, in 1066, to the Year 1803* (36 vols, London, 1806–1820).
Conring, Hermann, *Exercitatio de Germanici Imperii civibus* (Helmstedt, 1641).
Coxe, William, *Memoirs of the life and administration of Sir Robert Walpole, Earl of Orford* (London, 1816).

Davenport, Frances (ed.), *European Treaties bearing on the History of the United States and its Dependencies to 1648* (Clark, 2004).
*Declaration...: Außführliche Darthuung: Darinnen Deß...Ertz-Hauses Oesterreich/ gefaster Waffen Billigkeit...* (1635).
Dietrich, Richard (ed.), *Die politischen Testamente der Hohenzollern* (Cologne/Vienna, 1986).
Droysen, Gustav (ed.), *Schriftstücke von Gustav Adolf zumeist an evangelische Fürsten Deutschlands* (Stockholm, 1877).
Druffel, August (ed.), *Briefe und Akten zur Geschichte des sechzehnten Jahrhunderts*, iii: 1546–52 ([1823] Charlestown, 2011).
von Eggenstorff, Johann Joseph Pachner (ed.), *Vollständige Sammlung aller von Anfang des noch fürwährenden Teutschen Reichs-Tags... biss anhero abgefassten Reichs-Schlüsse*. Ed. Karl Otmar von Aretin (Hildesheim, 1996).
Europæische Zeitung. Mit Römisch=Kayserl. allergnädigstem Privilegio.
Faber, Anton(ed.), *Europäische Staats-Cantzley* (Frankfurt, 1697–1760), vols 12–13, 15, 29, 32–47.
Fassmann, David (ed.), *Gespräche in dem Reiche derer Todten* (Leipzig, 1720–37).
Gentili, Alberico, *De Iure Belli Libri Tres* ([1598] Oxford, 1933).
Grillon, Pierre (ed.), *Les Papiers de Richelieu. Section politique intérieure. Correspondence et papiers d'état IV (1629)* (Paris, 1980).
Grotius, Hugo, *The Rights of War and Peace* ([1625] Indianapolis, 2005).
Gundling, Nicolaus Hieronymus, *Ausführlicher Discours über das Natur- und Völcker-Recht* (Frankfurt, 1734).
Häberlin, Friedrich Carl, *Handbuch des Teutschen Staatsrechts* (Berlin, 1797).
Heineccius, Johann-Gottlieb, *A Methodical System of Universal Law, or: the Laws of Nature and Nations* ([1741] Indianapolis, 2008).
Heldmann, J. (ed.), *J.J. Schmaussens academische Reden über das teutsche Staatsrecht* (Lemgo, 1766).
Helfferich, Tryntje (ed.), *The Thirty Years War. A Documentary History* (Indianapolis, 2009).
Hofmann, Hanns-Hubert (ed.), *Quellen zum Verfassungsorganismus des Heiligen Römischen Reiches* (Darmstadt, 1976).
*Jubilæum Theatri Europæi* (Frankfurt a. M., 1738).
*Klagrede Uber den zwischen dem Römischen Keyser Ferdinand II. und Churfürsten Johan Georgen zu Sachsen... auffgerichten Vertrag* (1638).
Klüver, Hans Heinrich, *Beschreibung des Herzogthums Mecklenburg* (Hamburg, 1737–1742).
Kohler, Alfred (ed.), *Quellen zur Geschichte Karls V.* (Darmstadt, 1990).
Köhler, Johann-David, *Kurtzgefaste und gründliche teutsche Reichs-Historie* (Frankfurt, 1736).
*Königl: Majestät in Franckreich/wegen publication deß Kriegs wider den König in Hispanien gethane Erklärung* (1635).
Krause, Johann Christoph, *Lehrbuch der Geschichte des Dreyßigjährigen teutschen Krieges und Westphälischen Friedens* (Halle, 1782).
Lassberg, F.L.A. (ed.), *Der Schwabenspiegel* ([1275]Tübingen, 1840).
Laufs, Adolf (ed.), *Der jüngste Reichsabschied von 1654* (Bern, 1975).
Laufs, Adolf (ed.), *Die Reichskammergerichtsordnung von 1555* (Cologne/Weimar/Vienna, 1976).
Lautemann, Wolfgang et al. (eds), *Geschichte in Quellen* (Munich, 1996).

Leibniz, Gottfried Wilhelm, *Sämtliche Schriften und Briefe* (Berlin, 1983).
Lipsius, Justus, *On Constancy—De Constantia* (Exeter, 2006).
Löhneiss, Georg, *Aulico-politica oder Hof-, Staats- und Regierkunst* ([1622–24] Frankfurt, 1679).
Mably, Gabriel Bonnot de, *Le droit public de l'Europe, fondé sur les traits* (Amsterdam, 1761).
Machiavelli, Niccolò, *The Discourses* ([c.1517] London, 1970).
*Mémoire des Raisons, qui ont oblige le Roy de France Louis XIV. À reprendre les Armes...* (Paris, 1688).
[Moser, Johann Jacob (ed.)], *Merckwürdige Reichs=Hof=Raths Conclusa* (Frankfurt, 1726–48).
[Moser, Johann Jacob], *Reichs-Fama* (Frankurt, 1727–1738).
Moser, Johann Jacob, *Teutsches Staatsrecht* (50 vols, Leipzig, 1737–1754, reprint Osnabrück, 1968).
Moser, Johann Jacob, *Von der Garantie des Westphaelischen Fridens; nach dem Buchstaben und Sinn desselbigen* (np, 1767).
Moser, Johann Jacob, *Neues teutsches Staatsrecht* (20 vols, Frankfurt a.M., 1766–1782, reprint Osnabrück, 1967).
Parry, Clive (ed.), *The Consolidated Treaty Series* (231 vols, Dobbs Ferry, 1969–1981), vols 1, 6, 32.
Potter, David (ed.), *The Letters of Paul de Foix, French Ambassador at the Court of Elizabeth I, 1562–1566* (Cambridge, 2019).
Pufendorf, Samuel, *The Present State of Germany*, ed. Michael Seidler ([1667] Indianapolis, 2007).
Pufendorf, Samuel, *On The Law of Nature and Nations* ([1672] London, 1729).
Pütter, Johann Stephan, *Historische Entwicklung der heutigen Staatsverfassung des Teutschen Reiches* (Göttingen, 1787).
Pütter, Johann Stephan, *Geist des Westfälischen Friedens; nach dem Buchstaben und Sinn desselbigen* (Göttingen, 1795).
*Recueil des instructions données aux ambassadeurs et ministres de France depuis les traités de Westphalie jusqu'à la révolution française* (21 vols, Paris, 1884–present), vols 1, 4, 28.
Schauroth, Eberhard (ed.), *Vollständige Sammlung aller Conclusorum ... des Corporis evangelicorum* (Regensburg, 1753–1786).
Schmauss, Johann-Jacob, *Einleitung zu der Staats-Wissenschafft* (Leipzig, 1741).
Scott, Walter (ed.), *Somers' Tracts* (London, 1809).
Seckendorff, Veit Ludwig, *Christen-Stat* (Leipzig, 1685).
Sellert, Wolfgang (ed.), *Die Ordnungen des Reichshofrates 1550–1766* (Cologne/Vienna, 1980–1990).
von Senkenberg, Renatus-Karl, *Darstellung des ... Westfälischen Friedens, nach der Ordnung der Artikel* (Frankfurt, 1804).
Sinold, Philipp Balthasar (ed.), *Europäische Fama* (Leipzig, 1702–1735), vols 66, 206–16, 222–29, 234–9, 243, 281, 297, 316, 322–4.
Steck, Joh.-Chr. Wilhelm, 'Abhandlung von den Rechten und Pflichten der hohen Garans des Westphälischen Friedens', in *Abhandlungen aus dem deutschen Staats- und Lehnrecht zur Erläuterung einiger neuen Reichsangelegenheiten* (Halle, 1757), 99–132.
Stevenson, Joseph et al. (eds), *Calendar of State Papers Foreign: Elizabeth* (London, 1863–1950).
*Teutsche Kriegs-Canzley* (Frankfurt, 1757).
Vitoria, Francisco, *Political Writings*, ed. Anthony Pagden et al. (Cambridge, 1991).

Wilson, Peter H. (ed.), *The Thirty Years War. A Sourcebook* (Basingstoke, 2010).
Zeumer, Karl (ed.), *Quellensammlung zur Geschichte der Deutschen Reichsverfassung* (Tübingen, 1913).
Zwierlein, Christian, *Vermischte Briefe und Abhandlungen* (Berlin,1767).

## 2 Secondary Literature

Achenbach, Heinrich von, *Geschichte der Stadt Siegen* (Siegen, 1894).
Adams, Simon, 'Elizabeth I and the sovereignty of the Netherlands 1576-1585', *TRHS* 14 (2001), 309-19.
Affolter, Andreas, '"Freye Republiquen unter frembder Protection"? Die Beziehungen der eidgenössischen Orte zur französischen Krone im 18. Jahrhundert', in Tilman Haug et al. (eds), *Protegierte und Protektoren* (Cologne, 2016), 125-38.
Anderson, Alison Deborah, *On the Verge of War. International Relations and the Jülich-Kleve Succession Crises (1609-1614)* (Boston, 1999).
Aretin, Karl Otmar von, 'Russia as a guarantor power of the Imperial Constitution under Catherine II', *JMH* 58 (1986), 141-60.
Aretin, Karl Otmar von, *Das Alte Reich, 1648-1806* (4 vols., Stuttgart, 1993-2000).
Armstrong, David, 'The evolution of international society', in John Baylis et al. (eds), *The Globalization of World Politics* (Oxford, 2011), 34-49.
Arndt, Johannes, 'Kabale und Liebe in Detmold. Zur Geschichte einer Hofintrige und einer Fürstenabsetzung in Lippe', *Lippische Mitteilungen* 60 (1991), 27-74.
Arndt, Johannes, *Das Heilige Römische Reich und die Niederlande 1566 bis 1648. Politisch-konfessionelle Verflechtung und Publizistik im Achtzigjährigen Krieg* (Cologne/Weimar/Vienna, 1998).
Arndt, Johannes, 'Deutsche Territorien im europäischen Mächtesystem', in Heinz Schilling et al. (eds), *Heiliges Römisches Reich Deutscher Nation 962 bis 1806* (Dresden, 2006), 135-43.
Arndt, Johannes, *Herrschaftskontrolle durch Öffentlichkeit. Die publizistische Darstellung politischer Konflikte im Heiligen Römischen Reich 1648-1750* (Göttingen, 2013).
Arndt, Johannes and Esther-Beate Körber (eds), *Das Mediensystem im Alten Reich der Frühen Neuzeit (1600-1750)* (Göttingen, 2010).
Arnegger, Katharina, 'Der Einfluss Spaniens auf die hohenemsischen Herrschaften Vaduz und Schellenberg', *JhVFL* 108 (2009), 183-210.
Arnegger, Katharina, 'Vaduz und Schellenberg unter der Herrschaft der Reichsgrafen von Hohenems (1613-1699/1712), *JhVfL*111 (2012), 61-79.
Arnke, Volker and Siegrid Westphal (eds), *Der schwierige Weg zum Westfälischen Frieden. Wendepunkte, Friedensversuche und die Rolle der 'Dritten Partei'* (Berlin/Boston, 2021).
Asbach, Olaf and Peter Schröder (eds), *The Ashgate Research Companion to the Thirty Years War* (New York, 2014).
Asbach, Olaf et al. (eds), *Altes Reich, Frankreich und Europa. Politische, historische und philosophische Aspekte des französischen Deutschlandbildes im 17.und 18. Jahrhundert* (Berlin, 2001).
Asch, Ronald G., 'Estates and Princes after 1648: The Consequences of the Thirty Years War', *German History* 6, no. 2 (1988), 113-32.
Asch, Ronald G., '"Denn es sind ja die Deutschen ... ein frey Volk". Die Glaubensfreiheit als Problem der westfälischenFriedensverhandlungen', *Westfälische Zeitschrift* 148 (1998), 113-37.

Audisio, Gabriel, *Die Waldenser* (Munich, 1996).
Auer, Leopold, 'The role of the Imperial Aulic Council in the constitutional structure of the Holy Roman Empire', in R.J.W. Evans, Michael Schaich, and Peter H. Wilson (eds), *The Holy Roman Empire 1495–1806* (Oxford, 2011), 63–75.
Augner, Gerd, *Die kaiserliche Kommission der Jahre 1708–1712. Hamburgs Beziehung zu Kaiser und Reich zu Anfang des 18. Jahrhunderts* (Hamburg, 1983).
Babel, Rainer, *Zwischen Habsburg und Bourbon. Außenpolitik und europäische Stellung Herzog Karls IV. von Lothringen (1624–1634)* (Sigmaringen, 1989).
Babel, Rainer, *Garde et Protection. Der Königsschutz in der französischen Außenpolitik vom 15.bis zum 17. Jahrhundert* (Ostfildern, 2014).
Backerra, Charlotte, *Wien und London, 1727–1735. Internationale Beziehungen im frühen 18. Jahrhundert* (Göttingen, 2018).
Bahlcke, Joachim, 'Calvinism and estate liberation in Bohemia and Hungary (1570–1620)', in Karin Maag (ed.), *The Reformation in Eastern and Central Europe* (Aldershot, 1997).
Bahlcke, Joachim, 'Konfessionalisierung der Außenpolitik? Die Rolle der Konfession in den Außenbeziehungen der böhmischen Stände', in Friedrich Beiderbeck et al. (eds), *Dimensionen der europäischen Außenpolitik zur Zeit der Wende vom 16. zum 17. Jahrhundert* (Berlin, 2003).
Bähr, Matthias, *Die Sprache der Zeugen. Argumentationsstrategien bäuerlicher Gemeinden vor dem Reichskammergericht (1693–1806)* (Constance, 2012).
Ballschmieter, Hans-Joachim, *Andreas Gottlieb von Bernstorff und der mecklenburgische Ständekampf (1680–1720)* (Cologne, 1962).
Bass, Gary, *Freedom's Battle: The Origins of Humanitarian Intervention* (New York, 2008).
Beaulac, Stephane, 'The Westphalian legal orthodoxy – myth or reality?', *JHIL* 2 (2000), 148–77.
Behr, Hans-Joachim, '"Zu rettung deren hart getruckten Nassaw-Siegischen Unterthanen". Der Niederrheinisch-Westfälische Kreis und Siegen im 18. Jahrhundert', *Jahrbuch für westfälische Kirchengeschichte* 85 (1991), 159–84.
Beiderbeck, Friedrich, *Zwischen Religionskrieg, Reichskrise und europäischem Hegemoniekampf. Heinrich IV. von Frankreich und die protestantischen Reichsstände* (Berlin, 2005).
Bély, Lucien, *Les relations internationals en Europe. XVIIe–XVIIIe siècles* (Paris, 1992).
Bély, Lucien, *La Société des Princes XVI$^e$–XVIII$^e$-siècle* (Paris, 1999).
Black, Jeremy, 'When "natural allies" fall out: Anglo-Austrian relations, 1725–1740', *MöStA* 36 (1983), 120–49.
Black, Jeremy, 'The Anglo-French alliance 1716-1731: a study in eighteenth century international relations', *Francia* 13 (1986), 295–310.
Black, Jeremy, *The Collapse of the Anglo-French alliance 1727–1732* (Gloucester and New York, 1987).
Blanning, T.C.W., *Reform and Revolution in Mainz, 1743–1803* (Cambridge, 1974).
Blanning, T.C.W., *The Culture of Power and the Power of Culture. Old Regime Europe, 1660–1789* (Oxford, 2002).
Blanning, T.C.W., 'The Holy Roman Empire of the German Nation past and present', *Historical Research* 85 (2012), 57–70.
Blickle, Peter, *Landschaften im Alten Reich* (Munich, 1973).
Blickle, Peter, *The Revolution of 1525. The German Peasants' War from a New Perspective* (Baltimore, 1981).
Blickle, Peter, 'Untertanen in der Frühneuzeit', *Vierteljahrsschrift für Sozial- und Wirtschaftsgeschichte* 70 (1983), 483–522.

Blickle, Peter, 'The criminalization of peasant resistance in the Holy Roman Empire', *JMH* 58 (1986), 88–97.
Blockmans, Wim, 'Limitations to monarchical power', in Robert von Friedeburg (ed.), *Murder and Monarchy. Regicides in European History 1300–1800* (Basingstoke, 2004), 136–45.
Böhme, Klaus-Richard, 'Die Grossmachtstellung bewahren-Aber wie? Die schwedische Deutschlandpolitik nach 1648', in Matthias Schnettger (ed.), *Imperium Romanum-Irregulare Corpus–Teutscher Reichs-Staat. Das Alte Reich im Verständnis der Zeitgenossen und der Historiographie* (Mainz, 2002), 77–88.
Bosbach, Franz, *Monarchia universalis. Ein politischer leitbegriff der Frühen Neuzeit* (Göttingen, 1988).
Brady, Thomas, *Turning Swiss. Cities and Empire 1450–1550* (Cambridge, 1985).
Braun, Guido, 'Die französische Diplomatie und das Problem der Friedenssicherung auf dem Westfälischen Friedenskongress', in Guido (ed.), *Assecuratio Pacis. Französische Konzeptionen von Friedenssicherung und Friedensgarantie 1648–1815* (Münster, 2011), 67–130.
Brendle, Franz, 'Der Westfälische Frieden als Kompromiss. Intentionen, Grundsätze und Inhalte der Friedensverträge', in Claus-Peter Hartmann et al.(eds), *Der Dreißigjährige Krieg. Facetten einer folgenreichen Epoche* (Regensburg, 2009), 173–83.
Brewer, John, *The Sinews of Power. War, Money, and the English state, 1688–1783* (London, 1989).
Brightwell, Peter, 'Spain and Bohemia: the decision to intervene, 1619', *European Studies Review* 12 (1982), 117–41.
Brockmann, Thomas, *Dynastie, Kaiseramt und Konfession. Politik und Ordnungsvorstellungen Ferdinands II. im Dreißigjährigen Krieg* (Paderborn, 2011).
Brunert, Maria-Elisabeth, 'Friedenssicherung als Beratungsthema der protestantischen Reichsstände in der Anfangsphase des westfälischen Friedenskongresses', in Guido Braun et al. (eds), *Frieden und Friedenssicherung in der Frühen Neuzeit* (Münster, 2013), 229–58.
Brüser, Joachim, *Reichsständische Libertät zwischen kaiserlichem Machtstreben und französischer Hegemonie. Der Rheinbund von 1658* (Münster, 2020).
Burgdorf, Wolfgang, *Reichskonstitution und Nation. Verfassungsreformprojekte fürdas Heilige Römische Reich deutscher Nation im politischen Schrifttum von 1648 bis 1806* (Mainz, 1998).
Burkhardt, Johannes, 'Die Friedlosigkeit der Frühen Neuzeit. Grundlagen einer Theorie der Bellizität Europas', *ZHF* 24 (1997), 509–74.
Burkhardt, Johannes, 'Der Westfälische Friede und die Legende von der landesherrlichen Souveränität', in Jörg Engelbrecht and Stephan Laux (eds), *Landes- und Reichsgeschichte* (Bielefeld, 2004), 199–220.
Burkhardt, Johannes, 'Wars of state or wars of state-formation?', in Olaf Asbach et al. (eds), *War, State and International Law in Seventeenth-Century Europe* (Farnham, 2009), 17–34.
Canning, Joseph, *Conciliarism, Humanism and Law. Justifications of Authority and Power, c.1400–c.1520* (Cambridge, 2021).
Carsten, F.L., *Princes and Parliaments in Germany from the Fifteenth to the Eighteenth Century* (Oxford, 1959).
Chance, J.F., *George I and the Northern War 1709 to 1721* (London, 1909).
Chance, J.F., *The Alliance of Hanover. A Study of British Foreign Policy in the Last Years of George I* (London, 1923).

Clark, Christopher, *Iron Kingdom. The Rise and Downfall of Prussia, 1600-1947* (London, 2006).
Claydon, Tony, *William III and the Godly Revolution* (Cambridge, 1996).
Close, Christopher W., *State Formation and Shared Sovereignty. The Holy Roman Empire and the Dutch Republic, 1488-1696*(Cambridge, 2021).
Conrads, Norbert, *Die Durchführung der Altranstädter Konvention in Schlesien, 1707-09* (Cologne/Vienna, 1971).
Croxton, Derek, *Peacemaking in Early Modern Europe. Cardinal Mazarin and the Congress of Westphalia, 1643-1648* (Selinsgrove, 1999).
Croxton, Derek, 'The Peace of Westphalia of 1648 and the origins of sovereignty', *IHR* 21/3 (1999), 569-91.
Croxton, Derek, *Westphalia. The Last Christian Peace* (Basingstoke, 2013).
Cuno, Friedrich, *Geschichte der Stadt Siegen* (Dillenburg, 1872).
Decker, Klaus, *Frankreich und die Reichsstände 1672-1675* (Bonn, 1981).
Delgado, Mariano, 'Die Kontroverse über die Humanitäre Intervention bei der spanischen Expansion im 16. Jahrhundert', *Historisches Jahrbuch* 131 (2011), 93-118.
Dickmann, Fritz, *Der Westfälische Frieden* (Münster, 1959).
Dickmann, Fritz, 'Rechtsgedanke und Machtpolitik bei Richelieu', in Dickmann, *Friedensrecht und Friedenssicherung* (Göttingen, 1971), 36-78.
Diestelkamp, Bernhard, *Ein Kampf um Freiheit und Recht. Die prozessualen Auseinandersetzungen der Gemeinde Freienseen mit den Grafen zu Solms-Laubach* (Cologne/Weimar/Vienna, 2012).
Dingel, Irene et al. (eds), *Handbook of Peace in Early Modern Europe* (Berlin/Boston, 2020).
Dreitzel, Horst, *Absolutismus und Ständische Verfassung in Deutschland* (Mainz, 1992).
Droysen, Johann Gustav, *Geschichte der Preußischen Politik*, 4/2 (Leipzig, 1869).
Duchhardt, Heinz, *Protestantisches Kaisertum und Altes Reich. Die Diskussion über die Konfession des Kaisers in Politik, Publizistik und Staatsrecht* (Wiesbaden, 1977).
Duchhardt, Heinz, *Altes Reich und europäische Staatenwelt 1648-1806* (Munich, 1990).
Duchhardt, Heinz, *Balance of Power und Pentarchie. Internationale Beziehungen 1700-1785* (Paderborn, 1997).
Duchhardt, Heinz (ed.), *Der Pyrenäenfriede 1659. Vorgeschichte, Widerhall, Rezeptionsgeschichte* (Göttingen, 2010).
Duchhardt, Heinz, 'Das "Westfälische System": Realität und Mythos', in Hillard von Thiessen and Christian Windler (eds), *Akteure der Außenbeziehungen. Netzwerke und Interkulturalität im historischen Wandel* (Cologne/Weimar/Vienna, 2010), 393-401.
Duchhardt, Heinz, *Der Weg in die Katastrophe des Dreißigjährigen Krieges. Die Krisendekade 1608-1618* (Munich/Berlin, 2017).
Duchhardt, Heinz and Martin Espenhorst (eds), *Utrecht-Rastatt-Baden 1712-1714. Ein europäisches Friedenswerk am Ende des Zeitalters Ludwigs XIV* (Göttingen, 2013).
Duchhardt, Heinz et al. (eds), *Der Absolutismus—ein Mythos? Strukturwandel monarchischer Herrschaft in West- und Mitteleuropa (ca. 1550-1700)* (Cologne/Weimar/Vienna, 1996).
Dunthorne, Hugh, *Britain and the Dutch Revolt 1560-1700* (Cambridge, 2013).
Dureng, Jean, *Mission de Théodore Chevignard de Chavigny en Allemagne, 1726-1731* (Paris, 1912).
Edel, Andreas, 'Auf dem Weg in den Krieg. Zur Vorgeschichte der Intervention Herzog Maximilians I. von Bayern in Österreich und Böhmen 1620', *Zeitschrift für bayerische Landesgeschichte* 65 (2002).

Edelmayer, Friedrich, *Söldner und Pensionäre. Das Netzwerk Philipps II. Im Heiligen Römischen Reich* (Munich, 2002).
Edelstein, Dan, *On the Spirit of Rights* (Chicago, 2019).
Egler, Anna, *Die Spanier in der linksrheinischen Pfalz, 1620-1632. Invasion, Verwaltung, Rekatholisierung* (Mainz, 1971).
Ehrenpreis, Stefan, 'Die Tätigkeit des Reichshofrats um 1600 in der protestantischen Kritik', in Wolfgang Sellert (ed.), *Reichshofrat und Reichskammergericht: ein Konkurrenzverhältnis* (Cologne/Weimar/Vienna, 1999), 27-46.
Ehrenpreis, Stefan, *Kaiserliche Gerichtsbarkeit und Konfessionskonflikt. Der Reichshofrat unter Rudolf II. 1576-1612* (Göttingen, 2006).
Eisenhardt, Ulrich, *Die kaiserlichen Privilegia de non Appellando* (Cologne/Vienna, 1980).
Eisenhardt, Ulrich, 'Der Reichshofrat als kombiniertes Rechtsprechungs- und Regierungsorgan', in Jost Hausmann et al. (eds), *Zur Erhaltung guter Ordnung. Beiträge zur Geschichte von Recht und Justiz* (Cologne/Weimar/Vienna, 2000), 245-67.
Elliott, John H., 'A Europe of composite monarchies', *Past &Present* 137 (1992), 48-71.
Ernst, Albrecht et al. (eds), *Union und Liga 1608/09. Konfessionelle Bündnisse im Reich* (Stuttgart, 2010).
Ernst, Hildegard, *Madrid und Wien 1632-1637. Politik und Finanzen in den Beziehungen zwischen Philipp IV. und Ferdinand II* (Münster, 1991).
Espinosa, Aurelio, 'The grand strategy of Charles V. Castile, war, and dynastic priority in the Mediterranean', *JEMH* 9 (2005), 239-83.
Evans, R.J.W., *Rudolf II and His World, 1576-1612* (Oxford, 1973).
Evans, R.J.W., Michael Schlaich, and Peter H. Wilson (eds), *The Holy Roman Empire 1495-1806* (Oxford, 2011).
Externbrink, Sven, *Le Coeur du monde. Frankreich und die norditalienischen Staaten im Zeitalter Richelieus 1624-1635* (Münster, 1999).
Externbrink, Sven, 'Frankreich und die Reichsexekution gegen Friedrich II', in Olaf Asbach et al. (eds), *Altes Reich, Frankreich und Europa* (Münster, 2001), 221-53.
Externbrink, Sven, 'Staatensystem und kulturelles Gedächtnis. Frankreich, das Alte Reich und Europa', in Eva Dewes et al. (eds), *Kulturelles Gedächtnis und interkulturelle Rezeption im europäischen Kontext* (Berlin, 2008), 89-102.
Ferrone, Vincenzo, *The Enlightenment and the Rights of Man* (Liverpool, 2019).
von Friedeburg, Robert (ed.), *Widerstandsrecht in der Frühen Neuzeit* (Berlin, 2001).
von Friedeburg, Robert, 'Natural Jurisprudence, argument from history and constitutional struggle in the early enlightenment: the case of Gottlieb Samuel Treuer's polemic against absolutism in 1719', in T.J. Hochstrasser et al. (eds), *Early Modern Natural Law Theories* (Dordrecht, 2003), 141-64.
Friedrich, Susanne, *Drehscheibe Regensburg. Das Informations-und Kommunikationssystem des Reichstags um 1700* (Berlin, 2007).
Friedrichs, Christopher, 'Urban conflicts and the Imperial Constitution in seventeenth-century Germany', *JMH* 58 (1986), 98-123.
Frommelt, Fabian (ed.), *Zwangsadministrationen. Legitimierte Fremdverwaltung im historischen Vergleich* (Berlin, 2014).
Fuchs, Ralf-Peter, *Ein 'Medium zum Frieden'. Die Normaljahrsregel und die Beendigung des Dreißigjährigen Krieges* (Munich, 2010).
Gehm, Britta, *Die Hexenverfolgung im Hochstift Bamberg und das Eingreifen des Reichshofrates zu ihrer Beendigung* (Hildesheim, 2000).
Gestrich, Andreas, *Absolutismus und Öffentlichkeit. Politische Kommunikation in Deutschland zu Beginn des 18. Jahrhunderts* (Göttingen, 1994).

Glanville, Luke, *Sovereignty and the Responsibility to Protect. A New History* (Chicago, 2014).
Goetze, Dorothée, and Lena Oetzel (eds), *Warum Friedenschliessen so schwer ist. Frühneizeitliche Friedensfindung am Beispiel des Westfälischen Friedenskongresses* (Münster, 2019).
Goetze, Dorothée and Michael Rohrschneider, 'Imperien und "composite states" in der Frühen Neuzeit', *Europäische Geschichte Online*, Feb. 2022.
Goetze, Sigmund, *Die Politik des schwedischen Reichskanzlers Axel Oxenstierna gegenüber Kaiser und Reich* (Kiel, 1971).
Gotthard, Axel, *Säulen des Reiches. Die Kurfürsten im frühneuzeitlichen Reichsverband* (Husum, 1999).
Gotthard, Axel, 'Wende des böhmisch-pfälzischen Krieges. Wie Frankreich und England 1620 die Großmachtposition Habsburgs retteten', in Sven Externbrink et al. (eds), *Formen internationaler Beziehungen in der Frühen Neuzeit* (Berlin, 2001), 396–417.
Gotthard, Axel, *Der Augsburger Religionsfrieden* (Münster, 2004).
Grewe, Wilhelm, *The Epochs of International Law* (Berlin, 2000).
Gross, Lothar, 'Der Kampf zwischen Reichskanzlei und österreichischer Hofkanzlei um die Führung der auswärtigen Geschäfte', *Historische Vierteljahresschrift* 22 (1924/25), 279–312.
von Gschließer, Oswald, *Der Reichshofrat. Bedeutung und Verfassung, Schicksal und Besetzung einer obersten Reichsbehörde von 1559 bis 1806* (Vienna, 1942).
Haakonssen, Knud, 'Early-modern natural law', in George Duke et al. (eds), *Cambridge Companion to Natural Law Jurisprudence* (Cambridge, 2017).
Hantsch, Hugo, *Reichsvizekanzler Friedrich Karl Graf von Schönborn (1674–1746). Einige Kapitel zur politischen Geschichte Kaiser Josefs I. und Karls VI.* (Augsburg, 1929).
Hartley, Janet, *Charles Whitworth. Diplomat in the age of Peter the Great* (Aldershot, 2002).
Hartmann, Anja-Victorine, *Von Regensburg nach Hamburg. Die diplomatischen Beziehungen zwischen dem französischen König und dem Kaiser 1630–1641* (Münster, 1998).
Hatton, Ragnhild, *George I. Elector and King* (London, 1978).
Haug, Tilman, *Ungleiche Aussenbeziehungen und grenzüberschreitende Patronage. Die französische Krone und die geistlichen Kurfürsten (1648–1679)* (Cologne/Weimar/Vienna, 2015).
Haug, Tilman et al. (eds), *Protegierte und Protektoren. Asymmetrische Beziehungen zwischen Partnerschaft und Dominanz* (Cologne/Weimar/Vienna, 2016).
Haug-Moritz, Gabriele, *Württembergischer Ständekonflikt und deutscher Dualismus. Ein Beitrag zur Geschichte des Reichverbands in der Mitte des 18. Jahrhunderts* (Stuttgart, 1992).
Havercroft, Jonathan, 'Was Westphalia "all that"? Hobbes, Bellarmine, and the norm of non-intervention', *Global Constitutionalism*1 (2012), 120–40.
Hayden, J. Michael, 'Continuity in the France of Henry IV and Louis XIII: French foreign policy, 1598–1615', *JMH* 45 (1973), 1–23.
Head, Randolph, *Early Modern Democracy in the Grisons. Social Order and Political Language in a Swiss Mountain Canton, 1470–1620* (Cambridge, 1995).
Heckel, Martin, *Deutschland im konfessionellen Zeitalter* (Göttingen, 2001).
Herrmann, Susanne, 'Die Durchführung von Schuldenverfahren im Rahmen kaiserlicher Debitkommissionen im 18. Jahrhundert am Beispiel des Debitwesens der Grafen von Montfort', in Wolfgang Sellert (ed.), *Reichshofrat und Reichskammergericht: ein Konkurrenzverhältnis* (Cologne/Weimar/Vienna, 1999), 111–27.

Hertz, Friedrich, 'Die Rechtsprechung der höchsten Reichsgerichte im römisch-deutschen Reich und ihrepolitische Bedeutung', *MIöG* 69 (1961), 331-58.
Höbelt, Lothar, *Von Nördlingen bis Jankau. Kaiserliche Strategie und Kriegführung 1634-1645* (Vienna, 2016).
Horstkemper, Gregor, 'Die Protestantische Union und der Ausbruch des Dreißigjährigen Krieges', in Winfried Schulze (ed.), *Friedliche Intentionen—kriegerische Effekte: war der Ausbruch des Dreissigjährigen Krieges unvermeidlich?* (St. Katharinen, 2002), 21-51.
Höynck, Franz, *Geschichte des Dekanats Siegen* (Paderborn, 1904).
Hsia, Ronnie Po-chia, 'The Jews and the Emperors', in Charles Ingrao (ed.), *State and Society in Early Modern Austria* (West Lafayette, 1994), 71-80.
Hughes, Michael, 'The Imperial Aulic Council as Guardian of the Rights of Mediate Estates in the Later Holy Roman Empire', in Rudolf Vierhaus (ed.), *Herrschaftsverträge, Wahlkapitulationen, Fundamentalgesetze* (Göttingen, 1977), 192-204.
Hughes, Michael, *Law and Politics in 18th Century Germany. The Imperial Aulic Council in the Reign of Charles VI* (Woodbridge, 1988).
Ibáñez, José Javier Ruiz, 'Les acteurs de l'hégémonie hispanique, du monde à la péninsule Ibérique', *Annales* 69/4 (2014), 927-54.
Ignatieff, Michael, *Empire Lite: Nation-building in Bosnia, Kosovo and Afghanistan* (London, 2003).
Israel, Jonathan, *The Dutch Republic. Its Rise, Greatness, and Fall 1477-1806* (Oxford, 1998).
Jahns, Sigrid, '"Mecklenburgisches Wesen" oder absolutistisches Regiment? Mecklenburgischer Ständekonflikt und neue kaiserliche Reichspolitik (1658-1755)', in Paul-Joachim Heinig et al. (eds), *Reich, Regionen und Europa in Mittlealter und Neuzeit* (Berlin, 2000), 323-51.
Jensen, De Lamar, 'The Ottoman Turks in Sixteenth-Century French Diplomacy', *SCJ* 16 (1985), 451-70.
Johnson, J.T., 'The idea of defense in historical and contemporary thinking about just war', *Journal of Religious Ethics* 36 (2008), 543-56.
Joost, Sebastian, *Zwischen Hoffnung und Ohnmacht. Auswärtige Politik als Mittel zur Durchsetzung landesherrlicher Macht in Mecklenburg (1648-1695)* (Münster, 2009).
Kaiser, Michael, *Politik und Kriegführung. Maximilian von Bayern, Tilly und die Katholische Liga im Dreißigjährigen Krieg* (Münster, 1999).
Kalipke, Andreas, *Verfahren im Konflikt. Konfessionelle Streitigkeiten und Corpus Evangelicorum im 18. Jahrhundert* (Münster, 2015).
Kampmann, Christoph, *Reichsrebellion und kaiserliche Acht. Politische Strafjustiz im Dreißigjährigen Krieg und das Verfahren gegen Wallenstein 1634* (Münster, 1993).
Kampmann, Christoph, *Arbiter und Friedensstiftung. Die Auseinandersetzung um den politischen Schiedsrichter im Europa der Frühen Neuzeit* (Paderborn, 2001).
Kampmann, Christoph, 'Das "Westfälische System", die Glorreiche Revolution und die Interventionsproblematik', *Historisches Jahrbuch* 131 (2011), 65-92.
Kampmann, Christoph, *Europa und das Reich im Dreißigjährigen Krieg* (Stuttgart, 2013).
Kampmann, Christoph, 'Der Festgeschnürte Frieden', *P.M. History*, May 2017.
Kampmann, Christoph, '"Der Leib des Römischen Reichs ist der Stände Eigentum und nicht des Kaisers": Zur Entstehung der Konkurrenz zwischen Kaiserhof und Reichstag beim Achtverfahren', in Sellert, Wolfgang (ed.), *Reichshofrat und Reichskammergericht: ein Konkurrenzverhältnis* (Cologne, 1999), 169-98.
Kasper-Marienberg, Verena, *'vor Euer Kayserlichen Mayestät Justiz-Thron'. Die Frankfurter jüdische Gemeinde am Reichshofrat in josephinischer Zeit* (Innsbruck, 2012).

Keene, Edward, 'International hierarchy and the origins of the modern practice of intervention', *RIS* 39 (2013), 1077-90.
Keller, Ernst, 'Fürst Wilhelm Hyacinth', *AVNAG* 9 (1868), 49-122.
Kennerly, Sam, *Rome and the Maronites in the Renaissance and Reformation* (London, 2022).
Kern, Ronny, *Der Friedenskongress von Soissons 1728-1731* (Osnabrück, 2017).
Kingdon, Robert, 'Calvinism and Resistance Theory, 1550-1580', in J.H. Burns et al. (eds), *Cambridge History of Political Thought* (Cambridge, 1991), 193-218.
Kintzinger, Martin et al. (eds), *Gewalt und Widerstand in der politischen Kultur des späten Mittelalters* (Ostfildern, 2015).
Kleinheyer, Gerd, *Die kaiserlichen Wahlkapitulationen* (Karlsruhe, 1968).
Kleinman, Ruth, 'Charles Emmanuel I of Savoy and the Bohemian Election of 1619', *ESR* 5, (1975), 3-29.
Klose, Fabian (ed.), *The Emergence of Humanitarian Intervention. Ideas and Practice from the Nineteenth Century to the Present* (Cambridge, 2016).
Klose, Fabian, *'In the cause of humanity'.Eine Geschichte der humanitären Intervention im langen 19. Jahrhundert* (Göttingen, 2019).
Klose, Fabian and Mirjam Thulin (eds), *Humanity. A History of European Concepts in Practice from the sixteenth century to the present* (Göttingen, 2016).
Klueting, Harm and Wolfgang Schmale (eds), *Das Reich und seine Territorialstaaten im 17. und 18. Jahrhundert* (Münster, 2004).
Kohler, Alfred, *Expansion und Hegemonie. Internationale Beziehungen 1450-1559* (Paderborn, 2008).
Körber, Esther-Beate, 'Deutschsprachige Flugschriften des Dreißigjährigen Krieg 1618 bis 1629', *Jahrbuch für Kommunikationsgeschichte* 3 (2001), 1-47.
Kremer, Bernd, *Der Westfälische Friede in der Deutung der Aufklärung* (Tübingen, 1989).
Krengel, Johann, 'Die englische Intervention zu Gunsten der böhmischen Juden im Jahre 1744', *Monatsschrift für Geschichte und Wissenschaft des Judentums* 44 (1900), 269-81.
Krieger, Leonard, *The German Idea of Freedom. History of a Political Tradition* (Chicago, 1957).
Lanzinner, Maximilian, *Friedenssicherung und politische Einheit des Reiches unter Kaiser Maximilian II* (Göttingen, 1993).
Lau, Thomas, 'Die Reichsstädte und der Reichshofrat', in Wolfgang Sellert (ed.), *Reichshofrat und Reichskammergericht: ein Konkurrenzverhältnis* (Cologne, 1999), 129-53.
Lesaffer, Randall, 'Defensive Warfare, Prevention and Hegemony. The Justifications for the Franco-Spanish War of 1635', *JHIL* 8 (2006), 91-123, 141-79.
Lesaffer, Randall (ed.), *The Twelve Years Truce (1609)* (Leiden, 2014).
Lewitter, L.R., 'Poland, Russia and the Treaty of Vienna of 5 January 1719', *HJ* 13 (1970), 3-30.
Lockhart, Paul Douglas, *Denmark in the Thirty Years' War, 1618-1648. King Chrisitan IV and the Decline of the Oldenburg State* (Selinsgrove, 1996).
Luard, Evan, *The Balance of Power: The System of International Relations, 1648-1815* (Basingstoke, 1992).
Lundkvist, Sven, 'Die schwedischen Kriegs- und Friedensziele, 1632-1648', in Konrad Repgen (ed.), *Krieg und Politik, 1618-1648* (Munich, 1988).
Malcolm, Noel, *Agents of Empire. Knights, corsairs, Jesuits and spies in the sixteenth-century Mediterranean* (London, 2015).
Malettke, Klaus, *Hegemonie—multipolares System—Gleichgewicht. Internationale Beziehungen 1648/1659-1713/1714* (Paderborn, 2012).

Malettke, Klaus, *Richelieu. Ein Leben im Dienste des Königs und Frankreichs* (Paderborn, 2018).
von Mallinckrodt, Rebekka et al. (eds), *Beyond Exceptionalism—Traces of Slavery and the Slave Trade in Early Modern Germany, 1650-1850* (Berlin/Boston, 2021).
Manzano-Baena, Laura, *Conflicting Words. The Peace Treaty of Münster (1648) and the Political Culture of the Dutch Republic and the Spanish Monarchy* (Leuven, 2011).
Marks, Adam, 'Stuart politics, English military networks and alliances with Denmark and the Palatinate', in Caldari and Wolfson (eds), *Stuart Marriage Diplomacy*, 173-86.
Marquardt, Bernd, 'Zur Reichsgerichtlichen Aberkennung der Herrschergewalt wegen Missbrauchs.Tyrannenprozesse vor dem Reichshofrat am Beispiel des südöstlichen Schwäbischen Reichskreises', in Anette Baumann et al. (eds), *Prozesspraxis im Alten Reich. Annäherungen – Fallstudien – Statistiken* (Cologne/Weimar/Vienna, 2005), 53-89.
Mauelshagen, Stephan, '"Die Freiheiten zernichtet". Die Stadt Rostock im Kampf mit Herzog Karl Leopold von Mecklenburg-Schwerin', in Sylvia Schraut et al. (eds), *Stadt und Land. Bilder, Inszenierungen und Visionen in Geschichte und Gegenwart* (Stuttgart, 2001), 75-87.
McEntegart, Rory, *Henry VIII, the League of Schmalkalden and the English Reformation* (Woodbridge, 2002).
McGraw, Anthony, 'Globalization and global politics', in John Baylis et al. (eds), *The Globalization of World Politics* (Oxford, 2011), 14-31.
McKay, Derek, 'The struggle for control of George I's northern policy, 1718-19', *JMH* 45/3 (1973), 367-86.
McKay, Derek, *Prince Eugene of Savoy* (London, 1977).
McKay, Derek and H.M. Scott, *The Rise of the Great Powers 1648-1815* (London, 1983).
Mediger, Walther, *Mecklenburg, Rußland und England-Hannover 1706-21. Ein Beitrag zur Geschichte des Nordischen Krieges* (Hildesheim, 1967).
Mediger, Walther, 'Die Gewinnung Bremens und Verdens durch Hannover im Nordischen Kriege', *Niedersächsisches Jahrbuch für Landesgeschichte* 43 (1971), 37-56.
Mevorach, Baruch, 'Die Interventionsbestrebungen in Europa zur Verhinderung der Vertreibung der Juden aus Böhmen und Mähren, 1744-1745', *Jahrbuch des Institute für deutsche Geschichte* 9 (1980), 15-81.
Milton, Patrick, 'Imperial law versus geopolitical interest: the Reichshofrat and the protection of smaller states in the Holy Roman Empire under Charles VI (1711-40)', *EHR* 130 (2015), 831-64.
Milton, Patrick, 'The early eighteenth-century German confessional crisis: the juridification of religious conflict in the re-confessionalised politics of the Holy Roman Empire', *CEH* 49 (2016), 39-68.
Milton, Patrick, 'Debates on intervention against religious persecution in the Polish-Lithuanian Commonwealth: European reactions to the Tumult of Thorn, 1724-1726', *EHQ* 47/3 (2017), 405-36.
Milton, Patrick, 'Guarantee and intervention: the assessment of the Peace of Westphalia in international law and politics by authors of natural law and of public law, *c*.1650-1806', in Simone Zurbuchen (ed.), *The Law of Nations and Natural Law, 1625-1850* (Leiden, 2019), 186-226.
Milton, Patrick, 'The mutual guarantee of the Peace of Westphalia in the law of nations and its impact on European diplomacy', *JHIL* 22 (2020), 101-25.
Milton, Patrick, Michael Axworthy, and Brendan Simms, *Towards a Westphalia for the Middle East* (London, 2018).

Mortimer, Geoff, *The Origins of the Thirty Years War and the Revolt in Bohemia, 1618* (New York, 2015).
Mout, Nicolette, 'Der Winterkönig im Exil. Friedrich V. von der Pfalz und die Niederländischen Generalstaaten 1621-1632', *ZHF* 15 (1988), 169-94.
Mühling, Christian, *Die europäische Debatte über den Religionskrieg (1679-1714). Konfessionelle Memoria und internationale Politik im Zeitalter Ludwigs XIV* (Göttingen, 2018).
Müller, Frank, *Kursachsen und der böhmische Aufstand, 1618-1622* (Münster, 1997).
Müller-Luckner, Elisabeth et al. (eds), *Konfessionsfundamentalismus in Europa um 1600* (Munich, 2007).
Münkler, Herfried, *Der Dreissigjährige Krieg. Europäische Katastrophe, deutsches Trauma, 1618-1648* (Berlin, 2017).
Murdock, Graeme, *Calvinism on the Frontier, 1600-1660. International Calvinism and the Reformed Church in Hungary and Transylvania* (Oxford, 2000).
Murray, John J., 'Scania and the end of the Northern Alliance (1716)', *JMH* 16 (1944), 81-92.
Mußgnug, Dorothée, *Acht und Bann im 15. Und 16. Jahrhundert* (Berlin, 2016).
Nagel, Ulrich, *Zwischen Dynastie und Staatsräson. Die habsburgischen Botschafter in Wien und Madrid am Beginn des Dreißigjährigen Krieges* (Göttingen, 2018).
Neuhaus, Helmut, '"Defension" – Das frühneuzeitliche Heilige Römische Reich als Verteidigungsgemeinschaft', in Stephan Wendehorst et al. (eds), *Lesebuch Altes Reich* (Munich, 2006), 119-26.
Nève, Paul, *Die Lütticher Revolution von 1789 vor dem Reichskammergericht* (Wetzlar, 1990).
Nicholls, Sophie, *Political Thought in the French Wars of Religion* (Cambridge, 2021).
Nickel, Veronika, *Widerstand durch Recht. Der Weg der Regensburger Juden bis zu ihrer Vertreibung (1519) und der Innsburger Prozess (1516-1522)* (Wiesbaden, 2018).
van Nifterik, G.P., 'Religious and humanitarian intervention in sixteenth-and early seventeenth-century legal thought', in Randall Lesaffer et al. (eds), *Sovereignty and the Law of Nations*, in *Iuris Scripta Historica* 20 (2006), 35-60.
Nubola, Cecilia et al. (eds), *Bittschriften und Gravamina. Politik, Verwaltung und Justiz in Europa (14.-18. Jahrhundert)* (Berlin, 2005).
Oberländer, Erwin, '"Ist die Kaiserin von Rußland Garant des Westphälischen Friedens?" Der Kurfürst von Trier, die Französische Revolution und Katharina II. 1789-1792', *Jahrbücher für Geschichte Osteuropas* 35 (1987), 218-31.
Obersteiner, Gernot, 'Das Reichshoffiskalat 1596 bis 1806', in Anette Baumann et al. (eds), *Reichspersonal. Funktionsträger für Kaiser und Reich* (Cologne, 2003), 89-164.
Oetzel, Lena, 'Zwischen Dynastie und Reich. Rollen- und Interessenkonflikte Ferdinands III. während der Westfälischen Friedensverhandlungen', in Katrin Keller et al. (eds), *Die Habsburgermonarchie und der Dreißigjährige Krieg* (Vienna, 2020), 161-76.
Öhman, Jenny, *Der Kampf um den Frieden. Schweden und der Kaiser im Dreissigjährigen Krieg* (Vienna, 2005).
von Oppeln-Bronikowski, Friedrich, *Der Baumeister des preußischen Staates. Leben und Wirken Friedrich Wilhelms I* (Jena, 1934).
Orford, Anne, *International Authority and the Responsibility to Protect* (Cambridge, 2011).
Ortlieb, Eva, *Im Auftrag des Kaisers. Die kaiserlichen Kommissionen des Reichshofrats und die Regelung von Konflikten im Alten Reich (1637-1657)* (Cologne/Weimar/Vienna, 2001).
Ortlieb, Eva, 'Die Entstehung des Reichshofrats in der Regierungszeit der Kaiser Karl V. und Ferdinand I', *Frühneuzeit-Info* 17 (2006), 11-26.

Ortlieb, Eva, 'The Holy Roman Empire: the Imperial Courts' system and the Reichshofrat', in A.A. Wijffels et al. (eds), *European Supreme Courts. A Portrait through History* (London, 2013), 86-95.
Ortlieb, Eva, 'Rechtssicherheit für Amtsträger gegen fürstliche Willkür? Die Funktion der Reichsgerichte', in Christoph Kampmann et al. (eds), *Sicherheit in der Frühen Neuzeit. Norm-Praxis-Repräsentation* (Cologne/Weimar/Vienna, 2013), 622-37.
Osiander, Andreas, 'Sovereignty, international relations, and the Westphalian myth', *IO* 55 (2001), 251-87.
Parker, Geoffrey, *The Army of Flanders and the Spanish Road, 1567-1659* (Cambridge, 1972).
Parker, Geoffrey, *The Dutch Revolt* (London, 1985).
Parker, Geoffrey (ed.), *The Thirty Years' War* (New York, 1987).
Parker, Geoffrey, *The Grand Strategy of Philipp II* (New Haven/London, 1998).
Parker, Geoffrey, *Global Crisis. War, Climate Change and Catastrophe in the Seventeenth Century* (New Haven, 2013).
Parker, Geoffrey, *Emperor. A New Life of Charles V* (New Haven, 2019).
Parrott, David, 'The Mantuan Succession, 1627-1631: A Sovereignty Dispute in Early Modern Europe', *EHR* 112 (1997), 20-65.
Parrott, David, *Richelieu's Army. War, Government and Society in France, 1624-1642* (Cambridge, 2001).
Parrott, David, *The Business of War. Military Enterprise and Military Revolution in Early Modern Europe* (Cambridge, 2012).
Peak, Thomas, *Westphalia from Below. Humanitarian Intervention and the Myth of 1648* (London, 2021).
Pečar, Andreas, 'Am Rande des alten Reiches? Mecklenburgs Stellung im alten Reich am Beispiel landständischer Repräsentation und kaiserlichen Einfluss', in Matthias Manke et al. (eds), *Der Landesgrundgesetzliche Erbvergleich von 1755 in seiner Zeit* (Lübeck, 2006), 201-23.
Pennington, Kenneth, *The Prince and the Law, 1200-1600* (Berkeley, 1993).
Petry, Christine, *'Faire des sujets du roi'. Rechtspolitik in Metz, Toul und Verdun unter französischer Herrschaft (1552-1648)* (Munich, 2006).
Petry, David, *Konfliktbewältigung als Medienereignis. Reichsstadt und Reichshofrat in der Frühen Neuzeit* (Berlin, 2011).
Philpott, Daniel, *Revolutions in Sovereignty: How Ideas Shaped Modern International Relations* (Princeton, 2001).
Piirimäe, Pärtel, 'Just war in theory and practice: the legitimation of Swedish intervention in the Thirty Years War', *HJ* 45 (2002), 499-523.
Pincus, Steven, *Protestantism and Patriotism. Ideologies and the Making of English foreign Policy, 1650-1668* (Cambridge, 1996).
Polišenský, Josef, *Tragic Triangle: The Netherlands, Spain and Bohemia 1617-1621* (Prague, 1991).
Press, Volker, 'Die kaiserliche Stellung im Reich zwischen 1648 und 1740', in Georg Schmidt (ed.), *Stände und Gesellschaft im alten Reich* (Wiesbaden, 1989), 51-80.
Press, Volker, *Kriege und Krisen. Deutschland 1600-1715* (Munich, 1991).
Press, Volker, 'Fürst Christian I. von Anhalt-Bernburg, Haupt der evangelischen Bewegungspartei vor dem Dreissigjährigen Krieg', in Konrad Ackermann et al. (eds), *Staat und Verwaltung in Bayern* (Munich, 2003), 193-216.
Pursell, Brennan, *The Winter King. Frederick V of the Palatinate and the Coming of the Thirty Years War* (London, 2016).

Rahn, Kerstin, '"Die Weide des Weissen Rosses von Braunschweig bis an die Ostsee erweitern..."? Kurhannover und Mecklenburg in der ersten Hälfte des 18. Jahrhunderts', in Manke et al. (eds), *Der Landesgrundgesetzliche Erbvergleich von 1755 in seiner Zeit* (Lübeck, 2006), 335–49.

Raitt, J., 'The Elector John Casimir, Queen Elizabeth, and the Protestant League', in D. Visser (ed.), *Controversy and Conciliation. The Reformation and the Palatinate, 1559-1583* (Alison Park, 1986), 117–45.

Randelzhofer, Albrecht, *Völkerrechtliche Aspekte des Heiligen Römischen Reiches nach 1648* (Berlin, 1967).

von Ranke, Ermentrude, *Das Fürstentum Schwarzburg-Rudolstadt zu Beginn des 18. Jahrhunderts* (Halle, 1915).

Rasche, Ulrich, 'Urteil versus Vergleich? Entscheidungspraxis und Konfliktregulierung des Reichshofrats im 17. Jahrhundert im Spiegel neuerer Aktenerschließung', in Albrecht Cordes (ed.), *Mit Freundschaft oder mit Recht? Inner-und außergerichtliche Alternativen zur kontroversen Streitentscheidung* (Cologne, 2015), 199–232.

Rebitsch, Robert (ed.), *1618: Der Beginn des Dreißigjährigen Krieges* (Cologne, 2017).

Rebitsch, Robert, Jenny Öhmann, and Jan Kilian, *1648: Kriegführung und Friedensverhandlungen: Prag und das Ende des Dreißigjährigen Krieges* (Innsbruck, 2018).

Recchia, Stefano and Jennifer Welsh (eds), *Just and Unjust Military Interventions. European Thinkers from Vittoria to Mill* (Cambridge, 2013).

Ringmar, Erik, *Identity, Interest and Action. A Cultural Explanation of Sweden's Intervention in the Thirty Years War* (Cambridge, 1996).

Roberts, Michael, *Gustavus Adolphus. A History of Sweden 1611–1632* (London, 1953–58)

Roberts, Michael, *Gustavus Adolphus* (London, 1992).

Rodogno, Davide, *Against Massacre. Humanitarian Interventions in the Ottoman Empire, 1815-1914* (Princeton, 2012).

Roeck, Bernd, *Reichssystem und Reichsherkommen. Die Diskussion uber die Staatlichkeit des Reiches in der politischen Publizistik des 17. und 18. Jahrhunderts* (Stuttgart, 1984).

Römer, Christof, 'Der Kaiser und die welfischen Staaten 1679–1755', in Harm Klueting et al. (eds), *Das Reich und seine Territorialstaaten im 17. und 18. Jahrhundert* (Münster, 2004), 43–66.

Rüde, Magnus, *England und Kurpfalz im werdenden Mächteeuropa (1608–1632)* (Stuttgart, 2007).

Ruppert, Karsten, *Die kaiserliche Politik auf dem Westfälischen Friedenskongreß (1643-1648)* (Münster, 1979).

Ruthmann, Bernhard, *Die Religionsprozesse am Reichskammergericht (1555-1648)* (Cologne/Vienna, 1996).

Sailer, Rita, *Untertanenprozesse vor dem Reichskammergericht. Rechtsschutz gegen die Obrigkeit in der zweiten Hälfte des 18. Jahrhunderts* (Cologne/Vienna, 1999).

Schama, Simon, *The Embarrassment of Riches. An Interpretation of Dutch Culture in the Golden Age* (New York, 1987).

Schenk, Tobias, 'Reichsjustiz im Spannungsverhältnis von oberstrichterlichem Amt und österreichischen Hausmachtinteressen: Der Reichshofrat und der Konflikt um die Allodifikation der Lehen in Brandenburg-Preußen', in Anja Amend-Traut et al. (eds), *Geld, Handel, Wirtschaft. Höchste Gerichte im Alten Reich als Spruchkörper und Institution* (Berlin, 2012), 103–219.

Schilling, Heinz (ed.), *Die reformierte Konfessionalisierung in Deutschland. Das Problem der 'Zweiten Reformation'* (Gütersloh, 1986).

Schilling, Heinz, *Konfessionalisierung und Staatsinteressen. Internationale Beziehungen 1559–1660* (Paderborn, 2007).
Schmidt, Georg, 'Die "deutsche Freiheit" und der Westfälische Friede', in Ronald G. Asch et al. (eds), *Frieden und Krieg in der Frühen Neuzeit* (Munich, 2001), 323–47.
Schmidt, Georg, '"Teutsche Libertät" oder "Hispanische Servitut": Deutungsstrategien im Kampf um den evangelischen Glauben und die Reichsverfassung, 1546–1552', in Luise Schorn-Schütte (ed.), *Das Interim 1548/50* (Gütersloh, 2005), 166–91.
Schmidt, Georg, 'Deutsche Freiheit', in Stephan Wendehorst and Siegrid Westphal (eds), *Lesebuch Altes Reich* (Munich, 2006), 113–18.
Schmidt, Georg, *Der Dreissigjährige Krieg* (Munich, 2010).
Schmidt, Georg, *Die Reiter der Apokalypse. Geschichte des Dreißigjährigen Krieges* (Munich, 2018).
Schmidt, Peter, *Spanische Universalmonarchie oder 'teutsche Libertet'. Das spanische Imperium in der Propaganda des Dreißigjährigen Krieges* (Stuttgart, 2001).
Schmidt-Rösler, Andrea, 'Princeps Transilvaniae—Rex Hungariae? Gabriel Bethlens Außenpolitik zwischen Krieg und Frieden', in Heinz Duchhardt et al. (eds), *Kalkül—Transfer—Symbol. Europäische Friedensverträge der Vormoderne* (Mainz, 2006), www.ieg-mainz.de/vieg-online-beihefte/01-2006.html.
Schnettger, Matthias, *Der Reichsdeputationstag 1655–1663. Kaiser und Stände zwischen Westfälischem Frieden und Immerwährendem Reichstag* (Münster, 1996).
Schnettger, Matthias, 'Konfliktlösung in Krisenzeiten. Der Frankfurter Fettmilchaufstand 1612–1614 und die kaiserliche Kommission', in Irene Dingel et al. (eds), *Theatrum Belli—Theatrum Pacis. Konflikte und Konfliktregelungen im frühneuzeitlichen Europa* (Göttingen, 2018), 91–109.
Schnettger, Matthias, *Kaiser und Reich. Eine Verfassungsgeschichte (1500–1806)* (Stuttgart, 2020).
Schnur, Roman, *Der Rheinbund von 1658* (Bonn, 1955).
Scholz, Luca, 'Leibeigenschaft rechtfertigen. Kontroversen um Ursprung und Legitimität der Leibeigenschaft im Wildfangstreit', *ZHF* 45/1 (2018), 41–81.
Schorn-Schütte, Luise, *Konfessionskriege und europäische Expansion.Europa 1500–1648* (Munich, 2010).
Schorn-Schütte, Luise, *Die Reformation* (Munich, 2011).
Schröcker, Alfred, 'Die Amtsauffassung des Mainzer Kurfürsten Lothar Franz von Schönborn', *MöStA* 33 (1980), 106–26.
Schröder, Peter, 'The constitution of the Holy Roman Empire after 1648: Samuel Pufendorf's assessment in his Monzambano', *HJ* 42 (1999), 961–83.
Schulze, Winfried, *Bäuerlicher Widerstand und feudale Herrschaft in der frühen Neuzeit* (Stuttgart, 1980).
Schulze, Winfried, 'Majority decision in the Imperial Diets of the sixteenth and seventeenth centuries.' *JMH* 58 (1986), 46–63.
Schulze, Winfried, *Einführung in die Neuere Geschichte* (Stuttgart, 1987).
Schulze-Wessel, Martin, *Russlands Blick auf Preussen. Die polnische Frage in der Diplomatie und der politischen Öffentlichkeit des Zarenreiches und des Sowjetstaates 1697–1947* (Stuttgart, 1995).
Scott Dixon, C., 'Urban order and religious coexistence in the German imperial city: Augsburg and Donauwörth, 1548–1608', *CEH* 40 (2007), 1–33.
Scott, H.M., *The Emergence of the Eastern Powers, 1756–1775* (Cambridge, 2001).
Sea, Thomas, 'Predatory protectors? Conflict and cooperation in the suppression of the German Peasants' Revolt of 1525', *SCJ* 39 (2008), 89–111.

Seger, Otto, 'Der letzte Akt im Drama der Hexenprozesse in der Grafschaft Vaduz und Herrschaft Schellenberg', *JhVFL* 57 (1957), 135–227.
Sellert, Wolfgang, *Prozessgrundsätze und Stilus Curiae am Reichshofrat* (Aalen, 1973).
Sellert, Wolfgang, 'Richterliche Unabhängigkeit am Reichskammergericht und am Reichshofrat', in Okko Behrends et al. (eds), *Gerechtigkeit und Geschichte* (Göttingen, 1996), 118–32.
Sellert, Wolfgang (ed.), *Reichshofrat und Reichskammergericht:ein Konkurrenzverhältnis* (Cologne, 1999).
Sheehan, James J., *German History 1770–1866* (Oxford, 1994).
Sheehan, Michael, 'The sincerity of the British commitment to the maintenance of the balance of power, 1714–1763', *Diplomacy and Statecraft* 15 (2004), 489–506.
Sibeth, Uwe, 'Gesandter einer aufständischen Macht. Die ersten Jahre der Mission von Pieter Cornelisz. Brederode im Reich (1602–1609)', *ZHF* 30 (2003), 19–52.
Simms, Brendan, *Three Victories and a Defeat. The Rise and Fall of the First British Empire, 1714–1783* (London, 2007).
Simms, Brendan, '"Ministers of Europe": British strategic culture, 1714–1760', in Hamish Scott and Brendan Simms (eds), *Cultures of Power in Europe during the Long Eighteenth Century* (Cambridge, 2007), 110–32.
Simms, Brendan, '"A false principle in the law of nations": Burke, state sovereignty, [German] liberty, and intervention in the Age of Westphalia', in Brendan Simms and D.J.B. Trim (eds), *Humanitarian Intervention. A History* (Cambridge, 2011), 89–110.
Simms, Brendan, *Europe. The Struggle for Supremacy, 1453 to the present* (London, 2013).
Simms, Brendan, 'Europe's shifting balance of power' in Hamish Scott (ed.), *The Oxford Handbook of Early Modern European History, 1350–1750* (Oxford, 2015), ii, 638–62.
Simms, Brendan and Torsten Riotte (eds), *The Hanoverian Dimension in British History, 1714–1837* (Cambridge, 2007).
Simms, Brendan and D.J.B. Trim (eds), *Humanitarian Intervention: A History* (Cambridge, 2011), 89–110.
Soder, J., *Francisco Suárez und das Völkerrecht. Gedanken zu Staat, Recht und internationalen Beziehungen* (Frankfurt am Main, 1973).
Sonnino, Paul, *Mazarin's Quest. The Congress of Westphalia and the Coming of the Fronde* (Cambridge, MA, 2008).
Stein, Wolfgang, *Protection Royale. Eine Untersuchung zu den Protektionsverhältnissen im Elsaß zur Zeit Richelieus* (1622–1643) (Münster, 1978).
Stollberg-Rilinger, Barbara, *Vormünder des Volkes? Konzepte landständischer Repräsentation in der Spätphase des Alten Reiches* (Berlin, 1999).
Stollberg-Rilinger, Barbara, 'Die Würde des Gerichts. Spielten symbolisch-zeremonielle Formen an den höchsten Reichsgerichten eine Rolle?', in Peter Oestmann (ed.), *Zwischen Formstrenge und Billigkeit. Forschungen Zum Vormodernen Zivilprozess* (Cologne, 2009), 191–216.
Stollberg-Rilinger, Barbara, *The Emperor's Old Clothes: Constitutional History and the Symbolic Language of the Holy Roman Empire* (New York, 2015).
Stollberg-Rilinger, Barbara, *Maria Theresia. Die Kaiserin in ihrer Zeit* (Munich, 2017).
Stollberg-Rilinger, Barbara, *The Holy Roman Empire. A Short History* (Princeton, 2018).
Stolleis, Michael, *Geschichte des öffentlichen Rechts in Deutschland* (Munich, 1988).
Stradling, R.A., *Europe and the Decline of Spain, 1580–1720* (London, 1981).
Stradling, R.A., 'Olivares and the origins of the Franco-Spanish war', *EHR* 101 (1986), 68–94.
Straub, Eberhard, *Pax et Imperium. Spaniens Kampf um seine Friedensordnung in Europa zwischen 1617 und 1635* (Paderborn, 1980).

Strohmeyer, Arno, *Konfessionskonflikt und Herrschaftsordnung. Widerstandsrecht bei den österreichischen Ständen (1550-1650)* (Mainz, 2006).
Sutherland, Nicola, 'The Origins of the Thirty Years War and the Structure of European Politics', *EHR* 107(1992), 587-625.
Swatek-Evenstein, Mar, *A History of Humanitarian Intervention* (Cambridge, 2020).
von Thiessen, Hillard, *Das Zeitalter der Ambiguität. Vom Umgang mit Werten und Normen in der Frühen Neuzeit* (Cologne/Weimar/Vienna, 2021).
von Thiessen, Hillard et al. (eds), *Nähe in der Ferne. Personale Verflechtung in den Außenbeziehungen der Frühen Neuzeit* (Berlin, 2005).
von Thiessen, Hillard et al. (eds.), *Akteure der Außenbeziehungen. Netzwerke und Interkulturalität im historischen Wandel* (Cologne/Weimar/Vienna, 2010).
Thompson, Andrew C., *Britain, Hanover and the Protestant Interest 1688-1756* (Woodbridge, 2006).
Tischer, Anuschka, *Französische Diplomatie und Diplomaten auf dem Westfälischen Friedenskongress. Aussenpolitik unter Richelieu und Mazarin* (Münster, 1999).
Tischer, Anuschka, 'Claude de Mesmes, Count d'Avaux. The perfect ambassador of the early 17th century', *International Negotiation* 13 (2008), 197-209.
Tischer, Anuschka, 'Grenzen der Souveränität: Beispiele zur Begründung gewaltsamer Einmischung in "innere Angelegenheiten" in der Frühen Neuzeit', *Historisches Jahrbuch*, 131 (2011), 41-64.
Tischer, Anuschka, *Offizielle Kriegsbegründungen in der Frühen Neuzeit* (Münster, 2012).
Tischer, Anuschka, 'Dynamik durch Gewalt? Der Dreißigjährige Krieg und die Wandlungsprozesse der Frühen Neuzeit', in Tischer et al. (eds), *Dynamic durch Gewalt? Der Dreißigjährige Krieg als Faktor der Wandlungsprozesse des 17. Jahrhunderts* (Münster, 2018), 13-39.
van Tol, Jonas, *Germany and the French Wars of Religion, 1560-1572* (Leiden, 2018).
Tracy, James D., *Emperor Charles V, Impresario of War. Campaign Strategy, International Finance, and Domestic Politics* (Cambridge, 2002).
Trim, D.J.B., '"If a prince use tyrannie towards his people": interventions on behalf of foreign populations in early modern Europe', in Simms et al. (eds), *Humanitarian Intervention. A History* (Cambridge, 2011), 29-66.
Troßbach, Werner, 'Fürstenabsetzungen im 18. Jahrhundert', *ZHF* 13 (1986), 425-54.
Troßbach, Werner, 'Power and good governance: the removal of ruling princes in the Holy Roman Empire, 1680-1794', in J.P. Coy et al. (eds), *The Holy Roman Empire, Reconsidered* (New York, 2010), 191-209.
Tschaikner, Manfred, '"Der Teufel und die Hexen müssen aus dem Land…" Frühneuzeitliche Hexenverfolgungen in Liechtenstein', *JhVFL* 96 (1998), 1-197.
Tschaikner, Manfred, 'Hohenemser Schreckensherrschaft in Vaduz und Schellenberg? Graf Ferdinand Karl von Hohenems und die Hexenprozesse (1675-1685), *Montfort* 64 (2012), 87-99.
Tuck, Richard, *The Rights of War and Peace. Political Thought and the International Order from Grotius to Kant* (Oxford, 2001).
Uhlhorn, Manfred, *Der Mandatsprozess sine-clausula des Reichshofrats* (Cologne/Vienna, 1990).
Ulbert, Jörg, 'Die Angst vor einer habsburgischen Hegemonie im Reich als Leitmotiv der französischen Deutschlandpolitik unter der Regentschaft Philipps von Orléans' in Thomas Höpel (ed.), *Deutschlandbilder-Frankreichbilder 1700-1850. Rezeption und Abgrenzung zweier Kulturen* (Leipzig, 2001), 57-74.

Vann, James Allen, 'New directions for the study of the Old Reich', *JMH* 58 (1986), 3-22.
Vincent, R.J., 'Grotius, human rights and intervention', in Hedley Bull et al. (eds), *Hugo Grotius and International Relations* (Oxford, 1992), 241-56.
Vitense, Otto, *Geschichte von Mecklenburg* (Gotha, 1920).
Walker, Mack, *Johann Jacob Moser and the Holy Roman Empire* (Chapel Hill, 1981).
Walker, Mack, *The Salzburg Transaction. Expulsion and Redemption in Eighteenth Century Germany* (Ithaca, 1992).
Weber, Hermann, 'Richelieu et le Rhin', *Revue Historique* 239 (1968), 265-80.
Weber, Hermann, *Frankreich, Kurtrier, der Rhein und das Reich 1623-1635* (Bonn, 1969).
Weber, Hermann, 'Vom verdeckten zum offenen Krieg. Richelieus Kriegsgründe und Kriegsziele 1634/1635', in Konrad Repgen (ed.), *Krieg und Politik, 1618-1648. Europäische Probleme und Perspektiven* (Munich, 1988), 203-17.
Weber, Matthias, 'Zur Bedeutung der Reichsacht in der Frühen Neuzeit', *ZHF Beiheft* 19 (1997), 55-90.
Weber, Ottokar, *Die Quadrupelallianz vom Jahre 1718* (Vienna, 1887).
Weiss, Elmar, *Die Unterstützung Friedrichs V. von der Pfalz durch Jakob I. und Karl I. im Dreißigjährigen Krieg (1618-1632)* (Stuttgart, 1966).
Weitzel, Jürgen, 'Der Reichshofrat und das irreguläre Beschneiden des Rechtsmittels der Appellation', in Leopold Auer et al. (eds), *Appellation und Revision im Europa des Spätmittelalters und der Frühen Neuzeit* (Vienna, 2013), 163-74.
Wendehorst, Stephan et al. (eds), *Lesebuch Altes Reich* (Munich, 2006).
Wendland, Andreas, *Die Nutzen der Pässe und die Gefährdung der Seelen. Spanien, Mailand und der Kampf ums Veltlin 1620-1641* (Zürich, 1995).
Wernham, R.B., 'English policy and the revolt of the Netherlands', in J.S. Bromley et al. (eds), *Britain and the Netherlands* (The Hague, 1960).
Westphal, Siegrid, *Kaiserliche Rechtsprechung und herrschaftliche Stabilisierung. Reichsgerichtsbarkeit in den thüringischen Territorialstaaten 1648-1806* (Cologne/Weimar/Vienna, 2002).
Westphal, Siegrid (ed.), *In eigener Sache. Frauen vor den höchsten Gerichten des Alten Reiches* (Cologne, 2005).
Westphal, Siegrid, *Der Westfälische Frieden* (Munich, 2015).
Westphal, Siegrid, 'The Holy Roman Empire of the German nation as an order of public peace', *GH* 36 (2018), 401-14.
Whaley, Joachim, 'A tolerant society? Religious toleration in the Holy Roman Empire, 1648-1806', in Ole Peter Grell and Roy Porter (eds), *Toleration in Enlightenment Europe* (Cambridge, 2000), 175-95.
Whaley, Joachim, *Germany and the Holy Roman Empire* (2 vols. Oxford, 2012).
Whaley, Joachim, *The Holy Roman Empire. A Very Short Introduction* (Oxford, 2018).
White, Jason, *Militant Protestantism and British Identity, 1603-1642* (London, 2012).
Wick, Peter, *Versuche zur Errichtung des Territorialabsolutismus in Mecklenburg in der ersten Hälfte des 18. Jahrhunderts* (Berlin, 1964).
Wieland, *Protestantischer König im Heiligen Reich. Brandenburg-preußische Reichs- und Konfessionspolitik im frühen 18. Jahrhundert* (Berlin, 2020).
Wilson, Charles, *Queen Elizabeth I and the Revolt of the Netherlands* (Basingstoke, 1970).
Wilson, Peter H., 'The causes of the Thirty Years War 1618-48', *EHR* 123 (2008), 554-86.
Wilson, Peter H., *Europe's Tragedy. A History of the Thirty Years War* (London, 2009).
Wilson, Peter H., *The Holy Roman Empire. A Thousand Years of Europe's History* (London, 2016).

Wilson, Peter H., 'Financing the War of the Spanish Succession in the Holy Roman Empire', in Matthias Pohlig and Michael Schaich (eds), *The War of the Spanish Succession: New Perspectives* (Oxford, 2018), 267-97.

Wilson, Peter H., 'The Stuarts, the Palatinate, and the Thirty Years' War', in Valentina Caldari et al. (eds), *Stuart Marriage Diplomacy. Dynastic Politics in their European Context, 1604-1630* (Woodbridge, 2018), 141-56.

Wrede, Martin, *Das Reich und seine Feinde. Politische Feindbilder in der reichspatriotischen Publizistik zwischen Westfälischem Frieden und Siebenjährigem Krieg* (Mainz, 2004).

Würgler, Andreas, *Unruhen und Öffentlichkeit. Städtische und ländliche Protestbewegungen im 18. Jahrhundert* (Tübingen, 1995).

Zurbuchen, Simone, 'Vattel's "Law of Nations" and the principle of non-intervention', *Grotiania* 31 (2010), 69-84.

# Index

For the benefit of digital users, indexed terms that span two pages (e.g., 52–53) may, on occasion, appear on only one of those pages.

Aachen, Imperial city 77–82, 166–7
absolutism 4, 35–6, 69–71, 110, 114, 125–6, 131–2, 164–5, 224, 233–4
Adolf Friedrich, duke of Mecklenburg-Strelitz 258–9
Alsace 95, 111–12, 118–19, 123–4, 135–6
Althusius, Johannes, theorist 41
Altranstädt, convention of (1707) 142
Alva, Fernando Álvarez de Toledo, duke of, Spanish military commander in the Low Countries 65, 74–5
Alvensleben, Johann, Hanoverian privy councillor 248–9
Anglo-Spanish war (1585–1604) 74–6
Anna Maria Josepha, princess of Nassau-Siegen 195
Annan, Kofi 3
Antwerp 68, 70–1
Aquinas, St.-Thomas, theorist 42–3
August Wilhelm, duke of Braunschweig-Wolfenbüttel 224–5, 258–9
Augustus II 'the strong', king of Poland and elector of Saxony 78–9, 235, 259
Austria 15–16, 19–20, 80–1, 85–9, 93, 95–6, 104–5, 112–13, 115, 118, 120, 135–7, 141–2, 145, 153–4, 162–3, 169–70, 174–6, 230–44, 248–9, 254–6, 261–2
Austrian court-chancery, Vienna (*Hofkanzlei*) 230, 237–8
Austro-British alliance (1731) 154
Austro-British defensive alliance (1716) 240–1
Austro-Ottoman war 1716-1718 236
Avaux, Claude de Mesmes, count of, French plenipotentiary at congress of Westphalia 129
Ayala, Balthazar, theorist 48

Baden-Durlach, margraviate of 116
balance of power 7–8, 20, 118–19, 152–4
Baltic sea 92–3, 101–3, 108, 118, 122–3, 224, 241–2, 244–7
Bamberg, prince-bishopric of 168–9
Battle of Breitenfeld (1631) 107–8
Battle of Lützen (1632) 107–8

Battle of Nördlingen (1634) 107–8, 112–13, 116
Battle of Pavia (1525) 60
Bavaria, duchy (after 1623 electorate) of 15–16, 61, 80–1, 83, 88–90, 95–7, 107–8, 135–6, 166, 258, 260
Becher, Johann Joachim, theorist 39–40
Behr, Burghard, Mecklenburg nobility's agent and envoy 244, 256–7
Bentheim, county of 179–81
Berlin 135, 145–7, 245–7, 252–6
Bern 147
Bernstorff, Andreas Gottlieb von, Hanoverian chief minister 243–5, 247–9, 261–2
Bethlen Gábor, prince of Transylvania 88–9, 91–2
Bodin, Jean, theorist 41–2, 44, 46–9, 106, 267
Bohemia 15–16, 58, 85–96, 123, 154, 269–70
Böhmer, Justus Henning theorist 35–6
Boitzenburg, town 247–8
Bothmer, Friedrich, Hanoverian statesman 246–7
Bourbon dynasty of France and later Spain 58, 152
Brandenburg, electorate of (*see also* Prussia) 15–16, 19–20, 62–3, 78–9, 81–2, 100–1, 107, 135, 143–4, 151–4, 163–5, 186–9, 192–4, 207–8, 210–14, 218–20, 223–5, 235–6, 238–42, 244–7, 249–50, 252–6, 266, 268
Bremen-Verden, fmr bishopric of 240–1, 244–5, 252–3
Bruges 70–1
Brunnquell, Johann Salomon, theorist 35–6
Brussels 67, 112
Büllingen, Gerhard, Palatine envoy to Lower-Rhenish Westphalian Kreis diet in Cologne 111, 125–6, 151–2, 156–7, 202, 212, 244–7, 261–2

Calais 57
Calvinist International 66
Carl Friedrich, prince of Wied-Neuwied 183–4
Carl Leopold, duke of Mecklenburg-Schwerin 1, 185, 195, 223–66

Catherine II 'the Great', Tsarina and empress of Russia 148–9
Catholic League (France) 70–1
Catholic League (Germany) 81, 83, 92–3, 95, 97–8, 100–1, 103, 107–8
Cecil, Sir Edward, English MP 93–4
Cecil, William, English statesman 70
Censorship 115–16
Charles Emanuel, duke of Savoy 88–9
Charles I, King of Spain (see Emperor Charles V)
Charles V, Holy Roman Emperor 45, 58
Charles VI, Holy Roman Emperor 1, 144–5, 152, 189, 224, 230–43, 245, 247–8, 250–1, 259–60, 262
Charles VII, Holy Roman Emperor 28–9
Charles XII, king of Sweden 141–3
Charles, duke of Lorraine and governor of Upper Austria 174–5
Christian I, prince of Anhalt-Zerbst, governor of Upper Palatinate 79–80
Christian IV, king of Denmark 96–101
Christian Ludwig II, titular duke and administrator (later reigning duke) of Mecklenburg-Schwerin 224–5, 237
Church of England 94
Clemens August, archbishop-elector of Cologne 259–60
Cologne, archbishopric-electorate of 15–16, 79, 82–3, 136–7, 166, 169–70, 181, 186, 188–9, 199–208, 212, 214–15, 219–21, 257–61
Cologne, Imperial city of 197
Columba, Carlo de, favourite of Prince William Hyacinth of Nassau-Siegen 194–6, 214–15
Confessional crisis in Germany (1719–c.1723) 39, 144–5, 152–4, 180–1
Congress of Braunschweig (1710s) 237–8, 257
Congress of Soissons (1728–29) 144–5, 250, 261–3
Conring, Hermann, theorist 36–7
*Constitutio Criminalis Carolina* (criminal law code, 1532) 23, 201
constitutional law 1, 22–41, 132–3, 155, 225–6, 228–9, 248–9
Convention of Leipzig (1631) 107
Copenhagen 261–2
*Corpus Catholicorum* 218
*Corpus Evangelicorum* 38, 144, 151–2, 186–7, 211–14, 218–21
Craggs, James, British diplomat 247
Croatia 58
Cromwell, Oliver, English republican dictator 149–51

Cuban war of independence 2
*cuius regio eius religio*, legal concept 77
Customary law 16–17, 29–31, 37–8, 190

*Declaratio Ferdinandea* 77
Democracy 2–3
Denmark, kingdom of 19, 60–1, 64, 96–103, 105, 108
Diest, Reinhard, Brandenburg-Prussian envoy to Lower-Rhenish Westphalian Kreis diet in Cologne 212–13
Dömitz, town of 224–7
Donauwörth, Imperial (later Bavarian) city of 77–83, 166–7
Dubois, Cardinal Guillaume, French chief minister 262
Dunkirk 68
Düsseldorf 81–3
Dutch republic aka United Provinces (northern Netherlands) 5, 19–20, 44–5, 47, 58, 64–76, 82, 87, 90, 92–3, 96, 98–9, 110, 114–16, 122–3, 137–9, 142, 179–81
Dutch Revolt, aka Eighty Years War (1568–48) 44–5, 64–75, 79–80, 114, 122–4
Dynasticism 17–18, 41–2, 65–6, 81–2, 89–91, 96, 122–4, 161–3, 169, 185, 221, 267–8

East Frisia, principality of 162–3
Ecclesiastical Reservation (legal principle) 77–8, 97–8, 129
ecclesiastical territories 77
Edict of Restitution (1629) 100
Eichholtz, Johann, ducal Mecklenburg envoy to Vienna 226–7, 231–3, 235–6, 239, 256–7, 259, 261–2
Eitel Friedrich, prince of Hohenzollern-Hechingen 169
Elisabeth Farnese, Queen Consort of Spain 262
Elizabeth I, Queen of England 9–10, 19–20, 57, 69–75
Elizabeth, princess of England, countess consort of the Palatine 90
Eltz, Philipp Adam von, Hanoverian Privy-councillor 146–9, 151, 254
Emden, town of 79
Emperor, office of 14–16, 29–31
England/Britain, kingdom of 1–2, 9–10, 17–20, 33, 47, 57, 60–1, 66, 68–76, 90, 92–4, 98–9, 124, 142, 145, 149–57, 188, 218–20, 224–5, 238–42, 252–6, 261–3, 267–8
Enlightenment 39, 77, 270
*Entente* (Franco-British alliance, 1716–31) 153–4, 240–1
Erasmus of Rotterdam, theorist 42–3

Ertel, Anton Wilhelm, jurist 39–40
Eternal Territorial Peace (*ewiger Landfrieden*, 1495) 16–17, 22–3, 132–3, 193
Eugene, Prince of Savoy, military commander and president of the privy conference, Vienna 230, 238–9, 242
exemption (*Freistellung*), legal principle 77

Ferdinand I, Holy Roman Emperor 25
Ferdinand II, Holy Roman Emperor 87–9, 91–2, 117–18, 259–60
Ferdinand III, Holy Roman Emperor 129–30
Ferdinand Karl, Count of Hohenems-Vaduz 170–8
Ferdinand, Cardinal-Infante of Austria, governor of the Habsburg (Spanish) Netherlands 112–14
Feudalism 14–15, 29–30, 33–4, 65, 82–3, 90, 110, 114–15, 119–20, 161, 163–5, 184–5, 233–4
Finch, Edward, British diplomat 153–4
Flender vor der Haardt, Friedrich, ironworker in Nassau-Siegen 200–2
Flender, Johann Jacob, opposition leader in Nassau-Siegen 197
Fleury, Cardinal André Hercule, French chief minister
Foix, Paul de, French Ambassador to London 55–6
France, kingdom of 17–20, 26, 28, 33, 36–7, 44–5, 50–1, 57–73, 75–6, 79–80, 82–4, 95, 98–102, 107–19, 123–42, 144–52, 154–6, 166–7, 169–71, 188–9, 200, 217, 220–1, 235, 240–1, 245–7, 250–1, 254, 262–3
Franche-Comté 58, 95
Francis I, King of France 59–62, 110–11
Francis, duke of Anjou 68–9
Frankfurt, Imperial city 167
Franz Alexander, prince of Nassau-Hadamar 201–2
Franz von Sickingen, Imperial Knight and rebel leader 60
Frederick I, king in Prussia, elector of Brandenburg 201–2
Frederick II 'the Great' Prussian king 147–8, 163–4
Frederick V, elector-Palatine and king of Bohemia 78–9, 88–93, 95, 98, 122
Frederick William I, king in Prussia, elector of Brandenburg 146, 151–2, 163–4, 219–20, 252–6
French Wars of Religion (1562–98) 9–10, 19–20, 44–5, 55–7, 59, 66, 75–6, 121, 123–-4
Friedrich count of Leiningen-Güntersblum 181–2
Friedrich Karl Graf von Schönborn, Imperial vice-chancellor 230, 238–9, 244–5, 259
Friedrich Wilhelm Adolf, prince of Nassau-Siegen (Reformed line) 188–9, 192–4, 197–9, 201–2, 206–8, 210–14, 218

Friedrich, Count of Wied-Neuwied 169–70
Fronde, rebellion in France (1648–53) 137–8
Further Austria 174, 176

Gaddafi, Muammar 3–4
Gail, Andreas, theorist 41
Gattinara, Mercurino, chancellor of Emperor Charles V 58
Gebhard Xaver Count of Waldburg-Wolfegg-Waldsee 183–4
Geneva, republican city-state 147
Gentili, Alberico, theorist 46–9, 106, 267
George I, King of Great Britain 1, 151–4, 218–20, 224–7, 240–3, 261, 265–6
George II, King of Great Britain 154, 249–50
German Liberties/Freedom (*deutsche Freiheit*) 16–17, 19–20, 62, 64, 87, 99–103, 105, 107–8, 111–13, 115–18, 122–3, 125–6, 128, 140–1, 144–8, 229, 231–2
Ghent 70–1
Glorious Revolution (1688) 9–10, 149, 151–2, 156
Golden Bull (1356) 3–4
Great Northern War (1700–21) 142, 145–6, 186, 220, 223–4, 226–7, 235, 244–5, 252–3, 265–6
Great Turkish War (1683–1699) 177
Grey Leagues (Graubünden), Swiss-associated territory, 95–6, 170–2, 177–9
Grotius, Hugo, theorist 46–9, 102, 106, 267
Guelph dynasty 149, 224–5
Guise, House of, French noble family 57, 59, 70–3
Gundling, Nikolaus Hieronymus, theorist 35–6
Gustavus Adolphus, king of Sweden 101–9
György I Rákóczi, prince of Transylvania 119–21

Habsburg dynasty 15–16, 18–20, 22–7, 29–34, 36, 38–9, 42–3, 45–51, 128–33, 136–7, 141, 144, 147–50, 152–3, 155–6, 162–3, 169–70, 174, 177–9, 202–4, 236, 240–2, 259–60, 262–3
Haldane, James, British diplomat 152–3
Hanover (Braunschweig-Lüneburg), duchy (after 1692 electorate) of 15–16, 36, 145–6, 149, 151–2, 181, 213–14, 218–20, 223–8, 232, 239–53, 255–9, 261–2, 266
Hausschild, Johann Leonard, theorist 39
Havelberg convention (Prusso-Russian, 1716) 253
Heidelberg 90, 93–4
Henry II, King of France 45, 62–4, 125–6
Henry III, King of France 68, 71
Henry IV (also king of Navarre), King of France 83–4
Hermann Friedrich, count of Bentheim 179–81

Hessen-Kassel, landgraviate of 19, 78-9, 107-8, 116, 136-7, 161-2, 211-14, 218-19, 259
Heusch, Johann, Hanoverian envoy to Berlin 253-4
Hobbes, Thomas, theorist 35-6, 48-9, 267
Hohenlohe, county 116
Hohenzollern dynasty 20, 169
Holstein, duchy of 97-8
Holy Roman Empire, overview 10-11, 14-17
Huguenots (French Protestants) 67, 99-100, 137-8, 151-2
Huldenberg, Daniel von, Hanoverian envoy to Vienna 1, 231-2, 235-6, 238-9, 244, 247-8, 253-4
human rights 2-3, 271
Humanism 33, 41-3, 46
humanitarian intervention 2-4, 8-12, 271-2
Hungary, kingdom of 5, 58, 87-90, 119-23, 125-6, 142

Ilgen, Heinrich, Brandenburg-Prussian chief minister 252-3
Immediate subjects 15-17, 30, 59-60, 82-3, 85-6, 106, 127-8, 135-6, 144, 156, 181-4, 217-18, 232-3, 239, 266, 268-9
Imperial Arch Chancellor 257-8
Imperial ban (*Reichsacht*) 22-3, 28-9, 60, 80-1, 90, 96-7, 128-9, 177-8, 184, 203, 221, 250, 258, 260, 270
Imperial chancery, Vienna (*Reichskanzlei*) 138-9, 174, 230, 237-8
Imperial cities 11-12, 14-15, 77, 81-2, 165-8, 184-5
Imperial Estates 5-16, 22-3, 25-6, 28-35, 37-8, 50, 59-61, 63-5, 67, 77-83, 87, 105-6, 114-17, 123-5, 129-33, 135-40, 147-8, 155-6, 161-4, 174, 177-8, 184, 189, 194, 200, 217-18, 222, 224, 251-2, 256-61, 263, 267-8, 271-2
Imperial Italy (*Reichsitalien*) 5, 87, 109-10, 116, 166
Imperial vicar, office of 62-3, 189
Imperial Vice Chancellor 230, 238-9, 259
International Relations (IR), academic discipline 5-9
Iraq 3-4
Ireland 57, 73

Jacob Hannibal, count of Hohenems-Vaduz 172-4, 178
Jacobites 244-5
Jagiellonian inheritance (1526) 58
James I, King of England 90, 98-100
Jesuits 87-8, 90-1, 120

Jews 11-12, 154, 165-7, 267-8
Johann Georg II Fuchs von Dornheim, prince-bishop of Bamberg 168-9
Johann Philipp, archbishop-elector of Mainz and arch-chancellor of Germany 136-7
Johann Sigismund, elector of Brandenburg 81-2
Johann Wilhelm, duke of Jülich-Kleve-Berg 82-3
Johann Wilhelm, elector-Palatine 211-12, 214
John Casimir, elector-Palatinate 64-5
John Frederick, elector (later duke) of Saxony 62
Joseph Clemens, archbishop-elector of Cologne 258
Joseph I, Holy Roman Emperor 142, 189-90, 194-7, 201-4, 212-13
Joseph II, Holy Roman Emperor 148-9, 181-2
Jülich-Berg-Kleve-Mark territorial complex 75-6, 79, 81-4, 201, 220
Jülich-Kleve-Berg succession crisis (1609-10/1614) 81-4
Jung, Hermann, chancellor of Catholic Nassau-Siegen 188-9, 192-4, 197
Just War theory 42-3, 73, 102, 104, 113-14, 120, 122
Jutland, region in Denmark 99-100

Karl Magnus count of Rheingrafenstein and Grehweiler 183
Karl Philipp, elector-Palatine 259-60
Kirchner, Michael, Austrian diplomat (envoy at Reichstag) 237-8
Klerff, Friedrich von, Reichshofrat agent (advocate) 198
Klüver, Hans Heinrich, historian 40-1
Knights' Revolt (1522-23) 60-1
Knöringen, Heinrich, prince-bishop of Augsburg 80
Knyphausen, Friedrich Ernst, Brandenburg-Prussian envoy at Hanover and minister 253-4
Knyphausen, Friedrich, Brandenburg-Prussian envoy to Hanover 253-4
Kochenheim, Ernst, Münster envoy to Lower-Rhenish Westphalian Kreis diet in Cologne 186-222
Krane, Johann, Imperial envoy to congress of Westphalia and RHR-member 129-30
Kreise (Imperial 'circles'/districts) 1, 10-11, 14-16, 24, 26, 31-2, 64-5, 77-8, 80-1, 97-100, 104, 109, 136-7, 168-72, 176-84, 186-91, 195, 200, 202-5, 207, 209, 221-2, 236, 242

Lamberg, Johann Maximilian count of, Imperial privy councillor, RHR-member and plenipotentiary at congress of Westphalia 129–30
law of nations 1, 13–14, 34–5, 41–50, 55, 63, 67–8, 102, 104, 113–14, 121–2, 127, 132–6, 155, 248–9
law of nature/natural law 34–6, 38–9, 43–4, 46–51, 67–8, 90–1, 99, 104, 121–2, 155, 166–7
Lebanon 2, 57
Leibniz, Gottfried Wilhelm, polymath and philosopher 139–40
Leicester, Robert Dudley, 1st Earl of, English statesman and military commander 47, 71, 74–5
Leopold I, Holy Roman Emperor 136–41, 193–4
Letter of Majesty, legal document of Emperor Rudolf II (1609) 86, 88, 90–1
Liege, prince-bishopric of 137
Lipsius, Justus, theorist 67–8, 76
London 55, 70–1, 151–2, 227–8, 247–8, 253–4
Longueville, Henri II duke d'Orléans, French plenipotentiary at congress of Westphalia 135–6
Lords of the Congregation (Scotland) 57
Lorraine, duchy of 111–12, 124, 137, 139, 174–5
Lothar Franz von Schönborn, archbishop-elector of Mainz and arch-chancellor of Germany 215–16, 257–8, 260–1
Louis XIII, King of France 85, 107–9, 111–14, 117
Louis XIV, King of France 133–41, 148–9
Louis-Frédéric Bonet, Brandenburg-Prussian resident in London 253–4
Louis-Frédéric Bonet, Prussia's resident in London 253–4
Lutheranism 24–5, 27, 32, 39, 61, 77–83, 97–8, 130, 143

Machiavelli, Niccolò, theorist 42
Maes, J.J., electoral Cologne commission subdelegate in Nassau-Siegen 202
Magdeburg, massacre at (1631) 107–8
Mainz, archbishopric-electorate of 15–16, 136–8, 167, 181–2, 215, 226–7, 257–8, 260–1, 263
Mansfeld, Count Ernst von, mercenary leader and military commander 88–9, 98
Mantua 109, 111, 166
Mantuan succession crisis and war (1627–31) 111
Maria Theresia, Habsburg ruler 147–8, 154
Market economy 5–6
Marquard Rudolf von Rodt, prince-bishop of Constance 173–4, 178

Marquard, Graf von, Hanoverian *Oberappellationsrat* 244
Mary II, Queen of England 151
Matthias, Holy Roman Emperor 86–8
Maurice, prince of Orange, Dutch Stadholder 90, 93
Max Emanuel, elector of Bavaria 258
Maximilian I, Holy Roman Emperor 25
Maximilian II, Holy Roman Emperor 65
Maximilian, duke (later elector) of Bavaria 80–1, 83
Mazarin, Cardinal Jules, French chief minister 128–31, 135–6, 150
Mecklenburg, duchy of 1, 28–9, 35–6, 39–40, 62–3, 100–1, 103, 144–7, 161, 166, 177–8, 185, 223–66
Mediate subjects 11–12, 15–16, 23, 28–32, 35, 40–1, 59–61, 85–6, 127–8, 133–6, 156, 165–6, 203–4, 209, 217–18, 232–4, 254, 266, 268–9
Mediterranean sea 60–1, 240–2, 245, 262
Meierij, Netherlands 129
Metsch, Graf Johann Adolf von, Imperial diplomat (envoy at congress of Braunschweig) 163–4, 237–9, 257
Metternich, Ernst, Brandenburg-Prussian envoy to Reichstag 219
Metz 62–3, 123–4
Middle East 3–4
Milan, duchy and Imperial fief 58, 67, 95–6, 109
military intervention and war in Iraq (1991, 1998, 2003) 3–4
military intervention and war in Ukraine (2014/2022) 3
Mirandula 166
Monarchy 14–16, 33, 44–5, 66
Moritz (Maurice), duke (later elector) of Saxony 62–3
Moscherosch, Johann Michael, writer 115–16
Moser, Johann Jacob, theorist 29, 31–2, 36–9, 51, 134, 265, 268
Münster, prince-bishopric of 180–1, 203, 206–8, 211–14, 218–19

Naples 19–20, 58, 120
Nassau, dynasty and principalities of (*see also* Nassau-Siegen) 64–5, 186–7, 201, 207–8
Nassau-Siegen, principality 15–16, 144, 186–222, 229
Nationhood, nationalism 14–15, 41–2, 63–4
Neuhaus, Johann Wolfgang von, electoral-Cologne envoy to the Reichstag 256–7
New World (Americas) 43–4, 58

Newcastle, Thomas Pelham-Holles duke of, British secretary of state for the Southern Department (southern Europe) 145, 153–4
Nobility/aristocracy 1, 87, 98, 123, 224, 227–9
normative year (*Normaljahr*) 26–7, 130

Orléans, Philippe II, Duke of, French Regent (1715–23) 262
Osnabrück, prince-bishopric of 135–6, 259
Ostend Company, Austrian trading company 181
Ostend 68, 181
Otten, Ignaz Anton Freiherr von, electoral Mainz envoy to Reichstag 215, 257–8
Ottoman Empire/Turks 2, 8–9, 36–7, 57, 59, 64, 91–2, 119–20, 175–7, 236, 241–2, 244, 247, 254, 266, 271
Ottoman siege of Vienna (1683) 175–6
Oxenstierna, Axel Gustafsson Count of Södermöre, Swedish lord high chancellor and regent 104–6

Palatinate, electorate of 15–16, 64–5, 69, 78–9, 87, 89–98, 100–1, 114, 116, 122, 136–7, 141–2, 152–3, 156, 164–5, 169–70, 181–2, 188–9, 194–7, 202, 207–8, 211–15, 259–60, 269–70
Palmer, J. H., Palatine envoy to Lower-Rhenish Westphalian Kreis directorate in Cologne 212–13
Papacy/Pope 5–7, 17–18, 41–2, 48, 88–9, 95, 103
Paris 115–16, 138–9, 150, 182–3, 247, 262–3
Parliament of England, later Britain 93–4, 149, 151
Parma, Alexander Farnese duke of, governor of Spanish Netherlands and duke of Parma, Piacenza, and Castro 74
Peace of Lübeck (1629) 99–102, 104
Peace of Nystad (1721) 248–9
Peace of Passau (1552) 64
Peace of Prague (1635) 116
Peace of Teschen (1779) 148–9
Peace of the Pyrenees (1659) 137–8
Peace of Utrecht-Rastatt-Baden (1713/14) 240–1, 262
Peasants' Rebellion (1524–26) 60–1, 123
Perrott, Sir James, English MP 94
Personal unions (dynastic) 18–19, 89–90, 149, 151–2, 243–4
Peter I 'the Great', Tsar of Russia 224, 244–5, 248–9, 254, 261
Philip II, King of Spain 57, 65–7, 69–70, 72–5
Philip V, King of Spain 240–1, 262

Philip William, elector-Palatine 169–70
Philipp Christoph von Sötern, archbishop-elector of Trier 111–12
Plettenberg, Friedrich Christian von, electoral-Cologne to the Reichstag 260–1
Poland-Lithuania, commonwealth (kingdom) of 5, 19, 87, 89–90, 101–2, 104, 125–6, 142, 151–4, 235, 242–3, 245–7, 252–3
Pomerania, duchy of 103–4, 106–7, 244–5, 253
Portugal, kingdom of 19–20, 120, 122–3
Prague Jews (expulsions of, 1744) 154, 267–8
Prague 85–8, 92–4, 112–13, 116–17, 131–2, 154, 267–8
Praun, Daniel Hieronymus, Reichshofrat agent (advocate) 227–8
prince-electors, position in constitutional law 15–16
Princes' Revolt (1552) 62–4
Privy Conference (*geheime Konferenz*), governmental body, Vienna 162–3, 241–3
Protestant Reformation 7, 17–18, 59–61, 75–6, 122
Protestant Succession (England/Britain) 149
Protestant Union 81, 90, 92–3
Prussia, duchy (later kingdom) of 62–3, 252–3
Public sphere and print media 20–1, 93–4, 110–11, 151, 153–4, 216–17, 240, 263–5
Pufendorf, Samuel, theorist 38, 48–9, 133–4

Radclyffe, Thomas, 3rd Earl of Sussex, English courtier of Queen Elizabeth I 69
Realist theories of IR 12–13, 267–8
Realpolitik/raison d'état/reason of state 7, 12–13, 148–9, 210–11
Rebellion/revolt 3–4, 19–20, 23–4, 42, 44, 46, 48, 55–7, 59–63, 65–7, 74, 80–1, 85–97, 99–100, 114–15, 124–5, 137–8, 162–3, 166, 176, 203–4, 270–1
Reck, Johann, Hanoverian diplomat 250
Reformed Calvinism 24–5, 32, 100–1, 130, 190–4, 218–20
Regensburg, Imperial city of 9–10, 100–1, 107, 167, 214–15, 227–8, 237–9, 256–7, 260
*Reichsexekutionsordnung* (Ordinances of Imperial execution) 23–4, 80–1
Reichshofrat (Imperial Aulic Council) 14–15, 23–6, 28–32, 35–6, 38, 45–7, 49, 96–7, 127–8, 161–85, 192–212, 217, 219–22, 224–8, 230–7, 249–50, 257–8, 263, 265–6, 269
Reichskammergericht (Imperial Cameral Court) 14–15, 22–5, 38, 41, 77–8, 161–3, 165–6, 168–70, 183–4, 194

*Reichskammergerichtsordnung* (ordinances of the Imperial Cameral Court) 23
Reichstag (Imperial Diet) 14–15, 22–5, 28–9, 31–2, 38, 65, 77–8, 142, 144–6, 148, 153–4, 178–9, 182–4, 186–7, 189, 202, 209, 212, 214–21, 225–7, 237–8, 240, 243, 254–61, 263
religious toleration 26–7, 39, 77, 130, 155–6
Renaissance 41–2
Responsibility to Protect (R2P) 3–4, 269–70
*respublica Christiana /Christianitas*, 17–18, 114–15
Rheinfels fortress 161–2
Rhenish Alliance (*Rheinbund*) (1658–68) 135–40
Rhine river; Rhineland 65, 67, 82–3, 89–90, 95, 111–12, 124, 137, 139, 147–8
Richelieu, Cardinal Armand Jean du Plessis, French chief minister 98, 107–13, 117, 130–1
Right of Reformation (*ius reformandi*) 24–5, 27, 77, 129–30
Rostock, town of 224–6, 235, 246–7
Rudolf II, Holy Roman Emperor 76–7, 80–3, 85–6
Russia 20, 148–9, 153–4, 157, 223–4, 226–7, 231–2, 235, 240–9, 252–4, 261, 266, 268

Sachsen-Zeitz, Cardinal von, Imperial principal commissioner at Reichstag 145–6
Saint-Saphorin, François Louis de Pesme, Britain's resident at Vienna 238–9, 247, 249–50
Salvius, Johan Adler, Swedish privy councillor and plenipotentiary at congress of Westphalia 104
Salzburg expulsion of Protestants (1731) 154
Salzburg, prince-archbishopric 128–9, 175–6, 270
Sardinia 58
Savoy, duchy and Imperial fief 57, 88–9, 109, 124, 149–52, 156–7, 267–8
Saxony, electorate of 15–16, 36, 61–3, 78–9, 88–9, 95–7, 107–8, 112–13, 117–18, 135, 142, 147–8, 151–2, 156, 164–5, 220, 235, 242–3, 247, 255–6, 259
Scania, Danish, then Swedish, region 241–2, 245–6, 253
Schleinitz, Baron Johann Christoph, Braunschweig-Wolfenbüttel envoy to Paris 263
Schmalkaldic League 60–2, 166–7
Schmauss, Johann Jacob, theorist 37–8, 133–4
Schutte, Johann, opposition leader in Nassau-Siegen 197, 205–6
Schwerin, town (fmr. Bishopric) of 97, 224–7
Scotland, kingdom of 57, 74, 93–4, 244–5
Seckendorff, Veit Ludwig von, theorist 39–40
Senkenberg, Renatus Karl von, theorist 39
serfdom 32, 39–40, 55–6, 197, 224, 238–9
Seven Years War (1756–63) 129–30, 135
Sicily 58

Siegen, town of 187, 190, 192–3, 196–8, 200–7
Siena, republic of (until 1555) 62–3
Silesia 58, 86, 117–18, 129–30, 141–3, 247
Sinzendorf, Philipp Louis, Austrian court chancellor, plenipotentiary at Soissons congress 145, 230, 238–9, 241–2, 263
slave trade, slavery 2, 10–11, 32, 36–40, 67–8, 236, 238–9
Solemacher, Johann, electoral Cologne commission subdelegate in Nassau-Siegen 202, 212
Southern Netherlands (Spanish, after 1714 Austrian) 58, 69, 79–80, 112, 114–16, 137–9
Sovereignty 3–7, 10–11, 13–14, 26–7, 34–7, 41–2, 44–51, 57, 64, 67–72, 74–5, 99, 109–10, 114–15, 121, 123, 125–6, 128, 132–3, 135–6, 147, 179–80, 184, 188, 207–8, 221, 238–9, 265, 267
Spain, kingdom of 19–20, 44–7, 57–8, 62–76, 79–85, 88–9, 93–103, 105, 107–10, 112–16, 118–19, 122–4, 129, 131–2, 137–9, 149–50, 153–4, 162–3, 170–1, 240–2, 245, 261–2
Spanish Armada (1588) 74–5
Spanish Road military corridor 19–20, 33–4, 45, 49, 65, 80–1, 83, 95, 118–19, 150, 170–1
Speyer, Imperial city of 39
Speyer, prince-bishopric of 39
Stair, John, British diplomat 247
Stanhope, James, 1st Earl, British statesman and chief minister 240–1, 262
Stanhope, William (later Lord Harrington) British secretary of state and diplomat 145, 151–2, 240–1, 245–6, 250–1, 262
Starhemberg, Gundaker, Austrian statesman 230, 238–9, 242
States General of the United Provinces 67–9, 71, 74–5, 180–1
Stettin, Pomeranian town and district 240–1, 252–3
Stockholm 103, 118, 261–2
Stralsund, town of 103–4, 106–7
Strassburg 79, 82
Stuarts, Scottish and English royal dynasty 94, 151
Styria 87–8
Suárez, Francisco, theorist 48, 267
Sweden, kingdom of 19, 26, 28, 49–51, 92–3, 98, 100–19, 122–33, 135–49, 151–2, 155–7, 164–5, 235–6, 240–9, 252–4, 261–2, 265
Swiss Confederation/Switzerland 26, 60, 95, 147, 157, 170–2, 177, 179
Syria 2–4

territorial estates (*Landstände* – position in constitutional law) 15–16
Thierheim, Graf von, war minister at Vienna 238–9, 242–3
Thirty Years War (1618–48) 3–4, 17, 19–20, 26, 39, 75–6, 79, 83, 85–128, 131, 133, 155–6, 163–4, 166, 168–9, 177–8, 235–6, 259–60
Thorn (Poland) tumult and confessional crisis (1724–25) 153–4
Thurn, Heinrich Matthias von, Bohemian rebel leader 87–8
Tilly, Count Johann Tserclaes, military commander of German Catholic League forces 99–100, 107–8
Toul 62–3, 123–4
Townshend, Charles, British secretary of state for the Northern Department 245–6
Transylvania, Ottoman vassal principality of 85–9, 91–2, 95, 122–3
Trautson, Johann, *Obersthofmeister* at Vienna 238–9
Trauttmansdorff, Maximilian von, Austrian chief minister and plenipotentiary at congress of Westphalia 129–30
Treaty of Bärwalde (1631) 107–8
Treaty of Chambord (1552) 62–3
Treaty of Crépy (1544) 62, 64
Treaty of Greifswald (1715) 244–5
Treaty of Hanover (Herrenhausen) (1725) 257–8, 260–1
Treaty of Joinville (1584) 70–1
Treaty of Kuchuk-Kainarji (1774) 157
Treaty of Nonsuch (1585) 71
Treaty of Oliva (1660) 151–2, 157
Treaty of Pinerolo (1655) 150–2, 157
Treaty of Scheyern Abbey (1532) 61
Treaty of the Hague (1625) 99
Treaty of Vienna (1719) 247, 259
Treaty of Vienna (1725) 153–4
Treuer, Samuel Gottlieb, theorist 40–1
Trier, archbishopric-electorate of 15–16, 111–15, 164–5, 180–1
Tsar/tsarina of Russia 146–7, 224, 235, 238–9, 241–2, 244–5, 248–9, 252–3, 261
Twelve-year-truce (Spanish-Dutch) (1609–21) 75–6, 83–5, 93
Tyranny 1–3, 33, 38–45, 57, 63, 69–72, 105–6, 110–11, 115, 119–21, 166, 176, 184–5, 231–2, 238–9, 251–2, 270–1
Tyrol 96, 174

Ulrich, duke of Württemberg 60
UN Security Council 3–4

Vaduz and Schellenberg (present-day Liechtenstein), county of 170–9
Valois dynasty of France 58
Valtelline, subject territory of Grey Leagues 95–6, 98, 170–1
Vattel, Emer de, theorist 49–50, 267
Venice, republic of 19–20, 57
Verdun 62–3, 123–4
Vienna 1, 62, 87–9, 96–7, 100–1, 131, 137–8, 144–5, 161–2, 175, 181–4, 190, 193–4, 196–8, 201–3, 223, 225–45, 247–50, 255–9, 261–2, 266
Vilebois, Michel de, French diplomat 263
Vitoria, Francisco de, theorist 43–4
Volmar, Isaak, Imperial envoy to congress of Westphalia 129–30
Vorarlberg 174
Vossius, Imperial envoy in Berlin 145

Waldensians (aka Vaudois, Savoyard proto-Protestants) 149–50, 154, 267–8
Wallenstein, Albrecht von, Imperial general and military contractor 99–101, 103, 106
Walpole, Horatio, British envoy in France 250–1
Walsingham, Sir Francis, English principal secretary of Queen Elizabeth I 69–70
War of the Austrian Succession (1740–48) 154
War of the Bavarian Succession (1778–79) 148–9
War of the Spanish Succession (1701–14) 142, 151–2, 156, 166, 186, 188, 193–4, 220, 262
Weil der Stadt, Imperial city of 80–1, 166–7
Westphalia, Peace congress of (Münster and Osnabrück, 1643–1648) 108, 119–20, 127–32
Westphalia, Peace treaties of (signed at Münster 24 Oct. 1648) 16, 26–8, 34–5, 38–9, 48–51, 108, 117, 125–7, 131–7, 139–49, 151–2, 154–7, 166, 179, 218–19, 222, 224–5, 227, 231–2, 250–2, 254, 261–3, 266, 268–70
Westphalian system/myth of Westphalia 4–9, 26–7
Wetterau association of Imperial counts 67
Wettin dynasty 62
Whigs (English/British parliamentary faction) 56–7, 149, 151
Whitworth, Charles, British diplomat 245–7, 252–3
William 'the silent', prince of Orange, Dutch Stadholder 67
William Hyacinth, prince of Nassau-Siegen (Catholic line) 127–43, 186–8, 207–10, 214–18, 221–2

William III, king of England 151–2, 188
William, Duke of Kleve-Mark 61
Windischgrätz, count Ernst Friedrich von, president of the Reichshofrat 231–6
Wittelsbach dynasty 89–90, 166, 259–60
Wolff, Christian, theorist 35–6, 49–50
Wolfgang Wilhelm, count of Pfalz-Neuburg 81–2

Wrisberg, Rudolf von, Hanoverian envoy to Reichstag 219, 256–7
Württemberg, duchy of 36, 39, 60, 80–1, 116
Würzburg, prince-bishopric of 259

Zürich 60, 147
Zwierlein, Christian Jacob von, theorist 37–8